MARK BOULBY is a member of the Department of German at the University of British Columbia.

This is the first complete biographical and critical study of Karl Philipp Moritz (1756–93), German novelist, teacher, journalist, and philologist. His psychological novel, *Anton Reiser*, replete with insights into the sociological and psychological life of the time, was one of the most important eighteenth-century German novels. Moritz was in close touch with most of the major intellectual currents in Weimar and Berlin – from aesthetics and linguistics on the one hand to pietistical and mystical movements on the other – and he was a friend of Goethe and of other significant German literary figures as well. His career was a turbulent one, made all the more difficult by his many-sided psychological problems, which play a large role in his autobiographical writings.

Karl Philipp Moritz has never been totally forgotten, but scholarly interest in him has increased dramatically in the last few decades. His works, particularly *Anton Reiser*, have also generated considerable popular interest. This is the first comprehensive monograph on this multi-faceted modern writer – an amazing fact in light of the homage paid Moritz by such contemporaries as Goethe, Schiller, and Jean Paul. Mark Boulby has succeeded admirably in relating all the frequently disparate ideas of Moritz to the trends of the period, and has combined theoretical analysis and biographical investigation in a readable and lively book.

KARL PHILIPP MORITZ

Photograph courtesy Bildarchiv der Akademie der Künste, Berlin

MARK BOULBY

Karl Philipp Moritz:
At the Fringe of Genius

UNIVERSITY OF TORONTO PRESS

Toronto Buffalo London

Library of Congress Cataloging in Publication Data

Boulby, Mark.
  Karl Philipp Moritz.

  Bibliography: p.
  Includes index.
  1. Moritz, Karl Philipp, 1757-1793. 2. Novelists,
  German – 18th century – Biography.
  PT2435.M3Z555   833'.6 [B]   78-13651
  ISBN 0-8020-5414-5

Acknowledgements

I would like to thank the John Simon Guggenheim Foundation for awarding me a fellowship, which gave me, as well as time to begin a new project, the possibility of finishing this book. This book has been published with the help of a grant from the Canadian Federation for the Humanities, using funds provided by the Social Sciences and Humanities Research Council of Canada, and a grant to University of Toronto Press from the Andrew W. Mellon Foundation. I am especially grateful to the Social Sciences and Humanities Research Council (formerly the Canada Council) for its support during the years in which the book was written. Many people have assisted me in the undertaking at different times, but I wish to acknowledge in particular the readers of the manuscript for the Press and for the Canadian Federation for the Humanities, whose various suggestions were invaluable. A large number of the works cited are not translated into English, and many of them appeared only once, in the eighteenth century. The translations offered are invariably my own.

M.B.

Contents

List of Abbreviations

The following conventional signs are used:

A Anthusa
AB Allgemeine deutsche Briefstelle
AH Andreas Hartknopf. Eine Allegorie
AP Andreas Hartknopfs Predigerjahre
AR Anton Reiser
B Beiträge zur Philosophie des Lebens
BN Über die bildende Nachahmung des Schönen
C Die Neue Cecilia
D Denkwürdigkeiten
DM Deutsches Museum
DP Versuch einer deutschen Prosodie
DS Deutsche Sprachlehre für die Damen
G Götterlehre, oder mythologische Dichtkunst der Alten
IZ Ideen einer vollkommenen Zeitung
KL Versuch einer kleinen praktischen Kinderlogik
LP Launen und Phantasien
Mag Magazin zur Erfahrungsseelenkunde
RE Reisen eines Deutschen in England
RI Reisen eines Deutschen in Italien
U Unterhaltungen mit meinen (*or* seinen) Schülern
VA Vom richtigen deutschen Ausdruck
VO Vorbegriffe zu einer Theorie der Ornamentik
VS Vorlesungen über den Stil

Introduction

Generally speaking, Karl Philipp Moritz is a rather disorganised writer. To deal with him at all is none too easy a task, since much of his work has not been reprinted, and the greater part of it has largely been ignored. In this book I have taken into consideration his whole life, with a detailed examination of most of his works, but particularly of those which seem to make the most coherent and lasting impression on the reader – his novels perhaps, his travelogues and his dissertation upon aesthetic problems, *Über die bildende Nachahmung des Schönen*. The book has been arranged with some care, progressing logically through Moritz's life, and taking his works into account as the story progresses. Here and there – for example, in the case of the *Magazin zur Erfahrungsseelenkunde*, which lasted for ten years – it has been necessary to depart from chronology a little for the sake of order and clarity.

In Chapter 1 an account is offered of Moritz's life from 1756 to 1777, based largely, though not entirely, upon what is to be found in his autobiography, *Anton Reiser*. Chapters 2, 3, and 4 are concerned with the work of his adult years before his visit to Italy (which took place from 1786 to 1788), including his trip to England in 1782, and Chapter 5 then deals primarily with Moritz's time in Rome. Chapter 6 is essentially about his stay of eight weeks with Goethe on arriving in Weimar (December–January 1788–89), his return to Berlin in triumph and his success there, and the last chapter (Seven) is about his emergence as Hofrat Moritz, the *Hartknopf* novels, his final (unfinished) work, *Die Neue Cecilia*, and the events at the end of his life. In the course of the book an extensive survey is provided of Moritz's linguistic theories, and his principal essays are covered in some detail.

The last few years have seen an increasing interest in Moritz, although almost all work published has been in German. Perhaps he is becoming recognized at long last as a significant figure, one who deserves some consideration not only by specialists but also by the general reading public interested in the eighteenth century. His life was, after all, in certain respects an unusual one, and his writings, albeit often wordy and sometimes nondescript, are at their best extremely intriguing. August Langen, Robert Minder, Hans Joachim Schrimpf and Thomas P. Saine have expressed themselves at length, and admirably, on him. Eckehart Catholy published, some years ago, a distinguished monograph on Moritz. Arno Schmidt, on the occasion of the two hundredth anniversary of his birth, wrote entertainingly about him ('Die Schreckensmänner'). One may adduce various other authors of recent years (cited in the bibliography) who have made excellent contributions to Moritz scholarship. Going back a little further in time one comes across Hugo Eybisch, who published his massive – and irreplaceable – study of Moritz in 1909; there is Gotthilf Weisstein, in whose few pages of print a goldmine of information is to be found; and in Moritz's age itself there are of course many writers to whom we must be beholden. Chief amongst these is perhaps Karl Friedrich Klischnig, with whom Moritz shared his house for a while. Details about Klischnig's life are very hard to come by, and he is in fact important only as the author of *Erinnerungen aus den zehn letzten Lebensjahren meines Freundes Anton Reiser*, published in 1794, a year after Moritz's death. Not well written, this book remains nonetheless the most informative account of his later life, when he was well acquainted with Klischnig, that we possess. The inferiority of the writing, and the scanty background we can supply about its author, do not really detract too much from the value of the book.

There were many other writers of his own period who discoursed at length on Moritz, for example Karl Lenz (writing in Schlichtegroll's *Nekrolog*) who has hardly a good word to say about him. Moritz tended to produce violent reactions in people, was often provocative (sometimes intentionally, sometimes not), was contentious, and quite fertile with fresh ideas. Most of the research on him was done at the end of the last century and the first few years of this one, and then there was a fallow period, which now seems over. He deserves to be known outside Germany, certainly, if only because of his curious, interesting life, his friendship with Goethe which meant so much to both of them, and because he wrote *Anton Reiser*. But it is my opinion that he should be recognised for a further reason: that he was, despite – or because of – the inherent nature of much of his work, ahead of his time, a harbinger of the future.

KARL PHILIPP MORITZ:

AT THE FRINGE OF GENIUS

I

The Novel of the Self

With Karl Philipp Moritz, everything comes back to *Anton Reiser*. If this was not entirely true for his contemporaries, it is indubitably true for us today, whether our interest in him is lay or scholarly, and whether it is directed more at his work or more at his life. This latter has a fascination quite its own, for if Rousseau has been plausibly if rather grandiloquently described as 'a world-historical neurotic,'[1] then Moritz, who resembles him in a number of ways, is at least 'national-historical' in the same sense. The story of his early life is his one supreme, and incontestable, achievement, his only production upon which, in the final analysis, any permanence of literary reputation can conceivably rest. Its importance transcends the personal dimension, for it is also a social document of considerable value. But it is primarily to be seen as the convergence of a fate and an understanding at a moment in Western intellectual history when self-reflection has begun to reassert itself in a fresh and intenser form. It also happens that Moritz's life-work, which is full of interest, is centripetal to an unusual degree, and it is the reflective activity at the heart of *Anton Reiser*, the character of this systematic structuring of the remembered self as a kind of case history, which gives the book much of its more general relevance as well as its concentration of personal focus. For if the life of Anton Reiser as he lives it out incorporates modes of experience in typical flux and transformation at a critical time, the would-be objective interpretation of that life and the understanding of it, equally essential to the book, enrich its spectrum beyond measure. *Anton Reiser* is a centre from which the radii lead off in all directions, into every ramification of Moritz's career as novelist, psychologist, aesthetician, pedagogue and popular philosopher, a career which, in its very instability and kaleidoscopic quality, must be regarded in the literature of his own country as one of the very best contemporary portraits of his age. With his dilettantism, his journalistic foibles and his self-plagiarisation, his piece-meal cleverness and his constant divagation between self-serving attitudes and courageous idealism, Moritz belongs to that second rank of minds (and of men) which, given the right circumstances, can nevertheless generate works close to genius on singular, auspicious occasions. The inner demand made on him by his autobiography was such an occasion, and the reasons for its intensity lie more than anything else in the historical moment, as the culture of the Enlightenment began to take final stock of itself and of the rebellion with which it was faced.

These circumstances compel us, in approaching the life and work of Moritz, to do some small violence to chronology. We have to begin with *Anton Reiser*, if only because almost all the information we have about the first twenty years of his life is contained therein. But we cannot read *Anton Reiser* without encountering the mind of the mature man. Here we meet not merely the Moritz of the years 1756 to 1777, but also the Moritz of 1790, not too long before his death, when the book was finally completed. It is precisely this duality, even multiplicity, of level that makes *Anton Reiser* so rich and so engrossing. No doubt, a situation of this kind is inherent in all autobiography, but in this instance it manifests itself with peculiar sharpness as a set of narrative tensions and symbolic matrices which give the book its significant objectivity. The question, often asked, whether *Anton Reiser* is an autobiography or a novel is pertinent here, but it cannot be satisfactorily discussed except in the light of a full interpretation of the work. Equally germane is the problem of its 'truth,' which is of course a quite separate issue, since truth, at least as usually understood, is not a particularly common attribute of autobiography at all. In the case of *Anton Reiser*, this problem of autobiographical truth is accentuated by the commitment of the author to psychological analysis. If the book is, first and foremost, as Moritz himself called it, a 'psychological novel,' this makes it quite difficult to distinguish between the facts of the protagonist's life and the impact of these facts upon his mind. Though the biographer, whose initial interest lies in establishing the external outlines of Moritz's childhood and youth, can extract most of this from *Anton Reiser* without danger of being more than slightly misled, the instant he seeks to penetrate below the surface and to comprehend the meaning of these facts for his subject's life he is enmeshed in serious uncertainties, caused largely by the nature of his main source. For throughout *Anton Reiser* two intelligences are present, that of the protagonist and that of a narrator who at first sight is a didactic satirist, but in whom the pedagogic attitude masks a highly complex personality full of contradictions. Thus every event or fact has its external identity (which may, though rarely, be susceptible of confirmation from outside *Anton Reiser*), but the account we have of it will probably involve the protagonist's own circumscribed perception of it with the vision of the narrator superimposed. This 'fact' may also be utilised as an important piece in the interpretative structure the narrator is interested in erecting, an edifice as much a work of art as it is of science. What this means is that we cannot follow the story of *Anton Reiser* without forever taking account of this structuring process, as well as of a psychologising technique which analyses as it narrates. A satisfying insight into the design and meanings of this novel of the self can thus follow only when the details of the life and the commentary on the life have been summarised and to some degree separated.

In the course of retailing this 'history,' as a German 'Aufklärer' would have been inclined to call it, I shall naturally make use of what scanty external sources there are for confirmation and supplementation. We know, though not from *Anton Reiser*, that Karl Philipp Moritz was born on 15 September 1756, in Hameln, in the Kingdom of Hanover.[2] His father, Johann Gottlieb Moritz, was the son of a Prussian soldier, Albrecht Moritz, and had been born in Halle thirty-two years earlier. He served as a musician – an oboist – in two Hanoverian regiments, the von Hammerstein and the von Post. His first wife, Johanna Juliane (née Pottron) died in October 1753 in childbirth, leaving a son, Johann Peter. In April 1755 he married a woman three years his senior, Dorette Henriette König, who may well have been in service at the nearby Fischbeck establishment, a 'protestantische Damenstift,' which had once been a nunnery. Their first child was Karl Philipp, followed by a daughter, born in 1760, who died in infancy; they then had a further son, in 1764, and twin boys in 1767. Karl Philipp therefore had three younger brothers and an elder stepbrother (the reference to *two* stepbrothers in *Anton Reiser* fails to tally with these data).[3] The family was very poor, Johann Gottlieb's income amounting to less than two Thaler a month, a mere pittance.[4] The first years of Karl Philipp's life belong to the period of the Seven Years' War, when Hameln was at times in danger of siege. According to *Anton Reiser* mother and child spent a couple of years in a village in a securer location, while Johann Gottlieb was on active service. This time, which for the little boy was one of blissful tranquillity, although his sister died during it, lasted probably from his fourth to his sixth year. He implies that he remembers constant quarrelling between his parents going back to the time when he was two or three, which seems rather unlikely. At all events, when his father came home from the war in 1763 the Regiment von Post was transferred to Hanover, and any placidity there may have been in domestic life ended abruptly. The primary cause of the marital conflict lay no doubt in a deep incompatibility of character, but the *casus belli* was religion. Moritz had more than one reason for choosing to commence his autobiography with an account of the rather out-of-the-way sect to which his father had for some time belonged when he was born.

After the death of his first wife, Johann Gottlieb had quite suddenly turned devout.[5] He had fallen profoundly under the influence of a middle-aged nobleman, Herr von Fleischbein, discreetly referred to, like other characters in the first edition of this roman à clef, by his initial only. Of this gentleman a certain amount is known. Born in 1700, probably in Frankfurt-am-Main, Fleischbein was one of those many aristocrats caught up in the religious revival which was just then spreading through western and northern Germany in the form of a variegated sectarianism, of which the mainstream, Pietism, had developed in the late seventeenth century and had been particularly disseminated by the writings of P.J. Spener (1635–1705) and A.H. Francke (1663–1727). Pietism proper was in its origins an introverted, emotional modification of Lutheranism, seeking the realisation of the Kingdom of God on earth by the mystical transformation of the individual soul, and was a movement rooted in the lower middle classes. Besides encouraging devotion to feeling, which became especially effusive with such groups as Zinzendorf's Moravians, Pietism simultaneously imposed a severe, puritanical discipline upon its adherents. The Pietists met together in conventicles, did not go to church, and like the English Non-Conformists were often persecuted by the authorities. Some sects departed from the normal pattern, and one of these was Fleischbein's, which is more correctly designated Separatist. For many years Fleischbein had been associated with the Count de Marsay, a fanatical follower of the teachings of Jeanne-Marie de la Motte Guyon, the Catholic mystic and close friend of Fénélon, who had spent some time in the Bastille and is the authoress of a number of important works of ascetic contemplation. Her immensely long autobiography – parts of which Moritz was one day to republish in his *Magazin zur Erfahrungsseelenkunde* – provide a convincing insight into the inner life of a quite remarkable woman, no mere neurotic surely, but a person to whose authenticity, honesty and shrewdness of psychological perception all her work bears witness.[6] Her ideas seem to have percolated into Germany mainly through Huguenot families like Marsay's, and through the mediation of such mystical philosophers as Peter Poiret, from Metz, and Gottfried Arnold.[7] As so often in the Christian mystical tradition, the distinction between Catholic and Protestant is here quite thin. The doctrines of the Fleischbein Separatists differed from those of the mainstream of Pietism, however, not only in their more immediate sources, but in their essence, for they taught an extreme form of quietism.

In *Anton Reiser* Moritz describes it in this manner:

The teachings found in these writings are concerned for the most part with that total abandonment of the self already mentioned, and the entry upon a blissful state of nothingness, with that complete extermination of all so-called 'self-ness' or 'self-love,' and a totally disinterested love of God, in which not the merest spark of self-love may mingle, if it is to be pure, and out of this in the end there arises a perfect, blissful 'tranquillity,' which is the loftiest goal of all these strivings (*AR*, 7).[8]

This was in fact an austere teaching, requiring even for its embryonic realisation a spiritual understanding far more subtly honed than the majority of its disciples possessed. What it recommended was an emptying of the soul, and a submission to the work of God within – a passivity both delicate and pure, incompatible with sloth, apathy or any form of hebetude. Mme de Guyon warned continually against the perils of indifference, of torpor, and of the wrong kind of withdrawal from the world. What she proposed could not only be reconciled with but in fact exacted a proper devotion to the duties of daily life. However, in a teaching in which – unlike the traditional sectarian *praxis pietatis* – the essential was not self-observation and the struggles of self-denial but merely submission and utter stillness, the inevitable corruptions ensued: disregard of external, including family, obligations, unproductive, time-consuming contemplation, inertia, vacuity, and incessant brooding sometimes shading into melancholia. Into several of these vices Johann Gottlieb evidently fell.

As it happens, our sources of information about Karl Philipp's father are not limited to *Anton Reiser*. In 1790, in the *Magazin zur Erfahrungsseelenkunde*, his son published a summary account of Johann Gottlieb's life, and more details still may be gleaned from letters to him from Fleischbein, which appeared in this same periodical. In any case the portrait painted in *Anton Reiser* is rather ambiguous, as is that of Frau Dorette Moritz, and some inhibitions on this score were only to be expected. As a young boy Karl Philipp loved his mother intensely, and feared and hated his father. Yet when they were both away from her, he noticed that his father's behaviour towards him sometimes became almost kind. Much later he was to conclude that in the perpetual domestic strife which racked the Moritz household his mother's bigotry and intolerance had been the most at fault, and in later years his father, a widower again and a disillusioned man, was transformed from a mystical quietist into a sober and cheerful man of reason who enjoyed reading Voltaire. The storms which raged over the head of young Anton – as we shall now take leave to call Karl Philipp for the time being – arose superficially at any rate out of Frau Dorette's refusal to accept the harsh Guyonist doctrine of a total elimination of all the passions, including every form of tenderness. She was a pious, sentimental Lutheran with a hysterical streak; she loved the Bible, and her husband held her orthodox views in nothing but contempt. She was likely enough less intelligent than he was, and though she could read and write she had narrow horizons. She spoke in Low German dialect,[9] a language Moritz always connected with ignorance. If Johann Gottlieb was addicted to spells of morose withdrawal, and to occasional unfeeling and even cruel acts, his wife was given to making scenes, and to hysterical shouting and abuse. It was into such circumstances, as we are told with lapidary effect, that Karl Philipp Moritz, Anton Reiser, was born, 'and of him it can be said in truth that he was oppressed from the cradle on' (AR, 9). The most vivid, and most appalling, illustrations of his deprivation of affection are found in the story of his illnesses, in the first of which – 'a wasting disease' – he is given up for lost and is talked about in his own presence as though already dead, and in the second – a badly infected foot – when an amputation is finally proposed, 'Anton's mother sat and cried and his father gave him two pennies. These were the first expressions of pity for him he remembers from his parents, and owing to their rarity they made all the more impression upon him' (AR, 13). When the operation proved unnecessary, things reverted to normal.

At this time, Anton Reiser was nine or ten. This catastrophic environment, and in particular the relentless tyranny of Separatist fanaticism, led to a constant apprehension of failure on his part, of rejection and indeed damnation, as well as to a compulsive searching for compensations. A circle was formed and it began to spin. Johann Gottlieb tried to force the child through what he perceived to be the strait gate of salvation, but concerned himself with his son only in fits and starts. He taught him some of the *Cantiques* of Mme de Guyon, which had been translated into a stilted German,[10] and in which he accompanied himself on the zither. Music was just about the only solace the boy had, but the bliss of emptiness and the stilling of the passions of which these songs speak became wedded in his imagination with recurrent traumas of exclusion and withdrawal. Terrified by the inculcated sense of inadequacy and sin, Anton Reiser was shocked to learn from some pious tract, which spelled out the steps in spiritual advancement for children aged six to fourteen, that he was already at least three years behind. He sought refuge in the conviction that he was by now (as the grown-ups clearly were) on a conversational footing with God, and tried to practise a dimly apprehended prayer of the heart. In his tenth year Johann Gottlieb took him along to the little town of Bad Pyrmont, partly in order to treat his painfully inflamed foot at the spa. Here Anton was introduced into the strange household of Herr von Fleischbein, 'a little republic' (*AR*, 6) as such congregations often were, since among the sects the rigid class distinctions of eighteenth-century German society tended to be somewhat blurred. In the garden behind his father's lodgings in Pyrmont little Anton discovered a wheelbarrow, which he pushed around for many hours in deep conversation with an imagined passenger, none other than the child Jesus in person. It is not recorded whether Herr von Fleischbein ever learned of this barrow, and its somewhat unusual cargo.

One of the most spectacular insights of Moritz in *Anton Reiser* is in fact into the psychological significance of children's games, and in his maturer years he still indulged in mental games of various types, especially verbal, philological, onomastic ones – the best example being the game he and Goethe played together in Rome and which Goethe describes.[11] The notion of 'game' is an important one in his thinking, and emerges in various places, for instance in his influential *Deutsche Prosodie*. But in his boyhood the games to which he was addicted had – as it certainly appeared to him later – a sinister quality, as symptoms of neurosis. Herr von Fleischbein, who took some interest in Anton, had presented him with a copy of Fénélon's *Télémaque*, a work of fiction, but one dominated by quietist thought. Introduced thereby into the world of the Greek gods and heroes, he plays with these tales of blood and disaster. Slicing off the heads of nettles, thistles and other flowers with a stick he becomes in his mind a blind fate, striking out wildly in all directions eyes closed, and then sadly contemplating the fallen, visualizing himself – 'with strangely melancholic and yet pleasant feelings' (*AR*, 20) – as one of those slain. Back home from Pyrmont he made paper figures of the heroes, and destroyed them all with relish. Flies he also caught and killed, first tolling a little execution bell. His greatest delight was to construct a city of paper houses and then burn it down, and one night, when a fire did break out in Hanover, he felt the wicked longing that it might not be extinguished too soon. Looking back upon this last instance, Moritz sees in it more than 'Schadenfreude': it was to do with a sense of fate, of the unpredictability of the universe, it sprang from 'a dark premonition of great changes, emigrations and revolutions, through which all things would be quite altered in their form and the previous monotony would come to an end' (*AR*, 21). This formulation, committed to paper several years before the French Revolution, is really eschatological in character, for Moritz continues: 'Even the thought of his own destruction was not only a pleasant one, but actually aroused in him a sort of voluptuous sensation, when often at night, before going to sleep, he vividly imagined the dissolution and disintegration of his body.'

Aggression, like the horror of 'monotony,' lies at the heart of *Anton Reiser*, and much of Moritz's therapeutic self-analysis is indirectly concerned with defusing it. Its profoundest source was probably his relationship with his father, an absolutely classical complex with ramifications throughout his life and work. Moritz was aware of the presence of this up to a point, though, as his callow tragedy, *Blunt oder der Gast*, makes clear, its implications were much more far-reaching than he could possibly suspect. During his first stay in Bad Pyrmont, when his father, though otherwise preoccupied, treated him quite well, another important experience was reinforced – that of nature. The countryside had always seemed idyllic, an idyllicism which he calls (with a rather startling present tense) 'the foundation of all the illusions his imagination often produces' (*AR*, 10). By 1783, when he began writing his autobiography, his nature descriptions had certainly absorbed much of the sentimentalism of the day, and the language – though more detached – reflects the influence of Klopstock's poetry and of Goethe's *Werther*. But the core of memory is no doubt authentic – nature did function as a counter-balance in a pinched, overshadowed existence, increasingly afflicted with claustrophobic terrors. The idyll of 'soft hills ... green bushes ... blue mountains' (*AR*, 9–10) had early on opened up something in the soul that the ascetic tradition invariably denounced and denied, and which even as a grown man Moritz sometimes found it hard to believe in. A more enduring escape, in these years, was into reading. At the age of seven his father had begun to teach him to read, but thoughtfully gave him two books which contradicted each other entirely. One of these employed the traditional, grinding 'spelling method,' and the other a new phonetic technique (probably the 'Lautiermethode'); as a teacher and a writer on pedagogical matters, Moritz was one day to develop a professional interest in these conflicting methodologies; the little Anton Reiser gravely perused both volumes, and as soon as he discovered that words convey meanings, taught himself to read within a week or two. The world into which his repressed feelings then found their way was as idyllic, fantastic and 'unreal' as the countryside had been for the child from the streets of Hanover and Hameln. He began by devouring the Bible and *Télémaque*, unaware that the truth of the events described in these two was not supposed to be of the same order. A little later came the forbidden material – German popular novels, which his father threatened to incinerate should he find any in the house. Frau Dorette, however, indulged her son in this secret dissipation, and he consumed *The Arabian Nights*, *Die Schöne Banise*, and *Die Insel Felsenburg*. It was this last novel, by Johann

Elias Schnabel, which deals with the evolution of an insular society thousands of miles away from the corruptions of Europe, which had the most potent effect on the boy's imagination, and he dreamed of himself playing a great role as the centrepoint of an expanding circle of human beings, like the old patriarch in Schnabel's moralising – though also faintly lubricious – tale, in which animals, plants and things inanimate, as well as people, come under his sole sway. Anton's reading of novels thus encouraged in him the same thing his games tended to express, namely visions of authority and power, the classical accompaniment to a developing inferiority complex.

Anton Reiser recounts the process of an education which was desultorily eager but in its first years decidedly haphazard. In the course of time the boy was to learn Latin and read Roman authors, to absorb *Robinson Crusoe* (which he says gave him the very first thought of writing down his story), and even to encounter some of the German literature of his own day – bits and pieces of Lessing, a few specimen plays of the Sturm und Drang movement and, in his late teens, his beloved *Werther*. Early on, religious books were important, mixing oddly with his clandestine intake of novels. He was set to read *The Imitation of Christ* aloud to his parents over their breakfast, and was introduced to some of the writings of Tauler and other mystics, especially St John of the Cross while an apprentice in Brunswick.[12] Powerful religious conflicts were thus fed in him, and much confusion of the feelings. His inferiority complex grew rapidly, nurtured by the frustrations and disappointments which arose precisely from the fact that he was not entirely starved of learning and the chance for self-expression. Separatists did not usually send their children to school, but Anton was permitted by his father to attend a privately held class in Latin. There he could sit with boys from a higher social group and try to emulate them, though shamed by his mother's insistence that he should still fetch and carry water and groceries beneath the grins of his schoolfellows in the marketplace – 'like a woman, with a basket on the arm' (*AR*, 31). In the Latin class he moved up quickly along the bench. He received private lessons in writing from an old man, of whom he was fond. And then one day his father took him to see the centenarian Tischer, who sat in a back room in a tenement at the end of a labyrinth of stairs and corridors, stone deaf but still deciphering the small print of his Greek Testament without spectacles at the age of 105. Detached and serene, Tischer seemed to the boy the equal of a Disciple, 'a higher, superhuman being' (*AR*, 33), and his library of mystical texts was to be a rich source of new reading for Anton. At this point things seemed to floresce, life was getting better. But it is a prominent characteristic of the story told in *Anton*

Reiser that it is instinct with vicissitudes, with sudden turns of fate. The world is a game from which men cannot escape, and when the thistles are decapitated it is usually Anton who lies slain. So these few happier months of the year 1768 came to a precipitate end. His father informed him abruptly that he was to be taken out of the Latin class, and he was so devastated he reversed his efforts entirely and sought only to be demoted one place on the bench each day. Moritz brings out vividly the neurotic precision with which Anton Reiser organises his own decline, meticulously prescribing for himself the poison of his own disgrace. His writing teacher is dismissed, he is sent to the local elementary school, and he degenerates rapidly into a street lad, playing truant, brawling, and torturing the family dog. The nexus between a paranoiac sense of social rejection and the haunting shadow of spiritual damnation is made clear, and the vicious circle of exclusion, slight, withdrawal, and exclusion again, is exposed.

THE BRUNSWICK DAYS

To follow the twists and turns of this excruciating narrative is indeed, for the reader, to pick his way through an exploded minefield of psychological traumas. Life is perceived as it were horizontally through the narrow aperture of a claustrophobic vision, and simultaneously it is dissected from above and opened up vertically by a dexterous scientist of the mind. These two views, that of the narrated and that of the narrating self, are quite different, but of course the biographer of Karl Philipp Moritz has to take account of both. Not much exists in the way of external checks on Moritz's story, and in late 1768 a period begins for which *Anton Reiser* is the only source – the dark night in Brunswick, the apprenticeship to the hatter Lobenstein. For an obsessional nature such as Anton's, which greedily seeks out change, this great upheaval is at first exciting. Hanover with its narrow streets and its four dominating towers is left behind and with it that tedium which so often lays siege to the boy's mind, 'the eternal monotony of the same streets and houses' (*AR*, 39), so that he can imagine, as he is thereafter always quick to do, 'new towers, gates, walls and castles.' This, his first longish journey, takes place on foot with his father, tramping across the North German plain. As they approach the gates of Brunswick they see the sentry pacing to and fro on the walls, and Anton begins to play one of his word games. The name Hanover, before he went there to live, had always suggested 'a place with tall houses and towers, and bright and light to look at'; Brunswick had portended something darker and larger, and the name Paris had aroused pictures of a different kind again. As for Lobenstein, the sound of this name makes Anton imagine a tall, dignified very German-looking person, with an open brow, and here he was to be quite disappointed. Anton and his father enter Brunswick at dusk. Through many narrow alleys, past the castle, across the bridge and along a gloomy street they eventually come to the house, which is rather black in colour and has a black door studded with nails. The parlour in which they are received is panelled in dark brown, with an allegorical representation of the Five Senses still faintly discernible on the walls. Lobenstein turns out to be middle-aged and on the small side, 'with a face which, though still fairly youthful, was pale and melancholy, and rarely changed except into a kind of bittersweet smile.' He had

black hair, rather dreamy eyes, and something fine and delicate in his talk, movements and manners not usually found among tradespeople, as well as a pure but extremely slow, indolent and drawling way of speech, which made words last forever, especially if the conversation was about religion; he also had an unbearably intolerant gaze, when his black eyebrows pinched together over the abominations and wickedness of human kind, and in particular of his neighbours and employees (*AR*, 40-41).

The portrait is pungent and brilliant. It would be fiction of high quality if it were not drawn directly from life. These Brunswick episodes provide us with what is probably the most outstanding re-creation of lower middle and working class town life anywhere in eighteenth-century German literature, although the focus, a fanatical sectarian household, is somewhat specialised.

As for Johann Simon Lobenstein (as his full name appears to have been),[13] he was unfortunately all too real. Johann Gottlieb Moritz had met him a year or two earlier, possibly in Bad Pyrmont, and he had consented to be god-father to the Moritz twins. He was another of Fleischbein's followers, though what we learn of him suggests that he was not an exponent of the pure doctrine of Mme de Guyon, for Pietist and Calvinist influences mingled with Quietism in his mind. But he was certainly a Separatist, and when Anton Reiser started going to church in Brunswick he probably had to do so discreetly. Perhaps because the book deals with a period when both Pietism and Separatism in north Germany were already in decline, especially in the large towns, we hear nothing about any organised religious practice or conventicles. What the author offers is an imposing portrayal of a fanatical master hatter, quite probably psychotic, ruling over his family and apprentices with a rod of iron. The eighteen months of Anton Reiser's stay in Brunswick, autumn 1768 to spring 1770, had enormous ups and downs, but overall it was a grim time. His hopes were dashed as soon as he saw Lobenstein, and realised he would be treated like any other apprentice or perhaps worse. At first he was employed to clean out the workshop, and to hew wood and draw water. His imagination initially provided some compensation – the vast, dark shop with its paucity of glimmering lanterns turned in the chill early mornings into a temple where his task was to kindle, as he puts it Homerically, 'the sacred enlivening fire' (*AR*, 41). He was impressed by the tight organisation and apparent efficiency of the household, but the labour was burdensome and Sundays soon gleamed invitingly with their opportunity for flight into the fields beyond the city gates. This theme – the contrast between the simple but arduous workaday world of the apprentice craftsman, and the blissful domain of Mother Nature outside the walls (into which sooner or later the journeyman can hope to escape) – was to become a cliché of German Romantic and post-Romantic tales, a furrow still being plowed more than a century later, even by a writer such as Hermann Hesse. We can perhaps claim that *Anton Reiser*, the first, is also the most bitingly authentic of these accounts, and uncompromising in its way: even the escapism is seen with clinical detachment as a mechanism of compensation.

The compensatory dreams of Anton Reiser which arise in this penitentiary of Brunswick are called by the narrator 'novel-like' [*romanhaft*]. It is an important word, and in due course we shall examine its wider implications. These dreams transform people and places around him, and from time to time they even transform events. The school which stands forever out of reach just across from Lobenstein's house becomes for him a kind of sacred place, and the choir-boys who belong to it are beings from a higher sphere. But in the somber household the influence of its master is all-pervasive. Even Anton's fellow apprentice August, with whom he has groping discussions about religion, cannot help using the terminology favoured by Lobenstein. Only the journeyman, if the hatter prattles on too much about 'extinction and annihilation,' sometimes gives him a killing look. Lobenstein exudes misanthropy and inveighs continually against the sinfulness of men, an attitude which – as the narrator sardonically observes – brought him economic advantage: 'The utilitarian application, cunningly enough, was this, that he exhorted his people to loyalty and assiduity in his service, if they did not wish to burn forever in the fires of hell' (*AR*, 45).

Punctilious, a ferocious taskmaster, and miserly too – 'he made a cross over the bread and butter whenever he went out' – Lobenstein constantly criticises Anton's behaviour, his speech, his table manners, and the slightest smile or expression of pleasure. The lugubrious, hypocritical atmosphere of this tyranny seemed somehow translated into the odour of the fresh varnish on the panels of the Five Senses, an association which was to remain with Moritz-Reiser for good. However, the Brunswick chapter exemplifies the recurrent pattern of the narrative, in that it describes a rise to favour followed speedily by a precipitous fall. So Anton's fortunes start to improve, especially when his master, haunted by fear of death and of ghosts, takes the boy into his chamber with him at night. Resolved to save his soul come what may, he obliges him to pray out loud in terms of rigorous self-abasement, promising that the divine work will then proceed of itself within him. As a consequence his new-found favourite, or rather victim, half-imagines he can sense this process, and simulates the experience to himself and others. The hatter, duly impressed, then opens a correspondence about him with Fleischbein, and Anton is awarded the black apron of a full apprentice and is relieved of hard labour, to the envy of others. Lobenstein is sufficiently carried away to hire him a piano teacher.

The reversal of fortune, when it comes, is calamitously complete. As the hatter's irrational approval mutates into an equally irrational hatred, he attributes his spontaneous change of heart to an apprehended deterioration in his charge's condition of soul. He chides the boy for his clever conversation, his liveliness, his cheerfulness of visage. These things seem to him far too worldly, very bad signs. To Fleischbein he writes in terms designed to provoke the kind of answer he now malevolently shows to Anton: Herr von Fleischbein asserted that to all appearances 'Satan has built such a temple in Anton's heart that it can hardly be destroyed again' (*AR*, 50–51). Expelled, upon this, from his master's room in disgrace, the thirteen-year-old is put, in that severe winter of 1769, to work which exceeds his physical strength. Abandoning hope for his soul, Lobenstein feels all the freer to exploit his body. In the middle of the night Anton has to take the hats, steaming with black dye, and dip them in the river through a hole bored in the ice. He has to work for days in unheated rooms, sorting wool. And sometimes he is shut up all night with August in the drying-room, a cramped oubliette graced by a smoking cauldron and with an entrance so low they have to crawl through it on hands and knees. This tiny door, and the horror of such confinement, recur in Moritz's writings. Within this dark cavern [*Gewölbe*], however, the two boys' hearts overflow with friendship, but it is not surprising that overt depressive symptoms appear in Anton, culminating in a suicide attempt. Staring down into the river he thinks he hears the world laughing scornfully above him, and he totters and falls. Though he is dragged out by August, the incident causes sufficient sensation for Lobenstein to write indignantly to his father demanding his removal, and Johann Gottlieb, sullen and angry, duly arrives to collect his incorrigible son.

With this grim tale Moritz entwines a second, rather different one. This concerns the visits to church, instigated by August, in order to hear the best-known preachers in the town. Foremost among them is Pastor Paulmann, and here some external corroboration is once more to hand. Johann Ludwig Paulmann (1728–1807) was, from 1767 on, deputy pastor at the Brüdernkirche in Brunswick. The ecclesiastical histories make it clear that he was in most respects a rationalistically-minded clergyman of the type very common in the Enlightenment, who used his pulpit largely to purvey good practical advice on the care of the sick, the bringing up of children, and even the tilling of the land.[14] But there must have been some Pietistic influence in his background, for his style as a preacher could on occasion be highly emotional, and then he had a dramatic effect. As Moritz formulates it succinctly: 'he preached already just standing there, with his features, his quietly clasped hands' (AR, 54). Anton dreams of one day taking Communion from this elevated being, and more secretly still of emulating this tremendous performer, the centre of a great attentive circle. For Anton Reiser the pulpit presaged the theatre, and preacher and actor were always closely associated. He cannot imagine Paulmann eating and sleeping like other men, or even wearing a dressing-gown and a night-cap. But it is always this sphere, common subversive materiality, the very meanness of existence which erodes and disrupts Anton's dreams, and he is duly devasted one day to hear the pastor conversing with the verger in Low German. He is equally, but quite differently, affected by Paulmann's sermon on death. This terrifying address follows directly upon that climactic scene one day at dusk when Lobenstein, sitting in his bath, livid and sweating with ague, stares rigidly into the corner and screams out a warning: 'Anton! Anton! Have a care for Hell!' (AR, 62). Anton takes this to be a prediction of his own death, and perhaps this horror of dying and of what may come afterwards distills the essence of the benighted world of Brunswick; and the narrator perceives its unmistakable derivation 'from all the sad consequences of the superstition instilled in him since his earliest childhood ... the sufferings of the imagination' (AR, 64). Lobenstein must have been the victim of something of the same kind.

The sickness described was labyrinthine, and Moritz may have been aware that he had never fully emerged from it. But even in the depths of the Brunswick period the path to a liberation substantial if not total was discerned incipiently. It was not, as Anton falsely believed for many years, by analogy with Pastor Paulmann out into the triumphant circle of pulpit or theatre, but towards a quite different centre, that of self-knowledge. It shows itself on the occasion when, on a Sunday stroll, the boy arrives at the city gates through which he had entered with his father many months before. As he stares back down the long straight highway, lined with willows, along which they had marched, strange feelings assail him. As he recalls his first sight of the sentry on the wall 'his whole life from that time on ... was all at once there in his memory.' It is as though he awakes from a long sleep, and 'all the changing scenes of his life ... crowded close together, and the individual pictures seemed to grow smaller in accordance with a larger standard of measurement his mind suddenly acquired' (*AR*, 65). All at once the immediate past takes shape in Anton's mind, with the individual scenes printed out small so that it may be surveyed at a glance and comprehended entire, according to the criteria of a new insight. The first of a number of similar passages, this moment at the gates of Brunswick provides a glimpse of the symbolic superstructure of *Anton Reiser*, for there is something about it which transcends the vision of the protagonist and belongs to the level of the autobiographical narrator.[15] It occurs not far from the end of the first part of the book, which concludes shortly after the miscreant's return home to Hanover, with its welcoming towers, a journey on which Anton's father hardly says a word. The reunion with his mother is an immense joy, he takes flight into her bosom, tells her about Brunswick and particularly Pastor Paulmann, feels sure, when she falls ill, that he would expire too if she were to die. He passes the time teaching his little brothers games, 'besieging cities, conquering fortresses built with the books of Mme de Guyon, by bombarding them with chestnuts' (*AR*, 77). He even tries preaching to the twins, until his pulpit of chairs collapses on their heads, earning him a whipping. In due course it is decided – one must suppose at Frau Dorette's insistence, although by this time relations between Johann Gottlieb Moritz and Herr von Fleischbein had cooled – to send him to a local free school (run to train village schoolmasters), in order apparently to prepare him for Confirmation.

LIVING AND DYING

Part Two of *Anton Reiser* is in large measure concerned with life at school in Hanover, and considerable research has here elicited a number of details which both substantiate and clarify the author's story. However, it should be observed that for the psychological data with which the book is primarily concerned we are still entirely dependent upon Moritz himself, although of course we are by no means obliged to accept his interpretations at face value. The social environment can be sketched in briefly: Hanover in the early 1770s was still a smallish town by modern standards, with a population of some 18,000. Nevertheless it had a certain sophistication, being a seat of government with a number of fairly important nobles resident there. The effective ruler was Prince Carl von Mecklenburg-Strelitz, brother of the Queen of England, representing George III (who never came there), and the

English influence was quite noticeable (when just a child Anton had begun to learn the language from an Englishman in Pyrmont). Although, as in practically all German cities in those days, life was extremely limited and parochial by French or English standards, and the social system inexorably rigid, the effects of Enlightenment liberalism and of the Age of Sentiment were just beginning to weaken class barriers very slightly. Hanover possessed Masonic Lodges and gentlemens' clubs, it boasted a place of public entertainment called 'the Vauxhall,' and it was on the itinerary of the better travelling theatre companies such as the Schröder troupe from Hamburg with its star, Charlotte Ackermann. Good music could be had there – Handel was performed in Hanover earlier than in Leipzig or Berlin. There was also a literary periodical of sorts, the *Hannoversche Magazin*, and although the city had no university (Göttingen, not too far away, was at the time by far the best university in Germany), it could lay claim to a small reading public and even to a modicum of literary culture – the poet Hölty, who is mentioned in *Anton Reiser*, and the playwright Leisewitz lived there for a while. Most importantly, there was an excellent Gymnasium, the high school in the Old City, and it was here that Anton was to receive most of his formal education. This he got by a combination of stumbling determination and luck, for his father – though he did, rather surprisingly, arrange for private lessons in writing and in arithmetic – had no real interest except in finding his delinquent son a trade. Having obtained some kind of notary's position in a village some way from Hanover, Johann Gottlieb more or less washed his hands of him, declaring emphatically he would not provide another penny. But through a desperate application to the Inspector at the free school, Anton eventually managed to obtain a promise of tuition and books at the Gymnasium gratis, and thereafter a chance encounter with the pastor at the Garnisonskirche, Marquard, set in motion a series of events which brought about the intervention of none other than the Prince himself as his benefactor. A small scholarship was made available for this poor but clever and unusual boy, free lodging was found at the house of another military musician, Filter, and arrangements were made for free dinners with several families. The Hanover high school, to which Anton was now admitted, was an academically strong school, and fairly progressive for its day under its director, Ludwig Wilhelm Ballhorn, a modern-minded man well versed in contemporary German literature as well as in the classics, and in no sense a pedant. It appears to have been the kind of school where effort was very much rewarded, and where a lot depended on the exertions the pupil was prepared to make – little time was wasted on the stragglers and malingerers. The atmosphere, however, was relatively liberal, and the subjects taught included

Latin, Greek and some English, but also geography and history and of course religion (the absence of mathematics was corrected by the next Director, Schumann). Its records show that Karl Philipp Moritz joined the school early in 1771 in the Sekunda, becoming a senior ('Primaner') unusually quickly after one year.

An immense upswing, this good fortune was followed however not by a secure, plain-sailing career at school, but by a series of false starts, missteps, backslidings, and accompanying affective disorders. It is a tale tragic as well as ironic, pathetic as well as grotesque. The apparent triumph of escape from parental domination into some degree of financial independence, together with – when the source of Anton's support became known – a certain social prestige, generates 'the pleasantest fantasies' in the boy's mind, but these are at once undermined as the counterpoint of mean materiality and the spite of circumstance is heard morosely in the bass. The first disasters have to do with the free accommodation and dinners. The good will marshalled for him in this way by Pastor Marquard is soon eroded when his benefactors discover what their generosity costs them, and become tired of him and critical of his behaviour. By now Anton Reiser has become a fully-fledged neurotic, demoralised by the faintest breath of slight, suspicious, and compulsively driven to seek out derogation and rejection. As he regales his readers with the lamentable story of the dinners, the narrator insists on the importance of detail for the analysis of psychological chain reactions, for it is precisely 'these kinds of apparently trivial circumstances which make up life and which have the greatest influence on a person's mind' (*AR*, 103). That his clothes for example are egregiously awful, and the object of much mirth, is a small but for Anton Reiser deadly thing. And as the school years go on the narrative grinds out an apparently endless series of incidents of ridicule, shame and disgrace. Superbly observed, these constitute probably the best and surely the most clear-sighted and remorseless clinical depiction anywhere in eighteenth-century literature of the course of a paranoid illness, more detached and systematic than Rousseau's, less primitive if less spectacular than the Leipzig cleric Adam Bernd's. What is brought out is the manner in which a disastrous concatenation of circumstances and 'accidents' interacts with a psyche unusually predisposed to respond in such a way.

There is, for example, the case of the Christmas tree, intended by Anton's landlady for a little girl, which he vainly attempts to save from falling over and is unfortunately suspected of having tried to pilfer. This accusation produces in the boy 'a kind of paralysis of the mind ... Self-confidence, which is as necessary to moral action as breathing is to physical movement, receives a blow so powerful that it finds it very hard to recover from it' (*AR*, 120). The narrator, for his part, as usual both reflective and self-assured, notes that shame and confusion are far too often taken by ignorant people as proof of guilt, and we for our part might well be struck by the remarkable similarity here to the case of Rousseau, and to the incident of the broken comb in the *Confessions*. Nothing pierces 'so to his heart, to his innermost self' as does ridicule. Gauche as he always is, he is crushed to be snubbed when hastening to accept an ostensible invitation, with the words: 'But I didn't mean you' (*AR*, 121). Though he generates, in large measure, his own catastrophes, this scarcely mitigates their impact. The rebuke he receives for tearing a page of his Cicero while translating for Director Ballhorn shatters his self-confidence and sets the deadly circle spinning fast. The narrator calls this apparently minor incident, indeed, 'the source of all the miseries which Reiser had to face in his school years, and which were chiefly caused by the Director's lack of respect for him' (*AR*, 134).

One or two witnesses have recorded personal memories of Moritz in Hanover, though their substance is very slight. These include August Wilhelm Iffland (1759–1814), the famous actor, who was his schoolmate, K.G. Lenz who wrote so harshly of him in Schlichtegroll's *Nekrolog*, and anonymous contributors among whom may possibly be counted one or more of his teachers, as like as not Rector Sextroh of the Gymnasium.[16] While Iffland finds that Moritz's story is entirely true (and this no doubt means its psychology as well),[17] Lenz disagrees, holding that the whole account is founded upon judgments as unfair as they are anachronistic. Society, in particular Moritz's teachers and schoolfellows, should not be blamed for what happened to him at school, for after all this dirty, shifty, disorganised schoolboy was not yet recognisable as the successful professor and man of letters to come.[18] But this argument greatly oversimplifies the situation, and shows no insight into its nature as an infernal machine. Anton Reiser's decline, in his circle of exclusion and withdrawal, though slowed by pauses of resilience is quite relentless. Taken for a while, as a privilege, to live in the house of Rector Sextroh, he is expelled in the end for his impossible behaviour, his truancies, the time he wastes at the playhouse. He wears filthy clothes and goes hungry rather than show himself at the few homes where he still might claim a free meal. Just as he took pleasure, when a little boy, in contemplating his own future dissolution, he now finds satisfaction in the more immediate experience of his corporeal deterioration, which accompanies that of his attire. With clenched teeth he listens to the scornful laughter he thinks he can hear behind him in the streets. Psychopathic traits begin to manifest themselves as the shabbiness of the body and its demands take over his life. Cut off from his scholarship funds and from his free meals, he begins to starve in actuality, with nothing to gnaw on except the hard crust of dough used by his cousin, a wig-maker, in his trade, and which he begs for to give to a dog of his acquaintance. He lies torpid for days, on his hard garret bed, and even replays the games of yesteryear:

> He made a big collection of cherry and plum stones, sat on the floor and arranged them in order of battle ... then he took a hammer and closing his eyes acted the part of blind fate, hitting with the hammer at random – when he opened his eyes again he looked with secret pleasure upon the awful destruction ... (*AR*, 163).

It is a 'chain of circumstances' [*Verkettung der Dinge*] which drags Anton, that year of 1773, even to the brink of crime. The raid on the orchard, which he undertakes with his boon companions (social drop-outs like himself) 'did not seem to him to be robbery at all, but a sort of incursion into enemy territory' (*AR*, 166) – a perceptive illumination, quite unusual for its time, of an incipiently psychopathic attitude from the inside. How close he has come to total ruin is brought home to him traumatically when his room-mate, while singing on the street in the school choir, is arrested, charged with the capital crime of sacrilegious theft, and lodged in the town jail.

Legend has it that Goethe once observed he could have committed almost any crime, and since his day this has been a favourite reflection of those concerned to establish their credentials as outsiders. In the case of Moritz, his 'younger brother' as he was to call him, the brush with criminality was a fact. Years later, in his psychological magazine, Moritz was to publish many accounts of paranoiacs and depressives, and clearly he sometimes related these to his understanding of his own case. *Anton Reiser* was written over the period of his editorship of the *Magazin zur Erfahrungsseelenkunde*, and there are many connections.[19] The protagonist, though sometimes badly disturbed with psychotic symptoms, never lost his contact with the real world entirely. His depressions – seemingly more reactive than they were endogenous – he could often break out of in a manner which suggests they contained an element of pose, though this was also compulsive and therefore itself a part of the disorder. An amusing example is the incident when his melancholy is so profound his friend, Phillipp Reiser, whose ideas he claims were just as exaggerated and as 'novel-like' as his own, actually offers to shoot him before he gets even worse, and he has to decline hurriedly. An important character in the story, Philipp Reiser was in real life one Peter Israel Reiser,[20] who came from Erfurt, and was therefore considered a foreigner at school. He became Moritz's intimate friend, and must be regarded as the principal source of the protagonist's name. Much more worldly than the wretched Anton, and far better informed, 'Philipp' Reiser had the liveliness and wit, as well as the dialect, of the Saxon, and compared with him the native Hanoverians seemed stiff and dour. He had musical talents (he was to become a piano-maker) as well as a practical flair, and though also impoverished he was generous. His 'novel-like' fancies included the active pursuit of the opposite sex (an occupation which baffled Anton Reiser and bored him) and his equally ardent notions of friendship, philanthropy and self-sacrifice were also based partly on his avid reading of novels. The offer to shoot his bilious companion must have seemed to him a genuinely magnanimous proposition.

At the Hanover high school in the 1770s the life of the seniors, the 'Primaner,' appears to have been a rather free one, approximating to that of university students. They had their traditions, such as the torchlight procession at New Year, by which they put exceeding store. Anton Reiser is ignominiously excluded from this rite, since he cannot make the financial contribution exacted. This deprives him, as we are told in a significant phrase, of 'all the rights of his position [Stand]' (AR, 178). He feels so 'shut out, lonely and abandoned by the whole world,' that he even takes refuge in the Cantiques of Mme de Guyon! But this year of 1774, which thus began badly, was to be one in which his emotional life was sustained and nurtured by a huge expansion of his intellectual horizons. For the first time he becomes interested in philosophical questions and reads philosophical books. In the end, however, these perusings, especially Young's Night Thoughts, only contribute their part to the demonstration of 'the nothingness of life and the vanity of all things human' (AR, 184). Anton's discovery of philosophy, which is at first as though 'day was breaking in his mind,' leads rapidly to bewilderment and impasse, 'as if he suddenly collided with something that checked him and cut off any further view, like a plank wall or an impenetrable curtain – and then it seemed to him as if he had thought nothing but words' (AR, 181). Anton Reiser is not a book in which images and metaphors abound, but those it does employ are often so insistent that they acquire considerable symbolic force. One of these is that of the wall, which may be encountered within the mind as readily as outside it. In the instance quoted this image points to a fundamental, painful discovery, made early, often sadly disregarded, but never completely forgotten; this is the inadequacy of words, which Anton sees ultimately as mere toys of the mind and for ever separated from reality. The summer of 1774 brought some sort of crisis: burrowing dolefully in Young's Night Thoughts, tormented by perpetual headaches and unbearable boredom, Anton also had the pleasure of receiving his father's curse: clearly beside himself at his son's objections to his coat of coarse grey cloth, which made Anton look like a servant, Johann Gottlieb 'turned on his heel and gave his curse as a parting shot' (*AR*, 183). Everything now converges in a dreadful, paradoxical experience of finite and infinite horror as Anton is confronted by the tininess and the utter confinement of the individual. Once he had attended the execution of four criminals before the gates of Hanover, and had realised that all the watching crowd, himself included, could be equally well 'dismembered' [*zerstückt*] and that there is little difference between a man and a slaughterhouse calf. This episode is central, and 'zerstückt' is a key word. An obsession with dividing larger wholes (in this case human bodies) into smaller parts is combined with a neurotic terror of multiplicity, and a *taedium vitae* close to the melancholia of Romantic pessimists to come:

> That he had to get up one day and every day with this self, to go to bed with it – to drag this hateful self around with him every day.
> His awareness of himself with the feeling of contemptibleness and rejection became as burdensome to him as his body with its feeling of wet and cold; and he would have been just as willing to dispense with it as with his soaked clothes ... (*AR*, 188).

The confrontation with death, with the finite nature of the body, is linked with the realisation of its infinite possibilities of dismemberment, and the endless series of divided things. This fatal fascination with the infinitesimal is paralleled by visions of wholeness and circularity, and while both of these are significant as psychological symptoms they are obviously connected with Moritz's intellectual heritage, with Cartesianism and with a Leibnizian School philosophy which operated by means of deductive analysis and drew, at some remove, on Neoplatonist ideas. No doubt the rising tide of the empirical method, of which Moritz was to be a prominent German apostle, and the ebbing one of Pietistic mysticism also contributed. It is almost as if the constructs and principles of the High Enlightenment, of Leibniz and Wolff, of Gottsched and Mendelssohn, have become 'psychologised' in *Anton Reiser*, even to the point of turning into the degenerate property of an obsessional imagination. Crucial to Part Three of the autobiography, indeed to the whole book, is that conflict between the claustrophobic experience of confinement and smallness and the fractured vision of the Whole, which culminates in the most powerful description in the entire work, that of the encounter with the village churchyard. This passage is so remarkable it must be quoted in full:

Having escaped from the mocking circle of his schoolfellows – he wandered around in the lonely countryside getting further and further from the town without any destination in mind – He went across the fields until it grew dark – then he came to a broad path which led to a village he saw lying before him – darker and darker clouds began to cover the sky and rain threatened – the ravens started to croak, and two, which constantly flew along above his head, seemed to be keeping him company – until he came to the narrow little village churchyard which lay directly in front of him and was surrounded by stones piled untidily on top of each other to make some sort of wall – The church with the tiny pointed tower, covered with wooden tiles, in its thick wall on either side but one single small window through which the light could slant in – the door as though half sunken in the ground and so small it seemed it could be entered only if you stooped – and just as the church was small and unimpressive, so the churchyard was small and narrow, the rising mounds of the graves crushed together and overgrown with tall nettles – The horizon had already grown dark; the sky in the gloomy half-light seemed to hang down closely everywhere, the view was confined to the little plot of ground round about – the tininess and smallness of the village, the churchyard and the church had a strange effect upon Reiser – the end of all things seemed to him to run out to just such a point – the hollow narrow coffin was the last thing – behind this was nothing further – here was the plank wall nailed fast – which cuts off the view of every mortal man. The picture filled Reiser with disgust – the idea of this running out into such a point, this ending in a narrow, narrower, ever narrower spot – behind which nothing further lay – this drove him with terrifying force away from the churchyard and on and on in the dark night as though he were trying to escape the coffin which threatened to enclose him (*AR*, 265–66).

Tautologous, obsessional, this style – if style is indeed the man – points to the unbroken oneness of narrating and narrated self. Certainly we cannot re-tell the life story found in *Anton Reiser* without being continually engaged not just with fact but with mood, vision, art. The above passage brings together many of the dominant images of Moritz's autobiography – images of gloom and isolation, of low skies and glowering horizons, even adding in this case the birds of death. There are the walls – the one rough and untidy, the other almost windowless and very thick. Even more strikingly, there is the nightmarish half-sunken door which can only be negotiated half-bent, so similar to the door of the drying-room at Lobenstein's. There are also the graves and the coffin. There is the perspective of the coffin's shape, narrowing, running out to a point, so that the world terminates in a smallness without issue, whether psychological, theological, philosophical or mathematical. 'This smallness,' Moritz continues, 'approaches the point of disappearance, of annihilation,' and the transition from being to nothingness presents itself to Anton 'concretely' [*anschaulich*], while the fatal connection between concept and mood, idea and neurosis, manifests itself: 'Smallness arouses emptiness, emptiness arouses sadness – sadness is the beginning of annihilation' (*AR*, 266). The episode concludes in a wild, Ossianic coursing through the fields by night, with Anton temporarily transformed by a manic sense of inner liberation, aimless and free 'like the creatures of the desert,' then checked once again by yet another wall, high and strange, along which he staggers disoriented, afraid he is losing his reason, and being indeed, the narrator adds, 'maybe really close to insanity,' until the four towers of Hanover surge up before him in the mist.

The infinite sub-division of experience may be seen in *Anton Reiser* as the underside of that lucid analytical procedure which was the salvation of Karl Philipp Moritz. In his work the empiricism of the scientist is paradoxically related to the neurotic sensibility, and the writer's imagination is subject to a dialectic of expansion and contraction[21] involving a problematic encounter with time (to which we shall have to return for it is, I would submit, revealing for an understanding not merely of this writer but of his whole age). It was an age to which, of course, the young 'Primaner' increasingly belonged as a conscious intellectual being, growing up in the middle years of the literary Sturm und Drang. Things that modern, of course, could not be met with in school, where progressive attitudes meant at the most those of the Enlightenment rather than those of a rigid Lutheranism. But out of school Moritz participated in two current cults, that of Shakespeare and that of *Werther*. The response to Shakespeare was typical enough; we see how the plays wrench Anton out of his melancholy and help to make him manic again as he and Philipp Reiser sit up all night reading and declaiming them. *Hamlet* proved salutary, showing him that his spleen was not without its parallel in other men. And of the Werther cult Moritz-Reiser is perhaps the best documented aficionado, and an example of one in whom the effects were long-lasting. Goethe's novel, for which *Hamlet* no doubt prepared the way, went to his heart with its depiction of a morbid sensibility, its sense of existential isolation, and its rebellion against the class system, the limitations of society, and even the bonds of finite existence.[22] Many years later, after the completion of *Anton Reiser*, Moritz was to produce the outstanding critical commentary of his day concerned with *Werther*, and perhaps the first piece of incontestably immanent literary criticism written in German. This treats of Werther's letter of 10 May, but he always told people that it was that of 18 August which constituted the true 'centre' of the novel, the letter which speaks of the wings of the bird but also of the gaping of the grave. About the time of these literary experiences Anton Reiser starts keeping a diary again, and recounting to himself 'the inner history [*Geschichte*] of his mind.' For him the movement towards systematization is clearly synonymous with that towards health. He begins to grasp the importance of memory, without which the individual may possess neither identity nor coherence:

True existence seemed to him to be limited solely to the real *individual* – and apart from an *externally unchanging being who could embrace everything with his glance* he could not conceive of any such true individual.

At the end of his investigations his own existence seemed to him *merely an illusion*, an *abstract idea* – a combination of the similarities each successive moment of his life had with the one just past ... (*AR*, 192).

The discovery of the ineluctable nature of temporal succession goes hand in hand with a new conception of the possible nature of God. God, briefly, is perceived as that being who is not subject to succession, whose existence is not dismembered [*zerstückt*] by the flow of time. Anton comes to the point, as before at the gates of Brunswick, where as he walks one damp and gloomy day before the walls of Hanover he can see his existence as having form and shape, he can achieve 'a clear and concrete [*anschaulich*] conception of his own true, isolated life; which for a while was not attached to any circumstances but existed in and for itself' (*AR*, 197).

Circumstances [*Verhältnisse*] – these seem omnipotent, but they are the *details*. If a person looks upon the whole, he can learn '*to separate out the main lines [das Grosse] of life from its details*' (*AR*, 197). Here we come to another of the hinges of this book, which offers on the one hand a ruthless depiction of 'die Verhältnisse' in a manner unparalleled before the Naturalist writers of the later nineteenth century, and on the other gives itself structure as spiritual autobiography by drawing eclectically upon mystical, philosophical and aesthetic tradition. This dualism even means something in the cooped-up confines of the back streets of Hanover, where the world of the spirit still penetrates, as it did to Lobenstein's drying-room. There is for example the cobbler Heidorn, a mystic who has read Tauler and can even quote Bunyan. There is the cobbler Schantz, a metaphysician with whom Anton talks about space and time, and subjective and objective reality. And there is the astonishing vinegar brewer, 'who dwelt entirely in the shadows.' Like Tischer, the vinegar brewer lives at the heart of a labyrinth, a maze of corridors constructed out of barrels. His language is Low German, but he knows some Latin. He reads the novels of Fielding out loud with a fine declamation. A sort of Jude the Obscure, his grandeur resides in his ability to submit to a harsh destiny, to an oppressive society, to his exclusion, despite his intelligence, from almost all contact with that superior sphere in which he might have found some intellectual satisfaction. From his tiny wage the vinegar brewer saves enough to entertain young men of an evening, upon whom, surrounded by his barrels, he can bestow his Socratic advice. The modern reader might wish to see in this figure the unconscious herald of revolution, but 'the lofty patience of soul' (*AR*, 234) which Anton learns from him points as far as Moritz was concerned towards those Masonic ideals he was one day industriously to propound. *Anton Reiser* sees 'die Verhältnisse' as given and inescapable, though exceedingly bitter and difficult to bear; its resentments never turn into the beginning of an objective doctrine of revolution, though Moritz in other places criticises the aristocracy and even the idea of monarchy from time to time. Only in the molding of the single life, and in a resignation which originates in religious submission but makes possible in the end some degree of scientific understanding, can Moritz suggest an answer to the problem of the grip of history and of the moment of time upon the individual and the group.

LAST TWO YEARS

The last two years, 1774–76, which Anton Reiser spent at Hanover Gymnasium were a bewildering switchback of triumphs and disasters. What a triumph to be selected as the schoolboy charged with reading a formal address to the Queen of England on her birthday, 18 January 1776! What a satisfaction when Johann Gottlieb, on that very spot before the gates where he had pronounced his fatherly curse, now bestows his blessing! What an intolerable slight, however, to be excluded once again when the 'Primaner' stage their annual plays, and to be refused that role (Goethe's Clavigo) on which he has staked such hopes! At this moment he becomes so wild that he tears out his hair and cuts his face deliberately on broken glass. It is a defeat, after all, in the area of his dearest obsession, the theatre, which now begins to take over the book. It provides it with a climax, clarifies its meaning, and sheds light on its inner form. Linking the psychological analysis with the social in a firm mesh, it makes of the protagonist a figure of poignancy and, in a sense, of romance. He had begun to feel the pull of the theatre in 1773, when the Schröder troupe gave sixty-six performances in Hanover between April and July, including Charlotte Ackermann's portrayal of Emilia Galotti.[23] In April 1776 they returned for a further visit of three months (though Charlotte was now dead), and performed plays by Goethe (*Clavigo* and *Stella*), Klinger's *Die Zwillinge* and H.L. Wagner's *Die Reue nach der Tat*, all Sturm und Drang works.

Anton Reiser saw a good deal of this repertoire, which also included a lot of operetta, saw in fact much more than he could afford, to the great disadvantage of his school work, and even attendance. He had been gripped, ever since Pastor Paulmann, by theatricality, by the urge to stand at the centre of the circle of attention, and by the need to simulate emotions of which he felt deprived. Trenchantly, the narrator diagnoses this complex of impulses as 'the seed of all his subsequent miseries' (AR, 140). In his gluttonous reading – 'as much a necessity to him as opium may be to orientals' (AR, 144) – he swallows play after play, using his laundry money to pay off the bookseller, starving all day and then squatting half the night in a blanket living through the frightful hunger scene in Gerstenberg's Ugolino. The splendour of the theatre in his imagination increases in inverse proportion to the decline of his material circumstances and prospects, and it becomes linked with an unquenchable urge to travel, a connection which is called 'a peculiar romantic idea.' Anton Reiser is not alone in preferring the thought of the acting life to that of the University of Göttingen, and with him in this is Iffland, who was to follow in his footsteps along with several other schoolfellows. Moritz inserts a paragraph situating the cult in its social context: 'It really was then the most splendid period for actors in Germany, and it was not surprising that the idea of such a splendid career as that of the theatre fired the imaginations of a number of young people ... ' (AR, 254). The realities of the theatre, behind the wings, and of the travelling companies, were of course quite another thing, as Anton Reiser and certain other works, notably Goethe's Wilhelm Meisters Lehrjahre, show. But the furor theatralicus, as it spread among German youth, had a variety of causes: the florescence of the drama in the Sturm und Drang, the transient excellence of a few acting troupes, and more profoundly the psychological response to a social situation with little outlet for the imagination and energies of middle class children. Moritz is merely the outstanding recorded example of the depradations of theatre-mania, a widespread epidemic.

The winter of 1775–76, with its succès d'estime in January, was dogged by depressions and a sense of 'monotony' all the same. The hysterical face-slashing episode was still in the future, as was the village churchyard, and spring brought the trip to Bremen, Anton's 'first strange, novel-like journey,' from which moment on 'he put name and deed together' (AR, 237). He became, that is, an obsessional traveller [Reiser], and the hike to Bremen which took several days, has many of the characteristics of his subsequent perambulations. The name Bremen seems enticing, conjuring up for him the vision of a city grey and black. The impulsiveness which generally overrides rudimentary caution makes him spend more than he can afford on a barge trip down the Weser. Practically penniless, he discovers himself miles from anywhere on the open road, in a deserted [öde] countryside. Even in the town itself, where he cannot find the person on whom he meant to call, his 'novel-like ideas' are dispelled by an upsurge of mean physical reality, 'the cruel necessity of spending this night in the open, in the middle of a densely populated town, tormented by hunger and exhaustion' (AR, 240). On this occasion Anton Reiser succeeds in avoiding the worst consequences of his improvidence, and returns to Hanover his appetite for travel whetted. But this city is infernal, and intolerably monotonous, his life seems inexorably drab and hamstrung. Moreover, he cannot pay his debts. Therefore, with the help of his best friend, he plans his breakaway.

Their separation, as Philipp Reiser opens the gate leading on to the wall, is recounted with hyperbole, and the great journey commences with an epigraph taken from *Werther*: 'To knock so coldly, so stiffly at the iron gate of death' (AR, 272). Anton quits Hanover with urgent, hasty tread, as though 'the maw of the grave once more were opening up behind him' (AR, 272). The image tells us much about the ultimate nature of these wanderings, in the imagination of both protagonist and narrator. The chance of escaping at last from infinite smallness is appreciated again as the traveller looks back to see the houses of the city crowding closer and closer together, 'until at last the four towers, which marked the scene of all his affronts and miseries up to now, vanished from sight' (AR, 272).

Thus ends Part Three of the work, and Part Four, not published until four years later, is largely devoted to the adventures of Anton Reiser in the world beyond the walls. The composition of Part Four belongs to a period of still greater maturity, after Moritz had returned from his long stay in Italy and had established an intimate relationship with Goethe. This fact is, as we shall see, of some significance, and it is perhaps the reason why the dualism on which the book is founded emerges even more sharply in this section than before. Confined up to now very largely to the labyrinthine alleys and cramped chambers of oppressive, still half-medieval towns, the narrative opens out suddenly on to the highways of a wider world. Although such a thought goes far beyond the author's horizons, it is tempting to see this scene change as somehow symptomatic of social transformations to come. Now everything is in flux, the rigidly compartmentalised world of eighteenth-century Germany is broken open, and landscapes come and go, hills rise and fall, steeples materialise and fade again from sight, walls and gates confront this first of the German Romantic wanderers with emblems of hope and of despair. For Moritz-Reiser this was just one of what was to be a series of such break-outs, in search of self-renewal, of self-reinforcement, would-be major surgery in which 'the thread of his previous life seemed severed' (*AR*, 274). The probable date of his departure from Hanover was 30 June, 1776, and his initial goal was Weimar, where Eckhof's famous troupe was then performing.[24] With them he hoped to find employment, and to be quickly able to pay off the debts he left behind. To do this would salvage his bourgeois identity, and emerging thus into a new life he would be 'resurrected there after dying here a civil death' (*AR*, 270). The notion of palingenesis, it has often been observed,[25] is an important one in Moritz's writings, and translates a basic social experience into a psychology and terminology still influenced by Pietism, while also interpretable as a pattern of deep reinsurance.

It is not possible here to give a detailed account of Anton Reiser's wanderings, though they seem to invite it, making as they do a picaresque, often comic and always vividly realistic tale. For this major journey, one of some 120 miles on foot, he is typically very ill-prepared. His entire liquid funds amount to one ducat, so that even the impetuous Philipp Reiser tries to dissuade him from the undertaking. His clothes have already been mostly pawned to pay for theatre tickets, and all he is left with is the suit in which he delivered the address to the Queen together with a gilded dress sword, silk stockings (with a couple of pairs in reserve), an extra shirt, an overcoat and shoes. He carries with him, for relaxation, a copy of the *Odyssey* with Latin translation, and for identification nothing but the Latin poster announcing the ceremonial address, to be delivered by one 'Reiserus.' His magnificent get-up leads to solicitous attentions in the first inn he comes to, in Hildesheim, and these he cannot afford. He is thereafter compelled to restrict his rations to dry bread and beer, and to sleep on straw. Typically enough, his castles in the air become grander as his state worsens. He awakes on the straw before the hearth, to 'the beer mugs, the black bread and his weariness' (*AR*, 278). His mood follows the countours of the landscape as he labours towards his mirage, acting out in his fancy ferocious roles like that of Guelfo in Klinger's *Zwillinge*. Near Seesen, he wanders with near disastrous consequences on to a musket range. He sits romantically in a medieval ruin, compares himself to the Disciples as he plucks ears of corn, and remembers Ulysses. Approaching Mühlhausen he has to deal with an importunate recruiting sergeant who considers him easy prey, and gets through by brandishing his poster and his Latin, while the spite of material objects viciously attacks him in the rapid disintegration of his shoes. 'It is curious,' Moritz writes, 'how the most despicable real things can intrude in this way into the most glorious constructions of the imagination and destroy them and how a person's fate can depend upon these same despicable things' (*AR*, 290).

The town of Gotha to which, as he learns, Eckhof's troupe has moved, now becomes his goal. When he gets there the Director receives him quite well, his assistant Reichard somewhat less warmly. In Gotha he hangs around for a week or two, living on credit and counting on the imminent offer of a place with the company. When Reichard communicates the official rejection, one day in the theatre, Anton Reiser is all but paralysed with shock: 'he walked to where the stage with its last curtain bordered on the bare outside wall and leant in despair against this ... he saw no way out of this labyrinth into which his own folly had led him – here was the bare blank wall, the illusory play was at an end' (*AR*, 301). The language here is persistently figurative: the wall, the labyrinth, the inner theatre which is Anton's imaginative life. By such metaphors, as well as by overt moral judgments, Moritz seeks to interpret his past existence, and they have an integrating function as well. Eckhof's company refuse to engage him, not even as a prompter or a cleaner, and his absurd proposal to work for nothing is also turned down. His despair provokes death fantasies and the notion arises of becoming a building labourer, like those he sees at the castle. But at Eckhof's suggestion he rushes wildly out of Gotha on the road towards Eisenach, where another company is said to be playing, leaving his coat and his few other possessions behind him. The romantic landscape around Eisenach, and the old Wartburg, temporarily raise his spirits, but these are then dashed entirely by the discovery that the actors have departed that very morning for Mühlhausen. He spends his last pennies on ascending the Wartburg, where he stands, it seems to him, 'high above his fate.' But the unavoidable return from Eisenach to Gotha now takes him (like the unfortunate in the well-known Kafka anecdote) days instead of hours, and he becomes lost in a maze of his own contrivance: 'As labyrinthine as his fate was his wanderings now became, and he could find no way out of either' (*AR*, 308). Actually reduced to living off the roots of the fields, he staggers about the countryside 'crazily' [*wie in der Irre*], and the narrator follows this pun with the note that 'nothing but imagination' now ruled him, and yet 'his destiny was not as much a novel as he would have liked' (*AR*, 309). So he begins to pretend to himself he has committed some crime, has killed a nobleman of his acquaintance while at the University of Göttingen, a delusion which takes such possession of him that he tells it as truth to a friendly clergyman and it even invades his dreams.

This might well look like the ultimate outbreak of schizophrenia, and certainly Moritz often asked himself subsequently if he had always been sane. But the comment the narrator makes on this occasion points in a different direction; it is the observation that such dreams were in fact his salvation, for they insulated him from the true hopelessness of his condition. The book is full of evidence that, though Anton Reiser was a paranoid, he never developed a genuine schizophrenia. The author's subsequent labours as a collator and editor of cases of mental disease gave him certain standards of comparison, and he was aware that he had never suffered from true insanity [*Wahnwitz*]. He perceived, to use modern terminology, that his symptoms were essentially reactive, and often merely neurotic, since they emerged for the most part as ineffective behaviour. For Moritz they were clearly identifiable as the consequences of social misfortune and miseducation. If we cannot entirely agree with this self-diagnosis, especially in view of his conduct in later life, we can probably accept it in essence. It is unmistakable how, in the fields between Eisenach, Gotha and Mühlhausen, 'a dreadful desert,' this 'abandoned and disregarded creature' lives out again the fantasies of his Pietistic childhood. Accompanied by a journeyman cobbler he meets at an inn, who initiates him into what he calls the order of tramps (for whom life is always changing and free) Anton staggers on to Erfurt, close to collapse but revitalised by a spring on the city's outskirts, writing the poetry of this moment in his mind as he quenches his thirst. In this, the literisation of his life, Moritz-Reiser is something of a prototypical figure in German literature. To make a novel of one's life is to surrender to delusion, but to see the poetry of it, as of the spring at Erfurt, may be something else, a positive enrichment, which the narrator calls 'the only compensation for the necessary consequences of his folly' (*AR*, 313). In Erfurt too, as he drinks a last beer he thinks this portends 'the forgetting of all things, future and past,' and he becomes dissociated from himself, 'a strange creature for which he could no longer think, for it was irrevocably lost' (*AR*, 314). Here in Erfurt, however, once again, there comes an astonishing upswing of fortune. Benefactors materialise, and he finds himself a student at the university there, where he stays for a whole term.

In fact, the adventures just summarised took place in July 1776. By early August, Moritz was in Erfurt, where he matriculated as a *studiosus theologicae*, as did all those not in medicine or law. Erfurt was, in area, the largest town Moritz had seen, although its population (about 14,000) was less than Hanover's. But it was surrounded then by an extensive belt of gardens, while a fire at the end of the previous century had made space for further gardens within the walls. Thus Erfurt had a pleasant spaciousness which must have meant a good deal to someone as sensitive to the feel of place as a claustrophobic like Moritz. Under Catholic governance (it belonged to the Electorate of Mainz) Erfurt boasted several monasteries, in particular a Carthusian foundation in a romantic situation just outside the gates. This place caught the newcomer's imagination, and there began a period of his life characterised by a certain religious-romantic sentiment. He visited the Carthusian chapel frequently, and the lot of the monks acquired for him 'an inexpressible attraction,' for they had found the opportunity of giving up their dearest desires. These castration fantasies also occur in *Andreas Hartknopf*, which draws heavily on the Erfurt months. They may have been encouraged by his friendship with the unlucky Dr Sauer, a physician who treated the city's poor gratis, earned his own wretched living as a proof-reader and wrote poems, but who appeared to Anton Reiser as a classic case of a man crushed by the 'weight of circumstances' [*Druck der Umstände*], by public indifference and disdain.

Little is known of the course of Moritz's studies in Erfurt, an old but undistinguished university, although he claims to have done a great deal of reading there. This included the best-selling 'monastery novel' *Siegwart*, but we should note that Moritz-Reiser also set about writing a satire upon sentimentality. He came under the influence of Professor Just Friedrich Froriep, who also appears in *Andreas Hartknopf*,[26] whose classes in homiletics he attended. The Erfurt months were certainly of vital importance, providing as they did a temporary shelter from the savage goddess Fortuna, and some opportunity for stock-taking. It must indeed have been in Erfurt that systematic self-reflection began. Dr Sauer, in telling Anton 'of the many acts of oppression from his relatives and teachers to which he had been exposed from his childhood' (*AR*, 332), was holding up a mirror to his listener's life. Disgusted at the cruelty and indifference the world had shown towards this good man, Anton resolves to fight back in his own case, despite his old problems which still dog him – growing penury again, as the support he had pretended to himself and others was on its way from Hanover fails to arrive, the inevitable dinners on charity, and disreputable clothes. He has to contend with his own depressive nature, with his nausea over his own existence, with his recurrent sense of being a superfluous man, excluded from everything and wanted by no one. Outside the walls, the countryside seems to lie in wait, perhaps ready to swallow him up for ever. Drenched by the cold rain of winter, he takes to wandering about both inside and outside the town, quoting *King Lear* to himself ('to shut me out on such a night as this'), with the scornful laughter of the world about him. It is in Erfurt that the thought occurs to him of setting course for Weimar to seek a position as Goethe's valet, an idea which, had he tried to put it into practice, might quite well have ruined the rest of his life. Like the Carthusian monastery, the dark cathedral of Erfurt appeals to him as the longed-for refuge from the world, and agreeable dreams of Lethe provide a constant accompaniment to his sense of extrapolation and insignificance. He slips continually into what the narrator compares to 'dreams of a fever patient' (*AR*, 344), but also rises from time to time above it all as he begins to comprehend the etiology of his personality troubles. It is on the walls of Erfurt, to the sound of church bells, that he first glimpses the sense and pattern of his past:

... his existence was not limited by the present moment – on the contrary, this embraced once again everything already past.

And these were the happiest moments of his life, when his own existence first began to interest him, because he saw it in a certain pattern and not isolated and fragmented [*zerstückt*] (*AR*, 322).

To see his life as possessing a design and a meaning, to see himself as a case history, was to discover the possibility of autobiography and moreover of an autobiography that was scientifically based. On a deeper level still it was to recognise that an individual may, in his consciousness of himself, overcome fragmentation, succession, and the perpetual dismemberment of self-hood in time.

In Erfurt, Anton Reiser increasingly concerns himself with writing. He contributes to a local periodical, *Der Bürger und der Bauer*,[27] produces second-rate poems like *Das Kartäuserkloster*,[28] and absorbs in viscous doses both *Siegwart* and Klopstock's *Messias* – read out to him by a new-found friend, Neries, as they sit at the edge of the romantic Steigerwald. Built into the account of the Erfurt period are the reflections sub-titled 'The Sufferings of Poetry,' which contain Moritz's clearcut rejection of the literary aspirations of young men without creative gifts. They may confidently be dated to the Italian or post-Italian days, and are closely linked with his major contribution to aesthetics, *Über die bildende Nachahmung des Schönen* (1789). If this section of Part Four functions as a ritardando, the pace picks up again as Anton Reiser turns once more towards the theatre. From November 1776 until the beginning of February 1777, the Speich troupe was performing in Erfurt. Driven by his sleepless urge for 'the romantic and theatrical,' Anton secretly obtains an engagement with them, and delighted with himself he starts to study a role. But twin devastating blows of fate demolish this fantasy with little delay. There is the terror of the totally extraneous discovery that he is going bald, and when this gratuitous assault from the hostile universe has been temporarily parried there comes the thunderclap of the university's intervention on opening night, completely forbidding the appearance of one of its students upon a public stage. Even now, however, Anton's resilient day-dreams are not finally dispelled. Once more he resolves on abandoning everything else in favour of a theatrical career, and sets forth in the middle of a harsh winter for Leipzig, where the Speich company is due to play next, although it is obvious that they have already fallen on evil days. Director Speich has gone ahead with the wardrobe; and since Anton Reiser travels on foot he arrives at the destination last. In the inn in Leipzig his fantasy meets with its ultimate quietus: he finds the company penniless and broken, the Director having sold the wardrobe and absconded with the cash. The final line of *Anton Reiser*, Part Four, thus radiates a peculiarly cheerless gloom: 'The Speich troupe,' we read, 'was now therefore a scattered flock' (*AR*, 357).

AUTOBIOGRAPHY AND TRUTH

Moritz's autobiography, then, takes us up to the first days of February, 1777, the middle of his twenty-first year. Some of the lines along which it can be understood and interpreted have already been indicated, and it now remains to develop and connect these rather more systematically. The book was not intended to terminate where it did, and Moritz's contemporaries evidently expected some continuation.[29] As regards its genesis, the first part cannot have been composed prior to winter 1782–83, since it contains references to the author's travels in England that previous summer. The second and third parts were written in the period 1783–86, and the final part was finished in 1790, more than a year after Moritz's return from Italy. Had the story been continued it would, as we shall see in subsequent chapters, eventually – though not immediately – have found a more positive vein. That it was not is more likely to have been the result of other preoccupations than of any conscious decision (Moritz certainly did not regard it as his *magnum opus*). All the same, the manner in which the fourth part concludes cannot be considered to be wholly fortuitous, but is rather a calculated narrative effect. What we have here may be described as a fall-away ending, which nicely rounds off the satirical depiction of a misspent youth, and reinforces the book's pedagogical impact, something the author regarded as its main justification and purpose. By the time he came to write Part Four, Moritz had decided to go beyond the indictment of theatre-mania among the young and beyond an exposition of the internal machinery of his own development; he now wished to uncover the roots of the nefarious cult of the artist which had proliferated in the wake of *Werther*. In his decision to do this there was not so much the disdain and incomprehension of a man of the Enlightenment, like Friedrich Nicolai, but rather the self-insight of a perceptive psychologist, confirmed by the light his friendship with Goethe now shed on the errors of his life. *Anton Reiser*, however, cannot simply be classified as a therapeutic autobiography, of importance for German social history; it must also be treated as a work of literature, of art. The widespread reluctance to recognize this – more widespread among scholars than among creative writers – goes back no doubt to Moritz's own, exaggerated disparagement of his capacity as an artist, which was justified only in relation to his lyric poetry and his feeble attempt at a drama. Outmoded nineteenth-century genre theory causes confusion when applied to a work which, though it is certainly an autobiography, was called by its author himself, for good reason, a novel. Any adequate account of it has to begin by addressing this question.

The issue of the generic identity of *Anton Reiser* is an important one, though it should not be overinflated.[30] As was noted already, it must not be confused with the quite separate matter of historical truth. For all autobiography involves some shaping of the past, and tends to read sense into happenings by hindsight. Generally paramount is the author's concern to see his life whole, and he tampers with his past by the very selection and omission of details, and of course by fixing the relevance of events and sometimes expanding their implications.[31] But paradoxically this interference (as it appears to be) with historical truth may often be the precondition of another kind of truth which has its own value, for only thus can an autobiography become the faithful expression of the fully developed personality behind it, can it expose the relativity of human identity in time and perhaps attain to a profounder authenticity. This kind of veracity, therefore, is not unlike that of the novelist who, in writing his novel, discovers himself and creates a 'core of norms and choices' which comes to constitute the implied author.[32] Now there is incontestably a certain amount of fiction in *Anton Reiser*, and while this may not make of it a novel, it confirms the need to remember that autobiography is always art. Earlier versions of passages in the finished work show, for instance, that Moritz often polished up his material and sometimes altered matters of 'fact.'[33] Contradictions may be found which cannot necessarily be explained as mere failures of memory or carelessness, but which suggest conscious fictionalisation. The most grotesque 'error' occurs at the end of Part Three, in which Reiser sets off from Hanover 'in the middle of winter,' only to be found the very next day (at the beginning of Part Four) contending with the heat and chewing ears of corn! The most obvious piece of invention is in the game indulged in with the protagonist's name, to which we shall return; let us merely note here that the experience of meeting another boy at school with this rather unusual surname (Reiser) is entirely fictional, since the records show that there was at that time no other boy at the Hanover Gymnasium called Moritz.[34] Evidently it would be unwise to go in for bald distinctions and to assert that while *Anton Reiser* is not a novel the two *Hartknopf* books, written at the same time in a deliberately mystifying style but also containing much autobiographical matter, *are* novels. Nor would the term 'autobiographical novel' be a very illuminating alternative. In the end the degree of fictionalisation may have little to do with the degree of truth, because the creation of purely symbolic characters and situations may derive from a powerful will to get at the truth – the hidden inner truth or the broader, typical one. Dispute as to the veracity of *Anton Reiser* at the time of its publication was quite lively.[35] The obituary by K.G. Lenz actually attacks the book as fiction masquerading as truth, calling it, perjoratively, 'a work of the imagination.' Lenz argues that Moritz took no notice of the recognized requirements for writing 'the history of a life,' mixed up the events of earlier years with those of later ones, and – still more serious – was impelled to embellish his very ordinary existence out of sheer vanity. Hence he defines *Anton Reiser* as 'a semi-novel [*Halbroman*] similar to Rousseau's *Confessions*.'[36]

This contrast between 'semi-novel' and 'history' [*Geschichte*] is significant, in that it reflects the hostility of the German 'Aufklärer' to the novel [*Roman*], by which they understood a sensationalistic, meretricious form of literature without valid pedagogical function and favouring the exotic, the simply incredible, and the sentimental. Driven by an urge for verisimilitude, they much preferred what they had (after Samuel Richardson) come to designate 'histories,' by which they meant accounts of the lives of believable, ordinary and generally bourgeois people, true to life if not actually true, but first and foremost psychologically plausible. The question arises why Moritz, in accordance with this distinction, did not call *Anton Reiser* a 'Geschichte,' but chose the designation 'psychologischen Roman.' An examination of the Prefaces to the four parts combined with a study of the use of the terms 'Roman' and 'romanhaft' within the text itself suggests a reason, and illuminates the wider implications of the choice.[37] Moritz equivocates in the first two Prefaces between 'novel' and 'biography,' declaring in the second that 'what I called, for reasons I imagined not difficult to guess, a psychological novel is in its essentials a biography and moreover a presentation of a person's life down to its smallest nuances, which is as true and faithful perhaps as could possibly be.' This might appear to settle the matter, if the 'reasons' referred to are taken to be solely those of discretion. However, they may not be, and we do know that the author's own uncertainty dates from the very outset of the project, since it is reflected in a fragment published as early as 1783.[38] The confused nomenclature may derive partly from Moritz's perception that only biography can form the basis of a convincing psychological history,[39] but this explanation is inadequate to account for his use of the term 'Roman.' The Preface to Part Three provides an important clue: 'At the end of this part,' he writes, 'Anton Reiser's wanderings commence, and with them the real novel [*Roman*] of his life.' We can compare this with the employment of the terms 'Roman' and 'romanhaft' in the corpus of the book to imply, as they invariably do, illusion, departure from fact, exaggeration, fanciful imaginings, or simply lies. Anton Reiser and his namesake, Philipp Reiser, addicted as they are to the reading of popular novels, live in a world of dreams. When Anton proposes to act out, at the feet of his benefactor, Pastor Marquard, a hypocritical little scene of contrition, this is called 'playing at a novel' (*AR*, 172). When setting out to write an essay on the passion for novel-like experience [*die Liebe zum Romanhaften*] he considers the strangeness which can suddenly be evoked by a changed consciousness of the place one is in, and of the exotic allure of far away spots one may read of in novels. He is aware that everyday life can take on this 'unreal shimmer' too, and we can perceive here how features which belong historically to some variant or other of the traditional novel of adventure with its baroque origins (especially the travel novel) have become in *Anton Reiser* subjectivised, a function of the protagonist's imagination.

This leads to a useful insight: that Moritz's autobiography is in one sense a subjectivisation of 'Roman' material. Anton Reiser's dominant impulses may be described as 'novel-like,' or 'theatre-like' – for the genres, viewed as metaphors for patterns of behaviour, are practically synonymous. Thus Anton seeks to make a stage of his life because he cannot get on to the stage – or the reverse. He acts out his play, or he lives out his novel. *Anton Reiser* is therefore a landmark in being perhaps the first work in German literature which draws in a scientific way the negative consequences of the Sturm und Drang, analyses from within the often baneful results of the specifically literary imagination, and warns that a person must free himself at all costs from those urges which would have him turn his life into a novel or a play. There are obvious analogies between this subject-matter and the Quixote theme, which was popular in the German Enlightenment.[40] But there is more to it than this. The 'real novel of his life,' of which Moritz speaks so strikingly, is consubstantial with the period of Reiser's wanderings, his 'adventures' in the wide world into which he finally breaks out. Quite early in the book, when he leaves Hanover on a short trip to his parents' new home, he feels himself 'transposed out of the limited circle of his existence into the great wide world, where all those wonderful events he had ever read of in novels were possible' (*AR*, 132). We have already observed that the story is built upon a series of rises and falls,[41] as time and again Anton's bubble is pricked when his mistaken assessment of the situation, or some accident, results in a shattering reversal of his hopes. These endless peregrinations and vicissitudes are symbolic of the protagonist's whole life, and not merely of its lack of contact with reality, which is the groundwork of the book's irony; they point to something objective, that moving power of the old 'Abenteuerroman,' Fortuna, Chance, life's sheer unpredictability. In *Anton Reiser* the travel novel [*Reiseroman*], a sub-form of the adventure novel, becomes a symbolic structure, partly interiorised, but partly still objectively referential. Part Four thus brings the emergence of the underlying theme, as though at the close of some *Enigma Variations*. The pattern of Reiser's life may be seen as subjectively conditioned by the ambivalence of his feelings, the molding force of his neuroses (or psychoses), and thus eventually surmountable, curable. That is to say, until Anton becomes mature enough to write his 'history,' he cannot avoid living out his 'novel.' But it is a pattern which also objectively lays bare Moritz's understanding of the way the world is made, ruled mostly by the spite of circumstance and by blind chance. *Anton Reiser* contains the cases of others, the Amtmann's son and Dr Sauer, who are ravaged by this objective power. Although the narrator, sometimes censorious, sometimes serene, always superior, points out the follies of his hero with the clarity of a philosopher-satirist, we may also sometimes sense other dimensions in him, the presence of a richer and more ambiguous identity, an implied author who knows of the menace and hostility of the universe and for whom stoical ideals of resignation are the ultimate recourse. Thus we may conclude that this autobiography was meaningfully called a novel for it is in fact this too, and reflects an unresolved duality of vision in the author: a didactic contribution to the ironic mode, it is its simultaneous proximity to the tragic which gives it its most effective appeal.

It is fairly clear why Moritz failed to exorcise the demon of Fate which dominated the world of the old 'Roman.' Goethe, who confronted the same problem in his *Wilhelm Meister*, at least appeared to resolve it by restoring a rationalised Providence. But Moritz had the difficulty that his most original contribution to literature, his concepts of environmental influence and the importance of accidental and apparently trivial circumstances in childhood and adolescence are in some respects the secularisation of these old demonic powers. While struggling towards the freedom of the rational consciousness, he remained gripped by his insight into determinism, for the former, as it expanded, also illuminated the latter more intensely. This points, of course, to a profound paradox of the whole Enlightenment, which is rarely quite so obtrusive as it is in this work. If we enquire further into the sources of the notion of the 'novel-like' in Moritz's mind, we find that the idea is rooted psychologically in something more specific than an addiction to exotic fictions, or even a pervasive neurasthenia. He saw his early life in retrospect as a series of mishaps conditioned by a cruel childhood, a psychologically identifiable and interpretable 'Geschichte'; but he also saw it as a 'Roman,' being a flowing development of quasi-exotic events instinct with fluctuation and open to blind chance. And he saw it in this second way specifically because of something ingrained in him by his Pietistic education. When after one of his interviews with the centenarian Tischer Anton returns home deeply moved, resolved to turn again towards God and to fix his mind steadily upon him, he recalls with nostalgia that blissful period long ago when he felt he could converse with the Lord in high expectation of his mercies. The narrator then continues:

In these memories there was an indescribable sweetness, for the novel that the pious fancy of the faithful plays with the Highest Being, by whom they think themselves sometimes abandoned and sometimes accepted once more ... really has something lofty and grand about it and keeps the mental and emotional energies [*die Lebensgeister*] in constant activity ... (*AR*, 128).

In describing the relationship between the pious soul and God in terms of a novel, Moritz shows up its spurious nature; but at the same time he concedes the grandeur of this fiction, this 'romance.' *Anton Reiser* is the work in which he applies the model to the unstable relationship between the alienated individual and society, to the endlessly frustrated pursuit not of God but of community by this new type of Wertherian, extrapolated man.

I have connected the ambiguity, or more correctly the multivalency, of 'biography,' 'history' and 'novel' with the several realities of protagonist, enlightened narrator and implied author. There is of course no one-to-one relationship suggested here. *Anton Reiser* is an autobiography with overt fictional elements, having a complex narrator who treats his protagonist's life as both history and novel. Anton himself lives out his existence as though it were a novel, and the gulf between him and his narrator is much wider than is usual in autobiography, certainly wider than in Rousseau's *Confessions*. This narrator is first and foremost a rationalist and a pedagogue, distinguished by his informed, scientific objectivity and by his common sense. His detachment is such that he can bring in examples of other cases – one of enuresis is cited for instance. Occasionally, it is true, the use of a present tense betrays the continuing oneness of narrating and narrated self. But *Anton Reiser* is an important contribution to German satire. Irony is certainly one of its major devices and even the term 'psychological novel' might well be read ironically. Anton is seen in some degree as an *alazon* (to use Northrop Frye's term), a pretentious, self-deluded fumbler, brought into unusually sharp social focus. His theatricality is portrayed as his chief characteristic, and his theatre-mania understood as an externalization of this. Taught by those who bring him up to simulate feelings he does not have, he is perceived to impose upon himself even more than he does upon others. The sardonic narrator, shrewd and assured without being smug, never fails to point this out. But the cool bitterness of the account of the childhood is complemented by a more generalized satire, an acid portrait of the Pietist movement in some of its more fanatical aberrations, an indictment of parental unfeelingness as the source of much human misfortune, and a criticism of the insensitivity and short-sightedness of all too many teachers. Most importantly, Moritz in Part Four satirises the self-delusion of would-be artists led astray by the quixotic and undirected rebellion of their imaginations. Where else in German literature of this period, or for that matter anywhere in European literature then, do we find a title such as 'The Sufferings of Poetry'? Between 1786 and 1790 Moritz changed the emphasis of his work, as the difference between the Prefaces to Part Three and Part Four makes evident. He was now ready to press inexorably the argument that the cult of novels and of the theatre had seduced a whole generation into dangerous infatuations. In the orbit of Goethe in Rome he discovered once and for all the distinction between receptive aesthetic sensitivity and genuine creative genius, and put the *poète manqué* firmly in his place long before Romanticism had come to pass, never mind its agony. Indeed, *Anton Reiser* may be regarded in the history of German letters as a precocious attempt to dam the Romantic cataracts, near their source.

But the waters flowed over it and all around it, and in any case it really belonged to them. The most characteristic form of irony in *Anton Reiser* is itself of a proto-Romantic kind. It is that which springs from the constant subversion of Anton's fantasy structures [*Gebäude der Phantasie*] by the world of matter. Impressed by Werther's comparison of life to a puppet play, aware of an analogy between the human anatomy and the mechanisms of the wooden-limbed marionette, Anton Reiser is persistently haunted by the corrosive absurdity of corporeal restraints and necessities. It is the pain in his left foot which theoretically prevents him from going forth like St Anthony to dwell in the desert; it is the desire for his supper which exposes the inadequacy of Mme de Guyon's spiritual techniques; it is the freezing weather which soon dissipates his elevated excitement at joining the school choir; and it is eventually the imminence of starvation which brings his dream-châteaux crashing down around him. Anton Reiser leaning his forlorn head against the wall at Gotha is then outdone by the desperate wanderer tearing up roots for food. The tyranny of the body extends, in fact, beyond the realm of irony into that of tragedy. The tragic thing is that men have bodies, they are finite. But within the realm of irony the body serves very well as a harsh reminding factor, as the sheer tawdriness of the physical environment is constantly contrasted with the opulence of the dreams. In this meanness and absurdity all men are encompassed, as the novel makes abundantly clear – not only Anton Reiser, but also the piano teacher expelled by Lobenstein for spreading excessive butter on his bread, and Lobenstein himself sweating out his terror of damnation in his herbal bath.

Irony, tragedy, tragi-comedy – Moritz exploits this whole range. The grotesque is also an effect very near at hand. Thus the protagonist's incipient baldness is a blow which cannot be attributed to society or to the cruelty of men, but is one of those gruesome little strokes of wit of which the universe is so fond. Such grotesqueries, like the crowing hen in Lobenstein's yard, teeter on the brink of tragi-comedy in the modern sense. One thinks perhaps of Cyrano de Bergerac's nose, even of Joachim Mahlke's Adam's apple (Günter Grass's *Cat and Mouse* has some points of similarity with *Anton Reiser*). In Moritz's own period we can find parallel effects in Lenz's play, *Der Hofmeister*, and here begins a tradition in German literature.[42] Heinrich Heine's admiration for Moritz no doubt partly derived from his seeing in Anton Reiser a primitive prototype of his own sophisticated self-image, a character in whose experience the abrasive friction of ideal and reality issues aesthetically in an obsessional breaking-of-mood [*Stimmungsbrechung*].[43] This tragi-comical vein in the novel culminates in the curious account, at the end of Part Four, of the attempted dramatic performance of *Die Leiden des jungen Werthers* by the Speich troupe in Erfurt. Two rusty pistols, not properly tried out beforehand, failed to go off on the stage, so that the luckless player of Werther was forced to seize a bread-knife which happened to be lying before him and thrust it through his waistcoat, an action followed by the entrance of Wilhelm with the inappropriate cry: 'My God, I heard a shot!' We are reminded of course of Nicolai's *Die Freuden des jungen Werthers*, the celebrated Aufklärung parody of Goethe's novel. But the parody achieved by the Speich company is of a different order, for it is an accidental one, itself illustrative of the spite of life. This ought, the narrator implies, to have served to bring Anton to his senses, showing up the comic underside of tragic pathos ('Hardly can any tragedy ever have ended more comically'), and thus helping to render his favourite self-identification absurd. But Anton was so far gone that he could only think of how the performance might be improved and the Wertherian fantasy played out to a more fitting conclusion.

It is a fantasy which, far from being 'perfected,' needs to be abandoned. Only thus, the message goes, only by escaping from the self-created fiction of one's life, is there any hope of avoiding not a tragic but a banal and ludicrous outcome. A person can elude self-parody only by being careful to refrain from self-fictionalisation or, as it might be formulated, there will be no bang at the end in any case, and the whimper will sound funny. The irony of *Anton Reiser* is much more deeply rooted than is the case with other satirical novels of the German Enlightenment because it springs from this *insider's* grasp of the mechanisms of self-delusion. If the Pietists and their fraternity were responsible for warping the boy's early development, it was also paradoxically the self-observation of their *praxis pietatis*, 'noting every step, every smile, every expression and every word' (*AR*, 106), which provided the basis for his self-understanding. We may consider the central character either primarily from the point of view offered by a depth-psychological analysis or primarily from that suggested by considerations of social psychology. I have indicated that it would be wrong to regard Moritz-Reiser as a schizophrenic, that he was a marginal psychotic, and that the disorders from which he suffered were mostly affective ones. *Anton Reiser* is of course remarkable for offering a meticulous analysis of the childhood sources from which these derived: 'These first impressions were never erased from his mind [*Seele*], and often made of it a resort of black thoughts which he could not dispel by any amount of philosophy' (*AR*, 9). This refers to the altercations which filled the family home, and Moritz particularly suggests that his own morbid sensitivity and his hunting out of slight and rejection may well have been an acquisition from his mother. The combination, at any rate, of this agitated, largely love-shorn environment, the harshness of the father and the hysteria of the mother, with the pinching straitjacket of Quietism and the threat of hell, makes it clear enough how Anton Reiser became trapped in a vicious circle of rejection of the world and rejection by it. By the age of twelve he was already, in the words of the novel, a depressive: 'ein völliger Hypochondrist' (*AR*, 65). We must observe en passant that sexual problems are scarcely alluded to in Moritz's analysis, and the avoidance of this whole field of human pathology is characteristic of his psychological writings in general. When Anton's landlady, Frau Filter, warns him of the perils which beset young boys, 'luckily Reiser did not understand what she meant,' but resolved to fight 'wicked desires,' be they what they may. We are told that unlike Philipp Reiser, he has no interest in girls, because he cuts such a sorry figure in his unkempt clothes. He finds Philipp's stories of erotic escapades boring, and he skips all the passages in the many novels he reads which deal with such things. He even tries to disregard the love-story in

Werther.[44] The explanation he offers for this repression is simply 'the oppressiveness of his circumstances ... self-contempt, and even emotional fancies [*Schwärmereien*]' (*AR*, 328). That Moritz's self-analysis falters at this particular point is in itself a highly telling fact.

If he was therefore not aware of the Oedipal nature of his relationship with his father and of the consequences attendant on the stifling of his libido, this can hardly surprise us. The astonishing thing is that Moritz sees so much: symptoms such as the sadistic games, the link (scarcely perceived by anyone in his day) between childhood conditioning and deviant adolescent behaviour, and the functioning of various types of compensation mechanism. He carefully delineates the highly specific personality pattern of withdrawal and self-abnegation punctuated by explosive outbursts of self-assertion and muffled aggression. He perceives the machinery underlying the life of the recluse, and the escapism of the monkish cell. He even isolates something like the so-called 'oceanic' experience: 'Walking became so easy for him that the ground beneath him was like a wave on which he rose and fell feeling himself borne on from one horizon to the next' (*AR*, 281). Perhaps following a metaphor drawn from the mystics, he also speaks of losing himself in the ocean of mankind. If he does not fully grasp the nature of repression, he does actually use the word 'verdrängen,' which was to become a century later the technical term for it. As Anton hastens one gloomy day through the gates of Hanover out into the seclusion of his beloved woods, leaving behind him this infernal city 'where everything turns in a circle,' the thought of the vast but barren [*öde*] world before his mind, he feels 'crowded out' [*herausgedrängt*] from this cramped spot 'where human destinies converge,' and it has, he realises, been his fate since childhood to be thus 'pushed aside' [*verdrängt*]; Moritz continues this word-play, as Anton feels inspired and ennobled by the fact that he is not one of the 'crowd' [*Gedränge*], but stands outside it, confirmed in his individuality, for on this occasion the experience of exclusion has a positive effect, 'forced [*drängte*] him back within himself' (*AR*, 197).[45] Later on we learn that Anton's failure to be chosen to take part in the seniors' play exemplifies the identical process, and all social life is then summed up as 'this pushing and being pushed' (*AR*, 246). In the Preface to Part Four the word 'verdrängen' is given a perhaps decisive twist, by being specifically related to compensation, to sublimation, in fact: 'From the previous parts of his history we can see clearly: that Reiser's irresistible passion for the theatre was really a consequence of his life and his fate, by which he was forced out of [*verdrängt*] the real world, and since this was made painfully unbearable for him, lived more in fantasies than in reality.'

In these examples a term which was to acquire a figurative sense of central importance for psychology is already employed by Moritz in a manner which verges thereon. We see it beginning to expand from a meaning which is still for the most part purely social, to do with the relationship between the individual and the mass. Perhaps the psychology of *Anton Reiser* is best regarded as a social psychology, which in any case any viable psychopathology of the individual must comprise. We are confronted here with a personality disorder which Moritz seeks to account for – and which is no doubt best accounted for – as a result of environmental conditioning, aware as he nonetheless is of the darkness which shrouds the question of congenital predisposition. As the outstanding, and the most unsentimentalized, portrayal of lower class life in German literature of the eighteenth century, *Anton Reiser* must also be seen as an early study of alienation. The unallayed yearning for social acceptance and a meaningful existence within an idealised community has been isolated as the principal key to the protagonist's behaviour,[46] and this view has something to commend it. When Anton becomes a student at Erfurt, for instance, we read: 'He had a place in the ranks again, and was a citizen in a social class which tried to distinguish itself from all the others by a higher level of culture' (*AR*, 318). The elitism of this sentiment should not be overlooked, however, and it is this which constantly modifies Moritz's deep egalitarian instincts. Nevertheless, this author is more outspoken than almost any of his better known contemporaries in pointing to the source of the malaise he exemplifies so well, in the rigidity of contemporary society:

Fundamentally it was the sense of *the oppression of people by the social order* [*bürgerliche Verhältnisse*][47] which laid hold of him here and made life detestable ... What had he done wrong before his birth so as not to be a person like the others? ... Why did he have to have the role of *worker* and someone else that of *employer*? (*AR*, 262).

As we shall have occasion to note, there are several other equally unequivocal and historically precocious statements to be found in Karl Philipp Moritz's writings, but as the episode of the vinegar brewer clearly shows, the revolutionary impulse in him was muted and turned aside by a variety of factors, internal and external. This open indictment of social oppression and the exposition of its consequences for the individual's personality development is closely linked to that remarkable study of environmental conditioning which is the great achievement of the book. Moritz's understanding of economic oppression is purely subjective, his insight into political structures superficial. But he has an astonishing perception of the functioning of the psychological determinants of place and time. In *Anton Reiser* a powerful imagination has rendered the towns of Brunswick and Hanover positively demonic; they have become claustrophobic dungeons of psychic torture, overpowering labyrinths 'where the houses seemed ready to fall on him' (*AR*, 263). This is an innovation, and pre-empts the increased role of cities in the novels of the next century. We have noted the motifs of gloom and darkness, curtailed vision, tapering perspective and looming walls which culminate in the nightmare in the village churchyard. Such a scenario, not only Romantic – 'ein schönes Nachtstück' (*AR*, 268) – but practically Expressionistic, seems appropriate in a novel which reduces life to the hazardous encounter with a receding unknown, social but also transcendent, where 'every God ... his thoughts could envisage was too small and had to have a still higher one above him, compared with whom he was insignificant, and so on to infinity' (*AR*, 28).

This dimension of infinity is frankly peculiar in a novel written under the strong influence of the Berlin Enlightenment. Equally peculiar is the labyrinthine style, the almost total absence of dialogue, the punctuating dashes, the rhetorical questions, the repetitions of word, phrase and sentence. Agglutinative, graceless, Moritz's prose moves cumbersomely, with the trudge of a fearful treadmill, around and around the same patterns of recall. The labyrinth, a spatial concept, can be regarded as a figure for the process of Anton's existence in *time*, sustaining his hopeful fantasies about as often as it does his melancholia and despair. In the dreadful dead end at Gotha, and then in the fields beyond, his life becomes a labyrinth without issue. The labyrinthine nature of life in time is inimical to seeing an existence clear and whole and it therefore confounds all autobiography. Anton Reiser is long unable to visualise 'his entire life in Brunswick ... in a single, total vision,' essentially because of the grip of the moment of time and place which inhibits or precludes that freedom of vision which alone could so embrace it. But to see this labyrinth from above, 'spatially' laid out like a map or a city,[48] as one day begins to be possible on the walls of Erfurt, is tantamount to escaping from it. Such a liberation requires the severance of those 'threads' by which the consciousness adheres to 'the momentary, the everyday, and the dismembered (pieces) of life' (*AR*, 67). Thus the power of circumstance is ultimately presented in *Anton Reiser* as an unbroken chain, a circle or wheel, this elemental grip of the everyday moment, endlessly repeated, upon the subordinate mind. Moritz remained a Cartesian in his insistence that mind is distinguished from matter in having no extension in space, but he saw it as existing fatally in time, for all mentation involves succession. As in the executions before the gates of Hanover, any human life must always appear as *disjecta membra*, reduced by time to an infinite succession of moments of servitude, which defy the formation of any whole and persisting self that might transcend this condition.

In his *Kinderlogik* of 1786, Moritz insists that a human being must be able at all costs to expand his existence 'beyond the present moment, in which he would otherwise be swallowed up along with everything around him' (*KL*, 94). Here we can make the transition from the psychology of *Anton Reiser* to the logic, the philosophy which inheres in the book. Logical analysis, a procedure involving partition which can invite the neurotic fear of infinite smallness, also presupposes a rational understanding, an ideal, 'transcendental' domain. Moritz was certainly not a major philosopher, but he was nevertheless responsible for interesting aperçus and original probes. He did play an important – and until recently largely overlooked – part in the development of the theory of the symbol,[49] and incidentally offered, in his *Hartknopf* novels, an equally unremembered demonstration, years before its time, of a 'symbolistic' style. *Anton Reiser* contains a set of insistent motifs and images, and the process of symbolization in that work goes on on two levels: it is a technique employed by the writer to give his autobiography a coherent structure, but it is also the fatal ritual of the protagonist, an essential element in the machinery of his self-delusion. To find symbolic meanings in everyday objects and events was of course a habit among the Pietists, as they strove to gauge the condition of their lives, and read the pointers to the will of God. In just this way Anton Reiser tries to perceive in the *accidentia* of social intercourse the flickering indications of his fate. He is especially inclined to accumulate portentous, predictive fantasies around objects – the twin towers (church and theatre) of Gotha as he trudges over the plain, the clock-tower of Hanover with which he associates Pastor Paulmann's phrase 'the heights of Reason' (*AR*, 71), and which always brings to mind his dearest aspiration, to inspect the great clock from close at hand, to peer behind its face into 'the mysterious mechanism of the wonderful sound' (*AR*, 70). But the narrator dismisses this symbolization of his yearning for psychological knowledge as 'a game of his fancy,' and perhaps he does have good grounds for being critical of such mental processes as these. Closely analogous, of course, are Anton's word games, his response for example to the ineffable vocable 'Hylo,' which he thinks he hears in a hymn, but which turns out in the end to be nothing more exotic than 'Hüll' O ...' Thus symbolization may be seen to subvert the rational judgment in many cases.

Nevertheless, on the other level this process makes its contribution to the coherence of the book, lends this autobiography-cum-novel something of that self-centredness, that autonomy, which in Moritz's view authenticates the work of art. In *Anton Reiser* there is a structuring and patterning which is observable first of all in the language. Moritz's linguistic studies, many of which belong to the early 1780s, demonstrate a fascination with synonymic and homonymic elements, with the music and autonomy of words, with the suprasegmental, and generally with the verbal surface. The bare, reiterative monotonies of *Anton Reiser*, its agglutinative tautologies, have their own special impact, pointing as they do by their formal nature to the inescapability of the psychological patterns, a labyrinth almost without end. Various leitmotifs may be picked out, for instance the phrase 'so tot, so öde' ('so dead, so barren') which possesses its own peculiar rhythm of despair. Repetitive exclamations – 'Welch ein Donnerschlag!' or 'Was Wunder ...!' – knit different experiences and developments together, the first of these on the level of the protagonist, forever deluded and taken aback, the second more on that of the narrator, who has understood the law of causality. Anton Reiser's name, quite obviously, has a significance which might even be called allegorical. Moritz intended the self-evident allusion, although clearly the idea for the name must have come from that of his Erfurt friend, on whom he playfully bestows his own first name, Philipp. There is also a reference to St Anthony, who fled into the desert, and this may conceivably explain the choice of 'Anton.'[50] Moritz sometimes tended to see Anton Reiser as a typical sentimental traveller, while Anton felt himself to be a kind of Ulysses, tricking his way towards his goal, but it is on both levels, in the end, that he exists as both of these, and on both levels moreover that he plods over the sandy plain a pilgrim on the thorny path which leads to the City of God.[51] The landscapes through which he tramps are in some degree stylised as is the vagabond himself: plains and fields like deserts, low horizons cutting off the view, walls and towers which expand it whenever Anton, like his successor in Eichendorff's Romantic fantasy *Taugenichts*, climbs up over and above his fate. Wild nightscapes, discomforting, strange churches, graveyards, garrets, heaths – these *topoi* continually return, and the outlines of a genuinely symbolic topography begin to glimmer through, developed simultaneously and much more firmly in *Andreas Hartknopf*, which has been justly called 'the first symbolical novel in German literature.'[52] In this topography the city gates function so conspicuously that we may even speak here of a metonymic or synecdochal effect; they always point to the same connections, that moment of break-out which is also the moment of self-transcendence, when the labyrinth of streets and time is shed and the meaningful whole of the life discerned in the autobiographer's suddenly liberated vision.

The geometric metaphors in *Anton Reiser* have already been briefly referred to; they form a special group and link the book, as we shall see, with much that is important in Moritz's theoretical writings, where they are widely used. These metaphors – the straight line, the curved line, the point and above all the circle – derive from a common reservoir of mathematical imagery of which the German 'Aufklärer' were quite fond, but in Moritz's usage they hint fairly unmistakably at their descent from the mystical lore of the Renaissance. Geometry and topography, figural associations and onomastic games, all of these processes have in the end one and the same function, which is to be the bearers and bestowers of coherence within this at first sight straggling and gawky but in reality obsessionally concentric narrative, as Anton Reiser's ceaseless searching, his obscure groping after shape and integration is continued by the implied author on another plane. The atomising technique, empirical as well as analytical, by which events and feelings are dissected and individuality dismembered is itself subject to compensation. Upon the incoherent facts of his stumbling past Moritz imposes not just the cool order of his scientific understanding, vital though this is, but also an artistic form. *Anton Reiser* becomes through this very act the microcosm of a dichotomised self in which protagonist and enlightened narrator are both bound, as what is called in the *Kinderlogik* 'the art which transforms the dismembered [*das Zerstückte*] into a unity' (*KL*, 113), and which all autobiography demands, is actually put into practice. This is also a process of healing, and depends on an insight into neurosis and its causes. It depends upon the courage of a commitment to fact, and equally upon a heritage of philosophical idealism. The notion of the interdependence of part and whole, and the aesthetic doctrines founded thereon, provide the theoretical basis for a procedure of analysis and synthesis which makes sense of life by overcoming the process of fragmentation in time. Moritz continually returns in his work to the need to see the temporal in spatial form, to have a liberating overview of the labyrinth and a totality of vision comparable to that of God, the supreme biographer. To annul succession means to end its monotony, to disperse *taedium vitae* and the perpetual repetition of the moment with its inexhaustible ennui.

Anton Reiser should not be underestimated in this regard; it stands side by side with *Die Leiden des jungen Werthers* at the ceremonial inauguration of Romantic melancholia, more modern even than Goethe's novel as a systematic psychological case-book, more old-fashioned no doubt in its partial appeal still for rescue to the idealism of the Enlightenment, and in its pedagogical tone. 'The trouble with fiction,' Aldous Huxley once wrote, 'is that it makes too much sense. Reality never makes sense.' If this is true, then *Anton Reiser* must needs be fiction, for it certainly makes sense, and in more than one way. Part Four turns upon an unmasking of the cult of the would-be artist in a frustratingly confined society as it developed among sensitive but in Moritz's view inadequate personalities distorted by faulty compensation reactions. The perspective, like the Classical aesthetic which Goethe and Moritz devised in Rome, was of course in some respects too narrow. But Part Four also epitomises the underlying deeper theme, for it presents, visualised thus and therefore ultimately justified aesthetically, 'the real novel' of the protagonist's life. The novel of the self is a whole, it belongs, like all art, to a world of forms, and the attempt to write it, in the Germany of the 1780s, was a highly topical endeavour to save this integratable world in the face of an intellectual and social reality which seemed increasingly to deny it. In this, *Anton Reiser* belongs to the mainstream of modern spiritual autobiography, as it began to flow in the eighteenth century, and this impulse provides a key which can help to open up for us the rest of that life we have to recount and seek to understand.

2

Enlightened Man Emergent

When the principal of the Speich troupe of actors makes off with the funds, the last hopes of Anton Reiser are dashed and the autobiographical novel comes to an abrupt conclusion. This fall-away ending is aesthetically effective and appropriate, in the light of the author's purposes. It was, however, only partly intentional, since it was meant to be merely the dénouement of one part of the work, not of the whole. At one time the author had in mind to continue his story further, but in fact never did so. It was left to Karl Friedrich Klischnig to carry it on. Klischnig's 'fifth part' of *Anton Reiser*, published in 1794,[1] is our chief source of information on the rest of Karl Philipp Moritz's life, after the arrival of Moritz-Reiser in Leipzig in early February 1777. Klischnig had become his close friend, having initially been his pupil at the Kölnische Gymnasium in Berlin, where he attended Moritz's popular, if perhaps unscholarly class on Horace in 1783. From 1784 to 1786, before he went to university, Klischnig shared a house with his teacher and was thus well qualified to write about him from intimate personal knowledge. In the period after 1786 his subject's life became relatively public anyway, though for the early years (i.e. before 1783) Klischnig had to rely on conversational fragments, since Moritz apparently refrained from ever giving him a coherent account of his previous career. Klischnig writes poorly, and his half-hearted attempt to emulate the manner of *Anton Reiser* is a calamitous failure. As might be anticipated he is also by no means impartial, but strives to present as engaging a portrait as he can.

It is from Klischnig that we know how Moritz survived the final collapse of his attempts to become an actor. And in this case it was, as rather often in his life, chance which corrected the total failure of design. Penniless and more or less desperate, he encountered, in an inn near Leipzig, a member of the sect of the Moravians (Herrnhuter). A discussion of mystical matters, 'the nothingness of the human will,' ensued, and intrigued this gentleman, one Herr Meyer. At Meyer's suggestion Moritz thereupon accompanied him to nearby Barby, where the Moravians had their seminary, and where he is recorded as having arrived on 11 February. He apparently applied for formal admission there, declaring it was his hope and intention to save his soul, and he must have sounded convincing, since the Community – usually rather cautious about neophytes – accepted him provisionally. It is worth noting that the Moravians differed in fundamental respects from the followers of Herr Fleischbein and of Mme Guyon. Less narrowly sectarian, their religion centred on a doctrine of love which was affirmative and optimistic, although frequently inclined to emotional excess. No austere demand for total submission to the will of God dominated their faith. Their leader at that time, Bishop Spangenberg, an acquaintance of Goethe's, who had spent some time in America, evidently impressed Moritz as a man of broader experience and greater wisdom than anyone he had ever met before.[2] The Moravians, for their part, seem to have recognised their visitor's basic honesty of intent, but were discerning enough to be sceptical of his constancy of purpose. This may have been why his application for permanent residence, composed in Latin, was turned down for the time being. In any case, Moritz's enthusiasm seems to have begun to wane after a few days and a characteristic boredom and restlessness supplanted his sudden resolve to devote the remainder of his life to spiritual contemplation and the cultivation of the soul. After about a week, therefore, he decided or was prevailed upon to depart, being advised that he should complete his university education and then, if he wished to, come back to Barby. The Moravians gave him some money, probably little more than his travelling expenses back to Erfurt, but he used it to get to Wittenberg.[3] Afterwards, he kept in touch with Barby, at least for a while, writing to Professor Bossart, a lecturer at the seminary, in duly pious terms: 'I live alone in tranquillity, and ask God to bring me to the knowledge and love of him to whom we owe all our eternal bliss. If you did not object to my spending a day or two with the Community at Whitsuntide that would be a great blessing for me' (1 May 1777). Since visitors were generally recorded in the books at Barby, however, and there is no reference at all to any such second visit, we may assume that it did not take place.

Though the language of Moritz's letter to Bossart is certainly very forced, it would be an oversimplification just to label it insincere. For conscious insincerity presupposes a certain self-knowledge and even some stability of point of view, neither of which he possessed. His emancipation from the thraldom of Pietistic religious feeling and from mystical preoccupations of various sorts was certainly neither sudden nor was it ever complete. The context of Moritz's life over the next ten years, however, was one in which the hold such things had over his mind inevitably weakened enormously. About the first twelve months or so of this period, which were spent in Wittenberg, little is known. That they were far from being pious months, at any rate latterly, is clear enough, however. Moritz matriculated at the University of Wittenberg on 27 February 1777. This was at that time by no means the most distinguished educational institution in Germany, inferior to Erfurt as a university, just as Wittenberg was substantially inferior to Erfurt as a town. In 1760, during the Seven Years' War, it had been practically wiped out, and seventeen years later large parts of it still lay in ruins. No one had ever bothered to remove much of the rubble, or to repair the shattered walls. Out of some kind of piety the castle church had indeed been rebuilt but the castle itself had not. The town itself was confining and depressing, little more than a couple of streets.[4] The defects of the university, though no doubt less conspicuous, were equally discouraging. The Enlightenment had scarcely penetrated its orthodox halls, which at that time held a bare hundred students, most of them poor. A few years afterwards, Moritz wrote about the extraordinary cheapness of living there: two student houses actually providing without charge a bedroom and study, a table with a wooden stool, and a bed of straw. Many students received a small grant disbursed by the Elector of Saxe-Weimar, and it was not difficult to obtain free meals. In return for all these blessings the instruction offered was minimal. Many of the lectures and classes announced were either never given or soon abandoned for lack of interest. Much time was wasted in writing theses and conducting public disputations; this was old-fashioned, as was the dress – wigs being still very popular there, especially among the theologians. The chief amusements were, of course, drinking and fisticuffs, but both to unusual excess.

The atmosphere at Wittenberg was therefore, as Klischnig admits, 'still very rough,' and Moritz himself gives some account of it in *Denkwürdigkeiten*. These entertainments were apparently even more deplorable there than at most other universities in Germany, which is saying a good deal. Students were not infrequently killed or crippled, and those who were not spent much time sleeping off their hangovers. Moritz seems to have been a noisy participant in the tippling, though he probably kept out of the way of the fighting as best he could. He achieved some notoriety by delivering a speech from a window overlooking the market-place, in which he denounced certain actions of the Rector as infringing upon the rights of the student body. No more is known of this incident, and since the source is Moritz's own account to Klischnig, it may have been rather inflated. He also claimed to have acquired the sobriquet 'Genie' (genius) from an ill-disposed professor – a term which by this date had already become one of ridicule. That his alcoholic dissipations were especially wild in his times of depression we may well believe, for this is consistent with previous and subsequent patterns of behaviour. Periods of frenzied activity oscillated with long stretches of inanition and stupor. He would sit and brood for days, doodling and pondering gloomily where on earth he could go should he leave Wittenberg. He stayed there in fact until May 1778, a good two semesters.[5] Professor Titius, the professor of physics, was his particular patron, and helped him obtain his free accommodation at the Kollegium Fridericianum. Titius encouraged Moritz to study theology, a practical enough subject in those days. He also arranged for him to earn money as a translator and tutor in the English language, and so the lecture list (summer 1777) proudly announces: 'Herr Moritz gives instruction in English, and in reading the best English authors.'[6] He must have known rather little English at this time, but few would have noticed this in Wittenberg.

Perhaps in some degree these two semesters constituted a liberation which was badly needed. Academically they can have meant rather little, although Moritz did eventually (in 1779) proceed to the degree of Master of Arts.[7] In the spring of 1778 anyway, against the advice of Titius, he left the university for Dessau. He was on his way to the Philanthropin, the experimental school established in that town a few years previously by Basedow. Johann Bernhard Basedow (1729–1790), one of the most significant figures in the history of education in Germany, was to be a considerable influence upon Moritz's intellectual development, although without doubt a very mixed one. A passionate educational theorist, and a resolute practitioner of his own revolutionary ideas, Basedow had begun his career in the unenviable lot of a house tutor, but had gone on to teach at the Royal Danish Academy for Noblemen at Soroe and then at a high school in Altona. He had published works on philosophy and theology and had then turned to education. A gifted persuader, cajoler and fund-raiser, Basedow had subsequently badgered the plutocracy of Europe, from crowned heads to Free Masons, to support his plan for the publication of a massive instructional manual in three volumes, the *Elementarwerk*. This enormously successful and influential schoolbook began to appear in 1774, and provided a complete foundation for elementary education as its author conceived of this. The essential aim was to contribute to educational reform by stressing the cultivation of the personality rather than the exaggerated inculcation of learning, to impart both the exercise of the intelligence and the immediate actual practice of virtue, and (to quote from Christian Garve's very positive review):

... to elevate the lower classes, without eliminating distinctions, by better instruction and nobler practices; to liberate the higher and more learned from the illusion of a false superiority and wisdom and to join them with their brothers more precisely by means of an ideal primary purpose for their common education, [and] to rank our disciplines more according to the influence that they exert upon the happiness and individual perfection of everyone.[8]

The success of the *Elementarwerk* which, in the spirit though not in slavish imitation of Rousseau, is one of the high points of the new 'Philanthropist' pedagogy, encouraged Basedow to go further and seek to create an establishment in which his methods might be practised under his own direct supervision. He had been invited to go to Dessau in 1773, by one of the most progressive and intelligent princes of his day, Leopold Franz von Anhalt-Dessau, and now he launched an aggressive campaign of letter-writing to solicit funds for the new school.

Once again Basedow was, at first, remarkably successful, raising money not only in Anhalt-Dessau and in Denmark, but also as far afield as the Imperial and Russian courts (though not, apparently, from the thrifty Frederick the Great). His public appeals were generally couched in a sentimental hyperbole which is both personally revealing and also in some degree the style of his age: 'Nature! School! Life! Be these three friends, then the human being will become what he should be and as yet cannot be; happy in his childhood, cheerful and eager to learn in his youth, content and useful as a man.'[9] Basedow denounces contemporary schooling which, he claims, generally destroys the natural capacities of the mind. He complains that no one in Germany gives a thought to the practical training of schoolteachers nor even whether it matters what text books are used in school (it was here that the *Elementarwerk* was supposed to fit in). A pious Christian himself, though unorthodox (he later criticised the Wolfenbüttel *Fragmente*, that test case for free-thinkers), he is very insistent that the Philanthropin shall be a truly Christian school, but within the framework of Christianity he feels that liberty of conscience should be preserved. He wants to reform the antiquated teaching of Latin, by going over entirely to the direct method (he himself apparently conversed in Latin both fluently and incessantly and expected his assistants, and his pupils, to do the same). He proposes to teach French in a similar way, and maybe even English. For the rest, his school was intended to be eminently practical in its programme of instruction; entirely professional subjects, such as law, theology and medicine, were excluded, but otherwise Basedow purported to teach everything that was useful, including mathematics, history, political geography and rhetoric. This programme is, of course, much less extreme than what had been proposed by Rousseau in *Emile*.

The story of the Philanthropin is a picturesque and instructive commentary upon one vein of Enlightenment idealism, but at the same time a fascinating illustration of the single-minded devotion, not to say fanaticism, of one man. Basedow was an overbearing, hard-driving and in some ways ruthless individual, vain, opinionated and self-centred, and yet consumed by the passionate need to do good to his fellow-men. Goethe describes him vividly in his autobiography, and refers to him in a humorous poem.[10] The school, which opened in 1775, was an odd mixture of idiosyncratic rules and practices, and of pedagogical reforms which seem in retrospect astonishingly daring and progressive. Though Moritz never actually taught there, we can be certain that the goals and methods of the Philanthropin made a deep impression upon his mind, although as time went on he found more to criticise and even ridicule in them. At this school learning by rote was terminated at the age of twelve, students were encouraged to wander about the classroom during lessons (indeed, sitting down was limited, by statute, to three hours per day), and play-learning was developed among the younger boys. There were quaint authoritarian inconsistencies, however: uniforms were worn, and beating was permitted in 'incorrigible' cases. Geography, to take one example of the methods used, was supposed to be taught by means of 'two large hemispheres, the surfaces of which are divided into land, water (etc.), and which must not be completely spherical but merely somewhat curved, so that they can be walked and jumped upon.'[11] The geography class must have been a strange one, supposing further that much of the instruction was given in Latin. Equally muddled, though well-intentioned, was the institution of one day of fasting per week, the insistence on military drills and training, and the proposal that the pupils should live in tents for two months out of each year. A great deal of money was sunk into the Philanthropin, including Basedow's profits from the *Elementarwerk*, but from the outset the school's survival was problematical (it finally closed down in 1793). Basedow, as Curator, began with just two assistants, of whom at least one, Professor Wolke, seems to have been a devoted and gifted man. There was a struggle to get boarders from wealthy families, which was of course the financial key to the whole enterprise. Here the Philanthropin was not very successful, and the trouble may have been in part Basedow's reputation for flagrant heresy (he was a vociferous denier of the Trinity). Rather typically, the school also offered free education and board to a small number of poor boys so that they might be turned into superior domestic servants or house-tutors, for the ultimate purpose of improving (but not dispossessing) the gentry. The Phi-

lanthropın was scarcely viable with less than twenty-five boarders, but in
1775 it opened with only nine. The whole undertaking became the subject of
controversy, some of it malicious, and Basedow was forced to defend himself
against (probably baseless) charges of personal profiteering. In 1777 Johann
Heinrich Campe, an educationalist soon to be as widely known as Basedow
as well as personally much closer to Moritz, became Assistant Curator, but
when Moritz arrived in Dessau the next year Basedow was once more in
command for a short period of time.

Bushy-eyebrowed and domineering, and possessed of a rasping voice,
Basedow likely enough intimidated Moritz. At their first encounter he delivered, as he did to all and sundry, an excited speech larded with visions
and promises for the future. On this occasion there was no shortage of ma-
laga, a weakness of Basedow's as conspicuous as the stinking tobacco about
which Goethe complains, and Moritz may very well have been grateful for
the wine, since he had just walked from Wittenberg to Dessau in execrable
weather and had caught a serious cold. Basedow then asked him to translate
Horace's Ode *The Fountain of Bandusia*, no very rigorous test perhaps,
which he survived. Very soon after this meeting, which was inconclusive,
Moritz took to his bed at a local inn with a bad fever. This illness lasted
several weeks and his situation became truly dismal. He was indigent, having as usual made not the slightest provision for misfortune. He knew no one
in Dessau, apart from those he had met briefly at the Philanthropin. The
innkeeper begrudged him every spoonful of soup he was fed by a kind-
hearted maidservant, and remarked with curses that it seemed to be his fate
to receive in his establishment every tramp who happened to pass by. This
was of course neither the first time nor the last that Moritz was taken for a
vagabond, and he did occasionally come close to being just that. In this
instance he was finally rescued by Basedow, for all his faults a generous and
humane man, who found out where he was, paid his bill and sent Wolke to
look after him. Basedow probably took this further opportunity to involve
Moritz in his grandiose schemes. At some point, at all events, he said to him:
'Friend, if you had enough courage and were the sort of man I am looking
for, together we could move mountains. I have ideas, plans, like none conceived by anyone before – but I need participants, participants!'[12]

Moritz, certainly wisely, did not respond to this appeal. There was after
all a sober streak in him, despite his behaviour. More important, he was
probably beginning to identify success with access to the established order of
society, had perhaps always thought of it thus, and Basedow was distinctly an
oddity and an outsider. Moritz is that type in whom eccentricity is in part an
expression of frustrated conformism, and whose refusal to accept social

norms is a function of his sense of social rejection. Furthermore, Professor Titius and others at Wittenberg had like as not warned him specifically against Basedow, and first impressions probably confirmed for him that this man had indeed the makings of an egocentric tyrant. Many years later, in his novel *Andreas Hartknopf. Eine Allegorie* (1786), Moritz published a sharply satirical sketch of the educationalist in the figure of Hagebuck, the tipsy 'world-reformer,' staggering along through the night at Hartknopf's left hand, like an ambulatory and unrepentant Thief descended from the Cross: 'The leader on the left hand had great black bushy eyebrows and bristly hair and wore a velvet suit made of the sweat and blood of betrayed humanity' (*AH*, 10). This judgment of Moritz's maturity picks out the clownish, even charlatan element in Basedow and certainly fails to do him justice. In any case, however ambivalent the personal impression, Moritz was affected by the ideals and theories which were the basis of the *Elementarwerk* and of the Philanthropin. The view of the teacher's task held by the 'Philanthropist' movement, and reflected in the work of Basedow and Wolke, was one which in some ways he made his own. His reading of Rousseau certainly strengthened this direct impact. The need for learning, these theories of course held, had to be tempered not only by the inculcation of virtue or, better, by the release of the natural goodness of the self, but also more broadly by a genuine concern for the full development of the pupil's emotional life. Moritz, moreover, knew as well as Rousseau and better than Basedow what repression really meant, and later on indeed he was to come closer than Basedow ever did to formulating this problem consciously and in a manner that we can still recognise as relatively modern today.

THE BUDDING TEACHER

These weeks brought low in the inn at Dessau were a nadir equal to any that he had experienced before. Klischnig attributes to this period one of the very few poems from his friend's pen that may have some literary value. After first quoting the wholly undistinguished lament, *Die letzte Klage des Wanderers*, he then discusses another, and longer, example which he published under the title *Freund Hains Errettung*, calling it 'another poem written in the same spirit but of real poetic worth,' which Moritz saw fit to pretend was a translation from the Old English, thus causing one 'Herr Kriegsrat Ursinus, the editor of ballads and songs in the Old English and Old Scots' to ask him in vain for the original. This poem, which Basedow evidently saw and admired, was actually first published in 1791, as *Die Stimme drinnen und der Fremdling draussen*.[13] It takes the form of a dialogue between a stranger who comes to a tiny hut, and a voice from within the hut which bids him enter. To do this, however, the stranger needs to get down upon the ground, so low and narrow is the entrance. He is afraid of the voice and would fain flee but his feet will not bear him away. Drawn on inside the hut by a clammy hand, the stranger there finds death, or rather peace, for the latter is the overriding emphasis:

> Nun hab' ich dich, du Trauter,
> Nun bist du immer mein.
> Nun sollst du nimmer wieder
> Ein Spiel des Zufalls sein.

The lines of Death's lengthy concluding speech give expression to a moody adolescent nihilism, in which the discomfort of the inn at Dessau no doubt finds its expression. The death-wish partakes of the melancholia of contemporary graveyard lyricism, with something of the *frisson* of poems like Goethe's *Erlkönig* and Bürger's *Lenore*, which latter Moritz knew and admired. The stress on chance and on the vicissitudes of life belongs, however, very much to this particular author, as does of course the motif of the hut and of the man who has to bend to the ground to find its door, which we have already discovered elsewhere. Our interpretation of this does not need to be restrictedly Freudian. We can also see in it here once again Moritz's claustrophobic terrors, his sense of confinement and debasement, and of the minuteness, and sheer awkward inaccessibility of that Narrow Gate, to whatever it may lead.

Rescue by Death, however, remained a purely hypothetical solution. Soon after Basedow had paid his debts, the poet was on the road again, this time heading for Potsdam. Once again a chance conversation, with a Berlin merchant, had put a new idea into his head – that in Potsdam, the garrison city of the Prussian army, an appointment might be had for the asking as a regimental chaplain in view of increased requirements stemming from the new Bavarian war. Moritz was to be disappointed in this hope, for one or more of several reasons: either because he had no real qualifications, or because of a shortage of places, or because he could not produce a birth certificate, or because he did not possess the 70 Thaler needed for outfitting (indeed, he did not possess that many pfennige).[14] Faced with this situation, he formed the suicidal resolve to enlist as a common soldier, is said to have been dissuaded from this step by an acquaintance (we do no know, however, by whom), and was thereupon fortunate enough to obtain a teaching post at the Royal Potsdam Orphanage where an instructor had conveniently died.

He took up these duties on 23 July 1778, and continued in them until 9 October.

These were not happy months. On the positive side, however, it was an opportunity, which Moritz seized, to demonstrate for the first time his natural flair for teaching. At Potsdam he was a swift professional success, and the authorities at the Orphanage were sorry, if not surprised, to see him leave so soon. He 'did not settle down here either,' as they significantly observed, 'but during his short stay here he discharged his offices with skill, fidelity and honesty and gave the clearest evidence of his aptitude in teaching ideas to almost totally ignorant children.'[15] But such a performance was evidently compatible, on his part, with the blackest melancholy. His fits of apathy and depression culminated in days, and nights, of pointless wanderings on the Potsdamer Heide, and in a decision to starve himself to death – in fact he survived for two whole weeks on the petty sum of six groschen, sleeping rough and, Anton Reiser *redivivus*, devouring the roots of the fields. Most probably all this took place at the end of the Potsdam period (although the evidence is somewhat confusing), after he had resigned from what must have been a hardly bearable job. The physical conditions at the Potsdam Orphanage were appalling, and the institution was a disgraceful example of the King's disregard for the welfare of the poor. Moritz took refuge in his imagination, in which he was not deficient, and especially in self-dramatization, 'playing Lear rejected by his daughters, or Ugolino shut up in his tower of hunger, maddened, striking his son Anselmo down.' But a major change in his fortunes was now at hand, and it came through his being recommended to Probst Wilhelm Abraham Teller, a well-known cleric in Berlin. In his turn Teller recommended him to Anton Friedrich Büsching (1724–1793), Director of the Gymnasium zum Grauen Kloster (or Berlinisches Gymnasium) in the capital city. Helped by an excellent testimonial from the Orphanage, and after first giving the mandatory trial lesson, Moritz was appointed there, in November 1778, as a teacher in the lower school.

By the early eighteenth century there were already five high schools in Berlin, the Französische, the Friedrichs-Werdersche, the Joachimstalische, the Kölnische, and the Berlinische or Graue Kloster. These were reduced to four when the last was combined with the Kölnische in 1767, at Büsching's instigation. The Graue Kloster was the oldest, having been founded by the Elector Johann Georg of Brandenburg in 1574, on the site of a former Franciscan monastery, and astonishingly little had been done to improve or restore the buildings over the centuries (in fact, the school was not even partially rebuilt until the late 1780s). When, in 1766, Büsching became Director, conditions were little short of incredible:

The Kölnische Gymnasium had a few good classrooms, but the Berlinische did not have a single one. When I was shown round by Kriegsrat and First Burgomaster Riediger, he said they would be very good as wine-cellars, which was about accurate. They all looked like cellars, dark, unpleasant and unhealthy, since they were a yard or two below the level of the streets and courtyards. Two of these miserable classrooms were separated from one another merely by a wooden partition a few feet high, so that no one could raise his voice in either unless he wished to disturb his neighbour. It seemed as though the corridors to the classrooms and the rooms themselves hadn't been whitewashed for hundreds of years. The teachers' desks and the benches were in the worst possible condition. The writing class didn't even possess a few tables; the pupils had to put their writing books on the low benches and kneel down to write. Since classes usually started at 7:30 a.m. they needed light in winter; but though a minimum of candles were available there were no candle-sticks, so the pupils had to hold the candles in their hands.[16]

Anton Friedrich Büsching, the writer of these words, was a distinguished man. Originally a theologian and in orders, he had turned his interest to geography, in which field he became the most prolific, popular and important German author of his day. Best known for his *Neue Erdbeschreibung*, he may be said to have invented political geography in Germany, and he was also the first geographer to employ a statistical approach to the subject. As headmaster at the Graue Kloster he was energetic and effective, being like many another 'Aufklärer' a man whose conscience would not allow him to devote his career entirely to scholarship, as he would have preferred. In his long tenure (he held office until his death, when he was succeeded by the Director of the Werdersche Gymnasium, Gedike) Büsching improved the intolerable material conditions at the school as best he could, reformed and broadened the syllabus, laid down properly defined vacations and rescued the teaching staff from the penury into which they had all been plunged by the severe inflation of the Seven Years' War. His middle and later years were made more difficult by the tight-fistedness of Frederick the Great, whose replies to his pleas for money are hardly a model of enlightened despotism.[17] Reconstruction of the school, which took place after Frederick's death, was in fact made possible by a large bequest (not from the King). But during the period in which Moritz taught at the Graue Kloster he must still have had to contend with some of the bad conditions referred to above.

Nevertheless this opening, at a modest salary of 250 Thaler per annum, was a most gratifying one for a young man, especially for one who knew as little as Moritz did. There was at that time, as Basedow had complained, little or no provision for the training of teachers in the German states, despite the fact that laws imposing compulsory schooling (largely disregarded) existed in several of them. But the better teachers, at least, those who worked in the large towns, had normally enjoyed a less desultory education than had Moritz. He was master of barely enough Latin to understand Horace without a crib, and probably no Greek at all. His training in most other areas had been practically non-existent. It was a weakness which, in many respects, he never really remedied. For although it is true that he did become a well-known autodidact, he was never to be a formidable one, and to the end of his life he was sneered at as a dilettante. The sum of the evidence on Moritz suggests a man who possessed the ability to assimilate speedily, in almost any field, that minimum of knowledge necessary to give the impression that he was genuinely learned. He was unusually quick to perceive new issues, though often ill-acquainted with the old – a somewhat paradoxical capacity. His discoveries were often superficial ones, though now and then they were not. It is clear in retrospect that he was not simply a charlatan, although this possibility must often have occurred even to those who entertained no malice towards him. The frustrations and disasters of his early life seem to have sponsored the emergence of a compensatory intellectual self-confidence, even arrogance, in which real talent was combined with a certain blindness to his own limitations. His beginnings in Berlin, at all events, were modest enough – an elementary school master teaching Latin and German grammar, 'Briefstil' and 'Dichtkunst.' In this he was a success, just as he had been in Potsdam, particularly because he rapidly developed an excellent *rapport* with his pupils. In his early Berlin years he seems to have had few friends, as we shall see, but he was popular with the boys. He was, it is true, poorly organised, and possessed little in the way of style, form or even manners, but he did have, as Klischnig convincingly claims, certain emotional qualities to which his students could respond, a natural 'culture of mind and heart.' And of this something is reflected in his first substantial published work, *Unterhaltungen mit seinen Schülern* (1780).[18]

This little book, which was soon used as a reader at the Graue Kloster and elsewhere, is a collection of lectures and stories on moral themes. The direct influence of Rousseau's *Emile* cannot be discounted, that of Basedow and the 'Philanthropists' is certain. A central idea in the book is that of Natural Religion, something to be found and developed by means of intensive communion between the child and Nature, and there is evidence that Moritz had found particular support for this in the writings of Herder, an important source for much of his early thinking. The mood is otherwise reminiscent of the *Profession de foi d'un vicaire savoyard*.[19] The 'conversations' of which the volume is composed take place on class walks in the countryside, and several chapters relate specifically to the seasons and evoke the vision of God in Nature: 'Children,' exclaims the pedagogue, 'step out into free, open Nature and learn to pay heed to the voice of God' (*U*, 188). The purpose of the instruction given is properly practical: both prefaces, the first addressed to his pupils, and the second to other young readers, insist that the aim of the book is to turn them into 'good men,' which must necessarily mean happy men. Those who are not Moritz's pupils are asked to try to imagine these country wanderings, in all the seasons of the year, and not to forget that good thoughts are like jewels, though if these fail to lead on to good actions they will be but gems lost in the sea (*U*, IX).

Unterhaltungen mit seinen Schülern resembles other products of the new liberal pedagogy of the times, but is also in a wider sense representative of the Berlin Enlightenment, the influence of which was steadily undermining Moritz's residual Pietism as it was reinforcing his commitment to practical moral goals. The line between neo-Pietistic and fully-fledged 'Aufklärung' morality can, however, still be clearly discerned, since the former continues to be present here in an authentic form. For Moritz teaches the repression of the passions and concentration of the thoughts upon God. He gives his students a visual demonstration, when he disturbs the sediment in a stream to show the clouding that occurs when a man fails to bridle his instincts and desires. And it is a Pietistic exercise which he recommends when he advocates that his pupils note down, at the end of every day, what they have done with each hour of their time, and that they all keep a journal, secret from all except God and – tellingly enough – their parents and others set in authority over them. 'The slightest disobedience,' Moritz writes, 'against your parents ... can suddenly destroy your peace of mind.' (*U*, 96), and a cynic might take leave to think that imparting the need for submission to discipline and respect for parental authority is the author's deepest concern. Even the parable on death (*U*, 38f) is similarly authoritarian in effect: death is 'explained' by the story of an island, from which the inhabitants are removed one by one by a mysterious Lord (*Oberherr*); no one can think of suicide, for no one has the right to leave the island until called for; all those who have behaved well are then transported (so it is rumored) to a very nice place, the others to a much less pleasant one; therefore the thought of death, far from making anyone sad, should serve to encourage people 'to do their duty in life' (*U*, 51). This parable, quite agreeably told, is clearly meant to exhort and not to frighten, and it represents neither Karl Philipp Moritz's own deeper reflections on the subject of death nor anything of that instinctive terror which emerges occasionally elsewhere in his work.

The *Unterhaltungen*, despite such passages as these, do contain a few authentic images and thoughts, and even the seeds of social attitudes not entirely conventional. Injunctions to the reader to be thrifty with his time are amusing in the light of the way Anton Reiser dissipated his. Anton himself puts in a kind of surrogate appearance in the person of 'young Allwill,' hero of one of these tales, who is compelled, when his parents lose their wealth, 'to don a poor coat,' and who must endure the contempt of his fellows 'because of his poverty and his poor clothes' (*U*, 59)(the name 'Allwill' relates to Jacobi's novel *Aus Eduard Allwills Papieren*). The Pietistic argument that, if something unpleasant does occur, this is to be taken as God's will, has as its corollary that only those who keep God's commandments can safely put their trust in him. A quite other view, however, surfaces briefly in the story of Willich in 'The Merchant and his Four Sons,' where Moritz comments on the class system:

You know there are various classes in the world, and everyone has to live according to his class ... Assuredly it would be better if this difference were not so large ... but since it is so, we shall not be able to alter it, and we have to submit to the world (*U*, 139).

This proper but reluctant sentiment leads on to the sadness of young Willich at 'the great inequality among men' (*U*, 140). He is distressed to see that the children of the poor have no chance of an education, and feels compelled to reject the false solution of alms-giving, which is but a palliative and does nothing to heal the wound. Willich develops a kind of solidarity with the poor, deprives himself and acquires the reputation of a miser in order to accumulate the capital necessary to found an orphanage. But this whole story, like the rest of the *Unterhaltungen*, remains circumscribed by the sentimental limits of Enlightenment altruism as found in Germany. There is nothing of the passion of Rousseau, nor any glimmer of a modern critique of the class structure. Other German writers (notably Goethe and Lenz) had also taken a shot or two at such lumbering targets within the past decade. What is peculiar to Moritz, perhaps, is a certain quality of instinctive identification with the lot of the illiterate masses; indeed, this is intrinsic to *Anton Reiser*, where the criticism is stronger, and may be noticed repeatedly in his other writings. It is something not found at all extensively in the major figures of the Berlin Enlightenment, however, who were concerned almost exclusively with improving the minds of the already literate, privileged bourgeoisie.

This does not mean, as we have noticed in connection with *Anton Reiser*, that it would be right to see in Moritz a kind of incipient Jacobin. Far from it.

Nor was he even about to starve himself for altruistic reasons although, as we have seen, he was not without suicidal urges. His early Berlin years, in fact, are a period marked by the eager pursuit of advancement, punctuated by episodes of neurotic anxiety, withdrawal and despair, and they are not untypical, in these respects, of the rest of his career. His *Sechs deutsche Gedichte, dem Könige von Preussen gewidmet*, of 1781, are a conspicuous example of a tendency to truckle to the mighty. The first of these poems, *Gemälde von Sanssouci, 1779*, looks down from the terrace of the palace and studiously praises its absent royal master. *An den May, 1779* gives vent to artificial sentiments on the subject of fallen Prussian heroes, while *Das Manöver* lauds the army in a similar vein. Rather less specious is *Sonnenaufgang über Berlin*, which offers a few all but tolerable lines, as does the fifth poem, *Die Sprache*, with its elaborate personification of its subject, and its encomium:

> Du lassest auf der unumgränzten Fläche
> Des inneren Sinnes, Thal und Höhn,
> Beblümte Wiesen, Büsche, Silberbäche,
> In einem Augenblick entstehn.

The final poem, *Friedrich*, is quite alarmingly sycophantic:

> Er Selbst, o dass ich jetzt in Gluth zerflösse!
> Durchschauet Seine Heldenbahn,
> Er bebt zurück vor Seiner eignen Grösse,
> Und staunet über das, was er gethan.[20]

The King's cultivated French taste unhappily failed to protect him from admiring these poems, even to the extent of dropping their author an encouraging billet in his own hand. 'If,' Frederick writes airily, 'all German poets made the effort to mould their style that you have done, the German language would soon be able to compete with others.'[21]

THE PROFESSOR

It is at least to Moritz's credit that whatever illusions he may ever have entertained about his talents as a lyric poet were neither deep nor long-lasting. He probably valued the King's note more as an accrual of personal prestige than as a serious comment on the value of his literary work. As for the *Unterhaltungen*, they established his position among the Berlin 'Aufklärer,' and probably made an important contribution to his fairly rapid promotion at the Graue Kloster. In 1780 Moritz was appointed Conrector at the Berlinische Gymnasium, and then in December 1782 Büsching nominated him to be Conrector in charge at the linked Kölnische Gymnasium, and spoke of him most flatteringly as of one who 'had gained in high degree the love and veneration of the whole school of the Graue Kloster.' He was transferring him, the Director said, so as to advance him in his career, and to stimulate, strengthen and enlarge his commitment to education. Moritz's reply on this public occasion, a school ceremony, happens to have survived.[22] It combines appropriate expressions of gratitude and devotion with complaints about his physical condition. In fact, he had had a serious haemorrhage the day before, and it was only with difficulty that he had appeared at all.[23] He has, he tells his audience, been forced to curtail his address, and he concludes with a prayer to God for the restoration of his health. The facts clearly indicate that a tubercular condition had established itself in Moritz's lungs, and as we shall see, his situation in these next few years was often very serious. Collapses, short or protracted, were not infrequent. We may suppose that on this occasion he could hardly speak at all, but he does manage to proffer the proper sentiments in condensed form. To those pupils he is leaving behind at the Graue Kloster he expresses the wish that they shall all become 'good, happy and tranquil men,' and that they 'never extend their desires beyond the limits of their destinies.' To his new students at the Kölnische Gymnasium he promises, in the tones of the 'Philanthropin,' to be not only their teacher but also their friend. But if we were to imagine from these high-sounding words that for Moritz himself the four years just past had been a time of tranquillity and sanguine devotion to duty, we would be entirely misled. In so complex a period of expansion and maturing, restlessness had been his paramount state of mind and upheaval just below the surface of his life.

In reality, Moritz had made what amounted to several attempts to break loose from the Graue Kloster, which will be recounted in more detail later. He had for example applied for a curacy in Brunswick, had given a demonstration sermon there and had burst into tears when not offered the position.[24] By this time he did indeed rejoice in a certain reputation as a preacher, something to which (as we know from *Anton Reiser*) he had long ago aspired. According to Klischnig, Moritz's sermons were straightforwardly moralistic lectures, sometimes rendered comic by his gaucheries. He might conclude without the Lord's prayer or, rather worse, drop his Bible. His congregations were usually excellent, since he was 'gripping and yet down to earth (*populär*); he treats his subject thoroughly, speaks with warmth and conviction and it is apparent that this man wants to further the peace and happiness of his fellows.' Tieck, another witness, remarks that he used his sermons to display an eloquent command of language, and was often exceedingly histrionic.[25] The result was impressive, as long as the audience did not look too closely at this unhandsome, gawky individual with his awkward gesticulations. During his years in Berlin, as also on his various journies, Moritz preached from time to time, but for him, we may be sure, the driving impulse was to instruct rather than to save souls. He wanted to influence other men, to be the one who brought them well-being and who was known so to do. He could not bear to be inconspicuous, and no doubt he pressed Büsching hard for his promotion. As a conrector he quickly set his sights upon a professorship. Though the words of thanks he addressed to the Director and the Governors of the Köllnische Schule on 4 December 1782 were not actually insincere, they have to be weighed against his complaint that he had in fact been slighted in not being made prorector (despite Büsching's recommendation to that effect), and the uncontrolled outburst which had taken place but a week or two earlier to his friend Campe:

Oh who will deliver me from this miserable school dungeon in which I'm chained to the wall? All my philosophy is done for again. I don't want to become a tramp once more, but in these circumstances it's impossible for me to stay here (15 October 1782).

Joachim Heinrich Campe (1746–1818), who by this time had become the confidant of many of his woes, was a major figure in the educational reform movement of his day. Like Basedow, with whom he was briefly associated in Dessau, he was determined to improve the state of elementary education in Germany. In the eighties his path took him into publishing, and with his *Robinson der jüngere* (1779) he also wrote what was to become one of the most successful children's books of this and the next century. A strongminded and rather irascible man, Campe was associated with Moritz in various ways, some of them unpleasant. At first, however, a shared set of ideals led to plans for close co-operation between them. Campe had established a teaching institute of his own in Hamburg, and in July 1781 Moritz had gone so far as to resign at the Graue Kloster in order to join him there. But then that same August he wrote to the Berlin *Magistrat* seeking to withdraw his resignation (which was agreed to), and penned a long letter of apology to Campe explaining his change of heart (17 August 1781). The main grounds advanced are those of his health, intolerable headaches going on for three weeks, like those which, he says, he twice previously endured for a whole year (the true reason, however, may very well have been salary). An important biographical document, this letter to Campe gives us some insight into its author's egregious self-pity and his semi-conscious rôle-playing. In early 1781 Moritz had visited Hamburg, and been introduced into Campe's circle. The two of them had then come, in the words of the letter, to a firm agreement, 'on that solemn evening, in the open air before the face of God,' and all seemed arranged. But now Moritz is suddenly convinced that Campe is much better off without such a sick man on his staff, one for whom death cannot be far away:

All my most exciting prospects, my sweetest hopes have failed me. But I don't complain, and in the dust I worship God's wisdom, who is perhaps preparing me in this way for an early death which I await much more calmly now that everything has grown dark before me.

This hyperbole is capped by a plea to Campe not to withdraw his friendship, so much needed 'on my path of thorns,' and by a totally unconvincing offer to give up everything in Berlin and come in any case, should Campe exact this. These mournful sentences reflect one of those violent oscillations of mood and purpose to which Conrector Moritz was subject, and in which matters of health usually played only a superficial part. Even the modesty with which he pushes the candidacy of a replacement (one Empisch) is unpersuasive, because self-serving, though the candid admission that this gentleman knows more Latin and Greek than he does and possesses more of the social graces is unlikely to have been untrue. The letter to Campe stresses the favourable conditions of the job at the Graue Kloster: Moritz has little teaching to do, and has withdrawn to a house on the outskirts of Berlin where he can live quietly and pursue his private concerns.

Moritz was to take one further step in the school hierarchy, returning to the Graue Kloster (from the Kölnische Gymnasium) in 1784, when promoted professor. In some respects this advancement, though eagerly desired for the freedom as well as the prestige, was of doubtful advantage, since it reduced his salary from 330 to 120 Thaler a year, and he applied for it and accepted it against Büsching's advice. Since high school professors had to have a special field, Moritz selected history, knowing of course little or nothing about this subject. Meanwhile he strove from the heights of his new dignity as 'Ausserordentlicher Professor' to supplement his shrunken income by outside lecturing. He had by this time become, indeed, a well-known figure in the intellectual life of a rapidly growing and changing city. Berlin was by now as large as Rome – another metropolis Moritz was to know – having increased in size by half to about 150,000 people since the accession of Frederick the Great in 1740. Considerable industry had begun to develop but living costs remained reasonable and Moritz should have been, for most of this period, fairly well off. This does not allow, however, for his notorious extravagance and general thoughtlessness. The secluded and suburban mode of life for which he opted at least for a while in 1781 and returned to in 1783 did not prevent him contriving to dissipate his substance in foolish ways. He moved out, Klischnig tells us, from his accommodation at the Kölnische Gymnasium, a room where fungus grew on the walls and the best view was of a manure heap, into a 'garden house.' Living here (and sharing with Klischnig), he bought expensive clothes but failed to take care of them. A splendid fur coat (likely enough beyond his means anyway) he used as a dressing gown, or occasionally as an eiderdown. Rash and impromptu trips to Potsdam, Dessau and even Leipzig consumed as much as three months' salary all at once. There was also the long journey to England in 1782, admittedly financed by the profits of the very successful *Deutsche Sprachlehre für die Damen*. The motives behind all this travel are ambiguous; no doubt nervous instability and depressive tendencies were significant factors. And certainly nothing is more characteristic either of his personality or of its prototypical significance in the cultural history of his period than this dromomania.

Before turning to these matters, however, we should take fuller account of the 'positive' side. This may be seen in the emergence of Moritz's public persona as distinct from his shadow self, if we accept for a moment the value system of the group he was growing into, the Enlightenment intelligentsia. He was becoming a figure of some importance, and was now taken seriously by eminent men, though his shadow life, his tramp life, nagged at him continually. Certain qualities he possessed helped him to build upon the dignified but relatively minor status of a Gymnasium teacher and to transcend it in several directions at once. It was not merely that he wrote, as he did then and always, most prolifically. There was his energy in making contacts which at worst might be regarded as a rather impudent facility at imposing himself. This served him well all his life. There was also a less ambiguous asset: sheer inventiveness and initiative in the formulation of new projects. These latter, it is true, tended remorselessly to exceed his capabilities, but when part realised (like the *Magazin zur Erfahrungsseelenkunde*) or even hardly realised at all (like the reform of the *Vossische Zeitung*) they were still often of considerable influence and effect. As a public lecturer in Berlin Moritz professed the German language, the fine arts and (somewhat later and out of an even deeper ignorance) history. On the first two of these subjects, at least, he achieved a certain reputation, and his lectures were well attended, especially by ladies. In 1783 a Tübingen theology student, Christoph Friedrich Rinck, later to be 'Hof- und Stadtvikarius' in Karlsruhe, came to Berlin. He was on a journey, under the sponsorship of the Margrave of Baden, to visit 'the most famous men of Switzerland and Germany,'[26] and it is to him that we owe the only clearcut evidence that Moritz busied himself with the history of the plastic arts to any serious extent in the years before he went to Italy. On 17 December 1783, Rinck was taken by 'the Candidat [i.e. theology student] who lived in my house' to hear Conrector Moritz, 'who gives a few lectures for various amateurs of the arts.' Moritz, notes Rinck, is 'a person of quite peculiar genius and circumstances (*Schicksalen*),' 'a man who once studied at Halle and then became an actor' (both these statements are of course wrong, but it seems that the second one was widely believed).[27] He also travelled on foot through England 'a few years ago' (actually in the previous summer). He is, according to Rinck, a good poet, and wrote some poems to the King 'which are very much liked.' This young man of twenty-five (Moritz was in fact twenty-seven) is also said to be 'poor and good-natured ... and greatly loved.' The lecture Rinck attended was given to an audience of about thirty, in a room lent Moritz by a merchant, and it began with a discussion of the principles underlying the treatment of historical subjects in art, concentrating upon the paintings of Rode. The lecturer pointed out that artists should not restrict themselves to Biblical themes, 'since the other [i.e. secular] literature is much richer.' After having extolled Rode's pictures, 'with enthusiasm, fine taste, and most entertainingly,' it had got to six o'clock, and Moritz switched to the subject of the German language, seeking to prove that 'the language spoken here is the best one.' A few days later (31 December) Rinck visited the lecturer at his home, where the latter supposedly lived a 'very restricted and philosophical' existence. Like many of those who recount anecdotes of a meeting with Moritz, Rinck, albeit unintentionally, sounds a note of grotesque comedy: '[Moritz] could hardly get up when we arrived, for he had both feet in one boot.' They talked together of mutual acquaintances, including the Swiss Lavater, 'whom he detests.' Moritz gave some account of his trip to England, noting that he had returned with a troublesome bronchitis which he was trying to cure by means of ice-cold baths. The subject of his grandiose new project, the *Magazin zur Erfahrungsseelenkunde*, also came up. Moritz promised to visit Rinck soon in Karlsruhe, though we may presume that he never did so, since a planned journey with Klischnig to Switzerland in 1785 ended unexpectedly in Mannheim for lack of funds.

The glimpse we obtain through Rinck's account is of a lively if dilettantish teacher, now self-assured and well launched in intellectual Berlin, an

'Aufklärer' interested in encouraging the secularisation of the arts, enthusiastic for them and also (as many were not) for the cultivation of the native language, an eccentric who cannot resist displaying himself as such, and a hypochondriac raconteur. This picture is confirmed from other sources. An amusing record has survived of Moritz's classroom style, which must have been extremely odd. A pupil of his at the Kölnische Gymnasium in 1784 was Wilhelm Gabriel Wegener, who gives the following account:

> Professor Moritz taught us for two hours a week in the German language and the arts [*schöne Wissenschaften*], all sorts of things according to heaven knows what sort of plan. He usually appeared half an hour late and we grouped ourselves around him as though he were one of us. He was the greatest eccentric I've ever known. He evidently had some original genius and by his playful way of teaching he was useful to us; for through him we learnt to have some taste for thinking and speculating for ourselves. And even though we acquired no linguistic knowledge at all from him, his teaching in a formal sense was not futile. At the same time it was no doubt harmful that he showed not the slightest concern for manners and behaviour and this strengthened our delusion that the pernicious business of genius [*Geniewesen*] had something to do with an enlightened aesthetic philosophy. When he stretched out on his desk full length and, as though awakening from a dream, tore a page out of the *Idylls* of Theocritus and called this an excerpt, and then made all sorts of observations about the page in the 'genius' style, doubtless this theatrical tone did serve to keep us expectant and interested. But the sentimental effect it had and which we absorbed was certainly no more help to our eagerness for hard study than was his slovenly appearance and behaviour of any advantage to our *mores*. I know that some of us (particularly Klischnig) were infected by a certain pride and lack of modesty, by a certain self-satisfied clever-cleverness about serious work and – characterized by an appeal to Beauty and to superficial argumentation – by the ways of the 'genius.' Only later did I recognise what my disease was.[28]

Evidently Moritz tried to captivate his audience by means of eccentricity, and yet held their attention for more substantial reasons. This passage draws our attention to the degree in which this young man reflected in his ways the anti-establishment fashions of the day, although by the early eighties the cult of the Sturm und Drang hero had become, as we have already noted, something of a joke. The strange behaviour was, of course, not merely following a tired mode; it was innate in him, as a defence mechanism, a response to his terrible fear of being slighted and a part of the obsessional patterns of his personality. Despite such peculiarities, which were constantly commented upon, Moritz soon numbered among his acquaintances practically all the best known figures in the literary world of Berlin, though it is doubtful that many of them could be called his friends. He was obtrusive and importunate, but never really sociable. He had periods of rather forced gregariousness but was devoid of relaxed and easy affability. This is apparent from the testimony of such persons as Henriette Herz, who was quite fond of him. The wife of the celebrated Jewish physician Dr Marcus Herz (1747–1803) – Moritz's doctor, and the philosopher Moses Mendelssohn's too – Henriette Herz (1764–1847) was a great beauty and a famous Berlin hostess, rivalling Rahel Varnhagen, whose good friend she later became. Henriette is the source of a number of anecdotes about Karl Philipp Moritz.[29] One of her opportunities for getting to know him was the play-reading group which met regularly, in the early 1780s, at the house of Dorothea Veit (later Schlegel), Mendelssohn's daughter, in Charlottenburg. Members of this interesting group included Dr Herz, Mendelssohn's second daughter Recha, his prominent disciple David Friedlaender, Henriette herself and Moritz. Mendelssohn, we are told, occasionally attended meetings himself and sometimes read the part of Nathan when they took up (as they often did) Lessing's *Nathan der Weise*, Moritz usually playing the Templar or sometimes Saladin. In 1785 yet another reading circle, which convened at Frau Hofrat Bauer's apartment, included the poet Ramler, Probst Teller, Rat Dohm, Zöllner, the deacon at the Marienkirche, Henriette and Marcus Herz, Moritz and the two young Humboldts, Wilhelm and Alexander. This was a distinguished group, and Moritz's participation is further evidence of his established status.

Among all these people, if we exclude Mendelssohn as a special case, only the Herzes had a relationship with Moritz warm enough to rate as friendship. He was, however, also fairly close to both the editors of the important periodical, the *Berlinische Monatsschrift*, namely Johann Erich Biester (1749–1816), the librarian, and Friedrich Gedike (1754–1838), director of the Friedrich-Werdersche Gymnasium, a man scarcely older than Moritz, whose rise had been a rapid one. Both these people, though staunch 'Aufklärer,' were more open to the attitudes of the Sturm und Drang than, say, Nicolai and Mendelssohn were. Biester in particular was interested in the German Middle Ages and was a notable collector of old manuscripts. The unorthodox and qualified nature of Moritz's rationalism made him less acceptable on principle to the leader of the Berlin Enlightenment, Friedrich Nicolai (1733–1811), and his unpredictable conduct no doubt settled the matter. After his death, Nicolai wrote of him: 'Moritz was a good-natured fellow but half mad; I kept him as far as possible at arm's length and never had anything to do with him.'[30] He was probably exaggerating here, since we know that Moritz visited his house.[31] According to Klischnig, the young pedagogue found it hard to make friends, and in this category he mentions only Johann Georg Zierlein, who became a teacher at the Graue Kloster at the same time as Moritz, but of whom little else is known. Zierlein was apparently a sentimental hypochondriac and seems to have been very compatible with Moritz. His sudden death a few days after the occasion when, on an afternoon walk to Strahlau, he and Moritz had brooded together over mortality and the after-life (in which Moritz declared his disbelief), plunged the survivor into some very dark thoughts indeed. A funny story of Zierlein's, revealing his terrors on the subject of sex and marriage, is recounted by Klischnig, and is perhaps worth preserving as a *curiosum*. We have to note, at any rate, that Klischnig considered it to have been a powerful factor in dissuading Moritz from thoughts of marriage for years to come.

I am not very strong (Zierlein said) and afraid I could not satisfy a woman. What happened to that innkeeper in the Hennaberg district could easily happen to me. When I was going home from Halle I stopped at a village and the innkeeper allocated me a bed close to his room, where I could hear everything he said to his wife in bed. The man was a consumptive and he coughed whenever he spoke. Despite this his wife made impetuous demands for him to perform his marital duty and scolded him until he gave in and said 'very well then, as the Lord wills it, if you're determined to do me in.' From that time on I've hated the thought of marriage. Vestigia me terrent, Amice. And you too, Herr Kollege, can do nought but put your hand on your heart and say: God be merciful to me, a sinner![32]

This conveys either lubricious comedy or hypochondriac terror, and we do not know the tone of voice in which Moritz repeated the tale to Klischnig on whom, at all events, it did make a significant impression. It brings to the fore the issue of sexuality in Moritz's life and work, and on this matter we have to admit that the evidence is remarkably meagre. The absence of erotic themes and material in his early writings, just as in *Anton Reiser*, his most powerful work, is very striking. It is intriguing to note that in devoting himself to his beloved *Werther*, the young Moritz actually tried to exclude the love story from his appreciation of it, as a distraction. There may well have been a repression so powerful that it blotted out overt manifestations of sexual interest in Moritz until he reached his late twenties, and the eccentricities of his behaviour are no doubt in part connected with this. He was gauche with women, but by no means unpopular, without savoir faire, but an amusing raconteur at times. There is no evidence of perversion, although the ménage with Klischnig did lead to gossip in Berlin. It remains tantalising that this

psychologist and self-analyst of genius hardly ever ventures upon this perilous terrain.

Perhaps we can say that a native tendency in Moritz towards schizophrenia and paranoid behaviour is increasingly balanced out, in these years, by
the growing influence upon him of a social group highly rationalistic in its
ethos, pragmatic, and devoted to bourgeois common sense, but already in
some degree on the defensive against the incursions of the new irrationalism.
In Berlin Enlightenment circles, Goethe and his party were still very unpopular, and were to be resisted vigorously for at least another decade.
Others too were regarded in Berlin as dangerous outsiders, for instance
Klopstock, in Hamburg, whom even Biester, an early admirer of the *Messias*, had been obliged to abandon. Rousseauists and 'Philanthropists' were
also of dubious reliability. Kant, on the other hand, the Berliners considered
an ally against the Sturm und Drang, and in the famous 'Pantheismusstreit'
of the mid-80s his authority was invoked against Lavater and Jacobi. Kant's
close pupil Marcus Herz is an example of the clever and versatile rationalist
intellectual with whom Moritz was in intimate contact. Herz wrote a number of philosophical works, closely argued discourses in which he rejects
atheistic and materialist doctrines such as were now infiltrating rapidly
from France, and follows Kant and Mendelssohn in holding to a rationally
based belief in the soul and in immortality. As a physician (after leaving
Königsberg, Herz took his degree in medicine at Halle) he had the opportunity to develop that practical flair which co-existed with such formidable
powers of abstract reasoning in this remarkable man. His Kantian abstractions were therefore distinctly tempered by a broadly based empiricism. His
influence upon Moritz was obviously considerable and in one instance, as we
shall see, it was spectacular. As his doctor, Herz understood Moritz in many
ways very well, and had a real insight into his neuroses. However, among the
things he understood less well was Goethe's poetry, in which his patient was
well ahead of him. Once, Henriette relates, when she and Moritz were talking, her husband came into the room, brandishing a copy of the poem *Der
Fischer*, just recently published. 'Kühl bis ans Herz hinan!' Herz complained. 'Would someone please tell me what that is supposed to mean?'
'But who,' responded Moritz, tapping himself on the forehead, 'could want to
understand such a poem up here?' Herz could only stare at him. The story
points up nicely the ambiguity, and therefore the importance, of Moritz's
position in intellectual Berlin, as a kind of skinny Trojan horse in the very
citadel of the German Enlightenment.

Prior to 1786, the most vital single influence upon the development of
Moritz's mind, as well as one of the most famous thinkers of his day, was

probably Moses Mendelssohn. Even to summarise the career and significance of this extraordinarily gifted and many-sided man would of course transcend the limits of this study.[33] In any case much of what Mendelssohn wrote – the Hebrew works, quite obviously, but equally some of the German – was in books which his great admirer as like as not never opened. Moritz was something of a name-dropper, but whether he always read the works he talked about is justly a matter of some debate. In this instance, certainly, it was the personal contact with the philosopher he liked to call the German Socrates which was above all important. From 1782, certainly, until Mendelssohn's death in January 1786, Moritz was a frequent visitor at the Jewish philosopher's home, often spending time with the family in the evenings while Mendelssohn himself, who suffered from a nervous disease, was forced to look on from behind a glass door. Despite his many preoccupations and persistent ill-health, Mendelssohn kept open house for people of culture and letters in a way in which hardly anyone else in Berlin did. He probably had a warm enough relationship with Moritz, despite efforts by some of the latter's enemies to suggest the contrary. No doubt the two men were exceedingly different, but it is difficult to suppose, as has been suggested, that Mendelssohn left the selection of such house guests entirely to his family.[34] It is a matter of record that he more than once intervened to help Moritz out of his recurrent depressions, and the philosopher's serene and composed temperament must have had as positive an effect upon Moritz as did the sharp and systematic clarity, the consistency and conviction of his ideas. Perhaps no one, Moritz once said of him, ever left that man unimproved.[35] He must certainly have read such works as Mendelssohn's *Phädon*, a re-writing of Plato's *Phaedo*, and one of the great books of the German Enlightenment. The *Phädon* self-assuredly founds the doctrine of the immortality of the soul upon purely rational arguments, but makes an unusual appeal to moral necessity as additional grounds for such a belief. From Mendelssohn, Moritz learnt not only the loftier notions of Enlightenment moral idealism and its metaphysics; he also learnt much about aesthetics, about psychological analysis and about the empirical observation of the mind, and the body, as will be discussed in a later chapter. When Mendelssohn's last months were darkened by the controversy between himself and Jacobi over the issue of Lessing's religious views (the so-called 'Pantheismusstreit'), his affinities with the Sturm und Drang did not prevent Moritz from taking a belligerently pro-Mendelssohn stance. This was a petulant and very personalised dispute, in which Mendelssohn was deeply hurt, not only by Jacobi's allegations that Lessing had been a 'Spinozist' (which meant, according to the opinions of the day, something like an atheist), but by the imputation that the great critic had concealed his true attitude from Mendelssohn, his close friend. Moritz succeeded in raising the affair to a new level of acrimony by publishing in the *Vossische Zeitung*, just after the philosopher's death, the charge that it was the effect on Mendelssohn of Jacobi's intrigues and misbehaviour that was the whole cause of this misfortune.[36] This provocative tactlessness is perhaps symptomatic of an incautious tendency to take positions and express views without having first bothered to ascertain the facts, or to restrain himself from polemical non sequiturs. It is of the same order as a feature which is often apparent in Moritz's philosophical writings – an intuitive and essentially unscholarly attitude to truth.

A significant association Moritz had in his early Berlin years seems to have been with Hofsekretär Brandes, who is connected with his introduction to Free Masonry. He became a Mason on 22 November 1779, about a year after his arrival in Berlin, when he was admitted to the St Johannisloge zur Beständigkeit, over which Brandes presided. On 15 February 1781 he was made a 'Geselle,' and was raised to the rank of 'Meister' on 11 May 1784. At this time it was a comparatively easy matter to gain admission to a Lodge, since, as is well known, an enormous cult of Masonry, and also of other secret societies, had developed in Germany in recent decades. The existence of such groups and their activities had indeed become a staple of tea-party gossip. Some of the Lodges appear to have had a strong Pietistic colouring, and the St Johannisloge was one of these. Meetings began and ended with emotional, sometimes even tearful, prayers and supplications. It might be more accurate to call the fundamental tenor quietistic (as Schneider suggests of the whole movement),[37] and certainly the moral teachings of this Lodge stressed submission and resignation to the divine will. The young man's imagination, as Klischnig says, was no doubt richly fed by Masonic ritual and by the intimacy of the fraternal gatherings, and we may be certain that it was not just fashion that took Moritz there. The Masons clearly filled a gap in his spiritual life which had been growing ever since his childhood. The importance of the connection showed itself quite quickly in his writings. His inner life was changed by it in some degree, but especially, the Masons helped him strengthen his concern for ethical activity in the world. There is no indication that his membership involved him in conflicts, internal or external, although his Berlin associates Gedike and Biester, as well as Nicolai, had campaigned vigorously against the Lodges of the Strict Observance, which they even accused of crypto-Catholicism. Some mystery remains about the nature and extent of Moritz's commitment to Masonry. The cold water which Goethe, himself a renegade Mason, later poured on the whole activity had a powerful effect, but did not prevent Moritz from re-entering the

Lodge on his return from Italy in 1789,[38] perhaps just because it filled a religious need in him missing in Goethe. From a career point of view his membership certainly found him new contacts, some of them influential, such as Kriegskommissar Vieweg. However, Moritz's full emergence as a public figure in these years was fostered by two other factors of more overt significance, namely the successful establishment of the *Magazin zur Erfahrungsseelenkunde* and his editorship, brief as it was, of the *Vossische Zeitung*.

THE NEWSPAPERMAN

This last was at that time the only really important newspaper in Berlin. Founded in 1722 as the *Berlinische Privilegierte Zeitung*, it became known as the *Vossische Zeitung* after 1751, when the book-seller Christian Friedrich Voss acquired the 'Privilegium,' or licence, for it. In the 1780s its only real competitor was the *Berlinische Nachrichten von Staats- und gelehrten Sachen* (or *Spener'sche Zeitung*). Neither of these papers corresponded to the modern idea of a newspaper, and both concentrated very narrowly upon public affairs. Reform was certainly overdue, though Moritz, as Ludwig Geiger observes, was 'no doubt the most unpractical of men for such a practical undertaking.'[39] Nothing is known of the negotiations which led to his assuming the editorship, but it seems likely that the owner was impressed by his increasing reputation in literary circles. He took over from G.W. Burman on 1 September 1784, and moved into the publisher's house. He had the loftiest aspirations and hopes from this opportunity, and these are reflected in the pamphlet *Ideal einer vollkommenen Zeitung*,[40] where Moritz states that what made him wish to become editor was the belief that this would be the best way of achieving his aim: to see the establishment of a quite new type of paper, 'a paper for the people [*ein Blatt für das Volk*] which would really be read by the people, and thereby be of the most widespread utility.' Moritz conceives of the newspaper as potentially the most influential single organ of enlightenment and is surprised that this has occurred to no one before: 'It really is astonishing, as there has been so much said and written about enlightenment, that so far no one thought of such a simple means of spreading it as a newspaper' (*IZ*, 8). The dissemination of the printed word is, after all, synonymous with the advance of civilisation. A properly edited paper could well be an 'incorruptible tribunal' for assessing social behaviour, an impartial judge in matters of taste, and a vehicle for propagating whatever is of general interest in science and learning. It should describe the public administration of justice, and contain court reports. Doctors, clergymen and magistrates, in particular, might serve as the informants of the editor, whose task it would be to keep himself in touch with all sections of big city life, and to enter into its most hidden recesses.

Moritz's ideal editor (merely an aspiration, he concedes) is therefore charged with an approach to his task sharply in conflict with previous highly conservative practice. The most striking feature of this policy statement is perhaps the demand that the paper concern itself with all social classes, even the very poor: 'There should be no trade, no class, even the class of the despised and for the most part oppressed and tyrannically treated tradesman's apprentice, which it disregards' (*IZ*, 5–6). In the *Ideal einer vollkommenen Zeitung* Moritz indulges his penchant for social criticism, and expresses his impulse to reach out to the great unwashed as clearly as anywhere in his work. Not only people of title but the simple man in his smock or behind his plough may also, he maintains, achieve greatness if he has developed, in his own way, 'some human capacity' (*irgendeine menschliche Kraft*). This kind of sympathy is linked here with an equally significant insistence that only in the study of individuals can the social observer discover the sources of group manifestations and of large-scale events: 'For in a society of men, whatever it may be, it is only individual people who act ...' (*IZ*, 9) – society, in the last resort, being an abstract concept, as are such concepts as 'France,' 'Russia' and 'the Ottoman Gate.' Analysis is essential, events must be broken down into their parts, not merely recounted in the way they superficially present themselves. Individual facts from individuals need to be collected, so that the 'secret springs' (*IZ*, 11) of behaviour may be discerned. Moritz sums up this argument, bearing on the task of the newspaper editor, in an aphorism of far-reaching philosophical implication: 'For only the individual is real, the composite [*das Zusammengefasste*] exists for the most part in the imagination' (*IZ*, 12).

These ideas correspond, as might be expected, to the position taken in the first volume of the *Magazin zur Erfahrungsseelenkunde* and will be discussed further in that connection. They reflect some of the most characteristic principles of Moritz's mature thinking, in which analysis and synthesis, an objectively based empiricism and a holistically orientated subjectivism tend to complement one another. The former is determined by the realistic, even materialistic bent in Moritz, which shows up in *Anton Reiser* and makes that novel different from the typical fiction of the day, makes of it, among many other things that it is, such a vivid encounter with the world of disagreeably harsh fact. The latter is the discovery, made by a sharpened self-awareness, of the forming power of the 'imagination' [*Einbildung*] though this too is really to be seen as an empirical constatation, more psychological than logical in its nature, and not Kantian. It is strange but true that here, in a pamphlet aimed at describing and justifying the new editorial ideals of the *Vossische Zeitung* we find clues as to the manner in which this thinker was absorbing and modifying the rationalist idealism of the Berlin Enlightenment, extending the pragmatic purposes of the bourgeois moral propagandists and widening their social horizon, and canalising a strong pedagogical impulse in a concern for individuals as much as for universals. Moritz, far more than many other 'Aufklärer' with their normative preoccupations, recognised the irreducibility of the individual people who make up a society, the concreteness of the atoms which combine into the whole. Seen esoterically, it is no exaggeration to call the *Ideal*, and indeed the *Vossische Zeitung* itself for a short time, a document plotting new paths for the development of empiricism in German thought. Exoterically, however, what must be noted is a would-be reform which failed very quickly, partly because such a policy for a newspaper was in advance of its day, and partly no doubt because of the editor's own mistakes and his lack of tact and restraint.

Moritz lasted in the editorial chair for less than a full year.[41] As soon as the proprietor noticed a sharp falling off in subscriptions, he obliged him to depart. The practical changes carried out had been relatively modest. Moritz had introduced courtroom reports for the very first time into a German newspaper, he had printed reviews of exhibitions and theatre critiques, and had reduced the space devoted to official matters and political affairs. But the conservatively minded readers had responded unfavourably, and the intelligentsia offered no support. As for the ambition to produce a 'Volksblatt,' no readership was available for any such thing in the 1780s. A furore was provoked, moreover, by the theatre criticism, which was not congenial to the Berlin actors' fraternity. Indeed, Moritz was always inclined to underestimate the pungent effect which the written word may have, and to forget too easily that others were just as intolerant of criticism as he was sensitive to it himself. Already, before assuming the editorship, he had submitted a scathing review of Schiller's *Kabale und Liebe*, continued a few weeks later in still more strident tones.[42] Schiller's plays, Moritz felt, were not only performed too frequently, they should not be performed at all. *Kabale und Liebe*, currently a success in Berlin, he regarded as a disgrace:

With what kind of impudence can anyone write and print such rubbish? And what must be the state of head and heart of someone who can regard such products of his mind with satisfaction? ... To write like this is to trample on taste and healthy criticism ... Something might have been made of certain scenes, but everything the author touches turns to foam and froth in his hands.

When public resentment of these observations was expressed by Döbbelin, the director of the play, and by those around him, Moritz proceeded in the second instalment to try to justify his diatribe. The position he takes is so one-sided that it cannot be regarded as a serious critical contribution to contemporary discussion of Schiller's play, although other 'Aufklärer' certainly shared his disapproval of Schiller. With much selective quotation and a flow of sarcastic remarks Moritz on the one hand attacks the playwright's dialogue for its coarseness and naturalism, and on the other accuses it of being novelettish. The dramatist's hyperbole is taken severely to task. Schiller's characters are called monstrous and absurd – especially Franz Moor in *Die Räuber* and the Präsident in *Kabale und Liebe*. He feels obliged, Moritz declares, to make some statement, 'out of irritation that a man can blind the public with false brilliance and throw dust in its eyes.'

Döbbelin was so irate at these ill-considered comments that he is said to have confronted Moritz and threatened him publicly in the stalls. He certainly lampooned him, and one feeble example of his wit, apparently circulated with the playbills, has survived.[43] The unpleasantness thus generated just as Moritz took office as editor persisted into 1785, while subscriptions to the *Vossische Zeitung* faltered. Though Moritz seems to have given up his position in the early summer of that year, he continued to write for the paper, as witness his grandiose gaucherie of January and February 1786 on the subject of Mendelssohn and Jacobi. The savagery of the attack on Schiller, whom he had never met though he was to meet him shortly thereafter, is rather puzzling, but we have to recall that the dramatist was, at that time, not the imposing figure he later became. The underlying cause probably lay in Moritz's exaggerated and distorted idea of his pedagogical and moral responsibilities. The tone of his reviews of books and plays in the *Zeitung* shows clearly enough that he regarded his task as instructional, and as one of ethical guidance. He attempts moreover, in the Schiller articles, to hold on to a certain middle ground between the new 'naturalism' of the Sturm und Drang and the trashy style of the popular novel, both of which most 'Aufklärer' deplored. Moritz thus casts himself, with an opinionated vanity, in the ill-fitting role of tribune of the Enlightenment. Nevertheless, the *Ideal einer vollkommenen Zeitung* and the brief editorship which followed it may be regarded as the positive climax to Moritz's process of emergence from the shadows of vagabondage to mount the rostrum of the popular educator. And in this particular case, a rather sensible, forward-looking programme of press reform, liberal to a degree unusual for its day, was rendered nugatory by adverse circumstances and by sheer lack of savoir-faire. But the failure itself was only a lurch on the accelerating ride to reputation. By 1785 Moritz had come far. The enlightened man had emerged and found a place for himself on the public stage. Rashness – a function of deep and unresolved conflicts of mind – would continue to dog him, but was ultimately to be the harbinger of his further worldly success.

3

Poor Travelling Creature

In an age in which the bonds of social and moral tradition were rapidly weakening, as was certainly the case in the later eighteenth century, we can see in many philosophers and creative writers the frictions and instabilities generated by the conflict between a would-be autonomous subjectivity of the individual and his nostalgic conception of an objective, universal order. This antagonism emerges clearly in France by the 1750s, most conspicuously in the writings, but also in the life, of Rousseau; it shortly thereafter becomes intense in Germany, and its recognition must be regarded as an indispensable key to the entire work of Goethe. It provides the fundamental co-ordinates for understanding that author's development, and it continues in fact to be reflected in the ambiguities of the products of his old age. To some extent it epitomises the intellectual history of the whole era, and even Kant, a much less obvious example, cannot be properly situated in his philosophical environment without some appreciation of this confrontation. The German Romantics, later on, may well have obfuscated, but they certainly did not resolve the conflict. Moritz is a writer whose entire work exhibits it glaringly, not so much in the manner of one or two of his greater contemporaries, that is, by the masterly translation of the consciousness of it into art or into an imposing philosophical system, for such a thing was beyond his range, but through its direct manifestations – again, like Rousseau, not merely in his books but also in his life. Here it lies, stark and bare, with a number of its roots excruciatingly exposed. As for that universal order which is profoundly in question, this is both political and social, but it is also religious and moral, aesthetic and psychological, and the increasing cousciousness of its deterioration and perhaps irrecoverable loss is of course accompanied in the later eighteenth and early nineteenth centuries by diverse and persistent attempts at its restoration. In some cases (and we may think of *Emile*) it reappears paradoxically in the alienated and aberrent dreams of the autonomous subject himself. The preoccupation, in Moritz's work, with an ideal of wholeness, with 'das in sich selbst Vollendete'[1] can therefore not be seen simply as a derivative notion, with its origin largely accounted for by the aesthetics of Baumgarten or, conceivably, the mystical tradition; it must also be regarded as expressive of an energetic struggle for remedy and survival, topical and vital enough, and for the recovery of personal coherence. But Moritz's writings, more acutely than many, also display the countervailing trend, and this not merely as an act of subjective rebellion and insurgent individualism, but as an epistemological stance: that is, the concern with empirical observation, with induction, and patternless and apparently disassociated fact.

One route towards a profounder understanding of this paradigmatic antithesis in Moritz's work leads through a consideration of his study of language. During what may be called his first Berlin period, from 1778 to 1786, he became deeply involved in this area, and never lost his interest in it. If we include all those independent publications of his which are materially concerned with the field, they amount to more than a score, to which must be added a number of articles and short pieces that appeared in various periodicals, particularly his own *Magazin zur Erfahrungsseelenkunde*. He himself seems to have thought that these writings on language actually constituted his most important achievement. When *Kleine Schriften, die deutsche Sprache betreffend* (a collection, for the most part, of previously published essays) appeared in 1781, the author affirmed, in the initial dedication to his benefactor, Prince Carl von Mecklenburg-Strelitz, that this was the field of study 'which has been my chief occupation for some time.'[2] A decade later, after his rather lucky election to the Prussian Academy of Sciences, he evidently considered that it was the German language he was primarily expected to profess in that distinguished body; and it was indeed to this that he was to devote a good deal of his restless and rather disorderly energies during the last two years of his short life. Among his contemporaries, his standing as a linguistic scholar seems to have been relatively high, though this fact is perhaps merely a commentary upon the sad state of that discipline in those days. In 1782, when Moritz was still at the beginning of his career, Johann Christoph Adelung, the outstanding grammarian and lexicographer of this period, chooses to praise him as 'a linguist of the better kind,'[3] while the notoriously hostile obituary in Schlichtegroll's *Nekrolog* concedes that among his many (mostly hopelessly flawed) writings those on language are no doubt his best. Some of these did in fact become popular tools and ran through several editions, until well into the nineteenth century, and were far better known than *Anton Reiser*. However, as the intellectual climate and the style of philological scholarship changed, these books were forgotten or else a negative view was taken of them from which it would be difficult, on scholarly grounds at least, to dissent today. But though their scientific importance may be minimal, these writings taken as a group cannot be disregarded by the biographer, for in some respects they point to the very crux of this author's life's work.

In the dispute which developed between Adelung and some of the Berlin 'Aufklärer' on the issue of the standard language, we find Moritz siding with the latter. High German, according to their view, was not a dialect, but rather what Gottsched had once called 'a choice manner of speaking.'[4] The standard German language was, or ought to be, the written one, and no High German colloquial could exist that was different from this. No doubt Moritz's Hanoverian upbringing predisposed him to subscribe to such an opinion. He himself had noticed that High German was spoken more correctly in a district like Hannover, where the local dialect differed from it markedly, than it was in Leipzig where the two were relatively close. He even went so far as to propose that the Hanoverian pronunciation of 'sp' and 'st' was the correct one, and should be standard. His Berlin colleagues, Gedike, Biester and Nicolai, failed of course to follow him here, but in general his position is the same as theirs, a conservative and normative one. Moritz defends traditional orthography, as Adelung also does, but unlike Adelung he falls back for his reasons not upon the phonetics of Upper Saxon, but upon the written language.[5] Much of this is to be found in the little work, *Über den märkischen Dialekt* (1781), a typical production in that it blends philosophical reflections with pedagogical ends, the stress being upon the latter. It is here that we find the first demand for an academy: 'a society of scholars ... sufficiently supported to constitute our own Academy of German language.'[6] The book takes issue with provincialisms, and puts forward a puristic position. It was, however, quite justly taken to task by a reviewer in the *Allgemeine deutsche Bibliothek* for its careless failure to notice the distinction between the dialect of the Mark of Brandenburg and that of Berlin.[7] It is the Rationalist thrust of this essay, its pursuit of the 'sufficient cause,' and the implications of the arguments employed in defence of the *usus scribendi* which are still of some interest today. The attitude to language formulated here was founded on the commonly accepted principles of eighteenth-century grammarians, who generally understood little or nothing about evolutionary and historical processes; in turning however, as Moritz does, in a psychological direction he points up conclusions not too unlike those adumbrated by modern Chomskyite linguistics.

Various elements illustrate this, for example, the treatment of punctuation, which Moritz regards not merely as an aural or phonetic consideration but rather as a rationally based logically controlled concomitant of sentence and phrase.[8] Etymological questions, and morphological and syntactical ones as well, tend to be answered with a disregard for historical development as such. Like most eighteenth-century philologists, Moritz was blithely ignorant of Middle High German, and he makes at the most a few random allusions to sixteenth- and seventeenth-century usage. For him, the forms of language are created by the fundamental structures of the mind. In such phenomena as linguistic gender, and the personification of inanimate things, man imposes his consciousness upon the external world.[9] Language, as he was wont to formulate it self-assuredly towards the end of his life, should therefore be regarded as a set of norms entirely independent of fluctuating fashions – 'permanent and enduring, preserving its value through the centuries and not really capable of aging or wilting.'[10] He holds that it is hardly subject to historical change, and that it has a structure which, once grasped, makes it possible to derive grammatical rules of one's own, as the Introduction to *Vom richtigen deutschen Ausdruck* (1792) rather startlingly alleges:

This guide [*Anleitung*] should not merely contain the dry rules of correct German expression, but rather a natural development thereof out of the structures of the language, so that one may be enabled to employ them properly, with reflection, in each individual case, and in some manner to formulate the rules for oneself without learning them by heart.[11]

This is not all that far from a modern theory of generative grammar, and it puts Moritz firmly in the company of those who held language not to be an accidental discovery of man, by which he differentiated himself from the beasts, nor a gradual cunning adaptation, nor even the mysterious gift of God, but as the inevitable product of a mind thus constituted, different in kind from the animal mind.

Of all controversies about language in the later eighteenth century that as to its origin was the most widely pursued. In Germany, the most significant contribution to it to date had probably been Herder's prize essay, *Über den Ursprung der Sprache* (1770). Moritz follows Herder in rejecting many of the best-known theories of the day, including Condillac's view that language had emerged from instinctive exclamations. He adopts something close to Herder's own position that the first words must have arisen from the imitation of natural sounds, but then he goes further, resorting to the curious claim that the organs of speech themselves imitate in some fashion the external objects that are named.[12] This pursuit of a physiologically based explanation is, however, not of itself reliable evidence of a freshly empirical approach. For what counts for Moritz, as for Herder, is in the end the a priori conviction that language, developing hand in hand with rational thinking, illustrates and epitomizes the special nature of man. His (as he calls it) 'psychological' study of language is in any case really turned away from the question of historical origin, in which he is not greatly interested. When Moritz uses the term 'Ursprache,' he is speaking not so much of a primeval form of language as of an ultimate set of mental patterns, associated with particular sounds.[13] His morphological, syntactical and semantic notions, difficult to disentangle as they are, may be said to derive from a peculiar mixture of self-observation, intuition and logical premises, but with the greatest importance ascribed to these last.

He published a number of articles in the *Magazin zur Erfahrungsseelenkunde* under the title 'Sprache in psychologischer Rücksicht.'[14] Since he was, for entirely mercenary reasons, unscrupulous in re-using and reprinting verbatim the same material, we can also find it, both earlier and later than its appearance in the *Magazin*, in other places, though the *Magazin* is the most coherent source. These 'psychological' disquisitions, though often quaint, are both original and revealing, and we shall now consider the chief illustrations of Moritz's methodology, that is, his discussions of verbal inflexions, of auxiliaries, of impersonals, and of prepositions. The technique is always to examine (at first sight empirically enough) the psychological concomitants and associations of particular inflections and forms. Thus, in the present tense, *-st* and *-t* are found to be endings which express a sense of reality, of some real action done, which is why (so Moritz thinks) this *-t* has to disappear in other moods. It is also missing in the first person singular form, for the reason that it is unnecessary to reaffirm the reality of an act one is oneself performing. The less consistent failure of *-t* to appear in the third person plural, however, Moritz seeks to account for by positing a lost *-t*, since the proper ending, namely *-ent*, is supposedly still to be noted 'in old German authors.' His theory asserts that the need to emphasise the reality of an action is always strongest in the second person, where *-t* is therefore invariably found. As for *-t* as it occurs in the inflections of the imperfect, this is simply dismissed as another kind of *-t* altogether. Of the same nature is the author's discussion of Ablaut: the vowel change is said to be from a 'lighter' sound to a 'darker' one, since this properly accords with the relative darkness of the past! 'This is the way the past is related, in our imaginations, to the present, as distant, subdued music is to resonant and sonorous, as twilight is to light ... and how significantly this is expressed by the change from the higher vowel to the deeper one' (*Mag*, II, I, 122). Since, unhappily, there are numerous verbs in German in which the change may be more convincingly described as from 'darker' to 'lighter' (e.g. *blasen/blies*), Moritz is driven to label these unnatural perversions, the consequence of 'an exaggerated refinement of language.' A similar argument, in which he deals with the subjunctive, is likewise defective, though in this case its weakness is not conceded at all. The modified vowels found in the subjunctive mood, Moritz claims, are there to convey the half tones appropriate to what is uncertain, hypothetical and unreal. But the subversive appearance of -*t* in the second person endings of the subjunctive is then cavalierly ignored.

In the course of this 'psychological' treatment of verb forms, we also come across a passage on the auxiliaries. *Haben* and *sein* are accounted for in this capacity by their function in expressing a completed action. *Haben*, Moritz would have it, relates to events which either occur outside the speaker or else 'move outwards' from him, *sein* to what may be regarded as belonging to him. Such idiosyncratic, intuitive hypotheses reflect the explorative urges of a mind caught between deduction and induction. And to this confusion in methodology a further dimension is added in the discussion of the impersonal verbs, since this provides interesting evidence of a developing concern with the problem of the unconscious. This is in fact one area where Moritz displays an unmistakable, and innovative, empiricism, above all in the *Magazin*. As for the impersonal verbs, he finds that they exist to express the notion of something happening which is independent of the conscious will; they indicate 'both what occurs in our bodies and what occurs in the innermost depths of our minds [*Seele*], and which we can only formulate obscurely to ourselves.' This sentence contains terminology deriving from Leibniz,[15] but Moritz is by no means simply dependent upon the Leibnizian tradition, and he does break new ground. He is especially intrigued by those impersonals which have to do with psychological processes, and seeks to draw a distinction between verbs taking a direct and an indirect object. In the latter instance, the dative case is said to erect a barrier [*Scheidewand*] between the individual's innermost self and those feelings the impersonal construction seeks to render; such feelings are still outside the innermost circle and impinge upon it only 'from without.' The accusative impersonal, on the other hand, has 'a much more intimate and powerful relationship to us,' while the personal 'I think' presupposes the conscious will (the writer is able to point to a difference between 'ich denke' and 'mich dünkt').

Even here, in the attempts at observation and empirical analysis which underpin this discussion, we cannot overlook the presence of the normative impulse, and the Rationalist's grand design of establishing the ultimate parameters of the human mind, through an understanding of the structure and function of language.[16] One particular aspect of Moritz's work in the early Berlin years illustrates this purpose and interest excellently, and this is his preoccupation with deaf-mutes. It was a subject in which he had had his precursors, for instance Diderot and Locke.[17] Moritz was offered the opportunity by the Charité hospital in Berlin of conducting experiments with a deaf-mute in an attempt to teach him to communicate and eventually to read. This involved him in a study of sign-language, which he soon concluded was essentially metonymic. Such had, in his opinion, been the condition of all human language in its early stages of development, it had been a matter of metonyms, or of synecdoche, in which a quality or part represented the whole or, to put it another way, a sign was actually a thing. In time this changed, 'and signs became only signs.'[18] Moritz believes that the deaf-mute, through the metonymic, or synecdochal, nature of his sign-language, can learn what it is all-important to know, the relationship between part and whole, that the part can never be comprehended except in its relationship with the whole. To grasp this is perhaps no lesser thing than to understand 'the true purpose of our life on earth'[19] – an idea which Moritz develops in many forms, and which irradiates his entire thought. Equally important is the fact that the deaf-mute can respond at all, for this is decisive evidence

that language is not, as it were, an accidental discovery of man, by means of which he has differentiated himself from the animal, but that his power of thought [*Denkkraft*] in itself already differentiates him from the animal, surmounting as it does the lack of articulated sounds and creating a language, wherever it may take its materials from. – This much is taught us by those born deaf and dumb.[20]

Moritz's conception of language is therefore rooted in the notion of the generative powers of the mind, which is subject to its own innate laws. But the phenomenon of the teachable deaf-mute also enables him to resolve, to his own satisfaction, the contradiction between language as acquired behaviour and language as inborn structure. This is a contradiction not unrelated to the methodological conflict between deduction and induction, and to that between an empiricistic, at times even behaviouristic, approach and an overriding intent which is rationalistic and normative. In his pedagogical writings Moritz seeks to reconcile his fundamental belief in an innate 'Denkkraft' or 'vorstellende Kraft' with the notion that rationality can develop only if it is taught, and only by an interaction with the world. The case of the deaf-mute shows that this development will indeed occur, so long as the inborn faculty can be exercised in the appropriate manner, in this case by the learning of a metonymic sign-language. Thus 'Aufklärung' pedagogy, as Moritz represents it, may be seen as asserting its faith in the faculty of Reason, while equally insisting that this must be trained. But at the same time the psychological study of language as practised by Moritz has implications which bear upon the very concept of the Rational itself. A clue here lies in the definition of synecdoche as signifying the necessary relationship between part and whole. Rational thinking is an ordering dependent upon this relationship, and the metaphors for it are symbolic of the rational design of the world. Eighteenth-century thought is of course instinct with such metaphors of universal order, and Moritz draws frequently upon their resources. A consideration of his commentary on prepositions will further clarify this aspect.

The discussion ranges widely, but it is the speculations on the preposition *um*, meaning 'around,' which are most pertinent. Moritz begins with the use of *um* in a purely positional sense, maintaining that when we say 'The trees stand around the house,' we are unable to visualise all the trees simultaneously. We are obliged, in fact, to put the picture together piece by piece, and this is because 'around' is 'a composite idea,' made up of the ideas 'behind,' 'in front of,' 'at the side of,' and so on. In the author's view all prepositions have their psychological roots in relationships of bodily experience. *Um*, however, has the peculiarity that it is the sum of several different prepositions of motion and position, and designates proximity to an object on all sides. At this point in the argument a significant passage follows:

If we wish to imagine the continuous direction of an action towards a particular end and purpose, we think of this purpose as the centre about which our action turns ... The purpose for which [*warum*] I do something is an idea in me, around which my actions move as it were like a wheel around its axis, which goes forward in spite of this unchanging motion. If I therefore say, 'I am going (in order) to see the house,' 'going' always turns around the idea of 'seeing,' but in spite of this it preserves its direction towards the external object, i.e. the house, that I wish to see (*Mag*, I, 2, 108–9).

In examining in this way the 'psychological foundations' of the preposition *um*, Moritz does two rather interesting things: in the first place, he attempts to render what seemed to him an empirical observation of mental processes by means of a figure appropriate to the task; in the second place, he turns for this figure towards a tradition of metaphor which is readily identifiable. It is of course that of mystical literature, in which the circle is a symbol of wholeness and endlessness.

To pursue this question further is soon to realise once more that Moritz was a writer very much inclined to employ geometric metaphors, and particularly this one. Even allowing for his customary self-plagiarisation, he uses it astonishingly frequently. He exploits it in several ways, but especially in order to express the necessary connection, intrinsic (he believes), in all things, between periphery and centre, part and whole, surface and core, thing and consciousness, fact and meaning, or predicate and subject. The circle is taken as the symbol of that Oneness upon which all created things radially depend.[21] But Moritz uses it as an aid in the elucidation of a whole series of problems. It helps him, for instance, in his consideration of deaf-mutes, to indicate the nature of that process by which the mind awakens to rational knowledge, and of the processes of judgment. The circle expresses the fundamental truth that the part must always be seen in the light of the whole, and the whole constantly in that of its parts. The act of judging, in his view, involves the linking of a less general concept with one that is more so, and simultaneously with what Moritz calls 'the most perfect concept of existence.'

'Judgment is therefore ... making something, at a given moment, into the centre of the entire range of one's ideas – and describing a small circle, and at the same time the largest circle possible, around this centre' (*KL*, 24). If, goes the argument, we take a sentence such as 'The tree is green,' then the subject 'tree' may be regarded as the centre and the predicate 'green' as its circumference. If we then modify the predicate by adding limiting statements which more specifically define the tree, a series of diminishing concentric circles is thereby generated. Thus 'green' will produce a larger circle than will such a predicate as 'a body which grows.' Ultimately there appears the sentence: 'A tree is a tree,' and in this final case the circumference falls back into the centre, and the statement is simply reversible. The argument here is less interesting in itself than is the metaphorical device used in its presentation. In a similar way the figure of the circle is employed to explicate the Aristotelian syllogism. Yet again, the interrogative *warum* (which 'contains' *um*) is accounted for as a word which merely 'describes a great circle in which the concept can be contained' (*KL*, 125–9).

So far, the metaphor of circle and centre may be regarded as evidence not only of Moritz's persisting connection with the mystical tradition in his writings, but also of his inclination towards a mode of cogitation which is essentially a priori and analytic. However, the situation is not quite so simple since, as has been implied, Moritz's essays on language vividly display an unresolved dichotomy between deductive and inductive methodology. In an article in the *Magazin* he discusses the question of 'viewpoint.' Here he argues that the conceptualisation of anything requires the establishment of a central point, and that therefore achieving the *correct* point of view in anything presupposes the choice of the true centre. In trying to discover where this is, we have to test one hypothetical centre after another until we find that circle into which all relevant ideas will fit. But a process of this kind must surely be held to be an experimental one. Freedom of thought, freedom from the fixity of instinct, as well as openness to the possibility of error – all these are related to the choice of centre, and to its possible mischoice. The mind, Moritz asserts, functions naturally in this fashion, that is, it functions naturally empirically. But at the very moment he makes this claim Moritz adduces yet another overriding metaphor, more concrete perhaps than the former, and almost equally ancient and distinguished of lineage: 'It is in the nature of our mind, just as it is in the nature of the spider, to make itself the centre of its web ...' (*Mag*, IV, 2, 18). Again, therefore, what is ultimately true is already given, and enshrined in venerable imagery; it need not be sought out by the scientific method. The fullest exposition of this concept of mind in Moritz's work is perhaps to be found in the misnamed *Kinderlogik*,[22] already frequently cited. Written on commission and based on a number of copperplates originally intended for a different use, and surplus to the publisher Mylius's requirements, the *Kinderlogik* is supposed to be an instructional manual in reasoning and in understanding the order of the world, for the benefit of children. It does indeed begin on a level fairly appropriate to this intent, but the author clearly forgets his purpose more and more and inserts, especially towards the end of the volume, complex apodictical formulations of an epistemological and even metaphysical kind. The *Kinderlogik* makes much use of the distinction between body and mind, which is drawn with a near Cartesian severity. While physical objects are subject to fragmentation, concepts, so Moritz maintains, are not. Cognition is a process of forcing together [*Zusammendrängen*] elements otherwise disconnected and dispersed. Unity is defined as the inherence of one thing in another, but things, as they exist in the world outside the mind, do not have this characteristic of 'being within,'[23] hence they do not themselves partake of unity until they are cognised and thus become 'within': 'Not the thing, but our concept of the thing, has become one – thus the whole universe becomes one in our concept of it' (*KL*, 112). This means that coherence, and wholeness, are characteristics of mind, and of nothing else. Each thinking being, a kind of monad, is 'the point of conjunction of what is dispersed in its environment,' and God (the supreme monad) is therefore the point of conjunction of all dispersed things. Hence we may sum up that for Moritz, working deeply in the traditions of Leibniz, Wolf and Mendelssohn, it is the 'power of thought' [*Denk-*

kraft] or the imagination [*Vorstellungskraft*] or, in his later work, the 'active energy' [*Tatkraft*] of the mind which imposes coherence upon a disjoined world. Language, moreover, has a very special part to play in this activity. Without it, the human memory would be a desolate *labyrinth*, full of gaps and half-erased impressions: 'But language is the indestructible ball from which we unravel the thread that shows us the sole path out of this labyrinth of our ideas [*Vorstellungen*].' Language, Moritz says in this passage (which I take from a quite different essay[24]) was that faculty which enabled primitive man to make his initial distinctions between things, to see the part as a part in its relation to the whole. Although language was literally 'forced' from man's lips as he responded to the confusion of his environment, it is nonetheless still the noblest of man's creations. It is generated by the mind, and the mind is the central point of the circle, it alone possesses the art of converting 'the disjunctured' [*das Zerstückte*] into unity. Obviously the epistemology and ontology which underlies all this, the marriage of consciousness and wholeness, is that which also underlies Moritz's autobiographical novel, and gives *Anton Reiser* its most meaningful dimension.

It is easy to see that Moritz, as a linguist, was certainly no behaviourist, no proto-Bloomfieldian investigator. And yet the empiricist, experimentalist nuance (and it is more than a nuance) must not be overlooked. Most eighteenth-century grammarians, for good or ill, were far more conservative than he. And his plentiful erroneous etymologies were generally no worse than theirs. Adelung himself made serious errors because he used logical methods when he should have resorted to historical ones. Moritz, of course, blunders badly, and displays a curious obtuseness, in not realising that his theories, to be valid, should hold good for tongues other than German, at least in some degree. Nevertheless he does attempt to confront the perplexities of language where he finds them. And in the *Kinderlogik* we may discover a categorical defence of the empirical approach: 'The real inner nature of things,' Moritz notes, 'cannot be brought out by deduction, but only by experience [*Erfahrung*]' (*KL*, 130). He is certainly more inductive than Adelung, and his psychological approach shows that he has freed himself from the tyranny of traditionalist Latin grammarians. But his work, something of an oddity in the history of eighteenth-century linguistics, always had an overriding normative and didactic impetus, and it was from this angle that it was most appreciated in his own day. Moritz was a populariser more than he was a scholar. He made quite an impact in Berlin with his public lectures on the German language, apparently the first ever given in the Prussian capital, as he did with his pragmatic attempts to correct faulty usage and his appeal for an academy with the authority to set standards. The lack of knowledge of Latin, he argues, among the mass of the population should not prevent them from using their own language properly – 'for the knowledge of the mother-tongue ought really to precede all other knowledge of languages, and it is therefore never too late to study it' (*VA*, 1–2). Moritz wants to know why public lectures in so many fields are in great demand, but not in that of German. We should take note that his passionate desire to further the correct use of the mother-tongue is an important characteristic, for it can be linked with a strong commitment in him to public literacy, a more evident concern for the education of ordinary people than is the case with many men of the German Enlightenment. An instinctive sympathy, indeed, for the illiterate classes (a much greater proportion of the population than in France or England), a desire to reach out unto the great unwashed, never left him, and the essay 'Die Pädagogen'[25] sharply criticises the division of mankind into two segments, those who use their heads more than their hands and then those who serve them, for whom the contrary is true. Such a situation, in which 'a whole segment of mankind has become the head of the others, who have become its hands,' is contrary to nature, and for Moritz it demonstrates the failure of the new 'science' of education. Modern educational theories, he protests, are being diversified not so as to remove but rather so as to correspond to and thus preserve the stratification of society, and school books are only written by members of the upper classes, and only concerned with the improvement of others like themselves.

It thus turns out that Moritz's studies of language also have a political and social dimension which helps to complete the portrait of this young teacher, journalist and intellectual. The significance of the above remarks, and their asperity, should not be overlooked in an age in which many reformers could declare roundly that the lower classes were much better off illiterate, in which Frederick the Great wanted only a minimal capacity in reading and writing among the peasantry, Goethe and Schiller preferred servants without much education, and Rousseau made pejorative observations about the plebs.[26] All the same, much of Moritz's writing in this area is conventional Enlightenment meliorism, concerned with polishing up the duller brasswork of the middle class mind, a good example being *Deutsche Sprachlehre für die Damen* (1782), a tour de force of well over five hundred pages, catering for that rapidly expanding group of readers, the wives and daughters of the bourgeoisie. The style of the opening passage is flowery in the extreme:

You are thinking of resolving, worthy lady, now that the whole of nature is turning lovely again, to direct the ever wakeful attention of your thoughts away for a time from the scented violet, the rustling west wind and the softly rushing stream, to surrender them to the contemplation of those beautiful, wondrous sounds which your lips bring forth in order to name all those marvellous things of nature and their delightful totality [*Zusammenhang*]? ... You have screwed up your courage to persist in something where, instead of feeling, only the intellect is employed. – A resolve that does you honour (*DS*, 1–2).

I quote this passage for its fulsome and condescending absurdity. The attitudes reflected in it were, in that age, wholly unconsidered and quite usual. Women readers were hardly expected to be capable of much intellectual effort. Hence, when the *Sprachlehre* was reprinted a decade later, the phrase 'für die Damen' was dropped from the title, since Moritz had been persuaded that the work was 'too philosophical' for ladies. The book is essentially a re-statement, or first statement as the case may be, of a number of the author's psychological interpretations of language, based on an analysis of a short prose text by Salomon Gessner, the Swiss poet. A version of Moritz's lecture material, the work was very successful, and had been reprinted four times by 1806. Comparable with it in tone and purpose is the *Anleitung zum Briefschreiben* (1783), and the much later expanded version of this, *Allgemeiner deutscher Briefsteller* (1792), a still more popular work. Both these volumes are a contribution to the Enlightenment tradition (founded in Germany by Gellert) of manuals of epistolary style, decked out with exemplary letters and commentary upon them. Here we see Moritz at the very centre of his activity as pedagogue and pundit, but we also see, if we compare what are really two editions of the same work, an interesting development. In the earlier *Anleitung* there is a stress upon self-expression and spontaneity. Letters, the author asserts, should never be composed after models, but should be 'a faithful picture of human speech,' cast in 'the natural language of the heart.' The tone is reminiscent of Rousseau, and of course of *Werther*: 'Can there be any sensible person on earth who would not rather hear the simple, naive peasant speak in his honest tongue than in the imitative, artificial tones of city politeness?' (*AB*, 33). We may label these Sturm und Drang values, and to some extent Moritz always retained them. His *Vorlesungen über den Stil* (1793) also shows him still adhering to the 'modern' view that a writer's style must always remain native to him, 'characteristic' – and of course the doctrine of 'Eigenart' manifest in this means, in Moritz's philosophical vision, the insurgent autonomy of part against whole. But *Allgemeiner deutscher Briefsteller* displays something else, namely the results of a development, partly under Goethe's powerful influence, towards an increasing orthodoxy, an Enlightenment (and eventually a Classical) taste, in the service of universality and wholeness; for it reverses the disregard for models, and declares that any letter, if it is to be written in a good style, must clearly differ from everyday, natural speech.

THE BEITRAGE AND BLUNT

The assimilation of Karl Philipp Moritz into the Berlin intelligentsia was of course complete by 1792. The poor boy, brought up in the lower quarters of Brunswick and Hanover, had evolved by then from obscure schoolmaster into successful professor, a member of two academies, and a celebrated lecturer on language and the arts, whose courses were attended by some of the most distinguished members of Berlin society, including an unusually large number of ladies. At the same time, of course, he had become the first true proponent of the cult of Goethe in Berlin, and there was indeed a sense in which the neo-Classical ideals he had absorbed in Italy transcended, rather than corresponded to, the conservative intellectual environment of the Prussian capital. But it is clear that he never entirely abandoned the empiricistic bent, the individualism and the worm's eye view of his younger days. He could hardly have done so, for much of his work had been but a deepening of these furrows. His contribution to German thought was in some ways an original one, and cannot be subsumed under the heading of Enlightenment rationalism. It is to be found perhaps above all in the way he enlarged the horizons of contemporary awareness and subverted 'Aufklärung' norms by the achievements of the remarkable *Magazin zur Erfahrungsseelenkunde*. And this had been possible because first and foremost Moritz had developed a more scientific psychology, and a more potent technique of self-analysis, than had been seen in Germany before. Dreaming of wholes, he delved into parts with a determination approaching obsession. The most noteworthy document of these innovations before the *Magazin* itself is the *Beiträge zur Philosophie des Lebens aus dem Tagebuche eines Freimaurers* (1780).

Unterhaltungen mit seinen Schülern, which also appeared in 1780, is, as we have seen, a work of experimental didacticism with conventional moral attitudinising, and quite a residue of Pietism. In general, Moritz's pedagogical writings (and those of the 'Philanthropist' movement as a whole)[27] lack trenchancy, and are far less revolutionary than Rousseau's *Emile*. Unlike Rousseau, we do not find Moritz engaged in suggesting the construction of a new kind of order, by means of massive social engineering. At most he seeks a reform of existing pedagogical practice by the cultivation of spontaneity and natural feeling, and by providing scope for these in a more liberal curriculum. But in the *Beiträge* something different comes to the fore, namely introspection, or – to define it more precisely – the impartial observation of the self. The source here was not Rousseau's *Confessions*,[28] but rather the German tradition of the Pietistic autobiography, to which we have already referred, modified by secular writers, such as for example Christian Thomasius, who as early as the 1690s had suggested that it was possible to search out the hidden recesses of the human heart by carefully noting the minutiae of people's conversation. This was in the spirit of the keen and envious observation characteristic of the highly self-conscious courtly world. Germany never had her Saint-Simon, but nonetheless the bourgeois moral weeklies did propagate something of this lucid and urbane interest in the behaviour of the human animal. Another secular example is the work of Lichtenberg, who hoped for a 'psychological Newton' and was an expert observer of himself and of other selves. The Pietistic tradition in Moritz's case, is however more important. We might cite the autobiographical writings of Spener and Francke, and of Graf Zinzendorf, the founder of the Moravians. Equally relevant are the diaries of Haller, and of Lavater, whose theories on physiognomy are connected with the same impulse towards reliable psychological data.[29] Sectarian autobiography (as prominently in England) is in the seventeenth and eighteenth centuries the breeding ground of the 'spiritual autobiography' proper, in contradistinction to that type of autobiography typical of orthodox Catholic and Protestant writers which is concerned largely with deeds and events in the outside world, with *res gestae*. The autobiographical writings, and above all the diaries, of the Pietists are imbued with the so-called *praxis pietatis*, essentially the resolute examination of conscience. By means of the meticulous observation of his thoughts, feelings and sensations, as we saw in *Anton Reiser*, and through a careful stock-taking at the end of each day, the practising Pietist sought to establish the temper of his soul, and his exact place upon the ladder of salvation. At its most committed and intense this process required an exquisitely subtle scalpel. It could be practised on others, but this was subordinate to the necessity to practise it upon oneself. It appears at first sight (though this is only partially true) to divert the practitioner from the external sphere of moral, social and political activity. But it seemed to Moritz to function as an indispensable counter-balance. 'To observe with our gaze turned inward,' he declares, 'is just as necessary as to have an effect in the outside world. Mankind has been active outwardly for too long, without turning its gaze back upon itself' (*DW*, I, 197). Or as the *Beiträge* put it in a favourite image: 'We see how the pointer of the clock moves round, but we do not know the inner machinery that drives it' (*B*, 5). A similar idea is expressed more poetically, and pre-empting the very common German Romantic metaphor of the mine-shaft, in the *Magazin*: 'Man's audacious step goes down into the deep shafts of the earth, and should our thinking self, then, be afraid of descending into its own depths and searching for the noblest of metals in that place where so few look for it?' (*Mag*, VII, 3, 10). It is significant that this alchemical comment occurs in the context of Moritz's dispute with the 'Aufklärer' Pockels (for a while co-editor of the *Magazin*), whom he is accusing here of smugness and superficiality.

The *Beiträge* are in essence a re-vamping, with accretions, of Moritz's own diary material, ordering this systematically instead of chronologically. The most important probable addition is a didactic moral tract, which accommodates the material to Enlightenment rationalist values, although since most of the original diaries have not survived this must be mere surmise. An extensive diary fragment for the years 1778–80 was, however, published in the *Magazin* (*Mag*, VII, 3, 25f). Moritz had first learnt something of the techniques of psychological observation in his childhood, perhaps from his father, or from other pupils of Herr von Fleischbein. His first years in the teaching profession had helped him to expand, solidify and recodify this knowledge by the observation of his students. Schoolmasters, he notes, are in an ideal position to do research of this kind. His procedure at the Graue Kloster was first of all to notice what was striking about a boy, without committing himself to any firm conclusion. Then he would try to gain the pupil's confidence enough to question him, and after carefully watching his behaviour for a week or so would usually find that pattern [*Fazit*] emerging he had initially supposed to be there.[30] This is a classically scientific procedure: a hypothesis is proposed, tested, and refuted or confirmed. But of course the actual technique of observation remains highly subjective, since it depends upon personal evaluations of behaviour. More difficult still is the task of self-observation, which, as Moritz points out, requires an unusual capacity for detachment and impartiality. The observer must be aware of the 'ebb and flow' of his consciousness, without becoming lost in it or interested in what he sees (otherwise he will alter what he is attempting to observe). The mind must be seen in process, and not reflected upon. The student of self needs to learn the trick 'of suddenly withdrawing from the vortex of his desires to play the cold observer for a while, without having the least interest in himself' (*B*, 4). The *Beiträge* come back again and again to the point that a separation is genuinely possible within the mind – the self really can divide from itself – and also to the realisation that consciousness is a field of energy, ebbing and flowing throughout the day. Trite though the tone of the work sometimes is, and degenerating from time to time into the heavily denounced 'reflection,' there is in it a quality of direct personal experience which is unmistakable. And we encounter in the *Beiträge* the first clear statement of that major idea which was to condition Moritz's work, a recognition of the paradoxical nature of time as ceaseless flow and eternal present. Men, he says, in the section entitled 'Self-observation' (*B*, 19–21) lose their experience of what is present by too much reflection upon past and future. He is aware of his own failures in this respect, and also that reflection on self-observation is easily confused with observing. The *Kinderlogik* later states the central issue more philosophically: 'Man does not live in days and years, but only in hours and moments – carried onward from one to the next only by the power of memory and the history of each one' (*KL*, 118). Memory is the most obvious power which binds together the different moments of existence and makes a unity out of them; without it, all things suffer the fragmentation of successiveness. For Moritz the cruellest of truths was the recognition that all experience is by its nature atomised, disjoined, and devoid of coherence, except it be enhanced by memory or, if we press the matter to its epistemological extreme, by the clutch of cognition itself. Uncognised, and unremembered, facts are without wholeness – they are but points. Only the mind, knowing and remembering, draws through each such point the radius of a great circle.

The *Beiträge* are especially significant in that they stress the importance of the empirical observation of facts, of minutiae, of the smallest parts of things. The mind however finds it hard to confront facts dispassionately, it is 'easier to reflect about some circumstance or other in my life than ... to write a lot of circumstances down' (*B*, 21). As disjointed diary material (though made whole by the act of composition) the *Beiträge* are at least in theory factual, for they are concerned with immediately and supposedly unreflected experience. The clearest statement of the empirical approach is to be found a year or two later in the proposal to found the *Magazin*, the pamphlet *Aussichten zu einer Experimentalseelenlehre*,[31] to which we shall turn shortly. In this first comprehensive pronouncement on the subject Moritz brings out his notion of the atomisation of experience, its fragmentation in temporal succession, and relates it to his imperative, the observation of disparate facts, however minute: 'Noticing what appears to be small,' he says elsewhere, 'is a vital requirement for the observer of man ...' (*DM*, 5). Though Wolff had already distinguished between an empirical and a rationalist psychology,[32] Moritz here gives a fresh impetus to secular psychological studies. In Germany, at least, the new materialist approach, which had arisen in England and France and to which such diverse sources as Spinoza, Hartley and Newton had contributed their part,[33] had found difficulty in establishing itself. One author who may be said to represent it is Michael Hissmann (1752–1784), a professor at Göttingen. Hissmann edited a periodical, *Psychologische Versuche*, and published a volume on the theory of associations. In Hissmann's works, which Moritz no doubt knew, we find thoughts very similar to his own – the insistence, for example, that 'ideas' are normally composite in nature, that the mind co-ordinates individual sense perceptions into groups and that each act of perceiving involves a form of composition by association. Association psychology, as expounded by Hissmann, would therefore underpin a philosophical outlook such as that of Moritz nicely, since both are concerned with the relationship between parts and wholes. Marcus Herz was yet another who made observations and indulged in speculations in this area, as may be seen from his *Briefe an Ärzte* (1777) and *Versuch über den Schwindel* (1786).

In view of what has already emerged from our consideration of Moritz's work on language, it is not surprising to have to note also that the *Beiträge*, in spite of their empiricism, are written in a style which again makes no small use of metaphors deriving frequently from the mystical tradition. The sentimental tones of the prose often dilute the astringency of the psychological analysis, but the recidivist metaphors provide a superstructure by which the scientific independence of the methodology is still more constrained. Using imagery which recalls both Goethe and Mme de la Motte Guyon,[34] Moritz writes that 'the deeds of a noble man pour forth like a bright stream from the pure spring of his thoughts, and in their swift course absorb a thousand further good deeds of noble souls, until the stream turns into a mighty river, which spreads its benefits over arid land ...' (*B*, 20). The river of life is one on which a man travels composing pictures out of the fleeting things he sees; but life is also a landscape surveyed from a hill which will, the further it is away, the more likely become 'a beautiful painting' (*B*, 28), as its sharpness and its contradictions soften into harmony in memory; it is equally a path of thorns, and the soul can be thought of as a region where violent storms may rage (preferable as these are to the fate of being becalmed). Such parallels between nature and the mental and moral realms are the common stock of the eighteenth century. Moritz is especially enamoured of the storm, and also (as *Anton Reiser* demonstrates) of aridity and the desert. An overlay of poetry, piety and pathos covers, therefore (and sometimes all but covers up) the psychology of the *Beiträge*. But among all the hoary and portentous metaphors employed here, the most illuminating is perhaps that of life seen as a play. In words which bear us at once into the heart of *Anton Reiser* Moritz inquires where the coolness and serenity of mind might be found adequate to regard 'everything that happens as a play, and the people who offend me as actors? If only one were not oneself involved in it and if only there were no envy of the roles of others' (*B*, 30). It would be blissful to live like this, non-attached, outside the play, on a higher level of sheer spectatordom, and those who are blocked and oppressed by the roles accorded to others should indeed seek refuge in this state. No passage anywhere in Moritz's writings makes clearer the interrelationship between idyll of the Pietist mystic, passion for the theatre, and revolt of the repressed psyche. The rebellion of the autonomous subject against the universal order has, indeed, its well-known pathological dimension. In Moritz the philosophical vision of that wholeness which the disjoined world reassumes in the bond of the individual mind is thus linked not only with a developing psychology of self-observation and consciousness but also with the individual's own engagement with a calcified and crumbling entity of custom and tradition. Expulsion outside the circle circumscribed by this entity constitutes, for Moritz, the misfortune of alienation.

Once again, the terms Moritz uses to describe the state of expulsion and exile are often drawn from the Pietist's vocabulary. He is aware that he takes pleasure in seeing himself as a 'rejected creature' [*verworfenes Geschöpf*] (*B*, 131). He admits to being a melancholic not *malgré lui* but because the condition is secretly congenial to him. In *Anton Reiser* he employs the English expression 'the joy of grief,' and probably some of the attitudes in the *Beiträge* were fed in him by his reading of English authors, especially Young.[35] Moritz often asserts, in emulation not only of the Sturm und Drang but also of the Philanthropist pedagogues and of Pestalozzi,[36] the primary and supreme value of the individual, but he knows that the seeds of the individual's pride in himself are also the germs of his malady, and the literature of his period widely documents the spread of a dichotomy of self-realisation and self-pulverisation. The individualist as the exorbitant creator and at the same time merciless destroyer of himself: Rousseau is possibly the finest example of this cruel psychological mechanism, and the analogies between Moritz and his great French predecessor are often uncannily close. In Germany a terrifying autobiography, until recently largely forgotten, that of the petty Leipzig cleric Adam Bernd (1675–1748), parts of which the *Magazin* republished, had as early as 1738 provided an astonishing portrait of what might be called an eighteenth-century Steppenwolf, whose self-analysis seems like that 'of one who has returned from the kingdom of the dead.'[37] We do not know for certain whether Moritz had read this autobiography before he composed the *Beiträge* and the first volume of *Anton Reiser*, though it seems unlikely.[38] The former do not, at any rate, contain anything comparable with Bernd's creaking but nightmarish pathology. Though they illuminate melancholia and hypochondria, they are certainly not a document of grave mental disturbance. Into these latter realms the *Magazin zur Erfah-*

rungsseelenkunde was soon to take the plunge, but typically as a collaborative venture of altruistically-minded journalism and of concern for other men, for men in general, not as the alienated noctuary of a masochistic recluse like Bernd. Of Moritz we cannot say that he ever really lost his bearings in the outside world, apart from a few desperate moments in his vagrant years, nor that he ever, unlike Bernd, shows clear-cut symptoms of schizophrenia. His fascination with psychopathology is that of a man who is, or seeks to be, a social physician, and who in his more penetrating writings makes use of his own neuroses rather, in a minor way, as Freud resorted to his own dreams. He knew all about his own aggressive impulses, he saw the meaning of the destructive games described in *Anton Reiser* starkly and clearly. In a pessimistic essay entitled 'Die Unschuldswelt' he observes that 'we are all little Neros ... Since we cannot be creators, and like unto God, we turn into destroyers; our creative act goes backwards, since it cannot go forwards' (*LP*, 242–3, and *Schriften*). Man's imagination, writes Moritz, then finds a place for these annihilative procedures in the records of history, and in poetry and tragedy, where their 'grandeur' can emerge. He himself once tried his hand at this in his solitary contribution to the theatre, *Blunt oder der Gast*

Blunt is a revealing work, though astonishingly crude. It appeared first as a 'Fragment' in three numbers of the *Berliner Litteratur- und Theaterzeitung*, in the summer of 1780, and a year later in book form. Making use of the hackneyed horror motif of the parents who unwittingly murder their own son, the play also shows the ill-digested influence of Lillo, Klinger, and Shakespeare (especially *Macbeth*). The father, driven on by his poverty and his 'demon' (the latter having biblically promised him all the riches of this world) to stab his overnight guest to death, not knowing that this visitor is his long-lost son, is a ranting, lachrymose ogre, the victim of dire fate and of his own wickedness – the author is not quite sure which. The other characters (the mother, the sister, the son, the cousin who is to be his bride, and her father the mayor who has been feuding with his brother Blunt) are equally stock figures, roughly and haphazardly drawn. The plot is exceedingly weak, depending upon the visitor's strange decision not to reveal his identity to his parents straightaway. Indeed, the play might be regarded as of no interest whatever were it not for two aspects, first of all the peculiarity that it has a pair of parallel, contradictory, endings, and secondly (not unconnected with this) the almost schematic structures of repression which may be detected in it. In the version published first, the 'Fragment,' the murderer Blunt lies in prison repenting his deed and imagining the happy outcome had his hand only been stayed in time, had his terrified wife only knocked for a third time, and harder, on the door of the sleeping victim's room. Thereupon, his dream is transformed into an alternative happy ending, a sentimental reconciliation between father and son, and brother and brother, with a wedding to boot. This conventional Enlightenment dénouement replaces, so to speak, the Sturm und Drang tragedy of the murder accomplished, a substitution of fate which turns upon the critical moment of the third knock upon the door. Despite the general triteness and crass imitativeness of *Blunt oder der Gast*, which must make us wary of assenting to it as proof of anything about its author (except perhaps his incompetence as a playwright), we are probably justified in seeing in this motif of the hinge of fate something of Moritz-Reiser's suspiciousness towards the world and constant apprehension of the hostility of chance. Positivist literary historians tended to find the dual ending puzzling, seeing in it (correctly enough) a confusion of 'Aufklärung' conventions with those of the Sturm und Drang, and Eybisch notes that the egregious disregard of 'realism' in this feature is in fact a Romantic trait.[39] This is also true, but surely the outstanding significance of the parallel alternative endings is that they suggest the possibility of playing with reality, of interchanging the 'real' and fictional worlds at will. If serenely performed, such an activity controls the schizophrenia which lurks beneath it, and as in the dream of reconciliation the murder itself becomes a dream (*Son*: 'That you [father] say no word of this in the future – that you look on all of it as a dream now vanished'[40]) so the psychotic horror is incapsulated and rendered harmless.

Blunt oder der Gast, in fact, is a paradigmatic statement of the father-son conflict, so overt it seems hardly possible that so shrewd a psychologist as Moritz was could have been unaware of its true meaning. The son, for example, is made uneasy by an unmotivated 'Angst,' in a situation of homecoming which should surely generate only excitement and joy. We cannot then be surprised to find him, staring out of his window, oppressed just as Anton Reiser is by claustrophobic fears, and borne down (his name, by the way, is Carl) by an obscure sense of guilt which finds its way into his prayers. Guilt before God and guilt before the father are readily interchangeable, at any rate in German literature, and God, like the father, is treacherous because he fails to protect his loving children. But the father's treachery is utterly heinous, as is his guilt. His motive for the crime (his recent financial ruin) is elaborated upon to bring in his loss of self-respect, and his intolerable fear of dependence upon his brother's charity. We see the monstrous machinery of *Anton Reiser* spinning viciously in *Blunt oder der Gast*, and as the aggression becomes fully manifest the sole escape that remains is into a fantasy of reconciliation (*Blunt*: But if the father forgives his son, why shouldn't the son forgive his father too?'[41]). The happy outcome has the further significance that Blunt is not theologically damned, it is itself a 'sign' of his salvation, or at least that he is 'not quite rejected' [*nicht ganz verworfen*] by the Lord. This ending was the only one to be printed in the 1781 book version of the play, further evidence perhaps of how his Berlin environment helped Moritz gradually to dispose of the more sinister bugbears of his adolescence. And yet there was no total cure. On the contrary. The fact is that psychological disturbances are continually erupting in his life, no less than in his imaginative works, evident though it is that they are subject to a certain conscious as well as instinctive control. Moritz was often in collision with the established order of things, though the impact was commonly muted by the will to conform so as to 'succeed.'

In the German context, there are certain points of comparison with Jakob Michael Reinhold Lenz, yet another (much less fortunate) contemporary and acquaintance of Goethe's. Both figures, according to Minder, bridge the gap between 'poetic inwardness' and 'ironic subjectivism.'[42] Both had neurotic characteristics, both turned into vagrants. But Lenz, no doubt the greater poetic talent, had the lesser self-insight and the sicker mind. Thus his vagabondage ended in that insanity which Moritz-Reiser avoided by a skin surely a good deal thicker than that of his teeth. What for Lenz was inescapable, physiological fate was for Moritz, to some extent at least, an assumed rôle. As in *Blunt oder der Gast*, the curtain could always be dropped at the penultimate moment and the ending, or even the persona, changed. Though Moritz's follies were usually inadvertent, sometimes they sprang from a kind of design. The eye to success, to the main chance, was never entirely closed. And yet the disorders went deep enough, and the suffering was real enough. The early 1780s, in his life, are a period of grasping after recognition, which came in some degree as teacher and professor, journalist and linguist, and as popular moralist. But there was always the shadow life, contradictory, and even (in an ironic sense) compensatory. Klischnig tells us that in 1783 his friend was in the habit of lying on his bed for days on end, brooding and toying with notions of travel, to England again (whence he had recently returned), to Holland and the East Indies, even to America. Moritz imagined himself as a sailor, or alternatively in the army: it pleased him to visualize the state of subservience and compulsion that that would entail. Ulysses was his ideal hero, but his preferred reading was still *Werther* (and he offered his visitors long commentaries on the argument between Werther and Albert about suicide). He declaimed passages from Ossian, and inevitably, also, he showed a fondness for the Book of Job. Sometimes he would apologize to people for bothering them with his indecision, and with what he called his 'Verdrüsslichkeit.' Some of this restlessness dates from before the English journey of 1782, though most of it from rather later. But as early as August 1779 there is a diary entry along these lines.[43] The journey to England was certainly of great importance, although not such a watershed as the much longer one to Italy was to become. An expression of Moritz's need for personal freedom, it nourished his liberal political opinions and gave him perspective on his own society. It was made financially possible by the success of *Deutsche Sprachlehre für die Damen*, and by a leave of absence of several months granted him by the authorities at the Graue Kloster. This journey provided the material for one of the best known of all his works, and the only one to make a reputation for him outside Germany. This was the *Reisen eines Deutschen in England im Jahr 1782* (1783), which sold very well, and the reception of which will be discussed briefly below. The book is sometimes rather similar, in its style, to *Anton Reiser*, as Klischnig aptly notes, finding it more interesting 'as a novel and a part of Reiser's story' than as a mere travelogue.[44] The blurring here of the distinctions between novel, life-story and travelogue points once again to that problem of fictionalisation of the self so central to the emergence of the modern spiritual autobiography.

IN ENGLAND

The connection with England, of course, goes back to those days when Moritz lived as a subject of King George III in Hanover. He had encountered the English language at an early age, when he had got to know an Englishman in Bad Pyrmont, and had devoted a great deal of time to it. In Wittenberg, as we already noted, he gave English lessons, and later on he did some work as a translator.[45] He had at least a passing acquaintance with a number of modern English authors, and better than that with Shakespeare. The account of his visit to England (May–August 1782) is well-observed and vividly related, with much concrete description and rather less reflection; it is anecdotal, inquisitive, and on the whole eulogistic. Criticism and irony are largely reserved for things Prussian and German with which the ways of England are favourably contrasted. In May 1782 Moritz, who had travelled to Hamburg in the company of his friend Gedike, sailed for London, leaving some of his letters of recommendation behind inadvertently.[46] By his standards, however, the whole enterprise displays unusual preparation and foresight. He had not absconded, was legally on leave, and had a job to go back to. Though short of travel money he cannot have been too short, to judge by the number of coaches he hired while in London. This city, which of course dwarfed Berlin, impressed him extremely. It was a London which, Moritz observes, had recently passed through a period of serious civil disturbances (the Gordon riots), during which more people were found dead near the brandy barrels than were accounted for by musketry (*RE*, 16). Its buildings he finds less handsome than those of Berlin, but the people, even the beggars, are far cleaner. The coffins, which call to mind violin-cases, are 'very economically designed.' Passers-by seem indifferent to the ubiquitous funeral processions. Lots of people wear glasses which, he thinks, may be the result of excessive staring into coal fires (*RE*, 17).

Moritz had certain contacts in London, which he evidently utilised. He visited the Prussian Ambassador, Graf Lucy, and he preached in the German church on Ludgate Hill. Highpoints of his stay in the metropolis included going to the gardens at Vauxhall, and inspecting Parliament and St Paul's. But he shows little interest in historical monuments. At Vauxhall he is impressed by the fact that busts of 'the English Classical writers' – he mentions Shakespeare, Locke, Milton and Dryden – are on show and these authors actually seem to be read, as their equivalents scarcely are in Prussia; he goes on to relate that his own landlady, a tailor's widow, reads Milton out loud, and that her late husband first became enamoured of her because of the excellent declamation with which she did so (*RE*, 25). If these remarks seem somewhat exaggerated, they do at least illustrate his regret that literacy and interest in books were so limited among the ordinary people at home. England is, in fact, Moritz feels sure, much more the land of the common man than Prussia is. In this country political activity can have some meaning, whereas at home it is simply not worth the trouble. On his visit to Parliament he hears Fox speak, and being faced with a choice of attractions, hangings at Tyburn or a Parliamentary election, he selects the latter. He is astonished and impressed by the patriotic feeling in England, combined as it is with contempt for the monarch ('Our King is a blockhead'), and above all by what he finds to be the sense of participation and belonging among the common folk. 'You have a quite different feeling,' he remarks, 'than you have when you see the soldiers exercising in Berlin' (*RE*, 38). And children, adds Moritz-Reiser, are brought up here in England much more freely than in working-class homes in Germany, where the tyranny of the parents reflects the oppression under which they themselves exist.

The encounter with London, then, arouses in Moritz a sense of freedom and of social release, it reinvigorates his liberal instincts. And whenever his mind works undominated by the need to please or to gain advantage, it moves towards political emancipation and egalitarianism. His was naturally not an aristocratic temperament, by no means, and he stood well on the left of the Berlin Enlightenment in all his more authentic moments of self-recall.

The *Reisen in England* documents this side of his mind, but it also reveals a quite different aspect, what might be called a burgeoning romanticism. The comments on St Paul's draw a distinction between this vast empty church, impressive enough as a work of art, and the great temple of Nature, which is (as Werther had proclaimed) never empty, but rich with the presence of the divine. Thus there runs through Moritz's narrative a theme of nature worship, in which the English landscape is made to sustain a poetic encomium not unreminiscent of the style of Goethe's novel: 'O you blossoming, youthful cheeks, you verdant meadows, and you rivers, how you have entranced me in this happy land! But this shall not deter me from returning to those sandy plains [*Fluren*] where my destiny has established the place of my life and work' (*RE*, 65). So much for the Mark of Brandenburg, so much for the Graue Kloster! They are not (to cite Moritz specifically) 'romantic,' as the countryside of England is. And when he left London to continue his tour he headed for regions where he could, and did, use that word 'romantic' again. He went to Stratford-on-Avon, and there he sought to see how the landscape might have moulded Shakespeare as a child, since 'the first impressions of childhood,' this psychologist notes, 'always remain extremely important' (*RE*, 103). He then went off to Derbyshire, to that 'mountainous and romantic' district near Matlock (*RE*, 113), advancing upon it reading Milton's description of Paradise. The climax of this journey, several episodes of which are well worth reading for themselves, was the celebrated visit to Castleton Hole – no doubt the best known and most influential passage of prose Moritz ever composed.

The approach to the Peak cavern at Castleton is described in language which clearly prefigures the various conventions of the German Romantic nature tale. Accompanied by 'a philosophical saddler,' a journeyman met en route, Moritz first discovers a charming little valley, a blissful meadow where there dwells in isolation 'a great scientist,' with a bevy of strange plants before his door. Close by, however, is what may be called the Romantic alternative view: 'a terrifyingly beautiful outlook on bare mountains far and near, those covered with black heather being fearful to gaze upon' (*RE*, 118). As for the great cave itself, at its entrance there stands a man 'wild and rude in appearance, who asked me if I wished to see the hole, his harsh voice making a powerful echo.' With his black bristly hair and dirty, tattered clothes, this ferryman had 'such a wild appearance, like Charon's, that the strange delusions one experiences in inspecting this hole already commenced' (*RE*, 119). The way down into this Hades of Castleton, a gentle slope, induces melancholia, as though the thread of life had been severed painlessly; the two of them step, as it were, into a 'temple' of night, and the visitor lies prone in a boat which the guide, wading, then pulls under a low face of rock, a terrifyingly *narrow* passage, negotiated as though in a coffin. The recurrent nightmare of the author of *Anton Reiser* (and of 'Die Stimme drin') shows up again here. On this occasion, however, it is not Death beyond the narrow entrance, but 'a majestic temple with magnificent arches resting on handsome pillars,' finer than the most splendid buildings, revelatory of the Creator's majesty 'in the inner depths of Nature,' a grandeur 'which I worshipped here in this solemn silence and holy gloom' (*RE*, 123). Thus Castleton Hole. Nearby is another cave, Eldenhole, described with typical intensifying adjectives as 'a terrifying hole in the ground, of enormous depth' (*RE*, 127–8). Moritz exerts himself throughout, though he is not a colourful writer and his vocabulary is spare, to build up atmosphere, mingling Classical allusion with words resonant of sepulchral terror and religious awe. This first of the German Romantic wanderers descends here, in literal fact, into that mysterious kingdom of the Earth in which, less than a generation after him, the hidden, dark and often sinister workings of Nature were to be investigated, in the fiction of Novalis, Tieck, Eichendorff and Hoffmann. At the same time the inquisitive, enlightened observer is also present, and he recounts the curious superstitions of the area, and its legends, with the urbane notation that Castleton Hole 'is called here by a rather dirty name, the Devil's Arse' (*RE*, 128).

Between the fictional wanderer, Werther, and his still more fictional Romantic successors we have this actual traveller, real enough indeed but yet (as he peregrinates through the Peak district reading Milton's account of the Creation) himself in some degree the creature of his own imagination. We can see how, in a certain sense, in some of the actual episodes of Moritz's life the characteristics of a new kind of literary hero take on flesh. Not for nothing does Anton Reiser speak of the 'novel' of his life, for in the later eighteenth century a strangely equivocal relationship develops widely between autobiography and novel, and a new kind of interchange between fiction and reality.[47] This young man had come to Castleton Hole, by the way, on foot – an unusual manner of travelling in the England of that time, though not in Germany. Moritz suffered certain consequences from this eccentricity, arousing suspicion by it on all sides. Sitting in the hedge on the Oxford Road, perusing *Paradise Lost*, he had been the object of baffled stares. He had been ill received in an inn at Windsor, being taken for a tramp, as years before in Dessau. On the road to Maidenhead he had been held up by an aggressive beggar, to whom he had been forced to donate a shilling. In this last town 'they seemed to think I was off my head' (*RE*, 79). No one believed that he travelled this way partly for preference, and not wholly because of indigence.

In Oxford he stayed at the Mitre, and spent much of his time carousing.[48] He did not like this city, interestingly enough, because of its Gothic architecture, admiring only buildings 'in the modern style,' such as Queen's. After Stratford, the object of his particular attention since Shakespeare was 'perhaps the greatest genius Nature has ever produced' (*RE*, 102), came Castleton, and then further hiking in the Midlands. In one Derbyshire inn he was shown into the kitchen, where he dozed uneasily by the fire, overhearing a maid say of him in pitying tones: 'He's a poor travelling creature.' This phrase stuck in his mind. It seemed to him to epitomise the whole misery of the destitute wanderer he had so often been: 'all the wretchedness of a man who has no home, and the contempt to which he is exposed.' The risk of being slighted is, for him, the most intolerable of all the consequences of social exclusion.

In all this, the comic element in the narrative should not be overlooked. *Anton Reiser* depends, as we have seen, upon an effectively controlled division between observer and observed, and in the *Reisen in England* too there is distinct ironic detachment, leading in some cases to self-ridicule, like the humourous account of the hazardous journey by night 'in the basket' (i.e. on the roof) of the stage coach from Leicester to Northampton, in which Moritz was forced to scramble for his life among the sliding baggage.

There are clearly good reasons for the success of the *Reisen*, which is such a fresh, extroverted and largely sensible book. It created a vogue, but the imitations are all inferior.[49] The second edition was translated into English (1795), in which language it was also successful, and the author, referred to as 'Charles P. Moritz, a literary gentleman of Berlin'[50] in what was a very free translation, became so well known in England that he may be regarded as having given birth to a nineteenth-century stock (and stage) figure, the typical German professor, tall and gaunt, in Wellington boots and long grey redingote, carrying a staff and sitting eccentrically under a wayside tree with his copy of Homer or Horace, or perhaps his Bible. Hackemann notes that as late as 1907 there was in print a guide to London which quoted from Moritz's description of Richmond.[51] This Charles P. Moritz, who had after all preached a sermon while in the capital city, was widely held to have been a parson, as even nowadays, and Ian Watt refers to him as a 'Swiss visitor.'[52] In the 1790s there was considerable discussion of his book in England. A hostile review, accusing it of silliness, appeared in *The Gentleman's Magazine*, and in *The European Magazine* a friendlier one.[53] In Germany too there had been those who thought that they knew much better than its author. The reviewer in the *Allgemeine deutsche Bibliothek* finds the travelogue 'often too poetic,' the meagre fruits, moreover, of a shortish stay in which Moritz described what he heard and saw, 'but what he did not see he did not think of.

And if something is well enough known that does not prevent him from describing it in detail – he saw it, after all.'[54] But these sour tones are no reliable index of the book's influence, its wide impact. Goethe himself refers to it, alongside *Anton Reiser*, as the work which had first drawn his attention to his friend to be.[55] It particularly caught the imagination of the upcoming Romantic generation, especially the description of Castleton Hole, which swiftly became famous. Henriette Herz recalls Moritz giving a fascinating oral account of this exploit, just after his return home (he no doubt repeated it often).[56] The young Alexander von Humboldt actually followed in his steps, and visited Castleton on 15 June 1790, mentioning his predecessor in a letter to his brother Wilhelm.[57]

ILLNESS AND REJUVENATION

It was in the clammy interior of the great cave at Castleton, so Klischnig tells us, that Moritz caught the disastrous cold which supposedly led, in due course, to the breakdown of his health. No doubt the traveller himself half believed this – it was a romantic idea, after all. Certainly he did come home ill from England, and a severe bronchial infection later that year nearly killed him. In December 1782 he had a haemorrhage, and (as we have noted) he appeared at the ceremony of his induction as conrector at the Kölnische Gymnasium more dead than alive. This was the time of the episode which Dr Marcus Herz narrates so vividly, and which is so curious it has been remembered in twentieth-century pathographical literature.[58] Herz refrained from publishing the story during his patient's lifetime, not wishing to give Moritz's detractors further evidence of his eccentricity. This was for him an intriguing example of how psychological methods might be employed to combat physical symptoms. It was, he confirms, after Moritz's return from England that he first became concerned about the state of his lungs, and among other treatments recommended bleeding. But Moritz was too nervous of that, and Herz comments interestingly that 'one of the affectations of the flourishing cult of the 'genius' in those days, together with the open-necked shirt and cold baths, was a dislike of this bloody operation. They thought it unnatural.'[59] One day he was summoned in the early afternoon to the Scharnstrasse, where Moritz had collapsed and had been carried into a nearby surgeon's house, and lay there looking like a corpse, among a good deal of blood. He was taken home and put to bed. The next day, nevertheless, he had dressed and gone to the meeting at the school, subsequently lunching with Büsching. Despite recurrent attacks of fever, he refused to submit to treatment, or even to stay at home. A few weeks later

(January 1783 ?) Herz was sent for to find him in a dreadful condition of body and mind, and apparently in stark fear of death, obsessively taking his own pulse and complaining (in prose and verse) about the mishap of dying so young. Though the doctor managed to produce a temporary improvement, he had an impossible patient: 'whenever he suffered an attack of coughing, or noticed his pulse miss a beat, he rushed wildly around the room, cursing about his death in splendid hexameters.' The precise metrics were perhaps a sign that the illness was not yet mortal, but this disturbing state of affairs went on for several weeks. The doctor soon saw that the problem was largely a psychological one. Moritz, he says, was in essence more a man of 'taste' than of reason [*mehr Geschmacks-als Vernunftsmensch*], an obsessive intuitive often inaccessible to rational arguments, or sullenly unwilling to admit their cogency even when he perceived it secretly. Henriette tells us, moreover, that he was impervious to religious arguments, since he was an aggressive *esprit libre* (so she remembers him, but this casts a strange light on such works as the *Unterhaltungen*). In despair of anything else the doctor eventually resorted to the strategem of telling the patient the 'truth' about his condition, namely that he was dying. Herz then adduced a number of reasons why, when the situation was hopeless, a man should be able to quieten his mind and accept his own death. He even explained to Moritz psychological techniques for achieving such equanimity. To the patient's objection, 'But I haven't lived wisely,' he retorted, 'Then die wisely.' Almost at once Moritz calmed down and began to improve, and soon all that was left of the nightmare was the phrase 'Then die wisely,' with which he used to greet his physician in the street and to which, Herz says, he invariably replied, 'Then live wisely.' Though in the event, the doctor concludes, an unwise style of life years later carried his patient off.

There have been various comments on this episode. A famous contemporary hypochondriac, Lichtenberg, was impressed by one of Herz's methods for accepting death. The doctor had told Moritz to try to convince himself he had been born more than forty years earlier, in 1712. 'A funny idea,' writes Lichtenberg, '... naturally that's meant as praise in this instance. Not bad at all.'[60] The story was reprinted and discussed in Schlichtegroll's *Nekrolog*, with the persuasive observation that the vanity of dying had evidently served to dispel the fear of death. Ebstein has drawn attention to Karl Birnbaum's remarks on Moritz,[61] which however are based entirely on *Anton Reiser* without the knowledge of this story. Birnbaum defines Moritz as a pathological dreamer [*Phantasten*], who eventually becomes an unconscious swindler, playing a fantasy role instinctively and believing in it himself. This does indeed go close to the heart of the personality problem of Anton Reiser, and of whole generations of neurasthenics who came later, but it somewhat disregards the self-insight of the mature writer Moritz, insecure as this may have been. Relapses into states of histrionic fantasy do, however, continue to be recorded in these early Berlin years, and Moritz was no doubt fortunate in having clear-sighted friends, such as Mendelssohn, and a doctor, like Herz, who may have still believed in leeches but did have some basic notion of psychotherapy. In any case the English journey, though it may have unsettled Moritz considerably and contributed to a decline in his physical health, cannot be regarded as negative in its overall consequences. For it had given him a real taste of freedom, and of the richness of the wide world. It had also illuminated by contrast the extent of the restraints (and the cramping injustices) of Prussian society. His several other trips between this and the great one to Italy four years later are much more scantily recorded, and largely by other observers.

An important example is the visit to Halle in 1784, where Moritz spent some time at the house of Carl Friedrich Bahrdt (1741–1792), a notorious heretical clergyman. This was an attempt to recover from another severe bout of chest trouble, with haemorrhaging, which the victim first treated, according to Klischnig, by lying on his back with chunks of ice on his breast and, during the Halle journey, by a diet of parsnips, apples and water. In assaying such cures he was of course paying tribute to fashion. It was as uncustomary, among the open-necked geniuses of these decades, to be bled as it was fashionable to hike, ride, fence and swim, to take freezing baths and to cultivate the outdoors rather than the drawing room. Based on his garden house in a Berlin suburb, Moritz indulged in all of these activities, and added peculiar physical exercises of his own devising. To strengthen soul as well as body he practised standing for long periods on one leg, and on one occasion fell hard against the stove and lay prostrate, sending his servant to Moses Mendelssohn excusing himself for that evening, on the grounds of having broken both legs. According to the anecdote, a personal visit from the philosopher was necessary to persuade him even to get up. Even his friends regarded this behaviour as deliberate ostentation.

A story from the period spent at Bahrdt's house is even more grotesque. Moritz arrived there ill, but gradually got better over a stay of two or three months. At first he told Bahrdt (whom he was calling on officially in connection with their collaboration in Campe's *Revision des Erziehungswesens*) that he was resolved to wander indigent through the countryside until he expired of starvation or exhaustion. Bahrdt, who had never met him before, took him in out of kindness of heart and because he was interested in his pitiable state of mind, persuading Moritz (as he tells it) to await death in his house, and at his table.[62] With regular food and some clambering around in the local hills, the wanderer rapidly recovered. But peculiar episodes intervened. T.G. Dittmar recounts many years later[63] how he met Moritz that summer, when he himself was a student at Halle. He had previously had a very slight acquaintance with him in Berlin, and now visited him several times at Bahrdt's house. One day Bahrdt told him that his guest had repaired to the hayloft, from which he absolutely declined to emerge. Dittmar went up there to try to persuade him to come out. When he called his name, a sepulchral voice responded. On opening a skylight, he saw an alarming figure arise from the hay, 'like Macduff's (sic) ghost,' with ruffled hair, wild eyes and a terrifying grimace. Moritz declared that he was sick and was 'meditating in the hay.' All around were strewn pieces of paper – 'my reading ... medical things, economic, political, theological, philosophical, grammatical things ... then I forget my tormenting thoughts and my illness ...,' and he began to declaim irrelevant verses. He requested Dittmar to sit down at an old piano in the corner of the loft, denying it was totally out of tune. 'It has become,' he said, 'a-chromatic. Its tones are beautiful dissonances. Just try, and in the end you'll find a tone in which they are all resolved.' When Dittmar would not accept that an out-of-tune piano could simultaneously be in tune, Moritz declared with some contempt: 'If you don't understand that, then you must suppose me out of tune too [*verstimmt*], and you'd be nearer right on that score. I don't wish to continue to live, and you can die with me. Have you a knife on you?' When Dittmar politely refused this suggestion, Moritz abused him, and announcing that 'life is common prose but death-death is high poetry,' he tried to seize his visitor by the collar, whereupon Dittmar ran out and bolted the loft door. With Moritz now whimpering that it was all a joke and that he might well burn to death in there, Bahrdt and Dittmar solemnly discussed his case, the former speculating whether it was a matter of fits of delirium or of 'conscious experiments he is carrying out on the mind.'

We may assume, in this instance at least, that it was neither. Moritz is here merely posing as a psychopath – the pun on 'verstimmt' proves this adequately. The remarks about the piano contain more sense than nonsense and some of the language seems deliberately parodistic. It may be supposed that Bahrdt's guest was in an honest depression, and was defending his privacy and satisfying his resentments by a façade of paranoid aggression. The painful lucidity of a compulsive self-ironisation also flashes through such incidents as this, with which Moritz's career is well supplied. But they are surely very far from being symptoms of a full-blown psychosis, much further away from it than 'Anton Reiser's' behaviour had been a decade before.

We might profitably contrast the encounter Moritz and Klischnig had some twelve months later with a schizophrenic, the novelist J.K. Wezel, author of the best-selling *Hermann und Ulrike* (1780). In mid-summer 1785, on the termination of his editorship of the *Vossische Zeitung*, Moritz set off with his friend on a walking tour to Switzerland, equipped with a map, two copies of Horace, and what seemed adequate funds. On the journey they paid several important calls, one of which was on Wezel. Though forewarned that this poor man had become 'somewhat hypochondriac,' they found him far worse than expected. As they talked he kept on standing up and staring fixedly into one corner of the room, occasionally trembling all over. Moritz and Klischnig found this so unnerving that they made off as soon as they could, leaving behind them a man who indeed slipped not too long thereafter into incurable insanity. Another visit paid was to a crazy occultist Moritz had known in Wittenberg, who claimed to be on the point of discovering the philosopher's stone. Away from these dark basements of eighteenth-century life, a much more important call, in Leipzig, was on Schiller, to whom they were introduced by the publisher Göschen. In view of what Moritz had written in the *Vossische Zeitung*, the interview could well have been embarrassing, but in the event it went quite well. Schiller subsequently noted, however, that Moritz struck him at that time as affected, and as a would-be 'starker Geist,' a 'genius' – an impression to be modified favourably when they met again three and a half years later.[64] Apparently they discussed his objections to Schiller's dramas quite openly and he did not budge much from them (Schiller, for his part, was always a careful and fair-minded peruser of Moritz's writings, including the *Magazin*, which was not that much to his taste). During their meeting the dramatist read out excerpts from *Don Carlos* to his guests, and Moritz's approval of this play was no doubt the real key to their reconciliation.

After Leipzig the travellers moved on to Weimar, where they failed in their intention of paying their respects to Goethe, who was away. Herder was gone too, but they did meet Wieland, whom they found to their surprise rather shy and withdrawn. From Weimar they continued to Erfurt, Gotha, Fulda and Frankfurt, passing through country in which Anton Reiser had had some of his bitterest experiences. On the way to Mannheim they encountered a mad Englishman called Goodes, who claimed to have killed his wife's lover and was endeavouring to choose between the penance of a hermitage in the Swiss Alps and a leap into Vesuvius ('A truly English idea,' observes Klischnig sagely). Shortage of money then forced them to abandon the idea of going on to Switzerland, and so they set off home via Nürnberg, Erlangen, Bamberg and Dresden. A nobleman they met on route (one Baron

Hörwart) fired Moritz's imagination with dreams of Italy, and Klischnig recalls that as they reached Berlin again they seemed to talk of little else. Moritz also used this trip to try his hand again at poetry, composing part of an epic poem (since lost), entitled *Der Ritter des Geistes oder das Vehmgericht*.[65] It was not the only journey he took with Klischnig. Subsequently they visited Hamburg together, a city Moritz had seen before, when calling on Campe, and which pleased them both because the atmosphere was more open and 'democratic' than in Berlin, and even more startlingly superior to that of Nürnberg where they had come across an 'aristocratic tyranny' [*Aristokratendruck*].

On this occasion they paid a visit to the poet Matthias Claudius in Wandsbeck. The intention of continuing to Göttingen had to be abandoned, not for financial reasons but because Moritz was in haste to return home, being at long last in love. Göttingen was in any case a town he already knew. Knüppeln[66] refers to a journey there (autumn 1784?) in which the wanderer had certain 'adventures,' was practically press-ganged into the army,[67] and met a number of well-known writers. These encounters are said to have cooled his literary ambitions, since he discovered that these gentlemen were all of them in uncomfortable material circumstances – the most distinguished, Gottfried August Bürger, an author who by far exceeds Moritz in his talent for organising personal disasters, was at that time living uncertainly at the university as a *Privatdozent*.

The 'poor travelling creature,' then, was rarely at rest. His energy, since all these extensive journies were largely on foot, is extraordinary, and such activity is the more unusual in an age where travel was still a somewhat dire undertaking and much the exception rather than the rule. His illness seems to have encouraged his habit rather than to have limited it, perhaps because both had a common psychological origin – once again, in 1786, the journey to Italy was to be prefaced by a serious physical collapse. In the *Beiträge* Moritz calls himself, in conscious imitation of Werther, 'a wanderer upon earth,' and, as we noted, it has been the custom for commentators on *Anton Reiser* to link the dromomania of the hero, and of course his very name, to the symbolic figure of the pilgrim through this world. A similar interlocking of levels of meaning has of course often been proposed in the case of Rousseau, the prototypical *promeneur solitaire*. Some of these connections and analogies, we may well feel, are over-facile, although there is concrete evidence (both in the *Beiträge* and in *Anton Reiser*) that Moritz occasionally conceived of his life-pattern in such terms, thought of himself, that is, as the homeless wanderer before the face of God, *homo viator et peregrinator*. He had read Bunyan, and given his temperament it was inevitable he should posturize in this manner in the mirror of his imagination. But he also knew something of the novels of Laurence Sterne, and it would be wrong not to notice in his journies and his accounts of them an expression of that new subjectivity which travel in this period so significantly acquires. In Germany the restraints upon the self-expression of the individual were of course considerable, and the Romantic wanderer, both in literature and in life, owes something of his tortured perseverance to this. Moreover, in Moritz's case we can see a development of great importance: literature and life are beginning to be confused. This confusion, which the Werther-cult exemplifies well, had been noticed by Moritz in 1782 – nothing, he writes, makes people as false as do books, and those who have read no novels are for this reason the best subjects for psychological observation. As for the others: 'Instead of people, amazing thing, we now hear books talking and see books taking actions.'[68] Anton Reiser as a figure in European literature owes no little of his importance to the fact that he is one of the very first characters in a novel who tries to live out his life as if it itself *were* a novel. This is a complication of baneful consequence. It is, however, an inevitable result of the final shattering of the cosmos of Christian society in the eighteenth century, the crumbling of the authoritarian aristocracy and the arrival on the scene of the autonomous radical. In his untoward behaviour this last initiated an assault upon the world from an empirical point of view. In his imagination, meanwhile, he generates a new cosmos, which, like Anton Reiser's, takes the form of a fictional reassembly of the pieces of his own insubordinate and erratic life.

4

The Smoke and the Light

'For only the individual is real, the composite exists for the most part in the imagination' (*IZ*, 12). These are challenging words, suggesting, despite the terminological difficulties they entail, a philosophical position of a fairly radical nature. But we are entitled to inquire how far they represent a genuine insight, thought through and paid for by serious, well-qualified effort, and how far they are simply the hollow diction of a derivative rhetoric. Much more depends on this than the validity of a particular statement. What is hereby queried is the authenticity of Moritz as a thinker and writer, and this was an issue which divided contemporary witnesses roughly into two camps. The controversy aroused by the negative portrait presented by K.G. Lenz in Schlichtegroll's *Nekrolog* stimulated a lively discussion of Moritz's strengths and weaknesses, in which even those well disposed towards the deceased were often forced to admit the shallowness of his learning. A judicious reviewer in the *Neue Bibliothek der schönen Wissenschaften*[1] accords him the qualities of originality and acuity of mind, while conceding that his writing is more often than not hasty and careless. His unexpected aperçus, frequently of a psychological kind, are too commonly mixed with platitudes dressed up as novelty by means of an aphoristic, cryptic style of utterance. C.G. Salzmann says much the same thing: 'he had the capacity for quickly familiarising himself as much as he had to with the subject he intended to teach or write about, to appropriate the unfamiliar, to pick out what was important, and to gloss over gaps in his understanding by a certain opacity of style ...'[2] Better known witnesses for the prosecution include Klopstock, Nicolai and Tieck. Klopstock told Rinck that Moritz was a 'Schwärmer,' constantly making judgments on matters (he seems to mean linguistic ones) which he, Klopstock, though he had thought about them so much longer, could not yet resolve.[3] Nicolai sniffs that this 'good-natured half-crazy fellow' took to announcing all sorts of books which he either copied out of other works, or else did not write at all, the most glaring example being a Polish grammar, heralded though its would-be author knew not a word of Polish.[4] Tieck, who – as his friend, Wackenroder, seems to have thought – bore some resemblance to Moritz, is particularly virulent. He wants nothing more to do, he declares with this clown [Narr], whom he also describes as 'a petty, wretched fellow.'[5] He had observed him from fairly close at hand, having been personally introduced, had visited him and heard him lecture and preach.[6] He grants Moritz some modicum of intelligence and imagination, but has discovered him to be a dilettante of the worst kind, moreover spurious and vitiated in his emotional life and unbearably pretentious. It is evident from the shock with which Wackenroder greets these remarks that they constituted a sharp reversal, for Tieck had admired Moritz at first. It is just the sort of reversal which might be expected from a shrewd, maturing, but still youthfully intolerant observer, who thinks he has seen through a façade of intellectual authority set temporarily over his head.

But these criticisms are not conclusive, because the evidence for the defence is also impressive. If they were the whole truth, we should be obliged to reject the opinion not only of kind-hearted friends such as Henriette Herz, but of Goethe and Schiller as well. Schiller's view is especially important because it is a favourable one developed after an initial resentment towards Moritz and always qualified by frankly critical comments. When the latter arrived in Weimar from Italy at the end of 1788, Schiller (who, we must remember, was his junior by three years) found him much improved over the man he had first met in 1785. Moritz had moderated in his philosophical views, and no longer affected the 'genius.' Schiller notes that 'the things he is interested in are serious and of substance,' that 'his nature is a profound one,' and that 'he has an excellent mind.' He even remarks that 'by hard thinking [anstrengendes Denken] his mind has conquered his hypochondria.'[7] For Henriette Herz there was no question of Moritz being, as Tieck alleges in his most serious charge, 'false towards himself,'[8] and she attributes some of his odd behaviour to sheer naïveté. What Goethe thought of his friend we shall reserve till later. It seems evident that those who knew him personally, and fairly intimately, had on the whole a better opinion of him than those who observed him from afar, or merely in his public persona. To appreciate him it was probably necessary to be sympathetic towards an intuitive temperament (as Nicolai no doubt was not) and tolerant of eccentricity (as artists like Goethe and Schiller, and men of wisdom like Mendelssohn, might be expected to be). At the same time many of the more superficial animadversions upon Moritz's life and work, though they do not touch the heart, are difficult to rebut, and are certainly lacerating enough. The fact that he was so prolific, writing against the clock for money, and publishing fifty or more volumes in his short life, meant that he extracted from himself sheer quantity of production, often at the cost of the highest intellectual standards. Moreover, at the peak of his career, though he wrote so much, he read relatively little,[9] and was thus thrown back upon overdrawn imaginative resources or upon self-plagiarisation. He would sit up all night to complete his quantum of pages, often with the boy from the printers standing at his elbow. That he sometimes lost the thread of his discourse while doing this is less surprising than that he did not do so more often. His vanity, which had persuaded him to vacate the well-paid conrectorship at the Kölnische Schule in exchange for a half-salaried professorship at the Gymnasium zum Grauen Kloster compelled him to rely more and more, after 1784, upon the income from his writing. He found it difficult to refuse publishers' suggestions, and for his part he made many proposals and promises to which he could not possibly hold. Hence there ensued the notorious fracas with Campe and other quarrels. Such mercenary productivity is rarely endearing, especially if combined with intellectual charlatanry, the gravamen of the accusations made against Moritz. These charges, however, as we have noted, are not easy to accept in the light of the testimony of associates of unimpeachable intelligence and substantial powers of discernment.

In weighing the intellectual quality of Moritz's works, particularly his quasi-philosophical writings, due allowance must be made for their frequently derivative nature, and also for the overt effort to impress by means of an obscure and oracular style. But even so, a residue of insight remains which is indisputably authentic, and sometimes original, and this not only in *Anton Reiser*. The most essential ideas of K.P. Moritz are not vacuously derivative, but wear the flesh of experience. When he wrote of the antithesis between individual fact and composite understanding he knew well whereof he was speaking, for it was a contrast ingrained in his life. It is true of course that his thinking is far too much the child of intuition and feeling to rank as philosophical in the austerer senses of that term. And equally the mystification technique can be irritating, as in other writers. Thus K.G. Lenz makes fun of the *Hartknopf* novels, calling them a confidence trick upon the public. These works will be discussed in their proper place, but it is perhaps worth noting now that this critic's witty inversion of the *Hartknopf* epigraph, 'ex fumo dare lucem,' into its reverse, 'ex luce dare fumum,'[10] is certainly unfair. In Moritz's diverse writings, and not only in *Andreas Hartknopf*, there may well be not a little smoke, but there is also a good deal of light. And nowhere is this truer, of course, than in the field of psychology, where the empirical imperative was most able to come into its own.

The Enlightenment, according to Max Dessoir, writing from his vantage point at the end of the nineteenth century, was in the history of psychology in Germany essentially the period of accumulation of data.[11] More narrowly and precisely Goethe refers to his own youth as the time of the awakening of empirical psychology.[12] But evidently the emancipation of this science from its preconceptions of morality and value proceeded quite slowly. Even for Moritz, who broke fresh ground in this area, psychologist and moralist were basically one and the same, which is why he can speak in the *Magazin zur Erfahrungsseelenkunde* of the 'moral physician' and his functions (*Mag*, I, 1,37). Indeed, an unambiguous distinction between these two domains was not made until the next century. At the same time, psychology as an emergent discipline was nourished from all sides, from the philosophy of mind and from aesthetics, from ethics and metaphysics, and from physiology and medicine. It coalesced from all these. It is often overlooked that the philosophical systems of Leibniz and Wolff, which dominated German thought until the appearance of Kant's first *Critique*, are deeply psychological in nature. For Leibniz, after all, had made the autochthonous activity of mind the centrepoint of his philosophy. The monadology conceives of the universe as an infinite number of independent individualities. The extreme individualism of the system is merely concealed by the doctrine of pre-established harmony. The spontaneous, conceptual energy of the single monad is for Leibniz, and essentially for Wolff, the source of all knowledge. In Moritz's day, German philosophy and pedagogy still depend on this outlook, which the influence of Rousseau, as he was provisionally understood, only served to strengthen. It was a belief in the innate power of the mind, of the *vis representativa* [*vorstellende Kraft*] as the root of the various faculties [*Vermögen*], and these latter Wolff attempts to classify. But the 'Vermögenstheorie' was then subject to modifications as the antithetical ideas of the English and French Sensualists gradually became better known in Germany. These theories, of course, deny that the mind possesses any such creative power. The work of David Hartley was widely disseminated in Germany in the 1770s, partly through the agency of Hissmann's periodical, *Psychologische Versuche*. Hartley's ideas are based on association psychology, which viewed mental processes as fundamentally passive responses to stimuli. Their effect was underpinned by the spread of the influence of the eccentric Swiss polymath Charles Bonnet,[13] who also rejects the concept of innate ideas. Besides all this there was of course a more thorough-going materialism which infiltrated from France, notably through the popularity of Lamettrie's *L'Homme machine* (1747). The notion of pre-established harmony had to give way, in the main, to at least a dualistic view, founded on the so-called *influxus physicus*, an interaction between the two entities, body and mind.

As it is gradually conceded that knowledge is not principally, and certainly not exclusively, innate and subjective (only the better trained minds could make a distinction between these two), but is rather the result of the input of the senses, psychology, even in Germany, does indeed become somewhat more empirical. A number of significant writers emerge there who have at least in part shaken themselves free of the Wolffian tutelage, and whose approach displays at least a few of the characteristics of modern science, especially observation and analysis. Outstanding among these were Hissmann himself, and also Johann Heinrich Lambert (1728–77). At the same time major authors, such as Mendelssohn and the influential Johann Nicolas Tetens (1736–1807),[14] though accepting, partly as a result of the impact of Sensualism, the separation between intellect and feelings, do not abandon the idea of the creative power of the mind. The conception of the feelings themselves as an active, energetic and creative force is particularly developed by Johann George Sulzer (1720–79), upon whose compendious work on aesthetics, *Allgemeine Theorie der schönen Künste* (1777), Moritz in some measure depends. We can in fact say that out-and-out materialism, a fully-fledged physiological psychology, is not really characteristic of eighteenth century German thought at all (though there are exceptions), and moreover that the Sensualist position in all its forms, though influential, is normally found blended with Wolffian ideas on the mind.

Physiological explanations, and theories derived from clinical medicine, such as it was, must however be taken into account, as also must the development of some notion of the unconscious mind. Following Leibniz and his *petites perceptions*, his *perceptions sans apperception* and the *perceptiones partiales* of Wolff, thinkers of the German Enlightenment sometimes recognised that processes might occur in the mind of which the subject was not fully aware. But this usually amounts to little more than acknowledging the distinction between perception and apperception. The word 'unbewusst' (unconscious) is not found before about the year 1800,[15] though Moritz comes very close, in his *Magazin*, to a recognition of the functioning of unconscious processes and even of a mechanism of repression. His ideas on the physiology of the nervous system are also, of course, subject to the limitations and fancies of his age. The dried brain of Jeanne-Marie Guyon is not just mentioned in *Anton Reiser* for the sake of irony, it is there in reflection of current medical beliefs. According to Théophile Bonet in *Sepulchretum Anatomicum*, the brains of maniacs are invariably discovered, upon death, to be dry, hard and crumbly, and the well-known physician and poet Albrecht von Haller repeats this claim.[16] The treatment of the insane at that time, even in the most civilised centres, was of course still primitive and inhuman. And as the autobiography of Adam Bernd makes clear, dementia, hysteria and 'hypochondria' (melancholia) were usually regarded, at best, as all disorders of that mysterious organ, the spleen, and sometimes still as sin. Alternatively, a more general theory might be brought into play, that of the 'vapours,' which are supposed to rise to the head out of a sick stomach, or from diseased spermatozoa or menstrual blood.[17] Such *spiritus animales* were thought to infiltrate the nervous system via the blood vessels. Less common, but growing in importance in Moritz's day, was a theory of vibrations, developed particularly by Hartley. According to this, the nerves are simply tubes containing very fine fibres, which respond to stimuli by means of tension or relaxation, while their continuous vibration constitutes maniacal delirium. Both the *spiritus animales* and the fibres and vibrations may be found alluded to in various contributions to the *Magazin zur Erfahrungsseelenkunde*. In this periodical Moritz evolves a theory of mental illness and its treatment which is in some ways Leibnizian and derivative, but which draws all the same upon a fund of observations the very accumulation of which represents a new departure for psychological research in the German-speaking lands.

THE MAGAZIN ZUR ERFAHRUNGSSEELENKUNDE

It must at the same time be admitted that the *Magazin zur Erfahrungsseelenkunde* – in which a serious attempt was made to throw light into some of the murkiest recesses of eighteenth-century life, especially the area of personality disorder and the psychoses, where previously nothing but superstition and violence had held sway – is still however basically not a truly scientific but a popularising magazine. The full title is, ΓΝΩΘΙ ΣΑΥΤΟΝ *oder Magazin zur Erfahrungsseelenkunde als ein Lesebuch für Gelehrte und Ungelehrte*, and though the aim was to provide the means to new knowledge this was inseparable from the wish to inform and equip educated men. We find here combined, in an undertaking less specialised than such predecessors as the *Psychologische Versuche* or Unzer's *Der Arzt*,[18] the Socratic ideal of self-knowledge, the notion of empiricism, and the goal of popularisation. The term 'Experimental-Seelenlehre,' which Moritz had first intended to use, was already an established one,[19] 'Experimental-' denoting merely 'empirical.' At the suggestion of Mendelssohn, 'Experimental-' was replaced by 'Erfahrungs-,' because a differentiation between these two was emerging, and the *Magazin*, though it seeks to be empirical, has little or nothing to do with experiment in the modern sense. The influence of Mendelssohn upon the initiation of the project was certainly very significant and may even have been decisive. The manner in which the published material is organised also derives from his thinking. Marcus Herz was another who had much to do with the founding, and those involved in the preliminary discussions included Biester, Gedike, Zöllner and the unfortunate Zierlein. Moritz broached the proposal in three separate articles, which are very similar in wording.[20] In one of these, the 'Vorschlag,' he addresses himself to 'all those who seek to encourage knowledge and science for the common good,' everyone in any social station whose aims include the promotion of 'truth and happiness.' Moritz argues here that man has devoted far too little of his mental energies and his talents to the specific study of himself, and especially disorders of his psyche, for which omission various explanations – including the tendency to regard such manifestations as the result or expression of sin or the Devil – are proffered. Physicians preoccupied with the body must be complemented by 'moral doctors' of the mind, who must make publicly known the methods they employ to effect their cures. All true moral knowledge, just like all true pedagogy, has to be based on the study of individual cases, which must be reported notwithstanding any fears of a dereliction from privacy. Names can after all be withheld (and to ensure that the sick are not further disturbed by reading their own case histories it is charmingly suggested that subjects be selected who are illiterate). Potential material for the *Magazin* is to include excerpts from autobiographical writings and diaries (those of Jung-Stilling and Lavater are mentioned, as well as 'Rousseau's memoirs when they appear'), accounts of cures achieved by anyone, especially teachers, reports of the behaviour of the insane, of strikingly wicked conduct ('like that of Rousseau'), and perhaps discussions of characters found in novels and plays as well, but first and foremost observations of the real world, which are a thousand times more valuable than are those found in books.

Moritz appeals, in his 'Vorschlag,' for the submission of data from a vast area of medical, psychological and anthropological experience. Facts, hard facts, are what is required, and reflections must be withheld until enough of these have been collected and put in order. He draws upon the thoughts, and the actual formulations, of his *Beiträge* to argue once more that the precondition for observing other men is a capacity for, and experience in, observing oneself. And in doing both of these things it is noticing apparently minute details that counts for most. Men's minds consist of successive states, and they must learn to place whatever is successive side by side [*Nebeneinanderstellung des Successiven*], when unexpected patterns and harmonies may well stand revealed. Moritz borrows the passage from the *Beiträge* which speaks of the need to be able to see the world as a play, and people who offend as mere actors therein, a condition of detachment which would put a man (as he comments revealingly) upon a level comparable to God's. The perniciousness of the rules of politeness, and of the suggestibility and imitativeness of people, is denounced, and the author claims that children, under the influence of a good teacher, may yet be protected from the worst of these evils. The proposals for the *Magazin* may thus be seen to combine an inductive, strongly empirical methodology with a critique of social corruption after the manner of Rousseau, while the ideals and techniques of non-attachment also mentioned seem at first sight out of place in the context. The preface to the opening issue of the *Magazin* repeats the stress upon factual knowledge, calling this the sole purpose of the undertaking – 'facts and no moralistic verbiage, no novel and no play ...' (*Mag*, I, 1, 2). This preface is remarkable for the way in which it expresses the editor's own sense of commitment to the study of man by such a means, to which (as he says) it is his intention to devote the rest of his life. At the time of the publication of his proposals in 1782 Moritz had not yet read the first six books of Rousseau's *Confessions*, which had not appeared in German. His remark, however, to the effect that they contained accounts of 'wicked' conduct, implies that he must have seen reviews of the French edition. By 1783 he had probably at least dipped into this notorious work, one of the most sensational publications in the entirety of eighteenth-century literature, and there may even be some slight echo of it in his opening words in the *Magazin*:

Rousseau: Ich unternehme etwas, wovon man noch kein Beyspiel gehört hat, und dessen Ausführung keine Nachahmer finden wird ...[21]

Moritz: Mit Zittern schreite ich zu der Ausführung eines Unternehmens, dessen Wichtigkeit und Nutzbarkeit mir von Tage zu Tage mehr in die Augen leuchtet ... (*Mag*, I, 1, 1)

The utilitarian purpose of the latter statement is the first striking difference. And where Rousseau thereafter goes on to speak of 'moi, seul,' maintaining that no one has ever presented, or will ever again present, a portrait like his, Moritz writes in rational and Masonic tones of the untrod paths of the human mind per se, which are here to be explored, a perilous labyrinth from which escape can only be at the hand of Reason, and along the ways of tranquil wisdom. Of course, a psychological magazine is bound to be very differently oriented from a personal confession. We can say that the *Magazin*, an enterprise in some ways as significant historically as the *Confessions*, shows the imprint of its editor's Pietistic and Masonic background here and there but remains on the whole remarkably objective. Just as *Anton Reiser* too exceeds the *Confessions* in the objectivity and honesty of its self-exposure.

Who, then, were the contributors to the *Magazin zur Erfahrungsseelen-kunde*? They were many and various, although their identities can generally not be established, since most of the articles are simply initialled or unsigned. Moritz himself, of course, contributed a great deal, sometimes under his own name but also under pseudonyms (for example the account of the experiences of one 'K.St.,' probably his younger brother). Numerous well-known 'Aufklärer' participated, either directly or indirectly. One of the early cases, for instance, that of the free-thinking school inspector Johann Peter Driess (*Mag*, I, 2), though reported by Moritz, is based on information supplied by Mendelssohn. The article entitled 'Psychologische Betrachtungen' (*Mag*, I, 3, 47–75)[22] is directly from the pen of the distinguished Jewish philosopher. This essay discusses the effects of certain subconscious processes and the phenomenon of stuttering.[23] In the earlier numbers we discover excerpts from the autobiographies of Basedow and of Jung-Stilling (*Mag*, I, 2 & II, 1), and Moritz enlisted the co-operation of colleagues at the Graue Kloster, such as his fellow instructors Fischer and Seidel, as well as his partner as head of the Kölnische Schule, Conrector Schmidt. Marcus Herz made an important and lengthy contribution, the story of his own major illness (*Mag*, I, 2, 44–73), and we may suppose that the editor frequently turned to his physician and friend for material and advice. For the rest, if we exclude the matter provided by the three editors, Moritz, Pockels and Maimon, the *Magazin* is a miscellany of submissions from all over Germany, most of the contributors being professional men, especially teachers, lawyers and magistrates, clergymen and doctors – those groups, in fact, whose work brought them most often and most sharply up against the manifold peculiarities and abnormalities of the human psyche. At Mendelssohn's instigation Moritz assembled his material under a number of headings, of which the most prominent are: 'Seelenkrankheitskunde,' 'Seelennaturkunde,' 'Seelenzeichenkunde' and 'Seelenheilkunde.' There are also one or two other subdivisions which occur rarely, and contain fewer contributions (for example 'Seelendiätätik'). During the ten years of the periodical's existence the great mass of data falls in practice under the first two heads.

Under 'Seelenkrankeitskunde' we find the many cases of abnormality and psychosis in which Moritz was particularly interested. Some examples are the very first piece published, an account of a catatonic personality, and the second, a story of paranoia – one Johann Matthias Klug who, in the erroneous belief that he was being hunted down by the King of Prussia, became a total recluse and heavily fortified his room.[24] The *Magazin* is a mine of clinical *curiosa*, for instance the tale of Christian Gragert, who thought he could persuade cherries to grow on apple trees, or of an hallucinating housemaid who sees little grey men, or of a succession of schizophrenics or depressives who murder in order to be executed and thus enter heaven expeditiously, circumventing the anathema upon suicide. There are some really exotic cases, such as that of the woman who loses the first phalange of a finger each time she is pregnant. Premonitions of various types, including apparent examples of precognitive dreams, are recounted. Sadists and cleptomaniacs appear from time to time, as do other obsessives, notably compulsive shouters in church (a widespread pestilence in those days). Melancholics, of course, are at the centre of interest, as also are religious maniacs and 'Schwärmer' of many kinds. The inclusion of much of this under the heading of 'Diseases of the Mind' seems reasonable enough, but the modern reader is more puzzled to find such 'moral disorders' as stubbornness, envy, greed, promiscuity, and so on, treated under the same rubric. In contradistinction, the reports published under 'Seelennaturkunde' purport to offer evidence of man as a psychological being, other than in his manifestations of illness. Here are found the discussions of language previously dealt with, but also such phenomena as left-handedness and stuttering. There is clearly therefore some overlap, and only a loose distinction between categories. Under 'Seelennaturkunde' fall Moritz's considerations on the subject of deaf-mutes, and on the influence of childhood and childhood memories upon the adult life. Biographical and autobiographical accounts are largely grouped in this section, those of Basedow and Jung-Stilling, the story of Zierlein's demise, and (in the later years) the letters of Herr von Fleischbein and selections from the autobiographies of Mme Guyon and Salomon Maimon[25] (the memoir of Moritz's father is rather amusingly included under 'Seelenheilkunde'). Further, certain paranormal and occult phenomena are regarded as belonging to this 'Natural Science of the Mind.'

A comparison between the chief sub-divisions is not really very helpful in understanding the foundations of the editor's psychological ideas, since the editorial principles employed are lax. 'Seelenzeichenkunde,' or 'semiotics,' offers a narrower band of materials, delving into the fashionable 'science' of physiognomy and introducing as specimens of characterology examples drawn from Moritz's study of his pupils at the Graue Kloster. 'Seelenheilkunde,' 'psychotherapy,' is, as Pockels complains (*Mag*, VI, 2, 50), rather sparsely represented; but it does contain a very interesting case of theatremania (*Mag*, III, I), now of course shown up without mercy as a form of neurotic fancy. Although the *Magazin*, at the beginning at any rate, was supposed to be nothing but a collection of factual data, there is commentary from the very outset, while in the fourth year of its existence Moritz begins a 'Review' [*Revision*] of the first three volumes, seeking to come to at least a few tentative conclusions (*Mag*, IV, 1 1–55). Though there certainly are inconsistencies and contradictions, a fairly clear picture does emerge of how Moritz interprets his data, and how he conceives of the human psyche and its proper and improper functioning. In the case of Johann Matthias Klug, the paranoid recluse, the editor makes two points: firstly, that there is a 'deeply melancholic streak' in the Klug family, and secondly, that Klug had held a position involving him in excessive mental effort over a long period of time. Here we can detect more than a glimmer of the notion of hereditary charac- teristics, although the most startling statement made is one with its sources somewhere in occult lore:

What is to become of our praise of morality, what of the compendia of the crimi- nologist, if the germ of my follies was deposited in the moment of my begetting by my drunken father? (*Mag*, I, 2,2).

The idea of environmental influences is stated somewhat more scienti- fically, in several cases, for instance that of Paul Simmen (*Mag*, II, I), whose murder of several members of his family is partly attributed to external pressures, including economic factors. As a psychologist, as *Anton Reiser* shows, Moritz was more inclined to pursue the environmental explanation than that based on heredity, but he never quite forgets this latter. His con- ception of the potentialities of heredity as a causative factor goes beyond the diffuse eighteenth-century notion of family resemblances, although it never achieves the systematic formulations of the century to follow. A few pages after his discussion of the Klug case, Moritz lays down some fundamental lines of approach.[26] Mental illness, he supposes, may very well be inherited, and may therefore infest whole families (or even nations!). It may actually turn out to be infectious. As he defines it, however, it is always a 'lack of the proportionate harmony [*Übereinstimmung*] of all the energies of the mind' (*Mag*, I, I, 33). What is critical is not the strength or weakness of any particular impulse, but the balance between impulses. Disturbances of this balance may occur frequently (this happens in dreams), but they become disease only when they persist for a great deal of time. Above all else it is necessary for the 'active energy' [*thätige Kraft*] to be in a harmonious rela- tionship with the 'cognitive' or 'representative' [*vorstellende Kraft*]. And 'ideas,' as Moritz calls them, absorbed from without need to be ordered in a balanced way, some of them having to be 'verdunkelt,' i.e. closeted in the unconscious or preconscious mind, if the thinking energy or faculty, the 'Denkkraft,' is to stay healthy. The task of the moral physician is to pre- serve, or if necessary re-establish, these harmonies, and to be ready when called upon to probe the deeper sources of any disequilibrium which occurs.

This is in fact a traditional view of the nature of mental disease, seeing it as a state of imbalance precipitated in the thinking function, and it differs hardly at all from the theories of Christian Wolff and the conventional psychologists of Rationalism.[27] Despite his disclaimers, it is clear enough that Moritz is, as we have noted several times before, inclined to impose a derivative superstructure upon his empirical data, and to attempt to persuade these data to support a Rationalist view of the nature of mind. Furthermore, an unmistakable Cartesian note is sometimes struck in the commentaries of the *Magazin*. Mind and body are distinct, and the science of 'Erfahrungs-seelenkunde' is supposed to be the study of the former alone. Thus not only is this periodical anything but an exposition of materialist psychology, there is even a suggestion that if real insanity [*Wahnwitz*] is of physiological origin and responsive to physiological treatments, it is out of place as a subject here. Admittedly, this position accords ill with the cases Moritz often selects. However, strictly physical causes of mental disorder are only recognised in a limited sense, that is, fever, sunstroke, an unlucky fall, or alcoholic indulgence may lead to disarray in the faculties of the mind; but about organic lesions of the brain little is suspected or supposed. One exception is the 'Genesungsgeschichte eines Jünglings von einem dreimonatlichen Wahnwitz' (*Mag*, III, 2), which goes so far as to speak of the 'physiological psychologist,' to decry overfacile criticism of the materialist viewpoint, and to stress the influence of body upon mind. Hardly any of the material, it is worth observing, has anything to do with sex, and sexual explanations of the phenomena recorded practically never occur to the various commentators. Adam Bernd, reticent though he was in this respect, seems to have been readier to acknowledge such pressures. But within these rather tight limits fairly extensive analyses are offered of the possible causes of mental disturbance. In the end, however, essentially the same explanations are suggested for clearcut cases of schizophrenia as for moral defects, and identical cures are proposed.

Curative methods, such as they are, consist in restoring by whatever means the upset balance of mind, in an absolutely literal sense. The chief method suggested is the re-direction of the wayward energy which has caused the trouble. Thus, in one instance, a doctor beats his patient's buttocks so as to draw 'the juices' away from the head towards the lower extremities. Moritz often proposes as a remedy a mental exercise such as the study of history or astronomy. It is occasionally explained that the vapours invading the mind need to be expelled, or the extreme vibration of the fibres reduced. But as a matter of fact the first 'Review' pays more attention to the cure of moral weaknesses than of insanity, and the general principle is quite specific:

Since the nature of mind [*Seele*] consists primarily in its representational energy [*vorstellende Kraft*], the origin of diseases of the mind must be sought in some improper [*unzweckmässigen*] outflow of this energy, which has become chronic (*Mag*, IV, I, 4).

Moritz spends time on the consideration of fixed ideas, and also attempts a scientific explanation of several examples of apparent precognition recounted in the first three volumes. Here he displays his shrewdness, for he arrives alone and unaided at the notion of the self-fulfilling prophecy (*Mag*, IV, I, 20). The first 'Review' then continues with an extensive section on treatments, once more making the Cartesian distinction between the mind as 'activity' and the body as 'extension,' and concluding that as in physical illnesses the patient must come to a crisis, so it is, ordinarily, with psychological ones. Moritz wonders whether such crises, of which little as yet is known, might resemble the 'breakthrough' [*Durchbruch*] spoken of by Pietist mystics. He comments further:

Although it is the case that this pious fancy [*frömmelnde Phantasie*] despite the wrong direction in which it has gone, has concerned itself far more with the inner state of the mind than has ordinary moral and pedagogical thought (*Mag*, IV, I, 35).

This interesting acknowledgement of the importance of Pietism for the development of insight into the mind, and especially into abnormal psychology, is also of course a pointer to Moritz's own emancipation from 'pious fancy.' But in its later volumes the *Magazin* documents the mystical tradition extensively, and 'spiritual psychology' becomes a major subject. Some of the editor's own diary material is used in 'Aus dem Tagebuch eines Selbstbeobachters' (*Mag.* VII 3, 27–44), and in the striking article 'Über Selbsttäuschung' (*Mag*. VII, 3, 45–48 & VIII, 3, 32–37). This latter shows a perceptive scepticism on the matter of self-observation and self-analysis. There is, Moritz alleges, no greater self-delusion than the resolve to tell the truth about oneself, and private [*geheime*] diaries demonstrate this only too well. When keeping a journal a person will endeavour to give his life an importance and a meaning which in fact it lacks. This results, in many instances, in the 'affected language of a forced religious feeling and morality,' and in 'the opacity, distortion and uncertainty of expression, and the staleness and superficiality often found in the development of the thought, beneath which the truth still struggles up towards the surface, until the desire for the truth becomes itself a lie, the hatred of deception becomes itself deception, and the fear of self-delusion delusion' (*Mag*, VII, 3, 47). Such severities derive, *mutatis mutandis*, and at long remove, from the merciless self-criticism of Mme Guyon, in whom the very word 'unselfish' is said to have aroused nausea. Whether or not they demonstrate, along with the decision to publish some of Fleischbein's letters and certain other things, the re-emergence in Moritz of an underlying tendency to mysticism (as Minder believes) is an important question. Much of this material, at all events, is classified as 'Seelennaturkunde.' Under this rubric also we find the preliminary excerpts from *Anton Reiser* already discussed. On the other hand the most dramatic autobiographical matter used in the *Magazin*, the selections from Adam Bernd, were quite properly placed under 'Seelenkrankheitskunde.' These last, in fact, were not published by Moritz at all, who cannot therefore (I would argue) have known of them earlier, or he would most certainly have used them. They appeared at the instance of his replacement editor, Pockels, to whose activities we now turn.

POCKELS AND MAIMON

Karl Friedrich Pockels (1757–1814) was born near Halle, where he was subsequently a student of theology about the time that Moritz, one year his senior, was at Wittenberg. An enthusiastic exponent of standard 'Aufklärung' dogma, and a supporter of the Philanthropist movement in education, Pockels became, in 1780, house tutor to the two youngest sons of the Duke of Brunswick, and gradually made some sort of name for himself as a minor journalist and popular philosopher. By cleaving close to the ducal household all his life, he achieved a modicum of success, attaining to the title of 'Rat' in 1790 and 'Hofrat' in 1800, and to eventual installation as a Canon in Brunswick. He was certainly not a deep thinker, but a fairly shrewd observer, though stubborn, unimaginative, dogmatic and perhaps rather vain. Rinck, who met him in 1783, describes him as more concerned, in conversation, to create an impression of acute and ruthless logic than really to discover the truth about things.[28] A collaborator in the early days of the *Magazin*, he was left in charge of it when Moritz departed for Italy, as well as of the periodical *Denkwürdigkeiten*. Before this, we find his name appended to a number of articles. In one, 'Über den Mangel unsrer Jugenderinnerungen' (*Mag*, II, 2, 18–22) Pockels asserts roundly that all knowledge is acquired by way of the senses, but nevertheless his interest in epistemological questions led him consistently away from the purely empirical approach. Recounting how a declaration of love generates an irrational hatred ('Sonderbarer Eindruck einer Liebeserklärung,' *Mag*, IV, 2, 57–62) he becomes censorious, and indeed Pockels may, in many respects, be compared with Friedrich Nicolai, whose sobriety and intolerance he shared. At the beginning of the fifth year he picks up the reviewing of the first three volumes of the *Magazin* which Moritz had already started. He opens by pouring scorn upon superstition, especially the belief in premonitions. Dreams, visions, presentiments and prophecies cannot, Pockels declares adamantly, pass muster 'before the judgment seat of Pure Reason' (*Mag*, v, 1, 8). He prints a set of 'confessions,' observing that 'essays of this kind showing people in a healthy state of mind and will, and not just portraying ordinary (sic!) mental disorders, from which up to now so few significant results could be obtained, in our magazine, for psychology, will be especially welcome in the future ...' (*Mag*, IV, 1,76). The sous-entendu is obvious, it amounts to a criticism of Moritz's policy as editor, and of his predilection for cases of psychosis (no doubt partly with an eye to circulation). The 'Review' is then continued with marked self-assurance, ridiculing such phenomena as second sight, attacking the idea that God might speak directly within the soul, warning dissenting contributors not to be taken in by their imaginations (as even 'enlightened and impartial men' can be) and announcing as a new regular feature a series of articles on the subject of religiomania [*Schwärmerei*] as found in recent times.

A ponderous psychologist but not an unintelligent one, Pockels is concerned to explain away all curious data, and to reduce them to their rationally accountable denominators. In defence of 'Aufklärung' he is determined to repel 'the increasing spread of belief in the influence of good and evil spirits on the mind and on actions, with arguments from Reason, and by uncovering its insalubrious sources ...' (*Mag.* VI, 2, 1–2). In his 'Review' of volumes IV, V, and VI, later on, he makes a clean sweep not only of 'superstition' but indeed of any apparently inexplicable psychic phenomena upon which a less self-confident man might have felt it wiser to suspend judgment. Especially revealing are Pockels' remarks upon the excerpts from Adam Bernd, whose autobiography he recognizes to be a document of the greatest importance. Written (as he claims) with a precision the equal of Rousseau's – in some ways, in actual fact, it may be even more precise, though of course it is far less sophisticated and incomparably less elegant – he finds that Bernd's excruciating self-examination contains all sorts of vital psychological observations on thought processes, on the impact of early environment, on the nature of the imagination and on the 'weaknesses' which may sometimes beset the Reason. Pockels is interested in Bernd's terrifying attacks of conscience, and in their possible explanation, but he denounces the Leipzig cleric's methods of self-treatment, such as fasting, as 'stupid fancy,' and would like to burn without more ado the kind of book (for example, Lipsius's *De Constantia*!) which seems to him to generate such 'crazy' ideas in people. He comments sardonically upon Bernd's discourses on pleasure and pain, noting that the Turks are said to tickle the soles of the feet while making love and that Nature (Bernd himself had said God) was no doubt wise to limit the number of erogenous zones to only a few. This autobiographer's references to the devil provoke a sharp rebuke (in the footnotes with which Pockels peppers the excerpts) for such beliefs. His summing up of what is, after all, one of the most astonishing compendia of psychotic symptoms in eighteenth-century European literature, achieves a level of smug trivialisation only partly redeemed by a certain willingness to entertain sexuality as a major etiological factor. But even this advance is vitiated by the tone of moral censure which accompanies it:

The principal cause of all those things Bernd has observed and described in himself certainly resided in a weakness of his nerves, which he often complained of, and this weakness indubitably derived from his youthful dissipations, which he committed early on and was unwilling to call by their name. The consequences of these dissipations often reveal themselves very soon, often also later on, in nervous discomfort of the abdomen, subsequently degenerating into a stubborn hypochondria, as in Bernd. The imagination is very easily upset by this ... (*Mag*, V, 2, 37–8).

Pockels' belief that the schizophrenia of Adam Bernd could be reduced to an adolescent failure of the moral will is typical of the kind of approach to mental illness that made the eighteenth century an age of intolerance, ostracism and incarceration, in which, as Foucault has put it, the lunatics replaced the lepers. Perhaps not the idea itself, but certainly its ramifications as prejudice run counter to the declared purpose of the *Magazin* as Moritz had conceived of this, however much his own neo-Wolffian preconceptions may frequently have hindered his great project's execution. The counter-attack against Pockels could not be launched until the *Magazin*'s founder returned from Italy, and during his period abroad his substitute seems to have had a free hand. Moritz saw little or nothing of the *Magazin* while he was in Rome. According to him, he did not receive a single copy, although it had been agreed that he should get them regularly. He complains, furthermore, that Pockels failed to make agreed payments on his behalf, on the unreasonable grounds that Moritz, who had been incapacitated by an accident, had sent in no material.[29] This protest is not desperately convincing, since Moritz evidently continued to submit nothing at all, long after he had recovered from breaking his arm. The question, of course, is on what terms exactly Pockels had taken over responsibility as editor, and this we do not know. He may well have been misled by Moritz as to what these were. Stopping his predecessor's agreed honoraria, however, on whatever grounds, was provocative. At all events, and right or wrong, when Moritz returned to Berlin in 1789 he made short shrift. Though Pockels went so far as to threaten legal action, he was quickly forced out of the editorial chair, and in the next number Moritz addresses the readership in trenchant terms. He explains the background to the situation, criticises his deputy's stewardship severely, and denies outright Pockels' claim that his intervention, and the change of policy, had preserved the circulation of the *Magazin*. He then proceeds with pertinent irony to what he calls a 'Review of the Reviews of Herr Pockels' (*Mag*, VII, 3, 3ff), beginning with a sharp attack on the previous editor's attempt to dismiss premonitions out of hand as nonsense. This is not, Moritz points out, such a simple matter as Pockels thinks. It is not after all a question of whether it is useful or not for people to believe in premonitions, but of whether there are any grounds for thinking that such phenomena objectively occur. It is not the business of a magazine devoted to empirical psychology to teach morals expressly, still less to offer direct resistance to superstition. These are not its goals, though no doubt they will be the result of the disinterested pursuit of truth. Pockels' 'Reviews' have tended to reduce the undertaking to a mere moralistic journal, of which there are already too many, concerned primarily with criticising those beliefs and practices it considers harmful. Thus the dangerous urge to seek easy explanations has come to dominate it. Indeed, to be as sure of the answers as Pockels is really means that a periodical for the collection of data, such as this one, would be entirely superfluous. Psychologists should not be involved in stemming the spread of this or that belief, they are but observers and analysts. Such an enterprise as this magazine 'must be written absolutely against nothing, be opposed to nothing, if it is not to fail in its purpose.'

On Pockels' behalf one might adduce the attitude of David Hume, who declares in his *Essay on Miracles* that there are some things he will not believe no matter who the witnesses may be. However, as Moritz continues, the criticism of Pockels intensifies. He is even accused of outright incompetence, in that he unwittingly reprinted a case (the Simmen case) which had already appeared in the *Magazin* years before. He is constantly at fault for assuming what he ought to prove, and for forcing his facts to fit his hypotheses. He is, worst of all, smug and superficial, unwilling even to consider the need to venture into the unplumbed depths of the mind. In these irritated paragraphs against Pockels, although a personal animus does come through, Moritz is nonetheless strong and convincing as the prophet of a new empiricism, fired with the spirit of scientific enquiry in a genuinely modern sense. More distinctly than before we see here why this writer stands somewhat apart from the best-known representatives of the Berlin Enlightenment, not merely as a covert Stürmer und Dränger but as an inductive investigator offering the challenge to face a whole new, or rather disregarded, range of facts. The Enlightenment burns throughout Europe with two great torches, that of deductive reason, and that of empirical science, but the second of these had been barely flickering in the German states. Moritz, at least, was aware of this, and sought to make it flare up. If it did not do so very brightly, even then, this was not his fault. The urge to transcend the limits of a purely deductive Rationalism is that of a true *philosophe*. And it is, from the point of view of the literary and intellectual history of Weimar Classicism, rather striking that these words against Pockels are written *after* Moritz's Italian experiences, *after* the full impact upon him of Goethe's mind, and indeed *after* the completion of his own *Über die bildende Nachahmung des Schönen*. This means that Goethe, Italy and Classicism were factors compatible with the survival of the empirical imperative, and this compatibility is in fact the key to Moritz's work and to its importance as a historical example.

As things turned out, the *Magazin zur Erfahrungsseelenkunde* was never quite to recover the character of its early days. For this a variety of causes seems to have been responsible. They include of course Moritz's preoccupation with quite other aspects of his career, as well as the decision to unload a considerable amount of purely biographical and autobiographical material in the later numbers, in place of the concentration upon clinical cases. There is also the increasing influence of the new assistant editor, Salomon Maimon (1754–1800). This gifted young man who had taken his name from Maimonides was a Jew from Poland, who made his way in Königsberg and Berlin in spite of the incredible difficulties still in the path of people like himself. His fascinating autobiography, which was first published in excerpts in the *Magazin* under his patronymic, subsequently appeared as a book with a preface by Moritz.[30] Vivid and close to the bone, it offers a convincing and depressing picture of the unhappy situation of the Eastern European Jew. A student of Kant as well as of the Cabbala, Maimon is an excellent exponent of epistemological questions. Indeed, Kant declared him to be the only writer who had fully comprehended his work. Moritz published the newcomer's thoughts 'Über den Plan des *Magazins zur Erfahrungsseelenkunde*,' supposedly excerpted from a letter to the editor (*Mag*, VIII, 3, 1–7). The philosopher begins with definitions, dividing the study of the mind [*Seelenkunde*] into pure and applied psychology. He regards both the wholly empirical and what he chooses to label the wholly 'dogmatic' method as a pair of extremes, and sees as the only correct procedure the use of facts in order to establish general principles and laws. Maimon also distinguishes between the higher faculties of understanding and reason, and the lower ones of memory, feeling and imagination. He concludes that the proper field for the moral physician (the term he uses is 'Seelenarzt') is the lower faculties, especially that of the imagination, where serious disturbances most often occur. Maimon's approach, despite lip-service paid to facts and the inductive method, is predominantly theoretical and abstracting, as well as systematic. Discussing the work of psychological medicine, he lays down that it may proceed on the basis of any one of three assumptions: either the traditional view, that 'Seele' ('mind' or 'soul') has an existence quite independent of the body, or the materialist opinion that it is nothing but a subtle modification of the body, or the dualist view that there is an intimate relationship between these two, even though they can exist independently. He offers us an elaborate discussion of the pathology of the mind, arguing that mental disease is that condition in which it can no longer function freely, by which he seems to mean that the processes of thought cease to be voluntary, and are no longer subject to the control of the will.

The limitations of such a view hardly need pointing out. While Maimon, and Moritz, recognise the occurrence in people in general of uncontrolled streams of associations, they actually consider this to be a pathological symptom (so that even dreams are held to be a relative form of insanity) and not a normal mental process. Nothing could better illustrate the grandeur and the shortcomings of the eighteenth-century deification of the thinking mind. As far as the *Magazin* is concerned, the contributions of Maimon give it an increasingly academic slant, and in them we find restated some of those preoccupations which, from the outset, had tended to impede the pursuit of new knowledge. Maimon still regards the faculties of feeling and imagination, as he calls them, as of a lower order, which is no advance upon Leibniz; he is committed to the hegemony, within the mind itself, of Reason and of its handmaid, Free Will. Thought should, normally, be under the control of the will, but in the lower sphere of the imagination there is a passivity which exposes this latter faculty to grave disorders. And mental health, which depends upon a proper balance of the faculties, will be overthrown whenever the functioning of the faculty of rational thinking is upset by a disturbance emanating from 'below.' Maimon's emphases are such that he brings his psychological system persistently into the foreground of his discussions, to the detriment of the more factual analyses which Moritz had been accustomed to provide, so that any real gains in empirical knowledge made in the earlier numbers of the *Magazin*, the attention at any rate to concrete detail and the acknowledgement of such influences as environment or even heredity, tend to be obscured. Moritz had in a way made a virtue of the fact that he was not well trained in School philosophy. But Maimon constantly extends the argument into the philosophical sphere, eulogising the harmonious interaction of the various mental energies, or faculties: 'Human perfection and consequently happiness also consist in an equable exercise of all the energies of the mind [*Seelenkräfte*] together' (*Mag*, IX, 1, 91). Though more abstract than that of Moritz, Maimon's thinking nonetheless helps us to discern more clearly the framework of the other's psychological system (which, however, is too strong a word for it). Leibniz had scrupulously confined the association psychology of the English Sensualists to the lower sphere, leaving higher knowledge as the property of the Reason only, to be gained by apperception. Maimon is equally convinced that a man who is governed by his 'imagination' is not much better than an animal. Leibniz of course had distinguished between the 'état intérieur' of perception within the monad, and 'la conscience ou la connaissance réflexive de cet état intérieur,'[31] which constitutes apperception. In his *Psychologia rationalis* Wolff defined this latter crisply: 'Ex claritate perceptionum partialum nascitur apperceptio.'[32] Apperception according to him is the (spontaneous) act of the mind in which the light of consciousness binds the many partial perceptions together into a totality. The significance of this concept for the aesthetic ideas of Baumgarten, Mendelssohn and numerous other philosophers is well known.[33] In thinkers such as Maimon and Moritz, this activity of the rational mind, though it itself is spontaneous, constitutes an ethical test, for it depends upon the readiness of the will to resist passive, mechanical associations and to pursue a purpose. The presence, and proper functioning, of the active creative power of rational cognition is therefore for these psychologists the touchstone of mental health.

Hence, in any deeper sense, the psychology of the *Magazin* is by no means 'value-free,' but ethically bound. This was true, in essence, of almost all eighteenth-century psychologies, and of some physiologies too.[34] Moritz struggles manfully, though sometimes indirectly, to emancipate psychological research from its more egregious moral involvements, and he made a real contribution to this result. But his partial failure was the evident result of his own unacknowledged preconceptions, which were many and profound, although it also derived in some measure from the diversity of his interests. His aesthetic thought, which came to fruition while he was in Italy, is incomprehensible without some understanding of his psychological ideas, but it in its turn conditions these. By means of apperception, the mind imposes wholeness upon partiality, and this is paralleled in the aesthetic sphere by the artist's function of 'bildende Nachahmung' – i.e. 'forming' or (conceivably) 'creative' imitation. No doubt the main reason that Moritz in the end abandoned the *Magazin* to Salomon Maimon was that it had become too much of a burden to him, and little further help in his personal advancement. All the same, that Maimon, as editor, could be permitted to proceed, with his blessing, in so theoretical a direction points in itself to some change of attitude in Moritz, produced by the Italian years. However, as we have observed, the return from Italy was not merely accompanied by the publication of a major work on aesthetics, together with a developing commitment to what was to be called 'Classicism,' but also by the polemic against Pockels. And even unto its very last pages, the *Magazin* does retain something of that purpose which had been present at its foundation.

At the end of volume ten (1793) Maimon comments on the decision to close. It was, he says, a good idea to found such a periodical, and on the whole it has been a success. Enough material has been collected, and now it is time to proceed to construct the edifice of the science of psychology from out of all these fragments. The entire tenth volume is little else but a summary of what Maimon regards as the most significant *factual* content published in the *Magazin*, some final indication, maybe, of the continued honesty of the project's empirical thrust. What had specifically been achieved by it is not that easy to assess fairly. It goes without saying that a really scientific classification of data in the science of psychiatry had to wait until the nineteenth century, and the work of Krafft-Ebing, Griesinger and Alzheimer was still a long way ahead. Moritz came a hundred years before the real florescence of this subject in Germany; and it was only in the year of his death (1793) that Pinel took the risk of unchaining the patients at the Bicêtre Hospital in Paris. Moritz was not a physician either, but a pedagogue-cum-philosopher whose knowledge was scrappy to say the least. Clearly most of the case lore collected in his *Magazin* is, lacking as it does a truly scientific mode of classification and treatment, only of historical or curiosity value today, and can indeed never have been of much practical use to anybody. But the approach itself was at least salutary, and the weak flame it lit may nonetheless have served to burn off some of the soot and fog which enveloped the domain of mental illness. There were imitators, and this is some testimony to the historical significance of the initiative. J.D. Mauchart, who had made extensive contributions to the later volumes, produced something like a sequel to the *Magazin* with his *Allgemeines Repertorium für empirische Psychologie und verwandte Wissenschaften* (1792–1801), while the influential, three-volume work of Johann Christian Hoffbauer: *Untersuchungen über die Krankheiten der Seele und die verwandten Zustände* (1803) draws substantially upon the *Magazin* for its content. Moritz, in short, may be regarded as the initiator of clinical psychological journalism in Germany. The impact of his *Magazin* upon his contemporaries in letters and philosophy is probably even more important than its effect upon psychology and medicine. Very little notice has been taken of this influence, though we can surely assume that the *Magazin* was widely consumed – if only because the contents were not infrequently morbidly sensational. Schiller, for one, was a regular reader, drawn to it perhaps by his own medical background, but also finding it depressing, as he writes to friends:

> I gave him (Moritz) some advice about his *Magazin zur Erfahrungsseelenkunde* to which you will perhaps subscribe. I found that one always lays it aside with a feeling of sadness, often of disgust, and this because it rivets our minds upon nothing but regions of human misery. I advised him to accompany each number with a philosophical essay, to open up brighter prospects [*lichtere Blicke*] and, so to speak, resolve these dissonances again in harmony.[35]

Schiller's suggestion is typical of him, requiring as it does the imposition of certain optimistic tendencies of contemporary philosophical thought upon a project which, precisely because it had implicitly dispensed with these, had begun to uncover a social and anthropological dimension unpleasant for the eighteenth-century mind to behold. The kind of light Schiller sought to shed was, we may think, artificial. What Moritz had been struggling after, cumbersomely and stumblingly no doubt, had been the small but genuine light of day.

THE WAY TO ITALY

The ten years of the run of the *Magazin zur Erfahrungsseelenkunde* are the last ten years of Karl Philipp Moritz's life. They are the period of his success, and the relative transformation of his lot. But his public image, even then, was often beleaguered by ridicule, and his writings dismissed as unscholarly, or inconsiderable, or obscure. Perhaps it is true, as Arno Schmidt, in his enthusiastic rehabilitation of Moritz in 1956,[36] has claimed, that all the books of this 'Schreckensmann' are good only for the waste-paper basket, saving only *Anton Reiser* and *Andreas Hartknopf*, which however Schmidt holds to be creative works of international stature. Probably, however, this is a misrepresentation of the case. What seems certain is that the full impact of Moritz upon German literature in his own day has been consistently underestimated. Such things as the *Magazin*, the *Versuch einer deutschen Prosodie* and *Über die bildende Nachahmung des Schönen* were simply not minor literary events then, whatever dust may have collected upon them since. Nor was the friendship which developed between Goethe and Moritz in Italy a minor encounter, in the life of either man. The 'Italian journey' is the crux of Moritz's short and sputtering career, as it possibly is of Goethe's long and blazing one. Their Italian journey changed both of them, though in neither instance in a direction that was wholly new. The aesthetic ideas Moritz thought out in Rome had existed in embryo before he went there (which is, crudely and simply, why they cannot just be attributed to Goethe, as used to be the fashion). The pursuit of the cosmoplastic moment of insight may be traced in the 'ethical psychology' which underlies, and perhaps subverts, the empiricism of the *Magazin*, just as we may find it in its philosophical, neo-Leibnizian form in the *Kinderlogik*, as well as in the residual mysticism of the *Beiträge*. Moritz's escape to Italy, however, was not founded in any lofty desire to seek out new philosophical and aesthetic revelations. It was perhaps no more than irresponsible behaviour when in an awkward spot, or, if we wish to be psychological about it, we can see it as a resurgence of revolt against order and as the re-emergence of the obsessional *Wanderlust*.

There seems, at all events, to be little persuasive evidence for the view that the Moritz of the Italian journey was a very different man, more considered altogether and more disciplined, than the young travelling creature who had tramped the highways and by-ways of England some four short years before.[37] The circumstances of his leaving Berlin suggest the contrary, for although a number of factors converged remorselessly to drive him to this step, when it came it still had the hallmarks of rashness about it. His conduct in the months prior to departure, furthermore, was not very circumspect. The idea of going to Italy had been at the very forefront of his mind at least since the trip with Klischnig the previous summer, and his superstitious nature had been further influenced by the predictions of a mysterious visitor, the Conte Lanfranchi, to the effect that Moritz would one day go there and subsequently return to Berlin with his fortune made.[38] Such a pity, comments K.G. Lenz with sarcastic relish, that a *philosophe* and fighter against superstition like Moritz should be influenced by an incident of this sort![39] True enough, the prophecy did turn out to be self-fulfilling, although Moritz's success was in the end to depend more than anything else on the fortuity that Goethe came to Rome at exactly the same time. Italy was an obvious choice for him, given his situation and hopes. The date of the journey, however, depended on a combination of events which seemed to be turning 1786 into a very bad year. On 4 January Mendelssohn died unexpectedly, and shortly thereafter the acrimonious dispute with the Jacobi party broke out. Jacobi had known well what he was about when he made the deliberate allegation that Lessing had been a secret pantheist, in fact an atheist by the prevailing standards of the day. Moreover, Jacobi was a man of shrewd and powerful intellect, sufficient for him to detect a serious flaw, which Kant acknowledged, in the *Critique of Pure Reason*. Like his friend the Swiss Lavater, he was also a ruthless campaigner and intriguer, and Moritz was typically rash in taking on adversaries of this sort. Even more unwise was the manner in which he went about it, reducing the entire dispute to one of personalities. In the *Vossische Zeitung* of 24 January 1786, he reviewed Mendelssohn's posthumous reply[40] to Jacobi's claim, to which had been added an introduction by J.J. Engel, and Marcus Herz's vivid account of the philosopher's short illness and death.[41] Where Engel comments that Mendelssohn's end was perhaps caused in part by an unfortunate mischance, Moritz refers directly to the fact that he had been forced to visit the press on a very cold day about his forthcoming reply to Jacobi. He concludes his review with words which he presumably regarded as pulverising:

He (i.e. Mendelssohn) became a victim of his friendship for his Lessing, and died as a martyr in defence of the oppressed rights of reason as opposed to fanaticism and superstition. Lavater's importunity was the first blow at his life, Jacobi finished the job.

As Eybisch quite properly points out, Engel's introduction to Mendelssohn's book really implied much the same thing, though in far more guarded language.[42] Both statements were bound to provoke controversy, but Moritz's bald accusations aroused the sharpest resentment. The musician J.F. Reichardt thereupon published an account of a talk he had had with Mendelssohn in which the latter had seemed to take the whole matter far more lightly than his friends would admit. But a few days later Moritz returned to the assault, hardly modifying his position, and repeating the principal allegation that, had it not been for Jacobi's behaviour, Mendelssohn might still be alive. He had asked for, and now he duly received, buffets from every side, including the nasty suggestion that he had no justifiable reason to pose as Mendelssohn's friend, and did so only out of vanity. Engel publicly disassociated himself from Moritz. Even Herz, who must have found the whole episode immensely embarrassing, was forced to do the same, and to point out that to contribute to circumstances which might have predisposed a certain person to illness was by no stretch of the imagination the same as causing his death. Moritz, far from soft-pedalling his charges, seized on this, and expressed his satisfaction at not being in Jacobi's shoes, since the latter had evidently, in no small measure, 'contributed to the circumstances' of Mendelssohn's death. In another newspaper he then saw fit to distort Engel's words in order to shift the blame from his own shoulders on to the other's. This final step amounts to little better than dishonesty, and to cowardice besides. It was accompanied by complaints about the unfair treatment that he, Moritz, had received, and by a truculent unwillingness to withdraw his main charges.

This unpleasant affair, which Moritz brought entirely about his own ears, and which soured his whole existence in Berlin, certainly shows on his part neither wisdom nor even much stability of mind. The depression it caused in him was accentuated by a steadily deteriorating financial situation, and the misery of trying to remedy this by the hard labour of Grub Street. On top of it all came a love affair, the first (and almost the only) romantic episode to be recounted in the course of this whole life. Moritz's abstention from women had been widely noted, as had his ménage with Klischnig, and suspicions had been duly aroused which persisted after his death.[43] These were almost certainly unfounded. There had in fact been, as Klischnig himself tells us, a few occasions of passing enthusiasm for some lady or other, even thoughts of marriage, and the appropriate harvest of bad poetry. Moritz was in any case always inclined to the etherealities of passion, and seems to have shunned physical enjoyment. Klischnig takes it upon himself to swear an oath that his mentor and friend was still a virgin when he walked through the gates of Rome at the age of nearly thirty. Such a state of affairs (which by implication failed to survive Rome) cannot have been desperately unusual in eighteenth-century Germany, among the middle classes at least – similar claims, after all, have been made about Goethe.

However all this may be, the few known facts of the love affair are these: in the spring of 1786 Moritz was frequenting the house of Herr Bergrat Standtke in Ricksdorf, and fell in love with that gentleman's wife. Of the Bergrätin Standtke we know little or nothing, and it is dangerous to hazard an opinion on the basis of K.G. Lenz's probably biassed account. According to this, however, the lady 'turned her attention to his (Moritz's) living conditions and financial circumstances, and got the idea of marrying him off to her niece; which also gave him the hope of being able to come closer to the family'! The Bergrätin, we learn, was not unhappily married herself. Her relationship with Moritz remained wholly platonic, because they both respected their 'duty' (Klischnig). Moritz, however, did not miss the opportunity of emulating his beloved Werther, sporting for a while the famous blue and yellow breeches, and may have got more satisfaction out of this than out of the love affair itself (Lenz). This last narrator adds cruelly that Moritz, after all, 'was not capable of any true and deep feeling for anyone beyond himself.'[44] But while Klischnig's account of the episode is reserved and insipid, Lenz's is obviously in some degree a caricature. There was enough feeling involved to make Klischnig jealous, as he admits, and the connection persisted for a long time. Goethe, as Moritz's amanuensis in Rome, wrote several letters from him to Frau Standtke, and he renewed the correspondence on recovering from his accident. The prose poems printed by Klischnig entitled *Hieroglyphen*[45] express the lover's feelings in lofty and stilted tones, but we may guess that Moritz, though he may well have ranted to Klischnig and others, was in fact no very active wooer, and no threat at all to Standtke, who appears to have remained his good friend; he was most probably plaintive and passive, in search of that emotional protection he had nearly always lacked, while the Bergrätin, no doubt, was motherly enough. At Easter 1786, when this situation must have been at its height, Moritz and Klischnig were compelled to separate, the latter leaving the capital to commence his studies at Frankfurt-an-der-Oder. Moritz had at first intended to travel there with him, to escape his problem, but he had to abandon this plan when a further difficulty intervened, an attack of lung trouble with haemorrhaging and the inevitable doleful prognostications about his own imminent demise.

A few letters, and excerpts from letters have survived from the early months of this crucial year, and from these we can trace in outline the buildup to the decision to go away.[46] A pro memoria dispatched to the magistracy of the city of Berlin (17 January 1786) pleads for a salary increase, pointing out that Moritz receives less than other professors for the classes he gives at the Gymnasium, 'although these classes are so arranged that they spoil whole days of the week for other activities, on which I have so far depended to live.' A change in the staffing situation (this was the death of Professor Hermes) emboldens him, he says, to request an increase, however small, which would permit him to hope for better things and to devote himself the more wholeheartedly to his official responsibilities. Two days after it was submitted, this application was denied, and Moritz must have taken this to mean that there was little chance of any early improvement in his material lot. After Klischnig's departure at Easter the gloom seems to have deepened, accentuated no doubt by ill-health. Moritz congratulates his friend (18 May 1786) on being well established in Frankfurt, 'though I can't take any pleasure in my own condition, which is most unsatisfactory, both inwardly and outwardly.' He expresses the sepulchral wish that Klischnig at least may find happiness, if such a thing is possible for men. He enjoins him to devote himself 'to the present moment and to nature.' A few days after this he writes again, using characteristically claustrophobic language: 'The outlook, for me, is closing in more and more. Perhaps I'll be seeing you soon. A few days for a final farewell, and then out into the world.' The tone on the whole is disconsolate, and the letter makes a parade of resignation. But there is the clear suggestion of a break, and four weeks later a much more confident epistle discloses to Klischnig the determination to cut loose: 'It is settled! I have to leave, or I shan't survive. I'm being worn down by constant struggle with a passion I can never satisfy. I long to go to Italy, though I fear the parting ...' (26 June 1786). In this letter the overriding excuse offered is the frustrations of the love affair. The evidence, however, is too scanty for us to reach a balanced judgment as to the relative effects of the various pressures on Moritz's mind. Once it was made up, and he turned to the execution of his intent, it transpired that he had seriously overestimated his employers' good will. On 8 August he absented himself from the Graue Kloster, and sent a letter asking for two weeks' leave to go to the Harz mountains, for reasons of health; in this missive he informs the authorities that his colleagues are willing to stand in for him in the few classes he is responsible for. Naturally the magistracy first asked Büsching to confirm that he could in fact spare this member of his staff. A somewhat arrogantly toned note to the director from Moritz, also sent on 8 August, makes the identical request for a 'short leave,' and details the classes his colleagues will handle in his stead. In the case of a class not yet covered there is the bland suggestion that Büsching himself might like to take the five students in question into his own course. This note to the director concludes somewhat unsubtily with the presentation to him of Part Three of *Anton Reiser* (which had just appeared), presumably as a kind of douceur.

Büsching made hostile notes in the margin of this letter.[47] He seems to have been fed up with Moritz, and was not disposed to agree to the leave. He may have suspected what surely must have been the case, that this request was a disingenuous cover for some grander project. When the director told him he was rejecting the application, and criticised him severely for his unreliability, Moritz packed up and left Berlin in some pique.[48] From Potsdam (12 August) we find him writing to Göschen, the Leipzig publisher, announcing his departure for Italy and proposing a contract to accept from him 'various things' about that country. He tells Göschen that he prefers to work with him rather than with his publisher in Berlin, because Göschen's is a bigger firm, which seems to Moritz important when one is going to be dealing from abroad. By 'publisher in Berlin' it is not clear who is meant (no doubt deliberately not); it might have been Maurer (the house of *Anton Reiser*), or Unger, who published *Denkwürdigkeiten* and for whom Moritz was in arrears with the translation of an English novel, or Himburg, where he was in default with the *Geisterseher*. Besides these three, Moritz had dealings with Mylius, the publisher of the *Magazin*, and Wever, under whose imprint the *Versuch einer deutschen Prosodie* had just appeared. The erstwhile editor of the *Vossische Zeitung* had connections, therefore, with not just one but with practically every major publisher in Berlin, and was all too well known as an author who was always working against the clock, was unreliable, and ever ready to request a further advance. To finance his new, and prospectively very expensive, undertaking he therefore turned perforce elsewhere, namely to Göschen and to his old friend Campe.

From the former, who was away from home, he received for the time being no reply. Everything therefore depended upon Campe, now quartered in Salzdahlen, where the traveller duly arrived, also meeting with Pockels in Brunswick to make the arrangements for the continuation of the *Denkwürdigkeiten* and the *Magazin*. From Salzdahlen, on 21 August, Moritz mailed his resignation from his job at the Graue Kloster. He has an opportunity, he tells the magistracy, to go to Italy, and although this is the one and only way he can hope to become the fully proficient teacher of the humanities he is supposed to be, he cannot of course expect his position to be kept open until his return. Not rising to this bait, the magistracy accepted the resignation with some alacrity, though with a good enough grace, expressed satisfaction with his work over the years, and wished him godspeed. Moritz seems to have ignored his immediate superior, Büsching, altogether, to judge from a response by Unger to what must have been a baffled enquiry from the director as to his subordinate's whereabouts.[49] Such behaviour would be well in character. To Klischnig Moritz wrote an excited letter (late August 1786), informing him that he was actually en route to 'the Promised Land.' The tone now is close on ecstatic:

Now I am free – I've thrown off the yoke that I let them put on me so patiently without the least idea how it was going to oppress me, and I have escaped from the prison of the school [*Schulkerker*].

He tells his friend that he has managed to make an excellent contract with Campe, and that he feels very fit again, with no pains in his chest and his breathing as free and easy 'as if I were already enjoying the mild climate of Italy.' In flowery language he then expresses his regret that Klischnig will not be able to come along, and concludes with a Horatian injunction to him to gather his rosebuds while he may.[50] Klischnig calls the mood here 'changeable,' but the fragment we have is actually an outburst of near manic enthusiasm on which the memento mori of Horace pendulates like an artificial leaf.

With Campe, Moritz had previously had a number of connections. At one time, as we have seen, he toyed with the notion of working with him in Hamburg, and he had agreed to collaborate in the enormous pedagogical enterprise, the *Allgemeine Revision des gesammten Schul und Erziehungswesens* (1785–91, sixteen volumes). Campe, who had recently been appointed 'Schulrat' in Brunswick, with a commission to reform the schools there, was also expanding his activities into publishing, taking over the 'Schulbuchhandlung' attached to the Brunswick orphanage. A practical 'Aufklärer,' with plenty of ideals but also a good business brain, he is on record as having declared that the invention of the spinning wheel and the cultivation of the potato had done more for mankind than Homer had.[51] Moritz had expressed the wish, not long before leaving Berlin, to assist in Campe's new projects, hoping to escape the clutches of the ruthless (as he found them) publishers in the capital. He was later to claim that his arrival in Salzdahlen was in response to an invitation from Campe.[52] Before quitting Berlin he had borrowed some money – he says 100 Thaler from Bergrat Standtke (who was probably glad enough to pay it), but Campe alleges that other publishers had been induced to make advances to him.[53] The nature of the contract he agreed on with Campe became in due course the subject of a grand dispute. According to the publisher, Moritz arrived from Berlin in financial straits, and explained how he had recently been living a Spartan life in order to clear his debts. He then made the following proposition: Campe would provide him with the funds to go to Italy and live there for a few months. During this first period of his stay he would write a description of his journey, the manuscript of which, together with 100 Thaler payable in instalments by another trusted person (this turns out to be Pockels!) would repay the loan 'completely and without fail.' Once this had been done Campe would make a further advance, and the author would then begin his projected study of Roman antiquities, producing a book on the subject in due course. 'Of this unbelievably learned and finely written work,' notes Campe with the heaviest sarcasm, 'he was to send me completed fascicles month by month, and I was ... to make corresponding advances.' When the entire journey was over, Moritz suggested he would then settle down in Brunswick and, 'out of gratitude for the service I had rendered him,' work solely for Campe's publishing house.

Campe clearly anticipated a profit from the account of Moritz's journey, bearing in mind the considerable success of the *Reisen in England*. He did not, however, as he says, expect very much from the work on Roman antiquities, since Moritz clearly knew little or nothing about this subject and had borrowed a book on it from him! According to Campe, his visitor assured him gravely that he would never rue this agreement, and asserted on his honour that he was free of debts and commitments to other booksellers and printers, a statement which Campe, at the Leipzig book fair that autumn, was to discover to be entirely untrue. Much of the above account is denied by Moritz, and on this last point, his extraneous commitments, he observes reasonably enough that he could have hardly given the blanket assurances Campe alleges, since the *Magazin* and the *Denkwürdigkeiten* were ongoing obligations. Nevertheless, a number of details tend to support Campe's version, at least in outline, for instance the curious circumstances of the publication by Himburg of the *Fragmente aus dem Tagebuche eines Geistersehers* in its unfinished form, with a preface critical of the author. Moritz also denies that he told Campe he had been leading a pinched existence in Berlin in order to pay off his debts, he ridicules the suggestion that he could have bound himself to spend the rest of his career in Brunswick in return for 100 Thaler, and he declares that he never claimed it depended entirely on Campe's generosity whether the trip to Italy should ever come to pass.[54]

An account of the further development of this uncomfortable relationship and acrimonious controversy must await our treatment of the Italian years. An agreement of some kind was, at all events, reached, and Campe advanced a sum of money, not more than 150 Thaler.[55] Whatever the contract's precise terms, and whatever blandishments Moritz may or may not have employed, the incident further exemplifies a precipitate, hand-to-mouth manner of living by one's wits which had been a characteristic of his since Anton Reiser's days. He was, as yet, by no means cured of this. Flashes of disconsolate moods, unpredictable reactions to despondency, a careless readiness to cast himself upon the waters of the world – it tends to be these things, rather than anything concrete and more matured, which generate major changes in his life. Again one is reminded of the ill-considered comings and goings and the constant sponging of the young Rousseau, Karl Philipp Moritz's psychological cousin. At the end of August 1786, in the event, he finally set off for Italy triumphant, a freelance writer with a certain capital and no very pressing obligations of any kind. The dusty chambers of the Graue Kloster, the hackwork of his journalistic obligations, the complaints from his publishers, and the sourness of the aftermath of the Jacobi affair were all left far behind, while his love for the Bergrätin, though alive, was not (we may surmise) nagging too painfully at his heart. By early September Moritz had reached Nürnberg, from which he dispatched a letter to the poet Karl W. Ramler in Berlin, congratulating him on the award of a pension by the new monarch, Frederick William II. Here he refers to the recent publication of the *Versuch einer deutschen Prosodie*, saying that he has instructed Wever to let Ramler have a copy. He tells his correspondent that he intends to stay in Rome for a year, remembers himself to a couple of mutual friends, and notes that Biester will be sent his Italian address as soon as it is available. This is the sole letter which has survived from Moritz's journey down to Italy, which continued over the Brenner to Verona, where he arrived on 19 September. The only source to which we can turn for information is his own three volume *Reisen eines Deutschen in Italien in den Jahren 1786 bis 1788*,[56] which is very defective as a historical document, although interesting in several ways.

This was the work which had been promised to Campe, but he never saw any of it, apart from a few fragments. He must have been soon aware that he was unlikely to, and he hastened to deny in public that Moritz was travelling at his expense. In fact, the *Reisen in Italien* was composed for the most part after Moritz had returned to Germany, and was eventually published by Maurer. It is a miscellany of observations and anecdotes (some possibly culled from letters), with heavy and even verbatim borrowings from the chief contemporary guidebook, D.J.J. Volkmann's *Historisch-kritische Nachrichten von Italien* (Leipzig,1770f), and it lacks the relative coherence and the narrative flow of the *Reisen in England*. From it, however, we can follow Moritz's journey southwards, which proceeded uncommonly slowly even for those days. Ill-equipped, as he certainly was, to gain very much from the studious contemplation of Classical remains (despite constant pressure from Büsching, he had never really developed his competence even in Latin very far), Moritz meandered through Mantua, Bologna, Rimini and Ancona more or less as a pure tourist, making a detour to the Republic of San Marino, an out-of-the-way spot which attracted him for just that reason. He also liked this place because it was a republic, existing as such within the embrace of what he calls 'the papal despotism.' Its people had, he felt, a nobler spirit than did those in nearby Rimini (Cf. *RI*, I, 22f). In the event the early pages of the *Reisen in Italien* tell us little or nothing about any encounter with 'antiquities,' though there is a description of the amphitheatre at Verona, a few comments on several monasteries, and a tone of reverent enthusiasm for the landscape, which is frequently called 'romantic.' The liveliest passages are certainly those which come closest to the manner of the England travelogue, especially the picaresque episodes with the coachmen, the *vetturini*, including one with no vehicle to offer who nevertheless called himself *vetturino* and bestowed the title of *cavallino* upon his sole means of transport, his donkey (*RI*, I, 50). There are a variety of inquisitive, ephemeral and sometimes amusing observations of street and roadside life, stiffened only slightly by usually forced and irrelevant connections made with Roman history and the customs of the Ancients. That the traveller was uneasily aware of his incompetence in aesthetic matters is evident from a comment in which he excuses himself for not having paid more attention to the works of art in the churches and museums on his route:

> I only glance cursorily at all this, not having any standard and point of view from which I can consider it, as long as I possess no clear [*anschaulichen*] conception of what it is which holds together the dispersed, individual beauties that are lost among the faults of mediocre works of art, and escape the untrained eye ... (*RI*, I, 54).

The dilatoriness which was to characterize Moritz's behaviour for much of the next two years already makes its appearance here. Freed from the discomforts of his life in Berlin, from which he had in effect run away, he was also deprived of an external discipline which was important to him, and he began to succumb to an innate weakness, a passive vagabondage of the mind. He always slipped easily enough into a state of indolence, indeed of apathy or even endogenous depression, which frequently resulted, as we saw in *Anton Reiser*, in an inability to meet external requirements and thus in exposure to penury. It was hard for Moritz to live, either inwardly or outwardly, upon the fitful resources of his own creative energies, unless these were stimulated by the compulsions of duty or the immediate promise of social approbation. Long-term projects were never very likely to come to fruition at his hands, especially if they were financed in advance. Thus the remarkable thing about *Anton Reiser* is not that he did not bring it to a final conclusion but that he managed to produce such a sustained work over a considerable number of years. Just before he left Berlin, that summer, Part Three of the novel had appeared, as also had his *Versuch einer deutschen Prosodie*.[57] This latter is one of his major works. Consisting, as was rather fashionable, of a 'dialogue' followed by several 'letters,' a kind of thinking in public, it offers a relatively new approach to the vexed question of German metrics. It addresses itself to the longstanding confusion caused by the difficulty of adapting German verse, with its stress accent, to the Classical quantities. Any attempt to apply the rules of Latin prosody to the German poetic line leads inevitably to distortions. Moritz's attack on this problem, which had so beset eighteenth-century poets and theorists, is a novel one. It is based upon a distinction which he endeavours to draw between German and the Classical languages. The latter he calls 'languages for the ear,' in which the music of the poetic line is of the essence, containing as it does its melody within itself. Thought, on the other hand, is, in Latin and Greek poetry, supererogatory; it is but 'a noble dissipation ... it proffers the silver apple on a golden dish' (*DP*, 40). Indeed, Classical poetry is the child of feeling, and in it discourse and even sense are really secondary, so that all words are equally important in themselves. The textures of language exist here for their own sake, and not primarily for the meaning they have to convey (Cf. *DP*, 25f). Language, when used in this manner, ceases to be chiefly referential. Moritz then introduces into the argument a remarkable comparison with the dance, noting that walking, like discourse, is normally directed towards a goal. But feeling can produce an activity of the limbs which is not so directed, as in the case of dancing for joy. In dancing each step is of equal value, since each step is taken for its own sake. It is exactly the same, Moritz says, with each individual word in Latin and Greek poetry, and like the purpose of the dance so that of the poem lies within itself.[58] In both instances the decisive feature is autonomy, self-containment, and the absence of an external goal. German poetry, however, is dominated by thought rather than feeling, as German is 'a splendid language for the reason [*Verstand*] but not for the ear ...' (*DP*, 11). In German poetry the innate melody of the line is missing, and music must always be brought to it from without. The pursuit of meaning controls it, and thus a stress falls upon all the 'more important' syllables and words, in disregard of those which do not contribute towards the external reference of the poetic discourse.

These arguments enable Moritz to advance an ingenious theory of prosody, according to which in German verse the metre does not arise from the arrangement of long and short syllables following rigid rules, but on the contrary the quantities themselves derive either (in the case of monosyllables) from the arrangement of words in sentences or (in that of polysyllables) from stresses already inherent in each word. This therefore leads on to the claim that metre, in German, must be a function of thought – indeed of grammar. What is measured is not syllables, but ideas, although Moritz holds that this too, even in German poetry, is not done according to some absolute standard of reference outside the poem, but according to the relative significance of the ideas used among themselves. Hence the German poem is, like the Greek and Latin, potentially autonomous, but this autonomy depends upon a self-contained hierarchy of ideas rather than a self-contained pattern of words. German poetry, therefore, may be said to 'play with ideas,' 'in it the ideas are important more because of their relationship to each other than for themselves,' it is a question of the balance of principal and subordinate ideas (*DP*, 176). An elaborate systematic discussion ensues of the parts of speech in their relation to prosody. Each part is considered as fitting into a hierarchy, headed by the noun, which has the 'fullest' quantum of thought in it. Because nouns carry more meaning, they are more stressed than are other parts of speech; after them come adjectives, then verbs. In the last analysis it is natural intuition, however, which is called upon to determine such distinctions (*DP*, 150). The final conclusion is

that the quantity of the syllables in our language can be determined not by the number and nature of the letters and individual sounds they consist of but according to the prosodic value, as parts of speech of more or less significance; and that therefore the rules of prosody in our language must be derived from grammar, so far as this lays down the nature of the individual parts of speech and their hierarchical arrangement according to the measure of their meaningfulness [*Bedeutung*] (*DP*, 246).

The practical effect of Moritz's approach is to cut the ground from under the long-standing and wearisome attempt to force German verse into the straitjacket of Classical metrics. Its arguments themselves are of course highly debatable. Heusler regarded the *Prosodie* as a deplorably confused work, and its popularity as merely evidence of the ignorance of German poets in this technical area.[59] Schrimpf has summarised the weaknesses of Moritz's position, in particular the muddles of his terminology, and his failure to distinguish between stress (*Hebung und Senkung*) and length.[60] But he notes that Heusler did not take proper account of the innovative elements in the *Prosodie*, in which a real contribution is made to the study of German prosody on an independent basis. The actual discussion of the various metrical forms undertaken by Moritz is conventional enough, and hardly touches on anything except the Classical metres found, for instance, in Klopstock's *Odes*. Even the hexameter is only briefly referred to, and there is no consideration at all of free rhythms, folksong metre or *Knittelvers*, while the German poets adduced for illustrative purposes do not include Goethe. But the popularity of the *Prosodie* is a historical fact and its influence was clearly extensive. Goethe, as is well known, at least pretended that without this book he would never have recast *Iphigenie auf Tauris* in verse. Schiller told Wilhelm von Humboldt it was the only work on prosody he had ever read, and when he thanked Goethe for sending him a copy (23 August 1794) he observed how agreeable it was to find an 'instinctive process' thus codified into law. The *Prosodie* may not have changed the way in which poets actually tried to write, but it must have freed many from the uneasy notion that they were obliged to struggle to use the Classical system of quantities in their verse, and this was a great gain in the emancipation of German poetry from its dependence on Ancient tradition.

Moritz's separation between 'Gedankensprache' and 'Empfindungs-sprache,' as developed here, is not – though unconvincing as a point of distinction between German and Latin poetry – by any means a worthless differentiation, and the perception of the intellectual nature of much previous German poetry points forward to Schillerian aesthetic theory. Though Schiller did not read the *Prosodie* until 1794, it is likely that he had discussed some of its principles with Moritz five years before that. Schrimpf has brought out the connections between the *Prosodie* and Moritz's own aesthetic ideas, drawing attention to the contrast between straight line and curved line (or circle) in the latter, which is clearly related to the distinction between externally oriented discourse on the one hand and the language of poetry on the other as this language is, to use Moritz's own terminology, 'driven back within itself' (*DP*, 26). According to Schrimpf, Moritz's reference to 'game' may also be compared with the concepts of Huizinga.[61] Certainly, there are some precocious pointers in the *Prosodie* to much later critical ideas. The Classical poetic line is seen above all else as a self-contained entity, born of feeling and sustained in music, and even the unblessed German poem *ought* to be an autonomous structure of ideas. Superficially a technical contribution alone, the *Prosodie* actually stands at the very centre of Moritz's life-work, alongside *Anton Reiser*. As in his other writings on linguistic matters, we find in it a combination of empirical and intuitive insights, which are sometimes pressed too far (e.g. that stress ·d meaning coincide in German verse), with a scholastic yearning for system and order. Sanity, as the *Magazin* liked to define it, was a condition of balanced energies, in which the force of the individual impulse per se counted for little, and the poem is similarly a (quasi-musical) equilibrium of ideas in which the external reference is secondary. Further, we must not forget that the concept of wholeness retains its links, in eighteenth-century philosophy, with religious and spiritual ideals, including that of non-attachment. A flash of insight seems thus to have enabled the author of this curious work to prise loose, for the first time in German criticism, the conceptual pearl of the autonomous poem. It is, in sum, a highly personal, ingenious, opinionated and sometimes overstretched argument that is presented here, but one at any rate that is not at all fuliginous. For it has some of the clarity, as well as the arbitrariness, of an extended aperçu.

5

At the Fringe of Genius

It is commonly believed that German thought first arrived at the conception of the autonomous work of art in Kant's *Critique of Judgment*, which appeared in 1790. In fact, however, it was Karl Philipp Moritz who first gave unequivocal expression to this idea, in his *Über die bildende Nachahmung des Schönen* ('On the Creative Imitation of the Beautiful'), 1788.[1] This little publication may also be regarded as the only systematic statement made of what has been called Goethe's 'Roman aesthetic,'[2] but Goethe's influence upon it, though decisive, does not deprive its author of all claim to originality, and on balance Auerbach's recognition that the work was essentially Moritz's own must be upheld.[3] Before his departure for Italy Moritz was already beginning to lay the foundations of his system, which seems to have originated in an attempt to go beyond some of the ideas of Mendelssohn, to whom he owed most of his understanding of aesthetic problems and also perhaps his first acquaintance with Shaftesbury, the philosopher with whom he often seems in most accord. An 'open letter' to Mendelssohn, with the long-winded title 'Versuch einer Vereinigung aller schönen Künste und Wissenschaften unter dem Begriff des in sich selbst Vollendeten' (1785) shows the main lines of his position.[4] In the complex discussion which had accumulated on the subject of taste and judgment as a result of the development, in the mid-eighteenth century, of a new concern with subjective experience, Mendelssohn had sought to take account of feeling without surrendering the primacy of reason, the ultimate supremacy of the logical and the true over the beautiful. He had also concentrated on the issue of aesthetic pleasure, and the problem of the response to the work of art in general, while Moritz begins to restore the work itself to a position of central importance, discovering a creative faculty which transcends the reason *and* the feelings.

The connection of this essay (*Schriften*, 3–8) with the thought of the *Bildende Nachahmung* is manifest, and was duly noted by contemporaries.[5] It opens by postulating a fundamental distinction between the beautiful and the useful. Moritz inquires what, since the useful arts as well as the fine arts may inspire pleasure, constitutes the difference between these two principles? His answer is expounded with the aid of the metaphor of circle and centre-point. In the case of the merely useful object it is only a tool, while its user is its centre of reference and purpose, which lies therefore outside it. 'In contemplating something beautiful, however, I put the purpose back [*zurückwälze*] into the object itself.' Since the beautiful object is complete in itself and autonomous, 'I do not so much give it a relationship towards me as myself a relationship towards it.' How useful objects are structured is irrelevant, so long as they fulfill their end. But in beautiful objects their end and purpose lies precisely in their structure, in the harmonious balance of their parts, though they do 'have need' of admirers from whom they exact an abandonment of self and a surrender to their purer, higher power. The terminology of much of this bears striking analogies to the passages in the *Prosodie* on the self-contained hierarchy of words (and ideas) in poetry, and is even reminiscent of the reference in *Anton Reiser*, Part Three, to the autonomy of the individual outside the crowd ('drängte ihn in sich selbst zurück'). Beautiful objects possess what Moritz calls 'innere Zweckmässigkeit' ('inner purposiveness') and must always have a definite centre of focus. When creating such works the artist must be utterly pure and devoted, not concerned with approbation or effect. Moritz here perceives an analogy between the artist and the philosopher who pursues virtue for its own sake, and not in search of that happiness which is however its inevitable side-product.

The rejection of Enlightenment eudaemonism is clear-cut, while the connection between the ideas of the 'Versuch einer Vereinigung' and the doctrine of disinterested spiritual work fundamental to all *praxis pietatis* is self-evident. Minder's thesis is surely irrefutable that the aesthetic doctrines of Moritz's later years demonstrate the persistent underlying effects of his Pietistic education, even though much that is in them may be traceable to other philosophical influences. The intense personal quality, the passionate aspiration which may be sensed in the *Bildende Nachahmung* is partly attributable to this, partly however to something else: the new self-understanding and the re-evaluation of his own private situation which the meeting with Goethe brought about. The two years Moritz spent in Italy constitute, of course, a watershed in his life, leading to the transformation of his external circumstances as well as of much in his philosophical outlook. The biographical sources, while hardly plentiful, fortunately extend well beyond the rather stylized, often gazetteer-like paragraphs of his *Reisen in Italien*. They include a few of his own letters, those of one or two other persons, in particular Goethe, and anecdotal reminiscences by various hands. He himself portentously describes his journey to Rome *ex post facto* as a pilgrimage (*RI*, I, 2), but although he was no doubt persuaded on setting forth that much would come out of it, he cannot have anticipated the degree of good fortune that impended. When at long last he arrived, on 27 October 1786, he went at once to an inn in the Strada (or Via) Condotti, near the Piazza d'Espagna, which was managed by one Rösler-Franz and was one of several that served the largish German community in Rome.[6] On his first night there he slept badly because of carousing German artists in the adjacent room. Eventually he found satisfactory lodgings in the Strada Babuino, where he was to remain until the spring, moving after his trip to Naples to the Piazza Barberini and finally to the Via Borgognona. Rome was, by German standards, an extremely large but also a very insalubrious and chaotic city. At that time only the Corso possessed any kind of sidewalk, there was no street lighting whatever, and since torches were forbidden circumambulation after dark was hazardous. Enormous poverty went side by side with magnificence, the beggars were ubiquitous, and violence commonplace. Goethe, in his *Italienische Reise*, mentions a fatal *coup de main*, while Moritz in his journal refers to several murders. He complains that there is no effective police force and that justice is non-existent; those who have powerful protection can do as they like. People are often armed, and one may discharge one's pistol out of one's window with impunity. In the very first house in which he found accommodation the goings on made him so nervous he only remained one night. He was furthermore little comforted by the alacrity with which each and every disreputable-looking character introduced himself as 'un galant' uomo' (*RI*, I, 120–22).

Rome was then very much a place of amusements and displays as well, of course, as being a city of art, and it depended for its very uncertain economy to some extent upon an already developing tourist trade. Rich Germans played a role here, although the journey south was regarded as extremely difficult and their numbers were small. The Germans also constituted the largest national group among the artists. Connoisseurs and writers went to Rome inspired by the works of Winckelmann, and artists to sit perhaps at the feet of Anton Raffael Mengs, the great classicist painter, who had died in 1779 at the peak of his fame and with whose oeuvre and theoretical ideas Moritz soon became familiar. Most of the practice of the hordes of young German painters and sculptors apparently consisted in copying the Raphaels in the Vatican, studying the Laocoön and like masterpieces, and experimenting with every conceivable Classical, and especially mythological, subject. This particular bent was only reinforced during Moritz's residence in Rome by the success of the French Academy exhibition (August 1787), in which the hard, warlike quality of Jacques Louis David's *Oath of the Horatians* gave the coup de grâce to the dying roccoco. Moritz – like Goethe – lived almost entirely among the artists. He made friends, for example, with the painters Friedrich Bury and Alexander Macco (whose lifesize *Der Abschied der Adonis von Venus* he was to review), with Friedrich Rehberg, an old school-fellow from the Hanover Gymnasium whose best work was probably his portrait of Moritz, and with the young Konrad Gessner, son of the Swiss writer. He found his way into the circle of the luminous Angelika Kauffmann, Goethe's close friend and portraitist, and made the acquaintance of the antiquary and cicerone Aloys Hirt, with whom he was later briefly to co-edit an unsuccessful periodical.[7] Tischbein, to whom we owe the pen-drawing of Moritz, Goethe and the physician, curiously makes no mention of him in his autobiography. Unlike Goethe, who took lessons from Tischbein, Moritz did not try to acquire practical skills as an artist, and at the very end of his period in Rome, when he did study perspective seriously for a short time, this was again on an entirely theoretical basis. He was, after all, a very theoretical man, and must have known that there was no future for him with pencil, brush or chisel. Moreover he had no real interest in such concerns. He was a freelance writer and, as he wished to believe, a Classical scholar. As such he travelled with Gessner and other landscape painters in the environs of Rome, writing descriptions of the scenes they painted, the 'life and soul of the party' as Gessner called him because of his 'knowledge of Roman history and literature,'[8] occasionally reading to the group from a Latin poet or even giving them a brisk lecture on some Classical theme. In those days landscape painters were regarded as eccentric to the point of madness, and often went in peril of their lives. Gessner and Moritz and their little caravan were put down by the baffled peasants as treasure hunters, and the latter dangling on his donkey seems to have been an object of universal mirth.

This particular episode, the visit to Cora, dates from the autumn of 1787. At first of course the city of Rome itself absorbed Moritz's entire interest. Much of the life of the German colony centred on the Piazza d'Espagna, specifically on the Café Greco, sometimes rechristened the Café Tedesco owing to its clientèle, and on one or two neighbouring *trattorie*. In these restaurants each nationality ate in its own room, but the Germans are said to have spent more time than the English, French or Russians in the cafés after meals. There is no doubt that Moritz passed the time of day there too, and must have made a mixed impression. Although it is obvious from the sheer number of his contacts that he lived a by no means isolated life, he himself claims that he spent a great deal of time alone, wandering around the antiquities of the city. One writer singles him out as a conspicuously unsociable individual, sitting gloomily in the Café Greco of an evening, head propped in hand; according to this witness, the Italians – with whom it is here alleged that he had little or no contact, never even learning their language properly – were so struck by his eccentric behaviour that he was still widely remembered as late as 1796 as 'the German hermit.'[9] They awarded him, indeed, the sobriquet of 'philosopho,' which must have pleased him if he heard it. The *Reisen eines Deutschen in Italien* provides a casual account of Moritz's inspection of the monuments of the Eternal City and its countless art treasures, but it imports aesthetic judgments which depend upon principles developed later. Anecdotes of visits to museums and galleries alternate with quite lively episodes from Roman daily life, accounts of bullfights, of operetta, and of canonisation ceremonies. Though Moritz's life in Rome came to be dominated by the consequences of two singular events, his meeting with Goethe and the accident in which he broke his arm, he quite independently carved out for himself some kind of existence on the fringes of the artist community and was accepted by its members. He was in fact able to introduce Goethe to a number of painters and sculptors outside Tischbein's circle, whom the poet might not otherwise have met, and was not dependent upon him in this connection. His standing in the colony is indicated by one particular incident, the funeral of the young Dresden painter August Hirsch, a friend of Gessner's, which took place on 23 August 1787. Burials of Protestants were a tricky matter in Rome, and Hirsch had made things more difficult by dying out of town. Gessner relates how his body, held upright in the interior of a carriage by concealed strings, was driven back through the city gates like a gentleman with his equipage, and how Moritz and others then escorted his hearse to the pyramid of Cestius, outside the walls, where the Protestant cemetary lay, and where Moritz was the one selected to give the funeral oration.

Goethe and Moritz apparently met at the Café Greco on 17 November 1786. We do not know who introduced them. Travelling in secret under an assumed name, Goethe had reached Rome on 29 October, and had been received and assisted by his old friend Tischbein. On the afternoon of 17 November he and Moritz strolled together to the Villa Pamphilia, in the company of Bury and another painter, Johann Georg Schütz. Not long thereafter this same party and Tischbein went on an outing to Fiumicino,

three of them, including Goethe, returning by carriage, but two, including
Moritz, being on horseback; near the Ponte Sisto, Moritz's horse fell and he
broke an arm. In the eighteenth century such an accident was extremely
grave, and could well endanger life, although it would no doubt have been
much worse had it taken the form Henriette Herz mistakenly recalls – a
bolting donkey on which Moritz collided with a shop![10] The injured man was
at once surrounded by a solicitous crowd of citizens and transported home.
For the Italians, he later wrote wryly to Campe, care far more about someone
who is hurt and in pain than they do about the victims of those everyday
Roman killings, who are beyond it. In Goethe's correspondence there are
several references to this disaster. It probably happened in the very first days
of December, since it is not yet mentioned in Goethe's comment of 1 December: 'Moritz is here, whom we had taken notice of because of Anton
Reiser and the Travels in England. He is a fine [*rein*, one of Goethe's most
complimentary epithets] and good man, in whom we have much joy.'[11] On 8
December Goethe writes of how his new-found companion's horse slipped
on the ice, and that the event was a grievous blow to their 'little circle.' A
letter of 13 December makes use of the victim's own word-play in telling
Herder: 'Moritz the foot-traveller [*Fussreiser*] is here, has broken his arm,
and is suffering a great deal. We are all suffering with him, and he is a good,
sensible, mature and developed [*aus und durchgearbeiteter*] person.' High
praise indeed, and although this last judgment was one Goethe was to modify, he was clearly exceedingly taken with Moritz. The reasons for this liking
and sympathy, though not easy to determine with any certainty, constitute as
far as they can be surmised one of the more interesting indicators in Goethe's
own spiritual biography. The well-known letter to Charlotte von Stein of 14
December offers his own analysis of the emerging relationship:

Moritz, who is still sick in bed with his broken arm, told me when I was with him
things about his life and I was astounded at the similarity with my own. He is like a
younger brother of mine, of the same nature, only despoiled [*verwahrlost*] and injured by fate just where I have been favoured and preferred. This gave me a strange
retrospect into my own life. Especially when he told me finally that his leaving
Berlin had upset one who was dear to his heart.

It is all but comical that Goethe could be led to compare Moritz's relationship with the Bergrätin Standtke with his own to Frau von Stein. Discerning
as he usually was, he nonetheless seems to have taken this story at face value
and if later, as is highly probable, he saw through it, he was too fond of
Moritz to let this be known. The rest of the letter has to be taken more

seriously, and is revealing about Goethe's self-evaluation at this critical period in his life. He was, at least in his younger days, often attracted by, and sympathetic to, neurotic and alienated personalities, and we can cite the cases of Lenz, Plessing and Krafft. He tended to see in them something also present, but under better control, in himself, a kind of shadow existence. In this instance the identification seems to have been quite exceptionally strong. It had little to do with the externals of the younger man's life, which were as unlike Goethe's as could be, though for this very reason symptomatic of the selectivity of fate. But when it came to the inner condition, to the fundamental existential lot, then Goethe saw himself and Moritz as of a kind, common children of that Chance which governs all things, both of them excluded, extrapolated creatures, both – to use Werther's term – 'wanderers upon the earth.' The vagaries of Chance had forced Moritz to live out what Goethe had largely managed to contain within the safe walls of his creative imagination, and to taste the inner destiny of exclusion as cruel, pathetic and sometimes farcical physical fact.

Moritz's accident only served to cement the friendship more quickly. Goethe took it upon himself to supervise the care of his 'younger brother,' spent hours with him each day, and even drew up a roster of companions from among the German community to keep watch at his bedside. In the forty days or so that Moritz was house-bound at Strada Babuino 89, Goethe was continually coming and going, functioning, in his words, as 'nurse, confessor and confidant, as finance minister and private secretary.' As Moritz's amanuensis he wrote a letter to Bergrat Standtke in December, and three to the Bergrätin in December and January. Moritz also dictated two letters to Campe, to whom a short specimen of the proposed travelogue had already been sent. According to Campe, Moritz had himself written on 11 November (the letter is lost) promising to send material each week and claiming that the whole work was nearing completion, which was of course very far from being the case. But he was as yet not in any financial difficulties, and his relations with the publisher remained good. He had however secretly, but without success, renewed his efforts to enlist the cooperation of Göschen, proposing the establishment of a journal 'concerning the present state of the arts and sciences in Italy,' of which he was ready to produce the first issue, apparently alone and unaided, by January 1787! Surviving letters from the period before the accident include two to Klischnig, the first of which contains the rhetorical question: 'Am I really the same man who a few weeks ago was leading a vegetative existence hemmed in by monasterial walls and who went round in the same circle every day like a mill-horse?' In the second letter to his friend, Moritz refers to Goethe's arrival in Rome, 'like a beneficent genius.' He tells Klischnig he has given Goethe some account of their comradeship and travels together, on a number of walks he has already taken with him, and he exclaims in excitement: 'It is a delight [*Wollust*] to see a great man! – How warmly I feel this now!'

Whatever the motivation of the flight from Berlin, Moritz had had definite reasons for coming to Rome. His declared aims were to expand his horizons, solidify his knowledge, and make himself into the fully proficient humanist his vocation required him to be. He was there also with the intention of writing several works of literature and scholarship, which were to be published by Campe. Although in the very last months of his stay, in the late summer of 1788, there may have been some change of pace, he did in fact none of these things, except the first. Just before the accident he had written to Büsching requesting he make known in his periodical, the *Wöchentliche Nachrichten*, Moritz's proposal to compose a work on the Roman authors, in particular the historians, which would bring Roman history to life by 'constantly taking the reader to the places where the incidents occurred.' Büsching now took the opportunity to pay him back for his previous unconscionable behaviour by commenting sarcastically in the *Nachrichten* on his entire incompetence for such a task.[12] But Goethe, some months later, speaks approvingly of a project which was 'in progress,' and was in fact to lead, in the end, to both the *Götterlehre* and *Anthusa*: 'Moritz is now studying the antiquities and will humanise them and cleanse them of all their bookish and school-room dust ...' This was a bold plan, sneers K.G. Lenz, for one who knew so little of the Classical languages and literatures, though he concedes Moritz may have done some research in Rome. Nevertheless, according to Lenz he wasted most of his time, indulging in *dolce far niente*, in sleep, in food, even in women. This last suggestion is unsupported by other evidence, apart from Klischnig's faint imputation referred to previously, and only in the *Nekrolog* do we find the story of the tailor's widow with whom Moritz is supposed to have become so deeply involved that there was talk of marriage. This 'farcical comedy for all the Germans in Rome' is said to have reached its apogee when the tailor expired in hospital and the German artists 'persuaded a young doctor to skeletonize the body, and they erected this skeleton in her room for the purpose of anatomical drawings. This made possible all sorts of jocularities about the *cara sposa di due sceleti*.'[13] It may well have done so. Certainly Moritz was often laughed at, not least because of his skinny and gawky appearance. And it is doubtless true that he dissipated a lot of time in aimless peregrinations, moody seclusion, and sleep. Nevertheless his idling, his dilettantism and his fundamentally unscholarly attitudes and appetites also helped to preserve him from the pedantry into which

so many industrious German Classicists and aestheticians fell, and may in a
sense have made possible such innovative thinking as went into his theory of
mythology in the *Götterlehre*. His journey to Naples in the spring of 1787
actually shows him attempting to carry out his declared purpose, identifying
places famous in literature and history as he travels along (he went with
friends and with transport, the foot journies were largely a thing of the past).
On the trip he paid a call at a Carthusian monastery, but with thoughts much
more critical than a decade before in Erfurt; he met a Spanish monk of
whom he relates sardonically he believed Frederick the Great had just died a
good Catholic; he climbed Vesuvius at some physical hazard and peered into
its crater, an episode recounted vividly in letters to the Bergrätin Standtke
written in tones of almost filial attachment, and he inspected the excavations
at Pompeii. In Naples he made the acquaintance of the celebrated landscape
painter Philipp Hackert, and he found the Neapolitans gracious and himself
addressed as 'Signor Don Carlo,' but he was quite appalled to be informed in
Fondi that 'un uomo di conscienza' must invariably mean a man of property
or authority over others.

> To attribute conscience to just one class of human beings and not another – and
> this moreover in a religion which counts up the smallest sins and misdeeds ... Have
> the common people, who draw their daggers in revenge while Justice lets its sword
> rust in its sheath, a conscience less clear than the priesthood which crushes them
> into this state of animal apathy that knows no pity and no mercy? (*RI*, II,
> 100–101).

The most striking theme of the *Reisen in Italien*, despite its composition in
retrospect in Berlin, is oddly enough not art or aesthetic matters at all but the
concern for social justice, and the complaint at its absence, at the dreadful
poverty of Italy and the iniquitous tyranny of the Church. The book is in fact
exceedingly anti-clerical in tone. The priests are labelled 'all devouring;' the
monks observed wandering so inappropriately in the Forum have 'swollen
faces' and 'slothful expressions'; they return to barren cells to pursue 'their
eternally monotonous, dreary activities' (*RI*, I, 129). A papal procession is
good evidence to Moritz that for the parasitic Church 'appearances are the
chief thing' (*RI*, I, 133). The magnificence of the Vatican is seen in startling
contrast to the poverty of the streets around it, and while Moritz admits that
the sight of crowds on their knees outside St Peter's is impressive however
distasteful, he cannot resist noting a nearby peasant who reshuffles his rosary
beads in his hat during the blessing so that each one may absorb the full
dose! (Heine recalls this incident in his *Memoiren*). With the same genial

irony Moritz describes the canonisation ceremonies for three Franciscans one of whom (though he did bump his head) had performed the miracle of levitation, but he also describes with a shudder a visit to an underground church where the bones and mummified corpses are to be seen of people who had actually expired on the streets. His account of the way in which alms for requiems are extracted from those practically indigent is instinct with pity and anger, while he cannot withhold his amused approval from beggars who run from one monastery to the next to be in time for several helpings of the free midday soup. Rome is overrun with vagabonds, and in writing of those who sink back into the bosom of the earth having nothing to hope for any more, the pseudo-vagabond Moritz-Reiser puts the question: 'Who can decide where true unhappiness resides? In a submission devoid of hope, or in struggling on restlessly and aimlessly to the end of one's strength? In a decisive letting go, or in the anxious, uncertain effort to rise? (*RI*, III, 15). This antithesis is formed from the conflicting prescriptions of Quietist and Pietist, a basic mould underlying much of Moritz's self-understanding, and in this case his social commentary as well. This commentary indeed owes a good deal of its force to the undercurrent of personal experience of destitution, *and* of social climbing. Was it not better to be the beggar who sinks into blissful oblivion than the one who scratches a living with his finger-nails in the gutters of the city? Was it not equally better for Karl Philipp to drift with the tides and fade finally away into the ocean of the world rather than to be forced (or force himself) to do what might be necessary to achieve security and status? Was it, to put the matter succinctly, worth it to try to break into the circle of 'society' from outside? Perhaps the tramp's life was superior to the professor's, just as rational activity and control so often seemed more onerous than depression, the sweet vagabondage of the mind. This set of alternatives involves a threat with which Goethe, for another, was already well acquainted, and when he noticed its sinister presence in Moritz he felt quite reluctant to leave him on departing for Naples and Sicily in February, 1787. Though observing that his younger friend now seemed to be 'on a good path,' he added: 'When he is alone, however, he looks straightaway for favourite bolt-holes.' He encouraged Moritz to begin a correspondence with Herder, noting that the former was in need of those 'able, willing, indeed charitable enough to take the time to explain his condition to him;' but such people (says Goethe) had always been lacking (17 Feb. 1787).

Goethe and Moritz were apart from February until June 1787, but apart from this gap they were almost inseparable companions in Rome. Much of what we know of the friendship and its development comes from Goethe's side, and there is a succession of interesting comments of his on Moritz, from this period and later. On 8 January 1787, he told Charlotte von Stein that he had just been present at the unbandaging of his friend's arm: 'He can stand and walk very well.' This was the scene to be preserved by Tischbein's art, he being there also along with the physician, Dr Frey, a neighbour of his. Tischbein was greatly struck by the gentleness and sympathy which Goethe showed on this painful occasion, notwithstanding the patient's 'hellish cursing.'[14] In a letter a month later, Goethe makes a remark which has important implications:

Moritz is crawling round again, now I can be of some use to him once more and his acquaintance with me will have a significant influence upon his life in the future, he is good-natured, sensible, receptive, and grateful when you help him on a step.

And how hard [sauer] it is for a man without tradition, without instruction, to find himself and help himself at the right time. Tischbein for the last two days has been helping me to make almost hourly progress in drawing, for he perceives where I stand and what I need; it's like that in the moral sphere too, it's like that in everything. (7–10 (?) February 1787)

The analogy produced here is highly characteristic of its author. Goethe believed that just as he could learn how to draw from Tischbein, so Moritz could learn how to live from him. He was on the way, after all, to becoming something of a specialist in 'Lebenskunst,' and his observation that Moritz was without 'tradition' was shrewdly pertinent. Despite a certain cargo of popular scientific ideas, his 'younger brother' possessed neither objectivity towards his own situation and potentialities nor a concrete awareness of the cultural moment in which he stood. He lacked any focus for his thinking, and for his living he lacked any genuine centre of gravity. His mind, Goethe writes, seems to be 'a strange vessel, always empty and in need of content and thirsting for things to absorb and make into his own,' and in a letter of 2 October 1787, he goes on to sound an almost pessimistic note: 'Moritz has been my favourite companion up to now, though I did fear, and almost still fear, that his acquaintance with me might just make him cleverer, and not sounder [richtiger], better or happier, a worry which holds me back from total frankness with him.' Goethe cannot have been surprised to encounter episodes of withdrawal to the most convenient hayloft, like that a couple of years before in Halle.[15] But his influence upon Moritz was always salutary, and it worked itself out in a number of ways: in the general intellectual exchange in which the two friends participated as they read and studied together, in which Moritz made up by the novelty of some of his aperçus for what he lacked in wealth of knowledge and experience; in the receptivity

MORITZ, GOETHE AND THE SURGEON

Photograph courtesy Nationale Forschungs- und Gedenkstätte der
klassischen deutschen Literatur, Weimar

which made him into a good listener, so that Goethe could test out on him his new scientific theories as well as his poetic works; and above all through the radiant model which the intregration, the autonomy of Goethe's life appeared to provide.

What Goethe may have gained from his friendship with Moritz is not really our concern here. There can, however, be no doubt that he found him stimulating, in some degree intellectually, but much more as a problematic human being. We have already noted his claim that without Moritz's *Prosodie* (which he had acquired before travelling to Italy) he would not have dared to recast his prose drama *Iphigenie auf Tauris* in verse, and that his conversations at his friend's bedside finally clarified his understanding of German prosody. Some of this may well be slightly exaggerated – *Iphigenie* already existed, and would no doubt have been versified sooner or later anyway. However, Moritz's influence on the genesis of two other works, *Torquato Tasso* and *Wilhelm Meisters Lehrjahre*, may well have been quite extensive (a matter we shall touch on further in the next chapter). The views of the two men on literature and the arts were certainly convergent at this moment, and they shared a dislike for the Sturm und Drang, especially the work of its later exponents such as Schiller and Heinse. Moritz, as we saw, had expressed some rather forceful opinions on Schiller's plays just a year or two earlier. Commenting on the circumstances of his return from Italy and Moritz's visit to Weimar, Goethe was one day to write: 'I was trying to nurture the purest ideas [*Anschauungen*] and found myself squeezed between Ardinghello and Franz Moor. Moritz, who came back from Italy at the same time and stayed with me for a while, passionately encouraged me in these attitudes ...'[16] In the *Reisen in Italien* we find a distaste for the Gothic style even more pronounced than that in the *Reisen in England*: Gothic architecture is described with that rather negative term 'labyrinth' (see *RI*, I, 185). It is entirely compatible with the position sketched out in the 'Versuch einer Vereinigung' that Moritz, under Goethe's influence, came to see the plastic arts, especially sculpture – 'which turns man's gaze back to his inner self through the surface of his being' (*RI*, II, 194) – as the pinnacle of culture; ancient sculpture (e.g. the *Borghese Warrior*) is held to be better than 'modern' (e.g. Bernini's *David*), because it always communicates a sense of wholeness, the absence of this sense being, according to Moritz, the major difference between the inferior art of the new world and that of the old. The supremacy of sculpture derives from the fact that its principal subject is the human body and 'in the human form there is, with the greatest variety, the greatest unity' (*RI*, III, 228).

PREPARATIONS

Many of these ideas, of course, came directly from Goethe, others were clarified or reinforced by the contact with him. But it would be wrong to conclude that Moritz was merely a passive vehicle for the canalisation of Goethean insights in aesthetics, as has too frequently been suggested. Not only the 'Versuch einer Vereinigung' and the *Prosodie* point to the independent source of some of his basic notions, but so do the *Fragmente eines Geistersehers* (1786), and several other essays on the periphery of *Über die bildende Nachahmung des Schönen*. The study of this major work cannot be undertaken without automatically illuminating the eclecticism out of which it sprang, and thus the nature of the collaboration between Goethe and Moritz. The *Bildende Nachahmung* differs from typical academic discourses of its day on the same or similar themes, having an esoteric, even hieratic, quality about it. Very little is known about the circumstances of its composition, and until recently this matter, and its intellectual content, had never been thoroughly investigated.[17] It is clear that Moritz wrote the pamphlet (which is really all it can be called) during the winter of 1787–88, and it was probably essentially complete when Goethe left Rome in April 1788. At the end of May the manuscript was evidently dispatched to Campe in a sort of panic, in an effort to satisfy the publisher's increasingly peremptory demands. Curiously enough there is no reference to it in any of Moritz's surviving correspondence or elsewhere, until his letter to Goethe of 7 June 1788. It had certainly not been part of his original plans to compose anything of this kind, indeed aesthetic questions as such were not in the forefront of his mind at all when he first arrived in Rome. At that time, his interest was still in travel and in writing a travel diary, as well as in 'antiquities,' the study of Roman cultural remains. At some point in the course of 1787 there occurred a shift in the direction of art under the influence of Goethe. When he published his *Italienische Reise* in 1816 Goethe saw fit to include a longish extract from the *Bildende Nachahmung*, which he prefaced with certain much quoted remarks. The treatise, he said,

emerged from our conversations, which Moritz exploited and developed in his own way. However that may be, it can be of some historical interest to see what kind of ideas opened out for us at that time which, when developed, tested, utilised and disseminated, later coincided well enough with the thinking of the age.

This late comment is not his only public statement on the subject. He reviewed the *Bildende Nachahmung* when it first appeared, composing the review during Moritz's stay in Weimar.[18] In it he declares that the author had written his work 'so to speak out of the soul of the artist and into his soul,' an opaque remark borrowed from Herder who in his correspondence refers not to 'the artist's' but *Goethe's* soul,[19] but this coded allusion is not sufficient to justify the interpretation put on it by Pyritz that Goethe was thereby claiming primacy of authorship for himself.[20] In fact, the rest of the review totally fails to support such an argument, since it seems to be a considered attempt on Goethe's part to establish the independence and primacy of Moritz's contribution, especially in view of the widespread belief in Weimar that this had been quite secondary to Goethe's own. Hence the deliberate impersonality of the phrase 'soul of the artist,' and Goethe goes on to emphasise 'the profundity and the shrewdness of the author, which he has already shown in so many publications, and we find him true to those principles to which he had previously committed himself.'

'Those principles' can only refer to a number of ideas to be found in the 'Versuch einer Vereinigung,' the *Geisterseher* and the *Prosodie* which derived partly from Mendelssohn, and though developed in an original way reflected indirectly the tradition of Leibniz and Baumgarten and the influence of Shaftesbury. The most important of these is the concept of the aesthetic Whole, the perfect cosmos of the ideal work of art seen as a microcosmic reduction of that macrocosm which exceeds the bounds of human contemplation. 'This infinite universe,' Mendelssohn had written, 'is not an object whose beauty is visible for us.'[21] Mendelssohn, however, has a subjective view of the nature of imitation [*Nachahmung*], emphasising the image of the Whole as it is formed within the mind, a position reflected by Moritz when he writes in the *Kinderlogik* of the universe becoming one only 'in our concept of it' (*KL*, 112).[22] In the *Bildende Nachahmung* Moritz then changes the emphasis decisively, and as we noted turns away from Mendelssohn's concern with the psychology of the receptive subject, while also dropping his fundamental analogy with the Divine perception of the world.[23] A fresh stream of thought, bringing above all else a recognition of the uniqueness of the creative impulse as well as the primacy of the concrete domain of *objets d'art*, here coalesces with, and so transforms, the School-philosophical tradition, which had become, after Baumgarten, increasingly preoccupied with questions of reception, taste and aesthetic pleasure. The important essay, 'Die metaphysische Schönheitslinie' (*Schriften*, 151–57) offers further evidence here. It has not yet been conclusively dated, but it seems reasonable to suppose that it was written in Italy, about the same time as the *Bildende Nachahmung* and conceivably even earlier.[24] Here Moritz turns towards the problem of artistic creation, the functioning of 'genius.' He considers how 'the richness of great and noble ideas,' residing perhaps since childhood in the ar⌄st's mind, eventually come to find expression – 'so to speak when the measure is full' – in objective form, the creator's subjective delight being transformed into external contemplation, 'Genuss im Anschauen.' As the work takes shape, the ideas relevant to it dissolve their connections with other ideas in the mind, and by centripetal inclination begin to cohere around one single visualization [*Vorstellung*], for example, the figure of Achilles. That the essay is earlier than the *Bildende Nachahmung* seems likely, in that Moritz still points out in it that 'the only thing truly complete in itself' is the totality of the universe as perceived by God, who is said to 'cast back' [*zurückwälzen*] its purpose into itself.

The cumbersome key-word 'zurückwälzen' points here once again to the theme of autonomy. As the macrocosm is autonomous, so must the micro-cosm be also. Moritz now launches into a very strange argument built upon one of those geometric metaphors of which he was so fond. For the title of the essay, 'Die metaphysische Schönheitslinie', he was doubtless indebted to William Hogarth's *The Analysis of Beauty* (1754), translated into German in 1754,[25] with its concept of the serpentine line [*Wellenlinie*]. Hogarth's ser-pentine line was an empirical discovery, hence Moritz's decision to call his own line 'metaphysical.' He may or may not have actually read Hogarth, but if he did he cannot have found in the English painter's doctrines, which link the baroque with the roccoco, anything very compatible with his own neo-Classical tastes. Hogarth had been opposed to the English Palladians, whereas Goethe was now enthusing over Palladio, so it is not surprising to find a criticism of the serpentine line in the *Reisen in Italien* (*RI*, III, 114). 'Die metaphysische Schönheitslinie' conceives of Nature as 'a great circle the parts of which all have a centripetal quality [*eine Neigung gegen sich selbst*],' and which owing to its size has a curvature the human observer is unable to perceive. Therefore he sees only straight lines, and Nature's 'bending towards a [self-contained] purpose' must escape him. Nevertheless the artist, when he reproduces these straight lines in his drawings, gives them an inclination one towards another, 'as though within the great immeas-urable circle we desired to form a smaller one on a reduced scale.' Moritz sees the process by which a straight line can become curved as analogous to that by which the external purpose gives way to the centripetal coherence of autonomy: 'These curved lines we shall call the lines of beauty, and the lines in the immeasurable circle, which appear to be straight, we shall call the lines of truth. Beauty is therefore truth on a reduced scale.'

This is a typical procedure, showing as it does Moritz's trick of reformu-lating a School-philosophical idea, in this case the analogy between the cosmos of Nature and the cosmos formed in the artist's imagination, in a novel manner, utilising metaphor in an eccentric but consistent way. 'Die metaphysische Schönheitslinie' now takes up one of the central issues in Moritz's writing, the problem of temporal succession, an abstract issue for Leibniz and Wolff which he had personalized in his autobiography.[26] He links the process of transformation of the temporal into its spatial simulacrum with the act of artistic creation:

The complete in itself, which in Nature is achieved by *succession*, must be produced here in appearance [*auf eine anscheinende Art*] by construction [*Zusammenstellung*]. The imaginary line of beauty crosses a number of lines of truth, gradually imposing tighter constrictions on one after the other, and these limits constitute the essence of the line of beauty.

We might summarise thus: the open, endless universe, as it appears to human vision to be, is actually centripetal, although its circularity can be perceived only by God; but the artist bends the straight lines of which it apparently consists into a microcosmic model, by imposing upon them an artificial coherence by means of his creative act. In this process, infinite, discrete succession is transformerd into integrated structure, time into geometric pattern; as for example (Moritz argues) in a play the dialogue is curtailed and moulded by constant reference to the critical 'centre' of the drama; the more perfect the play, the more intensely centripetal the dialogue, and the more disconnected from referents outside the work.

In the *Fragmente aus dem Tagebuche eines Geistersehers*, which was published unfinished in 1787 with a sarcastic preface by the disillusioned printer Himburg,[27] and which might be called a typical 'Aufklärung' spiritual primer in which the author uses a tenuous fiction about a deceased philosopher in order to unload a number of improving miscellanea for cash, there appears an essay entitled: 'Gegenwart und Vergangenheit.' This poses the question squarely: 'Is it possible to think of what follows in succession as being adjacent?,' and Moritz then proposes the remarkable analogy already noted in connection with *Anton Reiser*, based on the contrast between the appearance of a city to a traveller who wanders through it street by street, and its appearance when viewed from a lofty tower. He suggests that what men call 'the succession of things' may be merely 'the succession of our visualization of these things.' The revolving wheel or the circle is employed as an image of the manner in which the Divine Intelligence perceives individual points of time – for God they are all equally and 'permanently' real so that there is no question of memory. A human being can but hope one day to be able to see his whole life in time laid out 'in space' [*neben einander*], and here the essay turns in an unmistakeably mystical direction by way, however, of a characteristic atomism: all that exists, Moritz asserts, is the present, the instantaneous, and therefore timeless, 'moment of experiencing.' This mystical tendency may have been the reason that the little piece, when republished a couple of years later, had acquired a fresh title: 'Sonderbare Zweifel und Trostgründe eines hypochondrischen Metaphysikers,'[28] perhaps implying that Moritz wished to distance himself from it. The writings of the Roman period show him indeed moving away from metaphysics in the narrower sense, and also from religious references of any kind.

Goethe's influence led his friend towards the world, and away from mysticism. But it should not be forgotten that Goethe was himself still very much involved with Neoplatonist ideas, and the *Bildende Nachahmung* certainly owes much to the Neoplatonic tradition. Goethe had of course had a grounding in occult doctrine early in life, and even knew something of the teaching of Mme de Guyon.[29] Together he and Moritz busied themselves with Spinoza, through the mediation of Herder's recently published treatise grandiloquently entitled *Gott*. Goethe's account in the *Italienische Reise* of the word-game he and Moritz amused themselves with in Rome is some evidence of their preoccupation with an *ens realissimum*. But Goethe saw reality as embodied in concrete things, as his doctrine of the symbol was in due course to specify. Thus he constantly sought to curtail the hypothesising, abstracting quality of Moritz's mind, as he tried also to modify its passivity, to counter the other's inclination to look for 'bolt-holes,' to walk away from the outside world. That he had a certain success is shown, for instance, by Moritz's letter to him of 7 June 1788, in which he states: 'It becomes clearer and clearer to me that the form of the human body is everything; and that as long as I live I shall have to contend with my nose; but also that I shall triumph.' The body, which 'provides the greatest unity,' was something Moritz had always neglected and loathed, the source, for him, of much of the universal spite. Now this was to change, at least in theory, as Goethe introduced his pupil to what may be loosely described as a philosophy of organism.

From Frascati, on 28 September 1787, Goethe wrote:

I am very happy here, the whole day until late at night we spend drawing, painting, colouring, glueing, craft and art really are practised *ex professo* ... Moritz and I pass good hours together, and I have started explaining my botanical system to him and writing down each time, in his presence, just how far we have progressed. This is the only way I could get my ideas down on paper. How intelligible the most abstract aspects of this way of seeing things [*Vorstellungsart*] become when expounded in the right way to a mind prepared to receive them – this I notice in my new pupil. He takes great delight in it, and is constantly reasoning his way forward himself.

It seems likely that some of the notions developed in Goethe's *Metamorphose der Pflanzen* (1790) made a significant contribution to the new aesthetic doctrines, although there is some room for argument as to how far specifically *organic* conceptions are entirely reconcilable with the system of the *Bildende Nachahmung*. One essential idea was that of 'inner form,' a natural unfolding from the seed. In January 1789, thanking Johann Heinrich Meyer for a drawing he had sent him, Goethe commented: 'It is a fine [*kostbare*] composition. Or as Moritz would have it, one should not say composition, for a work like this is not put together from without, it has been unfolded from within.'[30] This does not necessarily mean 'has unfolded itself,' and may still leave room for the conscious intervention of the artist; Moritz did not definitely hold a doctrine of the spontaneous, plant-like growth of the work of art, though he may well have favoured it. The remark does, however, attribute to him, rather than to Goethe, the formulation of and insistence upon a conception of inner form, as is indeed found widely in the Neoplatonic tradition and specifically in Shaftesbury (where again it should be noted that it is not associated with organicism).[31] Whether Moritz ever read the *Charackteristics*, entire or in part, is unknown. If he did so, he must have found there both the idea of inner form and the requirement that every work of art should have a focal point. In Shaftesbury also is the notion of the harmonious internal structure of the cosmos, which can only be intuited, a beauty which is furthermore known to the full solely in the process of imaginative creation. Shaftesbury's distinction between the creative and receptive functions was already somewhat blurred by the principal disseminator of his ideas, Hutcheson.[32] With him begins the stress upon the recipient, and the concern with taste, response and aesthetic sensitivity, which Moritz was to do something to change.

Other English writers, notably Young, whom he had read long ago, may well have a place in this eclectic set of sources. In the *Conjectures on Original Composition* (1759), Young had commented on the nature of genius, observing that: 'An Original may be said to be of a vegetable nature.'[33] Moritz's familiarity with the botanical metaphor, it is important to remember, precedes his acquaintance with Goethe. In the *Denkwürdigkeiten* had appeared in 1786 a short piece containing the following:

All things which Nature brings forth have more noble and less noble parts. The leaves of the tree are more refined than its trunk and branches are, the blossom more refined than the leaves, and the fruit is the noblest of all.[34]

This parallel between the hierarchy of botanical forms and moral character is not infrequent in neo-Pietistic writers in Germany (for example, in the novelist Sophie de la Roche). It is of course connected with the doctrine of the 'schöne Seele' or 'belle âme,' and has many ramifications in occult symbolism. Organicist ideas occur in fact in Leibniz, and their transfer to the aesthetic realm had already taken place by the time of Baumgarten, the principal aesthetician of the Wolffian School, who had interestingly enough himself been educated in the Pietist Francke's Orphanage at Halle.[35] We can therefore safely assume that Moritz, though impressed by Goethe's morphology of plants as it was now expounded to him, cannot have found in it very much that was totally and unexpectedly new. What was new however was the direction of his attention towards concrete works of art, as seen in the streets, the Villa Borghese, the Vatican and the other great Roman collections; new also was Goethe's interpretative method, as he approached these manifold products of genius. This involved recognising the body, the external form, as primary, at least in the sense that through this alone the inner nature of the object, and of beauty, could be grasped. 'Interpretation of the inner from the outer,' as Goethe once called it,[36] was a quite unfamiliar procedure for so rationalistic a mind, trained rather to operate in the reverse direction. But the empirical psychology which Moritz had discovered for himself, thus breaking loose from a priori reasoning, certainly made it easier for him to accept this change of direction, just as his speculations about the unconscious mind must have helped him to grasp the significance of the phenomenon of 'genius.' This was the other great thing that was new, his discovery, in his conversations with Goethe, of the unique character and quality of the creative act. As early as the first number of the *Magazin* Moritz had spoken of 'active energy' [*tätige Kraft*], which he distinguished from 'cognitive,' 'representative energy' [*vorstellende Kraft*] (*Mag* I, 1, 33–34). He had not, however, as he does now, singled out a unique 'Tatkraft,' 'creative energy,' the most conspicuously Goethean concept in the *Bildende Nachahmung*. Leibniz speaks of a *vis primitiva activa*,[37] and 'Kraft' is an important term for both Mendelssohn and Herder. In the *Bildende Nachahmung*, however, 'Tatkraft' is an energy possessed in adequate measure only by the genuine creative genius. When Goethe selected the excerpt for reprinting, so many years later, it may be significant that he chose to start with this passage.

At the end of August 1787, on his birthday, Goethe had received from Herder a copy of the latter's new book, *Gott*. He and Moritz proceeded to study this together, and to enthuse over it, as they were also to do over the third volume of Herder's *Ideen* a couple of months later. 'Moritz,' Goethe writes, 'has benefited very much from Herder's teachings on the divine

[*Götterlehre* – not *Gotteslehre*!], he regards it for sure as the beginning of a new stage in his life, he has turned his thoughts and feelings [*Gemüt*] in that direction, and was prepared for it by his contact with me; he flared up immediately like well dried wood.' Shortly thereafter he adds: 'Moritz is truly edified by it, it is as though this work were all that was lacking, and it now functions as the key-stone of his ideas, which were always falling apart ...' *Gott* is a document of Herder's renewed preoccupation with Spinoza, in which Leibnizian concepts, especially that of 'Kraft,' are introduced to modify the pure Spinozist equation of God and world, and in which the influence of Shaftesbury also shows itself. The $\dot{\epsilon\nu}$ $\kappa\alpha\iota$ $\pi\alpha\nu$ is used by Herder as the basis for an aesthetically orientated pantheism, which conjures with the notion of 'harmony.' One of his less successful ventures – Kant turned up his nose at it, while Jacobi lost no time in pointing out its numerous inconsistencies, deriving largely from its author's unwillingness to abandon a theistic position altogether[38] – Herder's *Gott* nonetheless gratified Goethe, whose organicist theories seem to have been reinforced by it, and it must have stimulated Moritz towards a view of art as the expression of the Oneness, the harmonious perfection, of the universe. As far as the third part of the *Ideen* is concerned, Goethe calls this 'a sacred book which I keep locked up,' and which he had only latterly (January 1788) allowed Moritz to read, who was completely 'carried away' by its peroration (Book Fifteen). This section is an encomium on the theme of the progress of mankind, in which Herder writes:

All the works of God have their being in themselves, and their beautiful coherence: for they all repose in their particular limits upon the equilibrium of conflicting forces by means of an inner power which brought these into order. With this thread to guide me I wander through the labyrinth of history and see all around me a harmonious, divine order ...'[39]

Moritz, as we know, was always in search of the thread which might lead forth from the labyrinth into the light of personal coherence. His *magnum opus* on aesthetics is in a way of being a claim to have found that thread.

ÜBER DIE BILDENDE NACHAHMUNG DES SCHÖNEN

Über die bildende Nachahmung des Schönen (*Schriften*, 65–93)[40] alludes of course in its title to one of the most persistent questions in eighteenth-century aesthetic thought. But Moritz offers no historical survey, and was likely enough only vaguely familiar with the complexities of previous debate. He probably scarcely knew any of those French authors – Diderot, for example, Batteux or the Abbé du Bos – by whom the problem of 'imitation' had been most thoroughly ventilated (indeed, the lack of any knowledge of French was a serious gap in his equipment, despite the proliferation of translations of the *philosophes*). In Rome it was difficult to obtain new German books, even supposing he could have afforded to buy them, and he may also have deliberately avoided direct reference and quotation in order to insulate his argument as far as he could from the unwelcome niceties of professional philosophical analysis. The *Bildende Nachahmung* is best considered a visionary, even a hortatory work. It begins, however, fairly soberly by developing a distinction between imitation in the sense of moral emulation and imitation in the arts. Moritz argues that the word 'nachahmen' (which he employs with a dative object) is equivalent, whenever it refers to the imitation of character and virtue, to 'nachstreben' or 'wetteifern,' that is, imitation means moral emulation. To clarify the difference between this and imitation in the arts, he attempts to distinguish systematically between the concepts of 'the noble,' 'the beautiful,' 'the good' and 'the useful.' His discussion of these terms is not without interest, since it epitomizes a number of distinctions fundamental to the aesthetic and moral philosophy of the German 'Aufklärung,' and indeed of Weimar Classicism itself. With the Rationalist's concern for an ideal domain of concepts independent of language, Moritz sternly separates the ideas themselves from linguistic usage. 'Das Edle,' 'das Schöne,' 'das Gute' and 'das Nützliche' may, he suggests, be arranged on a meaningful scale, which constitutes 'such a delicate game of ideas [*Ideenspiel*] that it has to be difficult for reasoning to separate out adequately what is continually blending imperceptibly together.' Games, as invariably for Moritz, are reflections of ultimate possibilities of structure, and windows into the mind. On his scale, the useful is deemed closer to the good than it is to the noble and the beautiful, but when attributed to actions it refers, unlike the good, only to external results, and not to the moral condition of the individual who acts. We love a good person, sensing his 'harmlessness' which may be of benefit to us. A noble person, on the other hand, arouses a loftier sort of admiration, having something in him which has no external reference and may actually bring no benefit to us at all. *Nobilitas mentis* is perceived as being entirely self-contained. Its beauty is inward, and is compatible even with a total absence of external beauty. Unlike such external perfection, furthermore, *nobilitas mentis* offers itself for emulation, an inward process. To imitate such moral beauty *in art*, however, requires the creation of an external replica of it. To depict a person's inner beauty of soul, 'in so far as it is reflected in his features,' the artist must externalise his intuition of the inner beauty 'not exactly by imitating these features, but so to speak by using them to help him reproduce outside his mind the beauty of soul of another being, which he has apprehended within.'

Turning now in greater detail to the problem of actions, Moritz considers the connotations of a number of attributes. He finds that a good act merits our respect both for its motives and for its consequences. But in the admiration of a noble act results have no place; this must depend purely on its motives. Such an act, therefore, possesses a certain autonomy, an inner worth which is precisely why we call it noble. If we only take into account its surface, 'from which it casts a gentle radiance into our soul,' we may also call it beautiful. The tale of Mucius Scaevola is then introduced as a parable to illuminate the distinctions between noble, good and useful acts, and also their negatives. The elaboration of the scale in this way shows that 'the bad is ... the starting point of the useless, just as the useful is the starting point of the good.' On this scale the concepts of 'the useless' [*das Unnütze*] and 'the beautiful' and 'the noble' (which latter pair Moritz becomes increasingly inclined to confuse) stand furthest apart, and yet paradoxically they are also close together, for 'the beautiful' and 'the noble,' exactly like 'the useless,' are characterized by their lack of any external purpose. The resolution of this paradox depends on recognising that the so-called scale is really a circle, around which the attributes revolve, or rise and fall: 'The three rising concepts of useful, good and beautiful, and the three descending ones of ignoble, bad and useless therefore constitute a circle, because the two extreme concepts of the useless and the beautiful are the least mutually exclusive.' Utility is pertinent neither to a noble action nor to a beautiful object; on the contrary. However, an object is beautiful not precisely because it is not useful, but because it has no need to be useful. Moritz goes on to define 'the useful' in a traditional manner, after Wolff, as a property parts have in relation to their Whole. Any useful thing has a purpose outside itself, and it subserves a Whole. However, the Whole itself need not possess this feature. If it is to have no need to be useful, a thing must have this quality of Wholeness, and it therefore follows that 'the concept of the beautiful is inseparably linked with the concept of an autonomous Whole [*ein für sich bestehendes Ganzes*].'

Other concepts – 'the majestic,' for example, and 'the sublime' – are also touched upon without affecting the central design of the argument. It may very well be (as Menz thinks) that this very curious 'game of ideas,' which depends on some notions already introduced in the 'Versuch einer Vereinigung,' had been conceived by Moritz well before he began his work on the *Bildende Nachahmung*, and that it was inserted at this point merely as a convenient device. Far from being trivial, however, we may see it as an ingenious 'diagrammatic' summation of certain issues prominent in moral philosophy at the time. German Classicism, as is well known, was soon to solemnize the risky marriage between the ethical and the aesthetic, although Kant strove to arrange a separation; and Goethe's work, particularly at this period, displays a persistent concern with the problem of *nobilitas mentis*.[41] The idea of the autonomous Whole having once been introduced in this manner, Moritz now uses it to establish the doctrine of the work of art as cosmos. Though all Wholes, except the macrocosm itself, are merely imaginary [*eingebildet*], they are all centripetal in structure, and therefore all analogous to the macrocosm. If the work of art is a copy of the macrocosm, the beauty (i.e. the curvature) of which is imperceptible to human eyes, the question arises how the artist is able to produce such a simulacrum. The answer is: by intuition. The beauty of the macrocosm can be apprehended only by the 'creative energy' [*Tatkraft*] of the artist; it expressly cannot be apprehended either by the senses or by the imagination [*Vorstellungskraft*]: 'The beautiful cannot, that is, be perceived, it must be produced – or *felt*.' In certain respects this is manifestly a Sturm und Drang doctrine, and some of the interest of the *Bildende Nachahmung* is in the light it casts on the subterranean connections between that movement and the aesthetics of Classicism. We might note in particular the assertion that:

the *living* concept of the creative imitation of the beautiful can only arise [*statt finden*] in the experience of the active energy which produces the beautiful, in the first instant of its birth, in which the work, as though already complete, having passed through all the stages of its gradual emergence, suddenly materialises, obscurely apprehended, before the mind's eye, and in this moment of its first conception is so to speak present before it *really* exists ....

By definition, however, only the creative artist can enjoy such a moment as this.

It also goes without saying that reason, in common with the senses and the imagination, has no possibility of perceiving and judging the beautiful, and in making this point Moritz took a further step beyond the position of the 'Aufklärung.' Because he himself does not create it, the person responding to the work of art can partake of its beauty only to a secondary degree, and his appreciation is in any case dependent not upon his reason but upon the much studied but still mysterious faculty of taste. Moritz separates the act of creation from that of response, while placing both artist and recipient under an uncompromising set of obligations. The perfect work of art is a circle, and should a single point be wanting (the so-called 'point of perfection' [*Vollendungspunkt*]) then the work inevitably fails and moreover sinks 'below the level of the bad down to that of the useless.' This austere doctrine proved devastating for dilettantes. Its associated corollaries, however, are equally severe. In distinguishing, as Shaftesbury had done before him, between the active creative faculty [*Bildungsvermögen*] and the passive receptive one [*Empfindungsvermögen*], Moritz points out that the latter may all too readily be mistaken for the former. In that event, defective works of art will be produced which have no value. The receptive faculty confuses itself with the creative essentially because of a vain wish to participate in that quite particular delight which belongs to 'das bildende Genie,' and to his creative act. Hence the sufferings of Anton Reiser, the poetaster, hence the miseries of the 'passive genius' (as Jean Paul was one day to call Moritz),[42] of which species, besides himself, Werther was the prominent example in Moritz's mind. The smallest particle of the wrong sort of egoism, of the pursuit of effect and of 'results,' will defile the creative act (as it would equally, of course, the mystic's pursuit of the divine). Such a pollution means that 'the focal point [*Brennpunkt*] or point of perfection of the beautiful is situated beyond the boundaries of the work, in its effect; the radii fall apart; the work cannot be rounded.' To overstress the biographical relevance of all this would not only be superfluous, it would impair the quite genuine integrity of the aesthetic system here presented. But we can scarcely forget how often chasing an 'effect' prevented the rounding of the circle of Anton Reiser's life.

This crushing judgment upon pseudo-genius must have had a bitter flavour for its author, and it has often been observed that the abstract arguments of the treatise actually disguise a kind of tragic personal confession. The distinction between active and passive principles, which was the great and simple illumination that came to Moritz through his contact with Goethe and that finally clarified his understanding of his own life, has, like much else in the *Bildende Nachahmung*, other roots as well. Practically everything in the essay may indeed be said to be 'overdetermined,' and in this case the sources are once again Pietism, Neoplatonism and occult lore. The nature of this debt emerges strikingly when Moritz writes: 'Creative energy [*Bildungskraft*] and capacity for acceptance [*Empfindungsfähigkeit*] are related to one another like man and woman. For the creative energy, at the moment of the first arising of its work, the moment of the highest pleasure, is simultaneously capacity for reception, and like Nature produces a copy of its own being from out of itself.' The *vis primitiva activa* is found to divide into two: 'In so far as this active energy comprises everything not included in rational thinking [*Denkkraft*], *in its process of creating*, it is called creative energy: and in so far as it comprises what is beyond the limits of thinking, *in its openness to what has been created*, it is called receptive energy.' Moritz writes here of a faculty more fundamental than that of reason, and situates the sources of both artistic creativity and of response decisively in the irrational.

The Classicism which the *Bildende Nachahmung* adumbrates may thus be seen to be based upon irrationalistic principles, squarely opposed to those of the Enlightenment. After progressing thus far, the discussion enters a sequence of gnomic and mantic assertions. This second half of the book has caused its commentators much trouble, and has generally been underplayed or even ignored. Various explanations have been proffered for its outstanding obscurity, including the not unlikely one of printer's error.[43] Goethe refrained from going into it in any detail in his review (contenting himself with reprinting a few paragraphs), and he omitted this section altogether from the excerpt in the *Italienische Reise*. He no doubt considered it not only enigmatic but also of secondary importance. For the student of Moritz, however, the second half of the *Bildende Nachahmung* is most interesting, being reflective of much that is characteristic of his mind. Certain ideas – annihilation, sacrifice and love, and the fulfillment of the species [*Gattung*] – now become prominent, and the author conjures with the notion of hierarchy, and of the great chain of being. Lower levels of organisation are held to be annihilated and absorbed by higher ones according to law, less intense energies succumb to those more powerful; thus plants submit to animals, animals to men, and the weaker men to the stronger, while those sensitive to beauty are overcome by 'the unquenchable yearning' for it. The aspiration after a level of experience one cannot attain, the futile longing of the 'passive' temperament to participate in 'active' experience, causes suffering; but this suffering is declared to be necessary for the very existence of the beautiful, as the suffering of individuals is apparently indispensable for the survival and development of the species. In a rather moving passage in which the visionary historicism of Herder's *Ideen*, shorn however of its simplistic conception of progress, blends with another, more intimate current of religious inwardness, Moritz goes on to point to the way in which individual suffering may be transfigured in the perfection of the species, which is now itself seen as an autonomous Whole, timelessly self-contained in purpose. The individual's sufferings 'are only terrible to the individual, in the species they become beautiful.' Moritz, who could not realise himself as he saw that Goethe could and had, never seems to have been jealous of that friend so 'favoured and preferred,' whom he became notorious for referring to as 'God.' For in his imagination he succeeded in converting the distinction between their fates into an illustration of a law of nature. Thus the unfulfilled aspiration after perfection may lead to the torments of hell ('Sisyphus rolls his stone'), but however painful and deprived an existence may be, however repetitive and infernal in its discrete succession in time, it still can have sense in the light of the harmonious totality, and a glimpse may be obtained of this harmony if the suffering is captured in art. When so portrayed, the sufferings of men like ourselves make us conscious of 'the continuous dissolution of our own nature,' and it appears as if, 'magically conjured up in beautiful reflection, there hovers before us a fragment of that great circle in which our diminutive lives may one day be absorbed.' The conclusion of the *Bildende Nachahmung*, which is a kind of apotheosis of being and an essentially optimistic celebration of the harmonious balance of creation and decay, Goethe chose to call 'touching.' But it is surely rather more than that. Like everything else significant that Moritz wrote, it centres on the tyranny of chance and time, and on the sublime solace of the coherent, the autobiographical, vision. The entire work is concerned in one way or another with the intuition of cosmos, indeed with its creation; the objective work of genius becomes a passionately venerated ideal speaking symbolically of the possibility of individual, and social, coherence restored.

The difference in level between this ardent, complex little work and, for example, the *Unterhaltungen mit seinen Schülern* with its derivative sentiment and occasional falsity of tone, is astonishing. Moritz had come very far in those eight years, had acclimatised himself to the values of the Berlin Enlightenment and was now leaving them rapidly behind. He had come, perhaps, further than he was ever to know, and was laying a foundation for things that were to be developed long after his death. It seems, for instance, entirely justifiable to regard the *Bildende Nachahmung* as an important step towards the emergence of the modern notion of the symbol. First of all, the reference to the concrete work of art, and the Goethean concept of 'Anschauung' ('intuitive appreciation') is implicit throughout, and secondly the *Bildende Nachahmung*, although it does separate the domain of ideas from that of ordinary language, acknowledges a higher language, that of art. Moritz may be found in the *Reisen in Italien* criticising Winckelmann for suggesting that there is an abstract world of beauty beyond nature (*RI*, III, 157), and under Goethe's influence (perhaps also that of Herder) he recognises ideas in art only in their embodiment in concrete forms. He is beginning to develop a distinction between symbol and allegory which is to be important for his *Götterlehre*, and of wide general significance. In the *Reisen in Italien* he also criticises the figure of Justice, blindfold and holding her scales: this allegorical representation he finds distasteful, for it is overloaded and unbalanced, and what unity it has is not in itself but only in the idea behind it: 'When in this manner the allegory contradicts and dissolves the inner beauty of a figure, it seems to me it has no place in the fine arts, and has merely the value of a hieroglyphic, not of a work of art' (*RI*, III, 91). Allegory, he maintains in 'Über die Allegorie' (1789) (*Schriften*, 112–15), is inimical to the autonomy of the genuine work of art because it points to a purpose outside the circle of that work. For Moritz, unlike the Romantics, 'hieroglyphics' have inferior standing for they are signs which belong not to the domain of art but to that of discourse, they convey a meaning quite separate from themselves. For the author of the *Kinderlogik*, of 1786, signs [*Zeichen*] and things [*Sachen*] belong, as for Wolff and his School, to quite different spheres; but in the fourth part of *Anton Reiser*, of 1790, the melancholy description of Dr Sauer staring down into a dark stream concludes with the comment: 'For if any meaningful picture could form in which sign and thing were one, then that happened here' (*AR*, 333). As sign and thing become one, so allegory – a word used in Moritz's day in the wider sense of 'figurative expression' – is exiled from the domain of art. As for the word 'symbol,' the older senses were three: abstract signs (as in mathematics), emblems, and signs of religious or occult import. Though Moritz does not yet use this word in a new way (it was left to Goethe and Heinrich Meyer to do so a decade later)[44] the *Bildende Nachahmung* may be held to contain more than the germ of the immensely fertile doctrine. For at its very centre stands the concrete, real, irrational object, the symbolic work of art, a kind of *numen*, a microcosm generated by the 'creative energy,' speaking a 'higher language': 'The beautiful is a higher language' (*RI*, III, 185). All form, Goethe was to pronounce, is symbolical,[45] and for the *Bildende Nachahmung* form is the imposition of Wholeness upon the world of disjoined experience by the active power of the mind, the only source of completeness, and this makes the microcosm thus created 'symbolic.' And in so far as the act comes from a level profounder than rationality or even perhaps than consciousness, it resembles the process of the generation of dreams. It comes as no surprise therefore to discover that G. Schubert's influential *Die Symbolik des Traumes* (1814) refers to Moritz.

FINAL MONTHS IN ROME

The *Bildende Nachahmung*, though it has serious faults, remains an extraordinary achievement. It may be summed up as a richly problematical working out of a variety of aperçus in the light of Goethe's passionately active concern with Classical art. Despite its undeniable opacity and terminological uncertainties, it gives a fresh concreteness to that cosmoplastic intuition by which the empirical imperative and the atomisation of analysis are compensated for and balanced. This polarity is, as we have seen so often, the most useful of all keys to Moritz's work. The uncompromising quality which is added here made the treatise appealing to some, and on the whole the better, minds, but its influence was scattered. Some of the debate which it engendered will be considered in the next chapter, but we may note here that Campe, who at long last and much to his surprise received this manuscript in June 1788 instead of the hoped for travelogue, could not make very much of it. Nevertheless he resolved to print it, hoping to recover at least something from the apparent wreck of his contract with Moritz. Their personal relations had grown tense over the past year. Already peeved by what seemed to him unmistakable evidence of his protégé's double-dealing, and baffled by the long absence of news, Campe had written a complaining letter on 15 January 1787, but had overcome his irritation on hearing shortly thereafter, first in a letter in Goethe's handwriting and then in one penned by Moritz himself, about the accident and its consequences. An assurance that the travelogue was nearly finished, which was of course quite untrue, helped to induce him to make a further advance, though on 3 February 1787 we find Moritz writing to him that such a work was not really an appropriate undertaking, that the *Reisen in England* could not serve as a suitable model, and that the new travelogue would have to be substantially fleshed out with learned matter about Roman customs and antiquities. The letter, in which Moritz begged for more time, was doubtless sincere enough, for Goethe also noted that his friend 'had become aware that a light, loose diary could not be composed without penalty,' and that he was therefore turning his attention to a more serious type of cultural study. At first Campe seems to have been reassuring (the actual texts of his letters are lost), telling his author that quality was more important than speed. Moritz's immediate financial difficulties were accentuated by the failure of Pockels to make the payments he had supposed were agreed, but then partially alleviated from an unexpected source when Biester organised a collection for him in Berlin which realised two hundred Thaler. In mid-June 1787, after his return from Naples, he wrote to Campe again for money, promising to return home soon and according to the latter was sent much more than his request. When the same performance was repeated in September, however, Campe's temper began to worsen,[46] since Moritz not only still sent no manuscript, but actually announced his intention of remaining at least a further six months in Rome, in Goethe's company, 'since it would be almost impossible for me to avoid remorse if I let this opportunity slip of further cultivating my taste and increasing my knowledge ...' (1 September 1787). In places this letter makes painful reading: Moritz is afraid of being penniless, 'which would be a terrible condition, since I am not on such a footing with anyone here that I could decently tell him I was short of money, and I wouldn't tell Herr von Goethe either under any circumstances, but would prefer to endure the most extreme want.' There are those in Rome, adds Moritz mournfully, who have the good luck to be funded by princes, 'whereas I have to twist and turn in every direction just to survive, though that is a matter of chance about which one can do nothing but submit to one's fate as best one can.'

There is some self-pity in this Reiseresque complaint, but he must indeed have been through many dark hours in Rome. His behaviour may often have been casual and irresponsible, but the passivity and the dilatoriness were obsessional, and he really could not help himself; he never quite knew why he so frequently did nothing at all. As for the sense of victimisation, even the envy, these are readily comprehensible, and forgivable, in a man whose life had been like his. That autumn Campe grumpily dispatched a further advance, accompanying it with an injunction to return at once to Germany, or at least to send something to print. But Moritz seems not to have bothered to write again until April 1788, having managed to survive the winter by borrowing once more from the charitable Bergrat Standtke. In May, therefore, he received a stinging rebuke from his publisher, which so alarmed him, as he wrote to Goethe, that he sent the manuscript of the *Bildende Nachahmung* off to Brunswick posthaste. Campe received the unexpected gift with kind words, and seems to have striven to mask his disappointment, calling the work 'maturer' than Moritz's previous writings; but in fact he had only glanced through the first few pages. Its author now informed him (5 July 1788) that 'everything I shall ever write on any subject is in the treatise on the creative imitation of the beautiful. And after this treatise it will always be impossible for me to write anything superficial again, even if I tried to make myself do so.' This may have been his sincere conviction at the time, but Campe inevitably thought the remark smug and intellectually arrogant. Having come to peruse the *Bildende Nachahmung* properly, he found some difficulty in understanding it, attributable no doubt to what he calls the 'fanciful' [*phantasierend*] nature of some of its arguments. Book dealers and readers reacted for the most part negatively to it, and in December Campe found himself forced to tell the author that his book was not selling, and might have to be pulped. He took this occasion to warn Moritz that if he meant to go on writing in such a style then subsequent productions, for instance the much vaunted study of antiquities itself, would certainly meet with the same fate. Stung by these remarks, which for his own good reasons he chose to regard as a rejection of his literary and philosophical work *in toto*, Moritz wrote from Berlin (31 March 1789) that he now considered himself absolved from all the terms of their agreement, and offered to repay Campe's various loans in full over the next twelve months. Confronted here by what struck him as a scandalous breach of contract, Campe demanded the return of all the money forthwith, accusing Moritz of bare-faced dishonesty, and when he did receive the repayment he acknowledged it in the most sarcastic terms.[47] The dispute soon thereafter became public with Moritz's attack on Campe in the *Jenaer Litteraturzeitung*,[48] and the exchange of pamphlets followed close upon this. The break was complete, and although the two were eventually reconciled, this took some time (according to K.G. Lenz, Moritz apologised in the end on his own initiative, but this is uncertain).[49] In trying to adjudicate the quarrel it is hard not to decide on balance in Campe's favour. He was, it is true, an irascible man, and he worried about his money; but he had lent Moritz far more than had initially been forseen, and had proved reasonably forbearing when the *quid pro quo* totally failed to materialise (he had even provided a small additional stipend for the support of one of Moritz's younger brothers). We see him as increasingly aggrieved, and his businessman's patience worn down, by the suspicion that he was being deliberately led on with a string of empty promises. Moritz, while in Rome, is in his letters always solicitous, flattering and sometimes entreating, with all the signs of a bad conscience as well as the fear of abandonment by his chief support; in his later polemics, however, after becoming successfully established in Berlin, he turns haughty and disdainful, and stands very much upon his dignity as a freelance. His attempt to dissolve the whole agreement after such a time on the basis of so flimsy and subjective excuse is hard to justify, and Campe may well have been right to assume this act was motivated by Moritz's belief he could sell the works he was now writing elsewhere for a better price.

On 23 April 1788, Goethe left Rome for Weimar. He was seen off by Bury, Rehberg and Moritz, of whom the last was particularly charming that day, and helped to take the traveller's mind off the significance of what was about to happen. Moritz, Goethe said many years later, had never been 'nicer, wittier, more forthcoming than at the time of parting, when the postillion had already sounded his horn.'[50] After he had driven off, the other three hired a carriage and went sadly to Frascati in the company of Goethe's servant in Rome, Karl Pieck.[51] For Moritz, the most brilliant period of his life must now have seemed over, and his future remained unsettled. The rash, eruptive flight to Italy had borne fruit beyond his wildest dreams, but it had not assured him of an income. He was therefore anxiously engaged in negotiations with the Prussian authorities in respect of a senior academic post in Berlin, the kind of matter in which Goethe's influence might very well turn out to be useful. And he had every reason to be confident that his connections with the famous writer would remain close. Goethe certainly regarded Moritz as being in a very special category of people. To Angelika Kauffmann, to Bury and to Moritz (who received a finely bound Livy) he gave parting gifts, and had noted as early as 25 December 1786 that only those would be admitted to his intimate circle who were

on the right path ... I am ruthless and intolerant with those who meander on their path and still want to be regarded as messengers or travellers. I work on them with wit and mockery until they change their way of life, or part from me. Here, of course, I speak only of good people; half-wits and idiots get baled out at once without ceremony. Two people already have me to thank for their change of mind and way of life, three in fact, and they will always have me to thank for it.

He knew what he could do for fellow-travellers through life and was to feel that he had done for Moritz, one of these three. He had not altered the fundamental pattern of this neurotic personality, but he had assisted it towards stability, and aided it in its vital self-recognition, above all by bringing it closer to the sphere of real things and allowing it to get a glimpse of that creative, active temperament from which it differed so much.

In June and again in August 1788 Moritz wrote to Goethe in terms which recall a pupil reporting to his master: since Goethe's departure, he relates, he has begun the serious study of perspective and of mathematics, he exercises his judgment continually in the contemplation of works of art, studies his Livy in the presentation volume, and pursues the antiquities. 'When I come to abysses,' he writes, 'I hear your warning voice, and I draw back my foot ...' That he did come to them even now emerges from Rehberg's letter to Goethe of 15 July 1788.[52] Though, Rehberg says, their mutual friend is well, he worries about him.

When he wants to he can very well learn what he needs to learn, but God knows if he will want to, and one can't ever be sure how he's going to see things three minutes later. You know him better than I do; whatever he does, he gets into such melancholy broodings ... The time since your departure has more or less passed that way, and the worst of it is that when something doesn't work out as it should he explains why it had to be like that, as though that was the end of it.

Moritz continually avoids taking decisions, adds Rehberg, 'however, since yesterday he has decided, and really begun, studying perspective under Verschaffeldt.' But if his manner of behaving had not altered that much, there may well have been some change in his understanding. He probably knew better now what he needed to learn and what was missing in him. He had a strong motive for work, to satisfy those in Berlin that he was a suitable person for appointment at the Academy of the Arts. The development of this matter, rather than his relations with Campe, was probably what decided him to leave Rome in October 1788. The last major incident of his residence there was the long-awaited arrival of Herder, in the third week of September. Herder, who was in pecuniary and other difficulties and in a sour state of mind, was introduced into the circle of artists and writers to which Moritz belonged. What correspondence had passed between them, apart from Moritz's first letter written at Goethe's behest, we do not know. However, Herder seems to have been favourably disposed towards him, and found him among all the others 'the best when it comes to intellectual matters.'[53] But apparently Herder also took it upon himself to advise his new acquaintance to leave Rome, a place he himself could not get to like, for it 'makes one's mind go slack,'[54] and his subsequent correspondence with his wife, Caroline, in Weimar reflects an increasingly ambiguous attitude. The last account in the *Reisen in Italien* of an episode in Rome describes Moritz standing with Herder on 'the tower of the Capitol,' in the setting sun, resolved 'to enjoy every beautiful scene in life to its ultimate moment, with no complaint or grumbling that it must end' (*RI*, III, 283). But such objective passivity still remained just an aspiration, a mystic's dream.

6

Subjunctives of Success

Moritz arrived in Weimar on 3 December 1788, with the post-chaise, in exceptionally cold, snowy weather. He was penniless and ill-clothed, with 'nothing but a thin, worn overcoat, so it was a near miracle he hadn't frozen to death in the open carriage.'[1] But he was still, remarkably enough, in reasonably good health. Quitting Rome on 20 October, he had naturally dallied on the way, visiting Florence, Mantua and Venice, and exhausting the limited travel funds he seems to have borrowed from friends.[2] He had given no notice of his impending arrival in Weimar, and Goethe happened to be away. Moritz therefore went forthwith to Caroline Herder, to deliver a letter from her husband, and pictures and other presents for her children.[3] To Herder he had written warmly from Florence, assuring him, as he had Goethe, of his continued devotion to self-improvement and to responsible preparation for his future career. The garrulous Caroline, to whose correspondence we owe much of what we know of Moritz's first stay in Weimar, received him with enthusiasm, and listened eagerly to his news of her husband in Rome. The next day he was back at her house for lunch, regaling the company on 'ancient Rome ... and the papal ceremonies. Everybody listened. You have to hear him narrate, he's a truly excellent, sensible man ... I had such a delightful lunch-time; we were his guests and he the host ...'[4] Tributes to Moritz as a raconteur are not infrequent, even from his enemies, and this facility probably contributed significantly to his astonishing social success in Weimar. Very soon he was being lionised all round, especially by the ladies: 'When we women are alone with Moritz,' Caroline writes to Herder, 'it's very nice; then he becomes our prophet, and we are constantly learning something' (25 December 1788). Goethe told this same correspondent two days later: 'Moritz has already been here for three weeks, and everybody likes him; in particular the ladies, whom he has enlightened in all sorts of ways, have taken him to their hearts.'[5] Schiller also comments on this phenomenon, noting the visitor's especial success with Charlotte von Stein, who had previously expressed a great liking for his *Geisterseher*, and who now paid him the most fulsome compliment of all: 'How much he has changed my ideas I simply can't tell you. He's like a supernatural being, so pure, so imperturbable, and he is affable to everyone but still retains his dignified reserve.'[6] The picture here is practically unrecognizable; perhaps it was the resemblance of the 'younger brother' to the 'elder brother' as he had been in his younger days that Charlotte found irresistible at this time of estrangement from Goethe.

Nevertheless, the face Moritz presented to the little world of Weimar was indeed a new one. Otiose, gossipy and intellectually incestuous as they were, they seem to have made of their visitor the sensation of the winter season. They apparently found him (and the unexpected opinion occurs several times) a calming influence, a man of wisdom and philosophy. At Caroline's, on 4 December, he was introduced to Major von Knebel, with whom he was to spend much time in the course of the next eight weeks. Knebel was an urbane dilettante, an admirer and a translator of Lucretius and an *esprit libre*. After lunch that day he took Moritz home, where the guest sat before the stove in his ragged coat, expounding a theory that '*Ein*heit' (oneness) was cognate with '*In*heit' (within-ness), a conceit almost the reverse of Coleridge's celebrated misunderstanding of the word 'Einfühlung.' That same evening Goethe returned to Weimar, and immediately took Moritz under his wing. He not only received him gladly in his house, but bought him clothes, and may possibly have advanced him money (that he subsequently saw fit to recover 81 Thaler from the Weimar privy purse in respect of expenses incurred on behalf of his friend is a curious footnote to this whole episode).[7] To the painter Macco, in Rome, Moritz wrote cheerfully on 6 December: 'Since yesterday I have been here in Goethe's house where, as you can well imagine, I am very comfortable.' He now enjoyed the introit to everyone who mattered in Weimar and, most importantly, he seems to have made an immediately favourable impression on the Duke. Karl August's letter to Herder of 21 December comments upon the shrewdness of his mind and the intellectual stimulation of his company.[8] The Duke soon arranged in fact to take lessons from Moritz in English, as much as two to three hours a day, as Caroline claims when she quotes Knebel's rather surprising belief 'that Moritz has had a tempering effect upon the Duke; God grant that it lasts' (26 January 1789). Charlotte von Stein observed with a touch of acidity that Karl August must have organised this 'so as the better to find the way to the heart of his Miss Gore,'[9] an English acquaintance just then in Berlin of whom the

Duke had become rather fond, but we may just as well assume that these lessons were at least equally a courteous device for providing the poor scholar with funds – Moritz was paid a considerable sum, 175 Thaler, in respect of them. He was treated in fact overall with the greatest honour, becoming a frequent guest at the ducal table.[10] At the tea-party which Frau von Stein gave at the request of the Dowager Duchess so that she might meet Moritz, Karl August called upon him to tell the rest of his life-story, which he is said to have done, beginning presumably with the events of the projected, though as yet unwritten, fourth part of *Anton Reiser*. Remarks of members of the Weimar circle and their various correspondents (for example the Langefelds) show what a deep impression Moritz's novel had already made upon some, and he seems to have talked of it often, indicating, though not absolutely explicitly, that he and his hero really were one and the same. That this was still occasionally disputed is proved by Schiller's reference to it as a mere supposition.[11]

'He is,' Schiller writes appreciatively, 'a philosopher and citizen of the world, who never thinks of sparing his own ego if it is a matter of serving truth and beauty.' Of course Schiller himself was at that time anything but a fully-fledged member of the Weimar inner circle, although he lived in the town. Indeed, he found Goethe quite unapproachable, and felt himself to be an outsider. It is just possible that Moritz sought to mediate in some degree between these two, speaking in Schiller's favour to his adamantly reserved friend. But there is no firm evidence of it. All that is known is that Moritz, while staying with Goethe, paid several calls upon Schiller, and that there was a lively interchange of ideas between them. After their first meeting on 8 December, Schiller wrote to Caroline von Beulwitz praising Moritz's profundity, his seriousness and clarity of mind, noting that he affected the pose of the genius much less than in 1785, but expressing reservations about his unbridled enthusiasm for Goethe:

[Goethe] has made a great impression on him, as he does on everybody who comes near. But it seems to me that the effect he has had is a good one ... Only I'm afraid that he [Moritz] selects models for his own self-development, and excellent though his choice may be, and is, imitation remains an inferior grade of perfection. He talks about Goethe too panegyrically for me. That does no harm to Goethe, but it does do harm to him (10 December 1788).

The same criticism is repeated in other letters, and in one it is joined to a complaint that Moritz 'recognizes no poet but Goethe and one other ... Herder perhaps,' but by the standards demanded by this new aesthetic, observes Schiller, even Goethe, not to speak of Herder, would not make the grade (3 January 1789). He goes on to accuse Moritz of nothing less than 'idolatry' (2 February), a word he may well have felt entirely appropriate if he had once heard him calling Goethe, as was his habit, 'God.' Schiller's irritation is quite comprehensible, given in particular his situation in Weimar at that time, and Moritz's provocatively ostentatious cult of Goethe was to become a thorn in the flesh of many (in the later *Vorlesungen über den Stil*, it is worth noting, Moritz quotes examples of felicitous style from various authors, but never from Schiller). On the other hand, Herder for his part was annoyed with Goethe (and perhaps others) for permitting and even encouraging the younger man's behaviour.

What you say about Goethe, [he writes to his wife from Rome], is quite true: my journey here had made more apparent to me than I would wish the selfishness of his character and his inner indifference to others. Though he can't help himself ... His dreadful enthusiasm for Moritz is a part of it. Moritz is a good fellow, even unusual in the way he confronts his ideas and is compelled to do so. But in them there is nothing that is clear, nothing that is finished, and it annoyed me to hear what kind of creature the ladies there have been making of him, and the way they behave with him. Even in your case I was surprised you felt his conversation to be so lofty and new. It leaves me neither illuminated nor restored, and at bottom he is a cramped [*gedrücktes*], sick individual, in his thinking too which isn't for me; we're further along than that (10 February).

The intellectual judgment may be fair, but these reproaches have to be seen as part of a crusty, embittered attitude to life which dominates Herder's correspondence from Rome. Always a rather envious man, he was prepared to speak well of Moritz as long as the latter kept to his proper place. Caroline, however, had been too adulatory altogether, as she quickly realised. She had described their visitor as a man in whose features one could read the triumph of his common sense (and his good fortune) over his imagination: 'In his deep-set eyes,' she declares, 'there is a firm gaze ...' (5 December). Herder's immediate comments were favourable. 'So Moritz has finally reached you,' he responds on 27 December, 'and everything you write about him is true.' Thereafter, however, he apparently repeated what his wife had told him to Rehberg, a close friend of Moritz, contriving to give it all a pejorative slant. When it got back to this last he became, as Caroline writes mournfully (6 February) 'rather reserved' towards her. As far as Herder's views on the *Bildende Nachahmung* are concerned, they may also be found in this exchange of letters. They reflect quite genuine philosophical objections to the book, upon which he had paradoxically exerted such an influence. Moritz had read his manuscript to Herder, and the latter, preempting the criticism most widely heard later, now declared it the work of a 'mystificator.' He was delighted, he said, to point out that Moritz had not made of him, as he had of Goethe, 'a bright mirror of the universe; I prefer to remain a dark glass.' The *Bildende Nachahmung* was 'entirely Goethean, out of his [Goethe's] soul and into it; he is the god of all our good Moritz's ideas ... this whole philosophy is ... repulsive to me; it is selfish, idolatrous, lacking in sympathy [*unteilnehmend*] and desolating to my heart' (21 February). Herder in short found Moritz's system narcissistic in the extreme. Moreover, it was very hard to understand, as he had told its author. All it was, in the end, was 'a coat cut and made for Goethe, but – for that reason even more – all but offensive' (27 February).

In these remarks of Herder's, with their peevish and faintly *ad hominem* tones, we may find the beginnings of the legend that the *Bildende Nachahmung* is really little else but a restatement, cast in deliberately obscure terminology, of Goethe's aesthetic ideas, even perhaps an essentially sycophantic work. This also seems to have been the pre-eminent view in Weimar, where the manuscript of the book was in circulation during Moritz's period of residence there. Herder of course could not have been expected to admire a line of argument so one-sided in its concentration upon the creative act, the perfect work and the perfect moment, and so unconcerned, moreover, with history. Indeed, the imperatives proposed in the *Bildende Nachahmung* correspond more nearly to Nietzsche's conceptions of 'critical' and 'monumental' history than they do to Herder's utopian evolutionism, and Moritz has here stepped out of the mainstream of the Enlightenment (something he did quite often) into a quite different tradition which was beginning to flow. Schiller could appreciate the nature of this side-step better than Herder. He could also distinguish between the cult of Goethe, of which he strongly disapproved, and the reverence for the beautiful as an ideal at the heart of the *Bildende Nachahmung*; it is only the former that is, for Schiller, 'idolatrous.' He makes a number of comments on Moritz's ideas in his letters of these weeks. On 12 December we find him apologising for his somewhat critical remarks of 10 December, admitting that he is inclined to make precipitate judgments. 'A moderate and beneficient philosophy' has taken hold in Moritz, according to Schiller, and he claims to find similarities between the ideas the former produced in their first discussions and some favourite thoughts of his own on 'life in the species, the dissolution of the self in the great totality of things, and the results which follow directly therefrom about joy and pain ...' (10 December). He had given expression to such notions in the so-called 'Theosophy of Julius,' published in 1786 (though written some-what earlier), but despite his claims it is doubtful how close this comes to the doctrine of individual sacrifice which is adumbrated in the *Bildende Nachahmung*.[12] Having, at the end of December, obtained the manuscript of Moritz's 'brochure,' as he called it, from Frau von Stein, Schiller now en-deavoured to read it. He found it hard going, not so much because of any inherent philosophical difficulty (he had after all a clearer and sharper philosophical brain than Moritz), but because Moritz

has no firm terminology, and in the middle of philosophical abstraction he wanders off into metaphor, and sometimes combines his own ideas with words which have a different meaning. But it is packed full of ideas, too full, for it won't be understood without a commentary. It is not free of fancifulness [*Schwärmerei*] and Herderesque ways of thinking are very visible in it (3 January).

Schiller goes on to object to the exaggerated demand for perfection in the work of art, which no artist can hope to meet. All the same he was evidently much impressed by the book and remarked weeks later that he was still trying to plumb its depths. An influence upon the poem *Die Künstler*, which dates from this period, seems likely.[13] His *Ästhetische Vorlesungen* of 1792–93 contain a section upon Moritz's theories of the beautiful, in which he expresses his agreement with the main distinctions of the first part of the *Bildende Nachahmung*, but then adds that later 'he confuses the effects of our reason with the effects of objects, the Whole of Nature, which we can never comprehend, with the Whole of Reason, which does indeed always seek unity.'[14] The next section in the lectures deals with Kant, whose *Critique of Judgment* had by now led Schiller away from Moritz's line of argument.

What Schiller found difficult, most of the Weimar circle must have found impossible, though they were not ready to admit it. Charlotte von Stein, with whom Moritz spent much time reading Shakespeare and to whom he first lent his manuscript copy of the *Bildende Nachahmung*, found its morality of individual self-sacrifice for the good of the species hard to accept. Caroline Herder finally read it in January, and thought the distinctions between the useful, the good, the beautiful and the noble 'very true, and the rest about the creative energy also enlightening, just as I felt everything that follows to be true and fine even though it wasn't completely clear to me' (11 January). A month after this she was still passing the copy round, announcing that it had given her 'a comprehensive principle for art' (13 February). She had at least some grasp of these matters, and came to agree with Knebel that the treatise had serious flaws. Knebel raised determined objections to the theory of beauty expressed in it, maintaining that Moritz had failed to distinguish properly between the beauty of Nature and that of Art. He felt threatened by the book, for it gave very short shrift to dilettantes. He even produced an answer to it, 'Über das Schöne,' which Schiller summarily dismissed as a feeble piece of reasoning.[15] This the *Bildende Nachahmung*, in his view, clearly was not, and for a few weeks in December 1788 and January 1789 Moritz's ideas were the burning issue in the intellectual conversation of Weimar. Their impact was doubtless reinforced by the extraordinary performance of their author. Holding the centre of the stage with astonishing ease, Moritz pontificated, elucidated and advised, conveying an overall impression of experience, self-assurance and sagacity. Of gaucheries, during the time, we hear nothing at all. It is as though a frustrated minor actor had suddenly floresced into a major role.

Moritz delighted all and sundry by the sheer poetry of his expositions, so that we can see here developing a bifurcation of great importance for the last years of his career: these cannot be understood unless it is perceived that his considerable impact came as much from his style as from his substance (and that the two did not really agree). Something of the ambiguity of Classicist and Romanticist characteristic of his influence resides, in fact, in this very distinction.

With a quite special clarity and feeling [writes Caroline wide-eyed], he told us recently how that man alone can be a poet, artist and creator who can give his work perfection of form and a living structure .... No poet must ever work for effects; solely the entire, and not fragmented [*zerstückelte*] creation that he now desires to bring forth must fill his soul. He put it so vividly [*bildlich*] that I can't repeat a single one of his words ....

She then adds, however, that she does not think he has an inventive mind: 'but what comes to his attention or what happens to interest him, which is – in particular – art, he can reduce to principles so clear and concrete [*anschaulich*] that it's a joy to listen to him' (19 December). These *fata morgana* of lucidity and self-assurance, we may suspect, partly concealed the 'real' Karl Philipp Moritz from view, obscuring his most original side, the 'Reiser' in him. His audience hung in almost ridiculous fashion upon his every perspicacious word. Caroline, Charlotte von Stein and Charlotte von Kalb, for instance, were dazzled by an impromptu discourse he gave on practical criticism, explaining how his study of perspective in Rome had taught him to look for the centre point in a poetic work, giving examples in the cases of Goethe's *Egmont*, *Werther* and *Clavigo*, but humourously declining to do the same for *Götz von Berlichingen*; he and Goethe, he said, had found the centre in that work too, and had laughed heartily about it (Caroline to Herder, 25 December). A week or two afterwards he proceeded to the unfriendly act of a public dissection of Schiller's *Kabale und Liebe*, demonstrating to his own satisfaction that it contained not a spark of poetry (Caroline to Herder, 19 January).

Though the *Bildende Nachahmung* had already appeared in print, no copies could as yet have reached Weimar, for there is mention only of the manuscript, a situation difficult to account for entirely. Moritz was beginning to think of reviews, and the first of these came in the spring. In May Rehberg said amiable things about the book in the *Allgemeine Litteraturzeitung*.[16] Goethe's review, which Moritz had already seen (it was composed while he was in Weimar) appeared in the *Teutsche Merkur* in July. The *Allgemeine deutsche Bibliothek*, when it got round to it in 1790, lauded the work, calling the author a good philosophical intellect, and declaring that the concepts employed, though indeed they may sometimes turn into a mere 'game of ideas,' are in fact analysed and differentiated with an unusual acuteness and profundity.[17] By far the most searching discussion of the treatise, however, came from a writer quite outside the circle of artists and men of letters in which Moritz moved. Karl Heinrich Heydenreich, Professor of Philosophy at Leipzig, examines it at length in his *System der Ästhetik* (1790). Heydenreich was the first to point to the 'Versuch einer Vereinigung' of 1786 as the foundation stone of the larger work. He stresses the importance of Moritz's concept of 'the complete in itself,' which has not been accorded sufficient attention. But then he begins a well-directed attack upon the terminological distinctions at the basis of the book's argument. What, in fact, is meant by 'the useful'? If it simply means the physically useful, then what Moritz has to say about it constitutes a truism. If it means more than this, however, then he has not established any compelling distinction between it and the beautiful on his own terms. For neither of these epithets can surely be attributed to anything unless the *effect* of the quality is allowed for: 'I cannot ... consider anything to be *beautiful*, without conceiving of a being who experiences it, and if I talk of things possessing beauty in itself, I invariably deceive myself and introduce a whole series of deleterious explanations.' That is to say, for a thing to be beautiful, just as for it to be useful, there must be an outside referent. Heydenreich then goes on to make further damaging points: even should it be true, Moritz's definition of beauty as that which causes pleasure without utility remains vague, while the argument that a beautiful object must always be a Whole has not really been substantiated; and Moritz has failed to notice that in his own usage 'contemplation of the beautiful' implies enjoyment of it, which again situates the centre of gravity somewhere other than in the work. If, Heydenreich asks sarcastically, the cosmic totality can be neither perceived nor comprehended, then how can we recognise works of art to be copies of it? If, moreover, as Moritz would have it, 'thinking' [*Denkkraft*] is incapable of grasping the beautiful since it has no standards of comparison, then what could have enabled the author to reach his own definition of it? 'Thinking could not bring him to it; could it perhaps be fancy [*Schwärmerei*] which did?'

Kantian reservations obviously condition some of these objections, and they may possibly have struck home, although it is all but certain that Moritz never really tried to read Kant's *Critiques* seriously.[18] He does, however, in his subsequent aesthetic writings, concede a certain utility to the beautiful. But his treatise was, as he well knew, not designed to fend off professional criticism of Heydenreich's kind. And the same charges of mystification against him, and of 'Schwärmerei,' are found throughout, as is the blunt complaint that the book is incomprehensible. With the reception of this work begins the complicated story of Moritz's influence upon the Romantic movement, one long overlooked, obscured and underestimated. To some extent a certain revival of scholarly interest in Moritz in the 1920s and 1930s went hand in hand with a recognition of his importance for the genesis of Romanticism in Germany. The approaches of Oskar Walzel, Rudolf Unger and even Robert Minder are predicated upon this view, while Joseph Nadler described Moritz as 'the first who can rightfully be called a Romantic.'[19] Here again, as in the matter of the relationship with Goethe, we shall do well not to seek a final and conclusive definition of Moritz's historical situation and role. It will remain multifacetted and ambiguous, complicated by the double effect of the presentation of the ideas and the self-presentation of the man. If looked at impartially, the historical and philosophical ambivalence even of the *Bildende Nachahmung* forces itself upon us. A gospel of Classicism, it not only cannot preclude but almost invites a Romantic interpretation of some of its tenets. A number of the early Romantics were fascinated by it, the most notable reaction coming from August Wilhelm Schlegel. In his comparatively little known *Vorlesungen über philosophische Kunstlehre*, given at Jena in 1798, he offered a detailed summary of the book's argument (directly followed, interestingly enough, by a discussion of Hogarth's *Analysis of Beauty*).[20] The listener's notes in which these lectures were recorded read in part as follows:

Philipp Moritz: more a poetic mind than a philosophical one. He had a divinatory gift, though no Classical learning ... He wrote *Über die bildende Nachahmung des*

Schönen ... after he had busied himself with the arts in Italy, but not thoroughly, just from a fanciful love which does not know its object. His treatise is extremely original, proceeding at the outset in gentle steps ... then turning fanciful [*schwärmerisch*].'[21]

Schlegel's explanation of the idea of 'Tatkraft' and of the intuitive perception of the forms of the universe relates this to 'the striving after the infinite,' and the same point is made again in the more widely known *Vorlesungen über schöne Literatur und Kunst* (1801–02), where however he expresses regret that this 'truly speculative mind' should have wandered off into the mazes of mysticism. In the *Bildende Nachahmung*, he concludes, 'both the relation with the infinite inherent in the beautiful and the striving of art to attain to inner perfection are ... most happily expressed.'[22]

Thus August Wilhelm Schlegel percipiently observes the paradox, as it seems, by which the fountain of Classical aesthetic theory springs forth from an encounter with infinity. But here indeed, in the history of German aesthetics, two highways part company. For unlike the thought of the Romantics, that of Moritz was dominated by the urge to escape from the infinite, rather than to pursue it. His Classicism is therefore ultimately related to his achievement as an autobiographer, and this connection, when perceived and understood, tells us something about the spiritual autobiography, as it does about Classicism. To convert an endless, discrete succession into a circumscribed geometric figure, which is what occurred when the wanderer climbed high above the town and saw below him the shape of his life, this act of autobiographical integration is a commitment to the finite. Where Eichendorff's Taugenichts, some thirty years later, gazes dreamily off into misty blue horizons from the tops of trees, Anton Reiser sees himself, at his various vantage points (the Wartburg for instance or the walls of Erfurt) 'elevated above his fate' (*AR*, 307), a man of achievement 'who had changed his standpoint in the world by his own effort' (*AR*, 320). When he left the Graue Kloster, Moritz had spoken of having been like a mill-horse, forever treading blindfold in the same circle. In *Anton Reiser*, Part Four, written in 1789, he points to the way people walk in the identical circle of conditioned impressions all their lives, their imagination hopelessly bound; the milieu then becomes 'a kind of second body' (*AR*, 322) from which it would feel like a crime to escape. Moritz's most original insight, as I suggested earlier, was precisely the grip of the environmental moment upon the mind, and its endless repetition; the specification of this marked the beginnings of social determinism in the novel, but it also marked out one of the sources of Romantic ennui. The terror of the infinite lies not only in Pascal's 'silence éternel de ces espaces infinis,' it lies also in the monotonous flow of subjective time. But *Anton Reiser*, Part Four, speaks also of the possibility of escape from this circle, of actually changing 'the standpoint' of one's life. The symbolic gates of Brunswick make it clear enough that to escape, and to integrate, are closely related if not identical acts. The labyrinth is overcome the moment it is seen entire. Thus the circle as the symbol of endless monotony and enslavement gives way to the circle as a figure for integration and containment. The straight lines of Anton Reiser's menacing great wide world, of which lines there is indeed no end, except at infinity – 'wo der Mond und die Sonne herunterfällt'[23] – these may be bent into a circle. This the autobiographer does, as does the artist. The infinity of the circle is manifest and visible, but for that very reason the endlessness of things has been effectively contained in this microcosmic symbol, and this containment, for Moritz, is the paradox of the perfected work of art. In this sense, the infinite nature of the beautiful, too, is not only compatible with limitation, with form, but depends upon it. And this is the Classical principle, the infinite embodied in the finite, and so disarmed.

PARTING OF THE WAYS

Thus it is correct to see in certain climactic works of Moritz, in the *Bildende Nachahmung* and equally in the *Götterlehre*, evidence of a critical parting of the ways. We stand here, as Sørensen observes,[24] at the point at which the paths of Classical and Romantic aesthetics divide. Moritz's *Götterlehre, oder mythologische Dichtungen der Alten*, which appeared in 1791, depends wholly upon the insights achieved during the Italian years, and is in some ways a natural corollary of the *Bildende Nachahmung*. The dominant idea in this general account of Classical mythology is the formative power of the imagination [*Phantasie*] – here no longer distinguished from 'creative energy' [*Tatkraft*]: 'The fictions [*Dichtungen*] of mythology must be regarded as a language of the imagination [*Sprache der Phantasie*]. As such, they comprise so to speak a world of their own and are separate from the totality of real things' (*G*, 7). This view of the Greek myths, as developed here, possesses a comprehensiveness and consistency unique for its day; it perceives in them a coherent, symbolical representation of 'the mastery of human existence through form.'[25] The language of the imagination which functions in this process avoids all abstractions, especially the idea of the infinite. It eschews the notion of existence without being: 'with it, everything is emergence, begetting and birth, back to the most ancient history of the gods' (*G*, 7), and its creatures are localised, are neither everlasting (though Moritz is inconsistent on this point) nor omnipresent beings. Such are, indeed, the exigencies of the artistic process, and equally its fictions are not allegorical: 'To attempt to turn the Ancients' story of their gods into mere allegories by all sorts of interpretations is just as stupid as seeking to transform these fictions by all sorts of forced explanations into nothing but historical fact' (*G*, 8). Moritz's Classical aesthetic, in dispensing with allegory, tends to regard it as the mark of an outdated Enlightenment rationalism. While a true work of art must be finished and perfectly formed, 'hieroglyphics and letters of the alphabet' (*G*, 9) can be as shapeless as they like as long as they convey their sense. Mythology, however, is art, a 'meaningful picture' in the words used of Dr Sauer (see above, p. 178), but a picture above all. How absurd it would be to put the question: 'What does *The Iliad* mean?,' and it is exactly the same, Moritz alleges, with the myths. This domain of symbols, for ever separate from the real world and yet so close to it, has no didactic purpose. The art of the myths, like all genuine art, has no end but itself, and here appears the gulf dividing Moritz from the moralistic aesthetics of the 'Aufklärer.' If the myths teach wisdom [Lebensweisheit – a new term!] then this is precisely 'because teaching is not their purpose, because the teaching itself is subordinate to the beautiful and in this way acquires grace and charm' (*G*, 9). The world of the gods, moreover, is totally amoral, it is a sphere into which human principles of good and evil do not even reach. Its characteristic is raw power: 'Power is their main idea, to which everything else is subordinate. The everlasting youthful strength that they possess expresses itself with them in its complete and abounding fulness' (*G*, 10). Man is but the toy of this unpredictable force, as he confronts the sublimity of the gods, a sublimity like that of the rage of the lion or the venom of the snake.

Moritz probably knew something of Burke, and the concept of the sublime [*das Erhabene*] must, as it develops in the eighteenth century, surely be seen in part, like that century's doctrines on wit, as the recognition of an element in the universe resistent to incorporation in any rational, moral cosmology. The use of the word 'erhaben' here may therefore be taken as evidence of the context in which the *Götterlehre* belongs: amid the crumbling walls of Rationalism, it stands for the search for a new principle of order situate in the subjective powers of the mind, as the Leibniz–Wolffian derogation of the faculty of the imagination is reversed. This power, it has been well observed, was conceived of in positive terms: that is to say, as forming, creative, and active, and not just, in the way of much later psychological theories, as a sublimative release. When we speak of the compensatory fantasies of *Anton Reiser*, we must therefore remember that these for Moritz were of a quite different order from the objective symbols of genuine poetry. In the

Götterlehre, it is also worth noticing, Moritz offers an interpretation of myth which makes only limited concessions to an historical approach: 'overhasty historical interpretations' he specifically declares, need to be avoided; though there are points at which imagination does touch upon history, at which 'the separate world' of myth is sustained by that of 'real things.' Unlike Herder, Moritz could not subscribe to the idea of a total resolution of the problems of civilisation through historical progress, in which the creative forces would inevitably triumph over those of destruction and decay. He was too much of a social, and above all a psychological, realist to swallow such optimism for long, his empiricism made it suspect. What he in fact did was to take refuge in an aesthetic consolation,[26] in which the perfect moment of the creative imagination, the stasis of the formed present in art, replaced the dream of a utopian future. Thus his realism led him to an irrationalistic solution.

He remained for all that a careerist, though we might go so far as to say that, at least in his more melancholy moments, he did not really believe in the future, and it was his nasty suspicion that the moments of time, empirically perceived, would always prove to be discrete, formless and dismembering, without teleological sense, which most profoundly separated him from the meliorists and eudaemonists of his age. It also attuned him to Goethe's cult of selfhood, and situated him in a tradition of which Schopenhauer and Nietzsche were to become the grandiose German exponents. The forming imagination, as he puts it, 'avoids the concept of a metaphysical infinity and limitlessness most of all, because its delicate creations would suddenly become lost in it, as in a barren desert' (*G*, 7). The *Götterlehre* here comes close to defining itself, for it is also a whimsical tissue of fancy, a delicate and all but lyrical work, free of pedantry – as Körner noted appreciatively to Schiller, remarking also that it was full of resonances of Goethe.[27] Several of Goethe's hymnic poems, including *Prometheus* and *Grenzen der Menschheit*, are included in the text. What the book offers is a poetic survey of the generation of the myths in the creative imagination, an exposition unredeemed, of course, by anthropological knowledge, but nonetheless modern in its central perception of the unity of the system, and given some credit for this by Kerényi.[28] In the *Vorlesungen über philosophische Kunstlehre* August Wilhelm Schlegel followed Moritz fairly closely here, making a similar distinction between allegory and myth, but attempting to modify the exclusively aesthetic mode of interpretation by arguing that myths are generated 'in accordance with the needs of the people.'[29] Schlegel's dependence is a good example of the influence of what was to be its author's best-known book. The *Götterlehre* soon became a standard text in schools, and was reprinted ten times in the course of the next seventy years.

In comparison with it, *Anthusa, oder Roms Altertümer* (1791) is perhaps less central, but was also most popular. Based on lecture material from the first two years of Moritz's professorship at the Royal Academy of the Arts, it represents the ultimate outcome of the project on antiquities. In the preface to *Anthusa* Moritz advances reasons for the study of Roman life and customs which emphasise the continued significance for modern times of these models from the past, stressing the unity of humankind which may be discerned through a familiarity with them. Goethean tones pervade the book, for instance the assertion that only on the civilisation of the Ancients can be founded any notion of a 'higher humanity,' as well as in the criticism of 'forced originality and a limited and exclusive patriotism which seeks to originate everything of itself' (*A*, 4).[30] Establishing the Classical ideal of universality as a barrier against emergent Romantic nationalism and particularism, *Anthusa* in its discussion of the Saturnalia combines this ideal with an unexpectedly political, Rousseauistic thrust: in the Golden Age 'no state had yet been formed to lay shackles on the equality and freedom of men,' and Moritz declares outright that all the advantages which may have been subsequently achieved through the existence of states have had to be purchased at the oppressive price of 'the inequality of the classes' (*A*, 223–24). We must never overlook these flashes of Jacobinism, which are found in Moritz's mature works as much as, or more than, they are in his juvenilia; but they cannot be regarded, despite their importance, as the essential burden of his later writings. He never expressed himself in public about the French Revolution, a silence we can perhaps attribute in part to caution, but it also came from the fact that his main interests were simply not political ones. It is of course in the fancy that *Anthusa* discovers the key to the pious cults of the Romans, summing them up as 'consecrations of real life' and a 'religion of the imagination.' Like the *Götterlehre*, this work is also intuitive and evocative rather than demonstrative and scholarly. Its second part was completed after Moritz's death by his colleague at the Academy, Professor Friedrich Rambach, who found it impossible to continue the book in anything like the original style. He could not, declared Rambach, imitate 'the peculiar relationship in which, in all the works of the late Moritz, thinking and imagination stand to one another,' nor could he emulate 'the inimitable art, in his lectures, by which, free of all pedagogical vanity, he seemed not so much a teacher as a student along with the others.' As for the subtitle Moritz had bestowed upon *Anthusa*, 'a book for humanity,' this had, complained Rambach, been retained against his will, and he could make no sense of it.[31]

If these two works were the only evidence they would suffice to show that the Royal Academy of the Arts, in the early 1790s, was graced with a profes-

sor more poet and dreamer than man of learning, who held the imagination
of his listeners, if Rambach and others are to be believed, by a naïve personal involvement in what we might describe as the attempt to evoke a coherent domain of monumental perfection, visualized as universally human,
limited, and yet free of all real constraint. In these works, and in his lectures
themselves, Moritz made his own particular contribution to the re-emergent
myth of the Golden Age. In their cultivation of this both Classicists and early
Romantics succumbed of course to a nostalgia which the Enlightenment, in
its smugness as well as its hopes, had largely avoided. We are reminded here
of Goethe's *Torquato Tasso* with its central lament: 'Die goldene Zeit, wohin
ist sie geflohen?,' and thus are brought to Moritz's important letter to
Goethe, written on 6 June 1789, a few months after taking up his new appointment in Berlin. Goethe understood something of his 'younger brother's'
true physical condition, and had no doubt been anxious about him; though
he was well till March, Moritz had in fact suffered a serious bout of illness in
April, as he told Duke Karl August on 23 May:

My state of health was so bad for a while, that I lost all real interest in myself, for an
existence without a future has little meaning; and serious physical disease is as
destructive of human relationships as moral disease is. For as soon as I myself feel
neither the courage nor the strength to go on living, I also cannot wish that anyone
else should take any further interest in me, I have to pass away calmly, without
complaint and with decency, so that something new and better may arise.

He now felt better, however, and the rest of this letter to his illustrious
benefactor is quite chatty: he speaks of a visit to the Crown Prince of Prussia,
of being urged by this latter to write a travelogue of his years in Italy after all,
of meeting with the Gores – 'they sent me an English doctor' – and of his
views on the English in general. Minister von Heinitz, he says, still comes to
his lectures, 'and finds the beautiful pagan doctrines ever more to his liking,'
while with Miss Elisa Gore 'I read through the first act of Goethe's *Tasso*,
which he has sent me.' To Goethe he then writes in appropriately warm
tones, apologising for his long silence:

For a while I have not been very sure of myself, and in that condition I did not want
to write to you; for we must only write letters of life [*Lebensbriefe*] to one another,
and everything must be of consequence. In this state of mind *Tasso* had something
balm-like for me, that turned however into something too close to death. Now the
green shoots have sprouted again, and I can breathe more cheerfully and easily, and
tell you with my whole heart how much *Tasso* has delighted me and given me

tranquillity and joy: tranquillity, because I see a point at which the most agonising and oppressive conditions of human life are transformed and perfected in the most delicate form; and joy because the point of perfection [*Vollendungspunkt*] has come into being so close to me. The clear small star hovers always before me, and everything else shapes itself accordingly.

These revealing words, in which we immediately glimpse the proximity Moritz felt between his own experience and that embodied with such intensity in Goethe's new play, are followed by a number of more detailed comments on the work, although he apologises for their cursoriness, telling his friend that in actual fact he is deeply involved just at the moment in the renewed study of *Werther*. In the figure of Torquato Tasso, as depicted by Goethe, he sees 'the highest intellectual quality, the most delicate humanity, oppressed by even the gentlest and softest of environments, and nearing its dissolution.' Tasso is a man who has lost his contact with reality, and who can be 'perfected' only in the world of art, of form [*in der Erscheinung*]. Such was the very doctrine of the *Bildende Nachahmung*, where the suffering of the individual had been declared ineluctable, for: 'The species is eternally at war with the individual, the sphere of form [*die Erscheinung*] with reality' (*BN: Schriften*, 88). Moritz comments acutely on the fine quality of the exposition in *Torquato Tasso*, the almost imperceptible subtlety by which the dialogue shades in great contours of life and fate, the harmonious totality which every line of the play subserves and the gnomic force of the language; but despite this objective criticism, nothing is quite so interesting as the unmistakable self-reference in this letter. Auerbach's statement, in his analysis of the links obtaining between Moritz and Goethe's drama, that the former suspected little or nothing of these connections, is misleading. True, it may have never occurred to him how directly he had contributed to the completion of the play, but he certainly did not feel 'no nearer than any other admirer' to *Tasso*.[32] For after all, it spoke of those things he knew so intimately, of paranoia, fear and social failure, and of the tragic awareness of the loss – perhaps irretrievable – of the coherence of the self and of the world. The 'small star,' the emblem of perfection, hovered just like 'a piece of that great circle,' as the *Bildende Nachahmung* had put it, 'in which our diminutive lives may one day be absorbed.'

How much Goethe saw of these analogies, or better, how much they truly influenced him, is the real unresolved question here. The sources of his Tasso characterisation have been well enough researched, and his primary dependance upon Serrassi's biography of the Italian poet long ago established. But the similarities between the psychology of his hero and that of

Karl Philipp Moritz remain striking. The oscillation between artlessness and mistrust, between avid clutching after recognition and embittered, psychotic withdrawal, the spinning of the circle of paranoia, the self-indulgence of the melancholic – these elements and much else were common to both. We have no need to follow Auerbach as far as his speculative parallel between the château of Belriguardo and the summer chalet of Bergrat Standtke and his Bergrätin princess(!), in order to realise that Goethe, working in the very private context of the transmutation of his own difficult relationship with the court of Weimar and Charlotte von Stein, was bound, when he got to know Moritz well in Rome, to discover a further set of approximate resemblances. Sitting at that bedside, he maybe slipped inevitably into the role of his own Antonio, with a mind before him to heal. It is surely worthy of note that, as Caroline Herder tells it,[33] Goethe, when working hard on *Tasso* in January 1789, made it clear he did not wish Moritz to leave Weimar until it was finished. Constantly involved with his play, he rushed off early from the famous tea-party (though it was after all at Charlotte's house) at which Moritz-Reiser continued his life-story, to return ostensibly to his labours. And in *Torquato Tasso*, over and above the psychological parallels, there may be other internal evidence of Moritz's impact upon it. The dialogue not only contains but in some degree structurally depends upon an elaborate manipulation of contending epithets, 'edel,' 'schön,' 'gut' and 'klug,' the first three of which are of course the foundation of the 'game of ideas' devised by Moritz in Rome. It is not inconceivable that the importance of these attributes in the dynamic patterns of Goethe's play owes something to the long discussions out of which the *Bildende Nachahmung* had also emerged.[34]

Be that as it may, we can surely say of Moritz that he understood *Torquato Tasso* peculiarly well, precisely because he had succeeded in writing the *Bildende Nachahmung*, which in a certain sense is the continuation of his autobiography upon another plane, motivated by the relentless need to understand, and justify, himself. Both works speak in different but subtly related ways of the failure of a life lived in the 'real' world, and of its consummation solely in a world of form, of an individual's suffering transmuted and justified in terms of aesthetics. Both stress the consuming power of the beautiful – 'das schadende und vernichtende Vollkommenere' (*BN*; *Schriften*, 89), 'Zu fürchten ist das Schöne, das Fürtreffliche/Wie eine Flamme ...' (*Torquato Tasso*, lines 1840–41); both investigate the enigma of *nobilitas mentis*, of 'inner form,' of that pure flow of the spirit of which Jeanne-Marie de Guyon had written in *Les Torrents*; both contrast the passive temperament with the active, and demonstrate, in differing modes, the consequences of the beseeching search for activity on the part of those eternally excluded therefrom; and finally both strive to balance a paranoiac atomism by a vision of cosmos accompanied by an ethical demand. The closeness of the *Bildende Nachahmung* to *Torquato Tasso* deserves to be brought out; it is even more striking than the similarities between the author of the one and the hero of the other, and it must be the case that the two months the former spent in Weimar in 1788/89 served, for Goethe, to complete the long poetic gestation of the year just ended. And yet when Moritz left that town for Berlin on 1 February, it was not *Tasso* which was in his mind but *Werther*, that single work of his friend's which obsessed him practically all his life. It was in the spring of 1789 that the significant piece, 'Über ein Gemälde von Goethe' (*Schriften*, 142–48) was composed.[35] In Weimar Moritz had discoursed at length on the famous novel. He had instructed Caroline that its 'centre' was the letter of 18 August, in which it was shown how 'Werther's intellect and feelings were too immense for his human nature, he had so to speak outgrown himself, and the slightest impulse, his love or some other thing, [would] bring him to his end.'[36] 'Über ein Gemälde von Goethe' was subsequently utilised in Moritz's *Vorlesungen über den Stil* (1793), and it deals not with the novel as a whole but with a single passage of description taken from the letter of 10 May ('Wenn das liebe Tal um mich dämpft ... Spiegel des lebendigen Gottes!'). Moritz considers the inner structure of this excerpt, pointing out that the picture has an outline or periphery [*Umriss*] (the valley, the sun, the dark line of the woods) from which the poet's attention moves downward and inward towards the 'centre' (the grasses, the insects, 'das Wimmeln der kleinen Welt') and then climbs again to a greater circumference still (the wide world, the heavens, the poem as the mirror of the soul as the soul is the mirror of God). The patterns of this short text are subjected to a form of practical criticism and are found to be topographically reflective of the progression of the poet's experience, a perfect mirroring of it. Such formal completeness, according to Moritz, comes only from the overwhelming urge for truth, as does such beauty, which would have been forfeited had it been pursued directly. 'Darstellungssucht,' the passion to portray, would have impaired the purity, the unbroken chain of responses, upon which such a verbal picture must, he believes, depend. The demand, once again therefore, is extreme and uncompromising: the artist has to stand before Nature in utter tranquillity of soul:

'But he who possesses such tranquillity of soul will usually lack the urge or the power to portray, and he who has this latter will rarely have the necessary degree of tranquillity of soul; that is why there cannot be many poets.' The true artist, that is, is one who possesses both active and passive capacities in a sufficient degree, neither the one nor the other being in itself enough.

Moritz quotes from *Werther* to illustrate Goethe's insight into the maiming of the creative faculty by the overdevelopment of the contemplative one.[37] He notes that this particular passage in *Werther* is perhaps unique, in that the 'passion to portray' may be found here depicting itself. In the manner of a more modern critic he emphasises the importance of individual words, especially the adjectives, and of details of phrasing, of the verbal surface in fact, but then adds that for someone to write like this a special relationship with Nature is required:

> In these moments at which such a description is to succeed, the individual consciousness itself must as it were lose itself in a co-consciousness [*Mitbewusstsein*] of the great Whole of Nature, as this streams through the thinking and feeling faculty [*Organ*].

The artist is conceived of as a vehicle through whom a tremendous power flows. However, the magical succession of Goethe's words, in which 'the succeeding impression never disturbs or displaces the one preceding,' is then converted in the mind of the recipient into an integrated, spatial structure, in fact a picture [*Gemälde*]. Thus once again we find Moritz pointing to the transformation into objective, visually apprehensible design of the infinite flow of spirit, word and time.

The empathy with which Moritz proceeds in this essay is remarkable, and as a piece of literary criticism it is unique in the Germany of its day. Its concluding section contains a paragraph of significant personal relevance, in which the author asserts that anyone who tries to create a work of art in this manner without having first experienced such a state of oneness with Nature ('co-consciousness') 'must become as untrue as someone who with an entirely commonplace and ordinary destiny still tries to compose a novel of his life.' These striking words belong to a time at which the 'real novel' of Anton Reiser's life, the fourth part of the autobiography, was being composed, and Moritz must have had himself in mind in writing them. By now he had become quite proud of his life, convinced that his had been an uncommon destiny. That he believed he was entitled therefore to write the 'novel of his life,' and to call it what it was, does not of course mean that he regarded *Anton Reiser* as a work of art like *Werther*. His own preconceptions effectively prevented such a comparison. For him among writers only poets, of whom very few existed, could be considered artists, in some degree like painters and sculptors. Novelists (of whom he certainly realised he was one) remained just novelists, a subordinate genus, as the 'Aufklärer' had always held them to be. In one respect alone Moritz might have thought his novel-cum-autobiography to be the equal of *Werther*, in its authenticity.

On *Werther* he became a sort of authority, and he used it as his *locus classicus* whenever he was expounding upon good style. He was never to have the opportunity to read Goethe's second novel, *Wilhelm Meisters Lehrjahre*, with which he has also been closely and convincingly connected. Some of the links here are more obvious than in the case of *Tasso*, and the interaction was perhaps simpler in kind.[38] *Anton Reiser*, and especially its fourth part, provided Goethe with an unexampled illustration and analysis of theatre-mania, which helped him transform his unpublished draft, *Wilhelm Meisters Theatralische Sendung*, into the *Lehrjahre*. That much is beyond contention. However, we may suppose that the really decisive impetus for this re-evaluation had come in Rome, when he had sat at Moritz's bedside and heard the sad and sometimes grim story of his youth from his own lips. Here he had found an apprentice, 'on the right path,' no doubt, but very much in need of guidance and training. Writing to Jacobi he was later to refer to him as a 'guter Geselle' – implying two senses, 'companion' but also 'journeyman.'[39] This alludes of course to the guild motif in the *Lehrjahre*. And Moritz may indeed have had an influence on Goethe's novel not restricted to his exemplary function as a victim of the obsession with an acting career. The Masonic or Secret Society superstructure of the book may also quite conceivably have had something to do with him. Goethe had tried to combat his younger friend's long-standing association with Masonry, but we must surely conclude that he was unsuccessful in this regard.[40] The continuation of Moritz's Masonic career after his return to Berlin is sufficient proof of it. From 1789 to 1791 he was 'Bruder Redner' in the St Johannis Lodge, and from 1791 to 1792 'erster Aufseher.' Both the *Hartknopf* novels (of which one post-dates Italy) are of course instinct with Masonic material, and in 1793 *Die Grosse Loge* appeared with numerous Masonic talks, essays and even poems in it. It is interesting to find the author of *Andreas Hartknopf: Eine Allegorie* nervously asking Goethe (7 June 1788) at least to 'leaf through' that book, should he 'come across' it! Possibly Moritz had no copy with him in Rome, but in any case he had probably not dared say much about it, quickly sensing the other's disapproval. These strong associations between his 'guter Geselle' and Masonry (towards which, as is well known, Goethe often wavered in his attitude) may nonetheless have played their part in the introduction into the *Lehrjahre* of the beneficent(?) Society of the Tower.

RETURN TO BERLIN

The two months Moritz spent as Goethe's house guest in Weimar in 1788–9 were possibly the happiest of his life. They were, however, by no means free of illness. Shortly after Christmas glandular swellings of tubercular origin became so agonising that Knebel was forced to drive him urgently by sleigh to Jena, so that one of Goethe's doctors, Professor Stark, could operate. Knebel's diary recounts that Moritz stayed overnight with him, and that despite the extreme cold they both rose early to watch the sunrise from the roof of his house.[41] The operation greatly relieved the patient, and by early January he was almost completely recovered. During the second month of his stay he spent most of his time with Goethe and Karl August, and certainly saw less of the ladies. His general effect upon the Weimar circle has been summed up by Nohl as that of an extraordinary combination of simplicity and originality, naïveté and comedy together with loftiness of mind. Such a blending of warmth of sentiment and intellectual concentration was felt as a rarity there.

In this sympathetic environment, in which his profound need for recognition and esteem was at long last fully satisfied, Moritz surpassed himself, in fact he escaped from a part of himself altogether. His external affairs also seemed to be developing favourably. Campe's letter, threatening to pulp the remainder of the *Bildende Nachahmung*, may well have not been received by the addressee for some time, since it had been sent to Berlin. According to the publisher, a message from Moritz reached him at the end of January 1789, promising that he was still going to honour all his obligations.[42] But he was actually not very much concerned with Campe any more. He was involved in far more critical matters, namely his negotiations with the Freiherr von Heinitz, who functioned in effect as the Prussian Minister of Education, although he did not bear that title. The contact with von Heinitz, which had been made more than a year previously, may perhaps have come in the first instance through Rehberg, who was on the staff of the Royal Academy of the Arts and had been seconded to Rome to supervise German artists receiving government stipends there. But it happened also that Bergrat Standtke, to whom it is clear that Moritz owed a great deal, was one of the two deputies in von Heinitz's office. Probably at his suggestion, a tentative offer had been made, in the late summer of 1787, of a position at the Academy teaching theoretical subjects: Greek and Roman history, antiquities and mythology. On 13 October that year, Moritz had written to von Heinitz expressing his pleasure, and asking for confirmation, but the Minister's reply had contained certain reservations: the Academy, he said, was short of funds and could not establish an additional teaching post; however the position of the elderly Professor Wagner might soon become vacant in the course of nature. On the other hand it would be mandatory that the person appointed should give instruction in 'architecture, perspective, and the mathematical sciences,' and he went on to suggest that Moritz might profitably utilise his remaining months in Rome acquiring competence in these areas, which ought not to prove impossible 'in view of your outstanding ability [*Genie*] and with serious and persistent work.'[43] He appended the offer of some financial support during this interim, and Moritz thereupon hastened to assure the Minister (1 December 1787) that he had in fact been developing an interest in these fields of knowledge for quite some time, because of their close connections with art. He then proposed for himself a stipend of one hundred ducats, so that he might devote himself fully to these studies rather than have to make his penurious living in Rome as a freelance. To this the response from Berlin was slow in coming. Moritz wrote again on 30 January 1788, and again on 21 February, requesting a firm offer of appointment duly approved by the King, and pointing out the financial difficulties he was now in due to his having been promised some support which had not arrived! 'It is enough for you that you have my word,' von Heinitz replied a trifle testily on 12 April, and he warned Moritz that it all depended upon his fulfilling the conditions laid down. A sum of two hundred Thaler was then granted for the calendar year 1788, during which it was assumed that the recipient would remain in Rome.

The outcome of the negotiations still remained uncertain. And Moritz may quite justifiably have feared that, in the end, he might be declared unqualified for the post, since he must have known that he was scarcely the man to develop a genuine competence in mathematical subjects in the time available. In fact, as we have already noted, he did not even begin to study perspective seriously under the resident authority, Verschaffeldt, until midsummer 1788. These well-founded worries may well have given the ultimate impetus to his long deferred departure from Rome. By that summer he had received no further assurances that we know of from von Heinitz, and no indication as to when Professor Wagner might be expected to expire. He may therefore have calculated that his best hope of resolving the whole matter favourably now lay in bringing other powerful influences to bear, which might be at his disposal, and it was possibly with this in mind that he arrived in Weimar. On 12 January 1789, no doubt with Goethe's assistance and advice, he composed a careful letter to the Minister: he had, he said, continued his studies in perspective and mathematics conscientiously, but had chosen to return to Germany since the latter subject could be much better pursued in Berlin; he was at present the guest of 'Geheimrat Goethe, with whom I spent eighteen months in Rome, and through whose instructive companionship and profound knowledge of art I learned a great deal which will certainly prove extremely useful in my future teaching.' Moritz proposed that as soon as the severe weather abated he should travel on to Berlin and present himself in person. But he probably guessed that for such a *coup de main* to be certain of success further assistance was necessary, and happily enough this was forthcoming. Duke Karl August was about to pay one of his regular visits to the Prussian capital, and so on 1 February 1789, at the crack of dawn, Moritz set off with him in style.[44] A letter to Macco (3 March 1789) refers to this quite glorious moment: 'I made a really magnificent entrance into Berlin because I came with the Duke of Weimar. But this was necessary too, to silence quite a few tongues. In fact my appointment did run into difficulties enough, which have however been resolved by the Duke of Weimar having personally intervened on my behalf emphatically with the King.' Karl August's influence at the Prussian Court worked like a charm. On 13 February von Heinitz recommended to Frederick William II that the 'well-known' Professor Moritz be appointed to the Royal Academy, to teach the theory of the fine arts, and also to edit its journal,[45] at a starting salary of three hundred Thaler per annum. The King consented immediately, and on 24 February the appointment was promulgated. What voices were silenced by these events we do not know, but they doubtless included those of numerous practical artists, some high school directors and professors, and several publishers.

Anton Reiser entering Berlin in triumph in company of the Duke of Weimar! – this in its way, is a spectacular moment in German literary history, and also one of considerable irony, to which Moritz was not insensible. If ever rashness was rewarded and undutiful behaviour went unpunished, this must have seemed to many observers to be the conspicuous occasion. Moritz was certainly now far better off than he would have been had he submitted to Büsching two-and-a-half years earlier, and remained to teach his classes at the Graue Kloster. No longer a 'mill-horse,' treading his daily round, he was suddenly accorded the opportunity of cutting a splendid public figure. And it was a chance which he seized. At that particular time the Royal Academy of the Arts, almost a century old, was entering on a period of florescence.[46] The new monarch was gradually being persuaded by von Heinitz to divert greater resources to its support than it had ever enjoyed before. Its staff was on the increase, and the celebrated engraver Daniel Chodowiecki (1726–1801), whose illustrations adorn several of Moritz's books, had just become its deputy director. Its purpose was twofold: to train practical artists, and to present new work to the public. In 1788 the Academy had begun to publish its *Monats-Schrift*, and in 1789 Moritz became editor of this journal. In 1790 he took over from August Riem as secretary of the Academy, and performed these duties in parallel with his academic ones. For the rest of his life he was the person responsible for all exhibitions and presentations, and he seems on the scanty evidence we have to have worked hard and to have done what he could to modernise the institution in various ways. 'The young artists,' he wrote to Goethe (6 June 1789), 'pay attention at my lectures – if only their teachers, the old artists, were worth something.' In the matter of criticism and taste he felt it was his duty to separate the wheat from the chaff. That meant upholding a determinedly Classical aesthetic, which he did with Romantic bravado. Both these things were new in Berlin, the citadel of Enlightenment with its moralistic and allegorical tendencies in the arts. Moritz was of course himself exposed to the inevitable and not irrelevant charge that he was not a practising artist, and that therefore his ideas were nothing but 'theoretical talk.' Such attacks struck home more cruelly than his critics may have realized, and he was sometimes thrown into one of his depressions on this account.[47] But his rapid achievement of fame and influence was not impeded thereby.

The intellectual style of the *Götterlehre* and of *Anthusa* is complemented in more lurid fashion by Moritz's platform performance, of which we have several reports. In 1789 and 1790 his lectures at the Academy became a great event in the cultural life of the city, if not *the* great event. He discoursed mainly on Roman antiquities, on aesthetic theory, and on forms of practical criticism, to an audience certainly more distinguished than that which had attended his earliest lectures on painting almost a decade before. Sometimes he organised his presentations as a private enterprise outside the Academy's framework – in 1790, for example, he lectured on the contents of the Königliche Gemäldegalerie, selling tickets for the series from his own house and falling foul of the Royal Gallery Inspector, Puhlmann.[48] Whatever instruction he may have offered the art students, we can be sure that it was not particularly technical. And it was his public lectures, commonly given on Sundays,[49] which brought him fame. These were exceptionally well attended, von Heinitz himself being generally present as well as a number of courtiers and (which was unusual in those days) a bevy of ladies. His style of delivery was always decidedly colourful and histrionic. The lecturer's manner is described by an unsympathetic observer as 'charming but often, from lack of proper preparation, too long-winded, and frequently slipping into the trivial [*das Tändelnde*] and the playful ... his students declare that they listened to him with great pleasure but – picked up only vague ideas ...'[50] Among those who sat at his feet were several later to become eminent, including Tieck and Wackenroder, then both schoolboys at Gedike's Friedrichs-Werdersche Gymnasium, and the brothers Humboldt. Tieck's initial enthusiasm for Moritz, which was to turn into a sharply negative attitude, has already been mentioned. To Moritz's influence on Wachenroder we shall also return briefly in the final chapter. But the earliest, and most informative, account of Moritz's Academy lectures is found in Alexander von Humboldt's letter to Wegener, Moritz's erstwhile pupil at the Kölnische Gymnasium:

Moritz is anyway in Berlin – at least until he goes tramping off again – and in fact appointed to the Academy ... He is still the same man, a true genius, a true eccentric. Only his external appearance has changed. He always wears his hair in a queue and has silk stockings on. He has started giving his course in the rooms of the Academy. He has fifteen or twenty of the most distinguished ladies in his audience. Minister Heinitz, Graf Neal and most of the people from the court never miss a lecture. The course is certainly the most brilliant being given anywhere in Germany. I went once. His delivery is noble, fluent and all too eloquent. But the material. What an enormous mixture of the most brilliant *errors* ...[51]

Observant people were clearly not altogether taken in by the new pose, which included the role developed in Weimar of mature classicist and wordly wise scholar. But while they may have been quick to notice the quirks of the old Moritz through the façade, they may not always have readily understood the ideas of the new. Alexander von Humboldt goes on to make fun of some of the content of the lectures, in particular the notion, figuring prominently in the second half of the *Bildende Nachahmung*, of the absorption of lower forms of existence by higher, more integrated forms. 'A real meal of monads,' he sums up sarcastically, but he does add that there are also 'many acute and genuine flashes of genius. However little Moritz's principles of beauty appeal to me I like listening to him. His eloquence is captivating and his brilliant period has now arrived.' It had indeed, but it was in some sense the brilliance of the frustrated actor which finally burst forth here in such a *feu de joie*. As Christoph Friedrich Rinck bore useful witness to the emergent public persona of Moritz in 1783–4, so now another traveller, this time a Russian, Nicolai Mihailovitch Karamsin, fills out his image in his time of short-lived glory. Karamsin's letters, which played a considerable part in introducing western European literature to Russia, contain an account of several days spent in Berlin and Potsdam in the summer of 1789.

'"Take me to Moritz," I said to my servant today. "Who's Moritz?" "Who's Moritz? Philipp Moritz, the writer, the philosopher, the pedagogue, the psychologist." '[52] There may well have been some who really thought him a polymath. As for Karamsin, he had been first impressed by *Anton Reiser*, which he compares with Rousseau's *Confessions*. He had also enjoyed reading the *Reisen in England*. Imagining the author of these works to be a man of forty or more, he was astonished to find 'a mere thirty-year-old, with fresh red cheeks. ' "You're as young as this," I told him, "and have done so many splendid things already?" He smiled.' There then ensued a conversation of some interest. Moritz said: 'Nothing is pleasanter than travel. All the ideas obtained from books can be called dead in comparison with those acquired through seeing [*Anschauung*].' Listening to Karamsin recite a few lines in Russian, he observed that one day it might be necessary to learn that language too, if something of quality should first be written in it (at which Karamsin sighed). Calling German 'better' than all other modern languages, Moritz explained this was because no other possessed so many 'versinnlichende Wörter' ('words which give body to ideas'), an odd expression showing once again how his mind circled the problem of the symbol, and forming links between his linguistic researches and his theories on art. Karamsin praises his host as a great authority on the German tongue, and refers to the essays published in the *Magazin zur Erfahrungsseelenkunde*. Forced to listen to an account of the quarrel with Campe, which had just become spectacularly public, Karamsin noted Moritz's claim that he had behaved moderately, and had abandoned an initial replique couched in Campe's 'own tones.'[53] German writers, Karamsin reflected, seemed to be queer fellows on the whole; there was scarcely a single one not engaged in some brawl or other, to the amusement of the educated public.

Of Moritz's lectures during this period no record has survived, which is a serious loss. For we may be quite sure that they would have shed a lot of light upon the genesis of the Romantic movement in Germany. The mishmash of ideas presented therein, in von Humboldt's 'enormous mixture of brilliant errors,' was of course one factor, the other was the presentation. Moritz spoke as though over the footlights, his style was unsystematic, aphoristic, full of flights of fancy and echoing with the rumble of apprehended philosophical coups. His aim was to entrance his audience, it was (to use Brecht's term) a distinctly 'culinary' performance. The extraordinary thing is that this was in the power of one in everyday life so often gauche and infelicitous, so permanently hobbled by his own terrible childhood. We can only conclude that there was something here released which was deep and genuine and by no means all façade. And as for the world about him, he was helping to alter that too. That such a presentation could take place in these halls (even if it was a school for artists) meant that things were changing in Berlin. For one thing the cult of Goethe now at last had an authentic, passionate apostle established there. It fell upon Tieck and the Schlegels, upon the Humboldts and upon Rahel Varnhagen to foster the spread of this influential religion which Moritz had founded (at his instigation, very probably, Goethe was made an honorary member of the Academy of the Arts). And in emphasising the picturesque externals we must not of course overlook the singular importance of the Goethean doctrines which Moritz professed. These contained the quintessence of the Classical ideal, but equally they contained many pointers towards a trans-Classical aesthetic, which was to be developed by others.

In the final stages of the negotiations preceding his appointment Moritz had submitted, presumably at official request, an 'Entwurf,' or outline, of his proposals for the instruction of the students,[54] and the same file in the Geheimes Staatsarchiv in Berlin also contains an undated précis of his major aesthetic concepts which was to be published posthumously a few years later.[55] In the 'Entwurf' it seems clear that he was writing to order, presenting von Heinitz with the exact case for his appointment that the Minister himself had outlined: the idea of the beautiful, he says, can be fully grasped and taste properly developed only if students are trained to appreciate the art of Greece and Rome, for which not only a knowledge of ancient history, of mythology and of antiquities must be deemed indispensable, but also (one suspects the addition was somewhat reluctant) a competence in perspective and in the elements of architecture. In the other document, the 'Bestimmung des Zwecks,' which was probably written a week or two earlier in Weimar, there is a more personal attempt to sum up the doctrine of the beautiful under a number of heads: in beautiful objects, the universal principles of order, integration and form become visible on a small scale, and their degree of perfection is directly related to the extent to which they reflect the macrocosm; beauty, it is now conceded, may be useful, since it does refine our perceptions of order, and it elevates our minds, showing us the relationship between part and whole; to appreciate any work of art, which must have its end and purpose entirely within itself and be completely autonomous, it is always necessary to discover the correct 'point of view' from which its integration can be best perceived.

AESTHETIC THINKING

For a fuller appreciation of the development of Moritz's aesthetic thought after the return from Italy the main source must be the *Monats-Schrift* of the Academy of the Arts, which soon became his personal responsibility. In this periodical he published a number of articles. Klischnig quotes one of these, 'Grundlinien zu einer vollständigen Theorie der schönen Künste,'[56] in full, as being the foundation for that general theory of the fine arts which Moritz had mooted in Weimar in conversation with Goethe and Wieland, but which he never managed to complete. A careful analysis of this catechism,[57] which its author however admits in a footnote is only a set of working ideas needing demonstration in practice, indicates that of the eighteen principles here stated the last eleven can be extracted from the *Bildende Nachahmung*, and are in some instances textually identical with it. The first seven, however, may be considered to be new, at least in their emphases. No.

1 asserts strongly (conceivably in reply to Kantian criticisms) that the beautiful is objectively real: 'The genuinely beautiful is not merely in us and our forms of perception, but *outside us* in objects themselves.' Moritz then argues (Nos. 2 to 4) for the existence of an essential point, in the work itself, from which alone the eye can perceive its beauty. Nos. 5 and 6 allude to the problem (so important in eighteenth-century aesthetics) of the relation between poetry and the plastic arts, which he goes into more fully in another essay of this period, 'Die Signatur des Schönen,', while No. 7 states the Goethean principle that 'the most perfect representation of the most perfect human form is the highest pinnacle of art, according to which all else is measured.' The remaining tenets, though reflective of the *Bildende Nachahmung*, are interesting for what they omit. Most notably, perhaps, there is no specific mention here of 'creative energy' [*Tatkraft*,] and the thoughts of the second half of the treatise are not touched on at all. Moritz does reiterate, however, the distinction between the creative artist, who alone can experience the beautiful in full measure, and the recipient whose possibilities are limited to the development of his faculty of taste, and he sums up the task of art appreciation as 'tranquil contemplation of Nature and Art as a single great Whole; for what ancient times brought forth has become one for us with Nature, and united with her must exert upon us its harmonious effect.' In these 'Grundlinien' an attempt has clearly been made to simplify the doctrines of the *Bildende Nachahmung*, to dispense with some of its more obscure and contentious speculations, and to move towards an utterly concrete, unmistakably Goethean aesthetic.

The publication of this essay had been preceded by that of 'Die Signatur des Schönen. In wie fern Kunstwerke beschrieben werden können?' (*Schriften*, 93–103). Begun in Rome and finished in Berlin,[58] this is one of the most significant summaries of the new doctrines. Its primary assertion is that the plastic arts are superior in kind to poetry, for in them a direct communication of beauty is possible, which is both immediate and utterly clear. In beautiful works the inner perfection of nature shimmers on the surface, 'and as in a bright mirror we are enabled to gaze through this into the depths of our own being.' The source of this beauty (once again the argument is conspicuously anti-Kantian) lies in the object itself. 'The light in which the beautiful manifests itself to us does not come from us, but flows forth from the beautiful itself, and for a while dissipates the twilight around us.' The nature of the relationship between thing and sign, on which Moritz had been developing a fresh view in the years since the *Kinderlogik*, is now seen, in the case of beautiful objects, as one in which 'the thing is identical with its designation.' Unorganised, accidental matter [*das Zufällige*] is here contrasted to determined form, the essence of which is always separation from its environment.[59] Goethe's morphology doubtless provided the main analogy employed here – the contrast between the amorphism, the contingency of rocks and stones and the predetermined form of the growing plant – just as Herder is surely the source for the claim that the highest manifestation of human nature is the use of language. In language, says Moritz, the totality of things is truly mirrored (the expression he uses, 'das Umfassende sich wieder selbst umfassend,' is almost certainly an echo of Goethe's poem *Ganymed*), but he still distinguishes this from the representation of beauty in a work of plastic art. He finds that there is a moment 'where form and sound divide,' and words can describe the beautiful only indirectly, by leaving behind them traces [*Spuren*] in the imagination, traces in time which (as we might justifiably paraphrase his meaning) can be converted only *ex post facto* into the simultaneity of structures in space.

An important point is Moritz's insistence that words, when they are poetry, constitute description for its own sake, and not, as is the case for example in the writing of history, for the sake of what is recorded: 'For it is evident that in poetry [*Dichtung*] we consider things for the sake of the description, whereas in history we consider the description for the sake of the things.' In poetry, then, words themselves, 'together with the trace they leave behind in the imagination,' constitute the beautiful, but since they follow one another in succession what they offer is not the experience of direct and immediate contemplation, of 'Anschauen.' Only perfection of visible form can convey that harmonious sense of 'love and tenderness' which can arise from the most violent, terrible and disharmonious subjects, and which is the essence of art (a point Moritz made anew in his description of Raphael's *Battle of Constantine*).[60] The human body is the supreme example of visible perfection, for in it there is an utterly satisfying relationship between the parts. Winckelmann's description of the Apollo Belvedere Moritz calls damaging, for his attempt to enumerate the manifold beauties of the work merely detracts from the sense of its centripetal unity, while his advice to turn towards a realm of incoporeal beauty is quite mistaken. As he pronounces elsewhere: 'Art with its spirit must penetrate deeper and deeper into the realm of physical beauty, and find expression for everything spiritual through the body ...' (*RI*, II, 185).

The Classical ideal of harmony, of unity and of objectivity, together with the cult of physical beauty and the more novel concept of the autonomy of word and work – these aspects were the basis for the teachings Moritz put forward in the last years of his life. In 1792 Goethe read out to the newly formed Weimarer Gelehrten-Verein a little essay, eight pages long, which

Moritz had published in 1791. It was entitled *Grundlinien zu meinen Vorlesungen über den Stil*. Karl August Böttiger, who was present at this session, summarises the main points.[61] He was particularly impressed by two: Moritz's insistence that clear and interesting thinking is an indispensable precondition for the successful use of language, that the idea comes before the word; and that this requires also a central point of view from which the thinker and writer must never entirely depart. Böttiger's account provides evidence of the respect in which Moritz was held in Weimar; what he was delivering himself of in Berlin was quickly debated there; he had become not merely an authority, but very nearly an oracle. His Classical principles produce, however, some curious results. In 'Der Dichter im Tempel der Natur' (*Schriften*, 160–66), for instance, which appeared in 1793, *Werther* is praised contrary to subsequent conventional wisdom as 'a work which, amongst all those produced by modern literature, comes closest to Greek simplicity, dignity and truth,' its subject matter being 'the only possible epic of our times which would still ring true.' But in this fragment we may also note the view that German culture must find its resources within itself, and in the *Vorlesungen über den Stil* themselves there is a stress upon individuality, 'das Eigentümliche.' Moritz argues that style cannot really be taught, although there are nonetheless precepts which should be followed, for example the need to keep the attention upon a part without thereby losing one's view of the whole. The dominant idea remains the rejection of the merely contingent, the superfluous; the mere removal of all superfluities in itself suffices for the beautification of any object.

Moritz clearly believed that he had found the key which would one day enable him to develop a consistent and comprehensive theory of the arts, what Goethe had called, when in Rome, 'Columbus's egg.'[62] In his last extensive contribution to such questions, the *Vorbegriffe zu einer Theorie der Ornamentik* (1793) we gain some insight into the way he made use of his teaching materials. He examines here the varieties of Greek architectural style, discusses terms such as 'arabesque' and 'grotesque,' criticises the excesses of the baroque, distinguishes between allegory and genuine art, and comments upon paintings, especially those of Raphael. Some account is also given of the private collection of Minister von Heinitz. Moritz rejects outright 'the false doctrine: de gustibus non est disputandum' (*VO*, 67–69), and maintains that not just the feelings but also the understanding has an essential part to play in taste. 'Curved lines,' he says, 'have no proper place in architecture, nor for that matter in furniture design: 'The improved modern taste in furniture began when curved lines gave way to straight ones' (*VO*, 69). Buildings, like serious works of poetry, must not in his view depend upon surprises or sensational effects [*das Auffallende*], but upon rational harmonies. The Ancients combined rational understanding with imagination in their art,[63] and degeneration resulted from the hypertrophy of the latter at the expense of the former. Those who fail to control their imaginations, he declares, will inevitably be led off into labyrinths (*VO*, 150).[64]

In these last years of his activity, as throughout his life, there is much in Moritz that is self-contradictory and paradoxical. Invoking a coherent Classical aesthetic doctrine, a *lucidus ordo*, which was indebted all the same both to the Enlightenment and to the Sturm und Drang movement, he bestrode the rostrum almost in the guise of an early Romantic *exalté*. Still preaching even now occasionally in church (Tieck once saw him drop his Bible during one of his sermons), this Rationalist Christian and one time apostle of Basedow and the Philanthropists had really turned into a kind of modern pagan. A proletarian outsider, moreover, in his beginnings, a soft-muscled rebel and an empirical tramp, he had by now metamorphosed into an academic grandee who consorted with the aristocracy and in his eloquent orations evoked the compensatory vision of an internalised Golden Age. Afraid of the labyrinths he had known so well in his life, Moritz denounced them in art, but continued, as we shall see, to construct them for his own bewilderment in practice. Famous at last, indeed a name to conjure with, he remained the object of envy and also of ridicule, though it should have been clear enough he was a dying man. Shrewd in many of his insights, occasionally brilliant in their presentation, capable even – should the occasion absolutely demand it – of dignified behaviour, he was still naïve, even child-like in his private life to a near pathetic degree.

To Hanover, and to Hameln, he now returned complete with servant, horse and carriage, driving around the villages in splendour, visiting some of his former teachers and his poor, astonished relatives as well. He was an orphan, Johann Gottlieb Moritz having died the death of a philosopher in 1788. Two of his surviving brothers, Johann Christian Konrad (born 1764) and one of the twins, came to live with him in Berlin. By this time he was reasonably prosperous, though still wasteful and very often in debt, even after his election to the Prussian Academy of Sciences when he was able to enjoy an income of seven or eight hundred Thaler per annum and a free house in Spandau. Despite these benefits, he chose to dwell in a hut in his own garden, and is supposed to have disliked visitors; according to Klischnig, who is probably unreliable on this point, only he and Salomon Maimon were always welcome.[65]

During this period, for obvious reasons, anecdotes about Moritz begin to proliferate again, providing oddly angled glimpses of this eccentric figure in

Berlin life. Tieck once found him fast asleep in his carriage, which to the embarrassment of his coachman he had ordered halted for this purpose in the middle of the street.[66] Both Tieck and T.G. Dittmar have more or less the same story of the way he would sit in a fur-coat in an overheated room, bewailing sunny Italy to which he wished to return, and the latter even records how Moritz once doffed this garment to stride up and down his orangerie, '*in puris* ... exclaiming: what a man!'[67] He had acquired a pair of white horses, and when taken to task for this ostentation is said to have replied that he was an admirer of Apollo and entitled to copy him. When he said things like this, it seems to have been with a disconcertingly straight face, but the not infrequent episodes of withdrawal do seem rather posed, even more so than in earlier years, as though merely the obvious props of the proto-Romantic fiction (or drama 'lacking in unity of action,' as K.G. Lenz called it)[68] which Moritz had made of his life, a fiction no profounder than that of most other men, but a bit more garish and more naïve.

He is a fool [Tieck exploded angrily] that's put rather abruptly, but it's all that needs to be said. However much I resemble him, I break from him herewith, he's a poor, wretched fellow. He's not without brains and imagination, has learnt a good deal but nothing properly, has sensitive nerves and a tendency to hypochondria, so from time to time he has had feelings ordinary people don't have, but he takes a silly pleasure in always appearing to be an extraordinary man, which he has confused with being a great man, though in minor matters great men are often amazingly ordinary – so instead of really feeling things he is constantly thinking up things to feel.[69]

At the house of the conductor and composer J.F. Reichardt, a rendez-vous for the younger, the Romantic, generation, Moritz was a frequent guest. Tieck was introduced to him there.[70] Attracted to and then sharply revolted by Moritz, he attributes many of the vices he finds in the famous professor to his excessive psychologising, which seems to him to have resulted in the loss of any moral centre, and to have brought Moritz to the point of thinking that all things, including the distinction between truth and untruth, are but fictions of the mind.[71] But such a doctrine is certainly not found in the essays we have just discussed, and is anything but Classical. Tieck was perhaps trying to account for a marked difference between the ideals Moritz upheld in his teaching and his own observable behaviour. Wackenroder reported, baffled, that the great man was becoming known as an egregious flatterer, and that this was especially noticeable in his conduct with the powerful Minister von Hertzberg. Wackenroder found such behaviour 'even less explicable than that he can write grammars.'[72] To this Tieck responded that only very exceptional people can dispense entirely with the need to flatter, and that Moritz was quite definitely not one of these:

Once again I say I break with him: my way of feeling is close to his [indeed Wackenroder had said they were like twins] but not my way of *thinking*, i.e. my way of applying my feelings. M. was in any case little admired, such a person commonly has a low opinion of himself, he has recently become a Hofrat and things like that, and now he's small-minded enough to want to rise still higher.[73]

This is a severe judgment and, as Wackenroder felt, an unfair one, but it shows the effect which Moritz must have frequently produced. How different in tone is the letter from the Dowager Duchess Anna Amalia of Weimar to her brother, the Duke of Brunswick (3 November 1791):[74]

Vous avez encor à Berlin un homme que j'estime infiniment tant pour son caractère que pour son esprit et talent, c'est le professeur Moritz je ne sçais, s'il Vous est bien connu, moi je sçais, qu'on le méconnait à Berlin et qu'on le taxe d'être un peu fol, mais je crois que cela [vient] de ce qu'on ne le comprend point, je suis sure qu'il Vous plaira infiniment et plus qu'on le connait plus il gagne il a été en Italie et nous a donné un livre sur les jours des fêtes des anciennes Romains qui est très instructif sur tout pour ceux qui veulent s'instruire dans l'Antiquité et voir les antiquité de Rome (sic).

Neither Tieck nor the Dowager Duchess, however, was wrong. In this peculiar case the biographical truth does not lie somewhere in between these polarised opinions, it manages to enclose them.

7

Departure Intestate

The Prussian Academy of Sciences had been founded at the instigation of Leibniz. Under Frederick the Great its affairs were conducted entirely in French, and at the King's death in 1786 only five of the eighteen members were Germans.[1] In the next few years there began a process of gradual Germanization, in which the driving force was the Graf von Herzberg. Herzberg had been a Minister under the late monarch, and had submitted to his prejudices; now he was flexible enough to recognize that the Gallic bias could not continue, but his recourse was to staunch and often elderly members of the conservative Berlin Enlightenment, such as the poet Ramler. The election of such a questionable outsider as Moritz (with his Weimar connections) to the Academy could not, therefore, have been expected to proceed entirely smoothly. Moritz took the publication of the *Götterlehre*, a copy of which he sent to Frederick William II, as the occasion to press personally for this honour. Not being, at that time, in favour with Herzberg, who regarded him as the protégé of his rival, von Heinitz, Moritz asked that the latter intervene on his behalf. Von Heinitz thereupon recommended directly to the Crown that, since there existed no current vacancy in the ranks of the Academicians, Moritz be appointed a supernumerary member without stipend, and on 26 January 1791 the King indicated his consent. The next day, however, von Herzberg lodged a resolute objection to any such step: the procedure was contrary, he protested, to the Academy's statutes, since its members were supposed to be elected; moreover, 'Professor Moritz [has] qualified himself for the Academy of the Arts by his elucidation of fables [presumably a reference to the *Götterlehre*], but not for the Academy of Science, which requires more, and he is regarded as a very mediocre scholar.' Von Herzberg then compared Moritz unfavourably with the distinguished 'Aufklärer,' such as Nicolai, Biester and Zöllner.[2]

The proposal was therefore dropped at the very last moment, and Moritz fell into the blackest despair. His resilience, however, had never been particularly wanting, and out of his depression he managed to inveigle von Heinitz into awarding him a valuable consolation prize, the title of 'Hofrat.' 'Extremely depressed,' he writes to his patron, 'by a hope of mine *again* [my italics] being disappointed contrary to all expectation, I dare to enquire most obediently of Your Noble Excellency, as to whether Your Excellency, would be ready to make good *the wicked blow which Fortune has this time dealt me* [my italics], by an act of grace which fundamentally depends only upon Your Excellency's decision.' This language is very revealing, for it discloses beyond misapprehension the Reiseresque patterns into which he still forced the events of his life, while the overlay of sycophancy and careerist calculation is unfortunately rather characteristic. Moritz goes on to point out that in the senate of the Academy of the Arts he is the sole 'literary' member, and that therefore no one else should envy him his elevation, but it might be just as well to bestow the Hofrat title upon one or two others at the same time, so that 'the artists might not feel themselves disadvantaged.'[3] Whether or not the Minister accepted this bit of political advice is not known. At all events, Moritz was indeed made a Hofrat on 26 April 1791. Almost six months later, on 6 October, his election to the Academy of Science ('Philosophische Klasse') in fact took place. The circumstances of this successful outcome are obscure, but it is possible that support from other quarters, for example the King's influential adviser, Wöllner, may have proved effective.[4] Johann Christoff von Wöllner (1732–1800) had been one of Frederick William's close associates for some years. He was a prominent Rosicrucian, as was the King himself. Between them he and his royal master mounted an increasing attack upon the rationalist party, and Moritz and his impact in Berlin may have been regarded as water over their mill. Certainly Nicolai and his group were in retreat in the earlier years of the new reign, and the famous 'Aufklärer' did not achieve his election to the Academy of Sciences until 1798.[5]

Moritz's joy, says Klischnig, was now complete,[6] and he must have regarded his success as a great victory over his enemies and detractors. It is curious that in the two years that remained to him he made no contribution to the publications of the Academy (at long last printed in German), and it is possible that there were those within that body who endeavoured to freeze him out.[7] He did, however, deliver several addresses at its sessions, including his inaugural, 'Über die Vereinfachung der menschlichen Kenntnisse,'[8] and he participated actively in the committee set up by von Herzberg in 1792 to find ways of encouraging the cultivation of the German language

('Deputation zur Beförderung der deutschen Sprache'), the purpose being to carry out 'le grand projet philosophique de Leibnitz, de faire toutes les recherches et méditations possibles, pour enrichir et pour purifier en même tems (sic) la langue allemande ...'[9] Moritz may have hoped that his expressed desire for a linguistic Academy which could preside over the standardization of the German language was at last in process of realization. The committee's long-term aims included the production of a great dictionary, as well as a standard history of the German language; but there is a certain irony in the fact that Herzberg formulated these proposals in French! He felt obliged to reassure certain members of the Academy that it was not intended to Germanize that institution and its proceedings entirely, but in the winter of 1791-2 Moritz and Zöllner were the first speakers on the floor of the Academy ever to address themselves to problems of the German language in German.[10] Moritz's speeches on the subject are reprinted in the *Deutsche Monatsschrift*.[11] Language in all its aspects was the subject he apparently felt himself called upon to profess in the illustrious body to which he now belonged. 'To be admitted,' he declares in his inaugural, 'to such a circle marks for me the finest period of my life.' He aims to prove worthy of the distinction in every way he can, including some modest scholarly contribution he hopes to make 'especially in the discipline of the philosophy of language.'[12] We see him therefore turning his attention once again to that area in which he had done some of his most original work, although the emphases are now somewhat altered. The pursuit of wayward psychological theories gives way to the standardization and purification of the national language as the primary concern.

The persistence of the pedagogical impulse is demonstrated by the appearance of such works as his *Italiäniche Sprachlehre für die Deutschen* (1791), his *Mythologischer Almanach für Damen* (1792), and *Vom richtigen deutschen Ausdruck* in that same year as well as a *Lesebuch für Kinder*. The year 1792 was also the one in which he edited Salomon Maimon's autobiography and translated from the English (although it may have been ghosted) Thomas Holcroft's long novel *Anne of St Ives*. This frenzied activity was crowned by the publication of all three parts of the *Reisen in Italien*. His major contribution in the language area, however, was to be his *Grammatisches Wörterbuch* (1793), incomplete at his death.[13] This was a work in four volumes, of which Moritz edited only the first, which is fulsomely dedicated to the Empress Catherine II of Russia. This first part contains a relatively small number of foreign words, most of which, however, are glossed in considerable detail, and there is also some treatment of prepositions, articles and grammatical terminology, concluding with Adelung's classification of irregular verbs. Johann Ernst Stulz, who took over as editor after Moritz's death, makes clear in the second volume that the primary purpose of the dictionary is to assist in the 'purification' of the German language and the re-establishment where necessary of valid German equivalents. Such preoccupations had, of course, been associated for hundreds of years with nationalist feelings in Germany (sometimes, indeed, with xenophobia), and this was as much the case in the 1790s as it had ever been. The Germanisation of the Prussian Academy is obviously a symptom of changes which were to become an element in the development of Romantic nationalism. Moritz was a moderate in the matter of foreign words. He recognised that some were very necessary, and equally that the elimination of all provincialisms and archaisms would cause rigidification and loss of subtlety.[14] He tried, characteristically, to preserve an area of organic freedom while establishing a set of rational principles of linguistic government. His position on the issue of nationalism is also rather ambiguous. He cannot be regarded as a German nationalist in the fully-fledged Romantic sense. Rather, his position in the matter of Germanisation evolved naturally from his schoolmasterly concerns, his pride in the language, and his long-term preoccupation with the spread of literacy.

Moritz's Classicism in aesthetics inevitably reinforced his Rationalist view of the foundations of language. Here, as so often with him, concepts of abstract, universal standards conflict with a certain awareness of evolutionary change, and Goethe's morphological ideas often helped to mediate, though inadequately, between these extremes. Indeed, the idea of a work of art that, though organic and autochthonous, is nonetheless not only perfect in form but also universal in meaning is itself a mediatory notion. Wackenroder found it hard to understand how such an avant-garde personality as Moritz seemed to be, Tieck's 'twin,' could also write grammars, that is, he could not fully grasp the other's Enlightenment heritage, and his Classicism. In seeking a German as far as possible purged of foreign words, Moritz was on the same side as Campe, with whom of course he had become reconciled, and who had now turned his versatile mind to these questions.[15] Some of Moritz's utterances do seem rather bald appeals to national feelings, as for example these passages in an address to the Academy given in January 1792:

Just as our German forbears resisted bending their necks beneath the yoke of Roman rule, so our language shall today resist absorbing and tolerating any admixture of foreign materials ... [German writers are in competition in the struggle] to restore our mother tongue to its rights ... their competition and their united efforts for the moulding of the language will surely not be without result, as long as German love for our fatherland inspires us, and as long as a German king protects the German Muses.[16]

At the same time he could also write, a year later, in these terms:

National taste, national arrogance is gradually disappearing along with hatred and prejudice between religions and nations ... and where is there a nation which is more free of self-pride, which is more solicitous of absorbing what has been produced outside of and independent of her, which learns more foreign languages, translates more, is readier to consider as worthy of note what has not grown out of her soil, than our nation? ... and that puts more value in her humanity than in all those things that separate men from each other ... such a nation must, and can, develop itself to the highest point of refinement, as soon as it can in tranquillity enhance what is noble and beautiful wherever it may find it, as its sense of the beautiful through calm contemplation naturally unfolds ...[17]

This cosmopolitan idealism rests clearly enough upon praise of Germany, and Moritz attempts to combine his Classical ideals with a concern for independence and nationhood. A study of the *Vorlesungen über den Stil* provides further striking evidence of the unresolved dichotomy of view. For these lectures (only partly by Moritz) are perhaps the first comprehensive statement ever made in the German language of that conception of good style which was to guide generations of schoolmasters.[18] They stress the virtues of clarity, naturalness, liveliness, conciseness, precision and individuality, and finally of beauty, all of which may be attained, Moritz thinks, by carefully emulating eminent poets. But these desiderata are themselves a mixture of rational and irrational principles. The *Vorlesungen* insist upon the distinction between words and things: 'The thing itself ... is the real object of thought, in so far as it can be imagined concretely [*anschaulich*], without words, and it is therefore something more than words are ...' (*VS*, 29). Moritz separates the language of the intellect [*Sprache des Verstandes*] from that of feeling [*Sprache des Empfindens*], and notes that figurative images always involve the latter, for it is a kind of admission that words as such are incapable of fully conveying the nature of things: 'What we call rhetorical figures are actually the language of feeling, which lacks words, and which tries various means for making up this deficiency.' Moreover: 'The language of feeling ... differs from the language of intellect primarily in the fact that it does not dismember but it puts together [*zusammenfasst*]' (*VS*, 68).

Moritz recognises an 'irrational' stratum of experienced things which cannot be expressed by means of 'rational' discourse. If language shows its irrational face in its archaisms, its provincialisms and even in its foreign borrowings, it does so even more indisputably in its figurative rhetoric. The language of feeling we met with already in the *Deutsche Prosodie*, and Moritz held that it was connected with music. It is because of its importance that style, in the end, cannot be reduced to principles ensconced in explanatory manuals, but depends upon individuality, upon the insurgent self. Hence the pedagogical and linguistic concerns of his later years cannot be regarded as fundamentally opposed to the emergence of Romantic points of view; his 'grammar,' for which Wackenroder felt much distaste, his dictionaries *et al* are vehicles for his ambivalencies too.

The points of contact between the late Moritz and the early Romantics are indeed many. Novalis (who mentions his name but once) possessed a number of his books.[19] Friedrich Schlegel knew his writings well – the Schlegels, after all, came from Hanover where *Anton Reiser* was rightly considered to be a local *roman à clef*, and Rector Ballhorn was a close friend of the Schlegel family. Like his brother, Friedrich was initially much impressed by the *Götterlehre*, although later on, when better informed, he was more critical of its obvious inadequacies: 'Moritz would have written splendidly about the Ancients if he had known something about them; but he was near to knowing nothing about them.'[20] At first he also liked *Anthusa*, and it is evident he got hold of all the author's works as soon as they came out. For years Friedrich Schlegel was to wrestle with the problem of the objectivity of the work and the subjectivity of the artist as discussed by Moritz in the *Bildende Nachahmung*, and gradually he transcended the latter's positions.[21] As for Wackenroder, he found in Moritz's work and in his personality the embodiment of that baneful conflict between artist and bourgeois, art and life, which he went on himself to present so uncompromisingly in his *Herzensergiessungen*. 'The Sufferings of Poetry' and the Preface to the fourth part of *Anton Reiser* emphasise the futility of seeking in art a refuge from life. It is fair to say that the 'bad conscience' of the would-be artist, with its enormous resilience as a theme in German, and European, literature as far as Thomas Mann, originated conceptually with Moritz rather than with Wackenroder. At the same time, there is a most significant difference between these two: Moritz glorifies the *genuine* artist, while Wackenroder's Joseph Berglinger in the *Herzensergiessungen* (which was printed by Johann Friedrich Unger, the publisher of Moritz's *Die Neue Cecilia*[22]) is not a dilettante. Moritz is a major exponent of the dilettante problem which has been discovered to be a central issue in the Classical and early Romantic period, but he fails to question the right to exist of the artist per se. In *Die Neue Cecilia*, however, which Wackenroder had most certainly read, we find presented the inevitability of the conflict between an art which is exclusive and indeed sacred, and the materialism of a profane and contemptuous world. Wackenroder's Berglinger is an artist much more inward in his nature than the sketchy figures drawn by Moritz in his last, unfinished, novel, and he is not a plastic artist, as they are, but a musician; however, music is mentioned in *Die Neue Cecilia* at least, and is conspicuously important in *Andreas Hartknopf*.

When Wackenroder writes of a 'language of art,' he is certainly thinking of something close to what is called, in the *Götterlehre*, the 'language of the imagination' (*Sprache der Phantasie*), and not far from the 'language of feeling.'[23] There are in fact passages in the *Reisen in Italien* which presage Wackenroder almost word for word, for instance the reflections upon Raphael's skull: 'Sacred is that organ, in which and through which such things could be created! The very speech of the divine glowed within it, and its remains are to be revered' (*RI*, I, 215). Moritz, in his more elevated flights of fancy, envisaged as we have noted already a 'higher language' (*RI*, III, 185), a symbolic tongue which would entirely overcome the inadequacies of language of the ordinary kind. Though he does not use the word 'hieroglyphic' in the Romantic sense, anymore than he does the word 'symbol,' his essay 'Die Signatur des Schönen' implies in its title a proximity to the occult tradition as filtered through Jacob Böhme, and Moritz does indeed invoke the occult language of Nature: 'Is not the fruit, besides its existence for itself also a sign, to the reflective and enquiring intellect, of the whole inner growth of the tree upon which it ripens? ... thus everything around it becomes a sign; it acquires meaning, it turns into language.' This seems far enough from the realms of the *Grammatisches Wörterbuch*, and it is perhaps closer to the mainstream of Moritz's influence, if not of his mind. His importance for the transmission, even for the elaboration of a numinous vocabulary in German literature in the pre-Romantic era is very considerable, as Langen has observed.[24] But as the vast wave of Romanticism rolled onward this source was largely forgotten.

MYSTICISM AND CURE

If the concern with language lies at the very centre of Karl Philipp Moritz's intellectual activity, then it is perhaps because here, as nowhere else, the paradoxical tendencies of his mind (and of his age) converge. Language is a matter which links pedagogue and popular philosopher, psychologist, artist and mystic. The vehicle of all ratiocination, it is in its nature both the object of deduction and also, with Moritz, of inductive investigation; its games disrupt the sphere of the logical and open up a dimension of aleatory truth; its structures and its vocabulary disclose the presence of an unconscious mind, but also imply a traditional domain of forms, while in its potential autonomy it can escape from all threads of external reference and become a microcosm. Yet language is also the simple basis of all social intercourse and thus of the common humanity of man; by teaching it, by spreading its literate use, it is possible to serve society in a modest but genuinely practical way. Such combinations of logical, mystical and pragmatic features could also be found in one or two other areas in which Moritz was involved, specifically in Freemasonry. His own Lodge – St Johannis zur Beständigkeit – had strong sentimentalist inclinations, but it placed due stress upon external activity: 'An unselfish, active man who is as little restricted as possible in his undertakings, is a Freemason' (*LP*, 26). Some of the Masonic doctrines to which Moritz subscribed are to be found stated in *Die Grosse Loge, oder der Freimaurer mit Wage und Senkblei* (1793), a collection of material for the most part of direct Masonic origin, upon which Klischnig expanded by adding several pieces when he republished it, after the author's death, as *Launen und Phantasien von Karl Philipp Moritz* (1796). This book has upon its title page a sphinx and other mysterious emblems. But on the whole, German Masonry, in the early 1790s, was a relatively sober, rationalistically inclined movement, although in this period of increasing reaction the Rosicrucians, who were far from being that, were rapidly gaining ground at its expense. Sharp critics of the Secret Societies, such as Nicolai, Biester and Gedike, did not distinguish very much between them, nor of course did the public in general.[25] Moritz's Masonry, which had much to do with the symbolism of his later works, can only have served to separate him still further from the camp of the arch-'Aufklärer.'

Masonry certainly influenced the development and formulation of his social attitudes, especially his stress upon the value of the individual and his criticism of a system in which some men seem to be merely the 'tools' of others. But it also helped to codify his stoicism, conditioned as this was by the experience of his early childhood. The *Launen und Phantasien*, taken as a whole, display a mind which tended to see the course of human life as a matter of blind chance, the only answer to which lies in resignation and non-attachment.[26] In these short essays, occasional pieces, and fragments of talks given at the Lodge, steadfastness in the face of misfortune and pain is the perpetual theme; what must be achieved is 'not a slothful calm, but a firm resignation ... ready for any successes and all the more active in the face of them, proceeding along the path of life and its steep abysses without terror or fear' (*LP*, 231). If effective, altruistic activity is regarded as the loftiest virtue, this is founded nonetheless upon self-possession in the face of death (*LP*, 31). 'Mors ultima linea rerum est' is the motto with which this volume concludes, and if the language is cliché-ridden, there is beneath it an authenticity of experience which *Anton Reiser* is sufficient to validate. Bitter though it may be, submission to the inevitable provides the only 'secure fortress,' from which the contemplative observer may watch the eventual resolution of all 'monstrous dissonances in general harmony,' for the good and the perfect do indeed exist and are everlasting: 'Should these sweet thoughts, however, themselves be only a dream, I still do not succumb, for I have learnt, when all things around me crumble, to withdraw into the moment of my existence' (*LP*, 121-2, and *Schriften*, 28)[27]

Jeanne-Marie de Guyon had said things much like this, but with a passionate sense of the Divine Love, a yearning for abasement and a recognition of the nothingness of the self which is not found in the mature writings of Moritz. He speaks after all of 'the moment of my existence,' not, as she does, of a 'désir de mourir à tout.'[28] Though he remained profoundly in the grip of Quietistically conditioned patterns of response to the very end of his days, he sought at least to give his life some quality of practical utility and rational ethical coherence. While in Rome he was led to a much more positive evaluation of the sphere of material things, and seemed to be done with asceticism and ideas of world-denial. Upon his return from Italy, however, he not only went back to the Masons but applied himself again to a consideration of mysticism, as though in order to reach a final and systematic view of it. 'If there is anything,' we find him writing in 'Über Mystik' (*Mag*, viii, 3, 75–76 and *Schriften*, 134), 'that deserves to be examined psychologically, it is the teachings of mysticism, which have always had such an astonishing influence, and still do, upon the minds of men.' He finds the phenomenon especially interesting because the higher forms of mysticism operate in a region beyond the imagination, seeking to dispel all mental images to make room for 'the true light.' He is thinking very likely of Nicolai but certainly of Pockels when he says that such things may not simply be dismissed out of hand, although it seems clear to his scientific intelligence that mysticism cannot possibly be well-founded, 'because it does not presuppose the other real kinds of human knowledge and science but pre-empts the outcome from the start.' Moritz sums up mysticism, in a few pregnant lines, as

a metaphysic without physics – a something that hovers and flickers [*schwebt und gaukelt*] above an abyss, but remains all the same as something that delicate sensibilities like to attach themselves to, because they are nervous of working their way through the coarser nature of wordly things; because they are crushed [*gedrückt*] by mankind's masses but now (can) rediscover themselves suddenly isolated in a lovely condition of loneliness.

Mystics, that is, are often afraid of people and life. The *Denkwürdigkeiten* of 1788 contain the subversive observation that his own impulses towards virtue and religion tended to arise while he was ill and to disappear as soon as his health returned (*D*, 11, ii, 6–7). The tone and the attitudes with which Moritz writes of mysticism in these later years are sceptical, and scientific: mysticism can have no ultimate foundation, but it is an undoubted phenomenon of human nature and society, and it needs to be properly understood. 'Über Mystik' is followed by the first instalment of the 'Mystische Briefe des Herrn von F. ...' (*Mag*, viii, 3, 53–74), which Moritz introduces as 'interesting for the psychologist in more than one respect.' It is worth noting that these letters of Fleischbein's to Johann Gottlieb Moritz, while stuffed with quietistic sermonizing, are neither fanatical nor absurdly eccentric, but temperate, friendly and humane. Moritz presents them in a light not entirely unfavourable, as he also does the excerpts he publishes from Mme de Guyon's autobiography. This latter work, he declares, exhibits a condition of mind that, 'in so far as it was delusion, certainly deserves closer investigation *as a delusion*' (*Mag*, vii, 3, 83). Fleischbein's letters had no doubt come into his possession on the death of his father, and he now felt it appropriate to publish an anonymous account of Johann Gottlieb's life. This is 'the case of a man who from his thirtieth to his fifty-fourth year was a keen mystic, but who later gradually moved away from this, and from his sixtieth to his sixty-fourth year was able to live happily, free of any prejudices' (*Mag*, viii, 3, 114). The 'cure' of Johann Gottlieb Moritz, we are informed, was brought about by his disappointment in the results of mystical practice. At the age of 54, some time after Fleischbein's death, Johann Gottlieb had apparently undertaken a journey to visit some of those who belonged to his sect, and had discovered that not one of them had developed spiritually as had been hoped. It took several more years, however, before his detachment from mysticism was complete. Losing his interest in mystical books, he turned to 'Aufklärung' periodicals,[29] and even to the works of Gellert; he gave up music, and changed his profession (this last step, of course, dates from much earlier, while Moritz was still at school in Hanover). After his wife's death in 1783 Johann Gottlieb was able to free himself from his debts, and this double liberation may have been decisive. He travelled around in his final years, Moritz relates, visiting various 'Aufklärer' whom he had come to admire, and finally died (if we may appropriate here Gibbon's epitaph upon David Hume), 'the death of a philosopher.' His son presents his case as one which would repay careful study, but is unmistakably well-disposed towards his father's transformation.

As Minder shrewdly points out, the development of Johann Gottlieb Moritz, his liberation from a state of neurotic isolation and enslavement, parallels in some ways what happened to Karl Philipp, and constitutes a kind of lower-class 'Bildungsroman.'[30] But in Karl Philipp's case the complexities of the matter are extreme. As we noticed, the empirical spirit which helped him achieve his own freedom derived in itself in some degree from Pietistic practice and analogies, if not connections, with his pervasive neurosis of infinitesimal dismemberment. The persistence of this childhood allegiance in his later years is found in his abundant use of imagery and motifs of mystical and occult provenance, and in his eventual canalisation of mystical passion in a vision of the beau-idéal. His advance towards a symbolic style near the end of his life is in some degree motivated by the need for a severe and pure order of forms, wedded, however, securely to things. This would fain leave behind it the allegiance of the Enlightenment, which sustained a conceptual style not resourceful enough to resist the recurrent insurgence of the unconscious. It would recognize the ubiquity of the unpredictable, the contingent and the irrational, while seeking to bind it firmly within apprehensible formal limits. Through the didactic and often schoolmasterly tones of his *Vorlesungen über den Stil* this policy may be discerned in outline. In *Die Neue Cecilia*, slight though it is, we may find his first and only clearcut practical attempt at realising such a style in narrative.[31] But what of *Andreas Hartknopf*, that weird melting pot of a variety of traditions and of several styles? If this work is (as Moritz's younger brother Konrad was one day to tell Jean Paul Richter) the best reflection ever published of its author's mind, this is partly because it is so strange a mixture. The two *Hartknopf* novels may be called 'allegorical' in Moritz's wide sense of the word, that is to say they are figurative. The characters and events they contain have a meaning which is continuously subject to commentary and interpretation, though often left obscure. Belonging as they do to the class of Masonic novels which proliferated in this period,[32] they are artistically superior to all the others mainly because their protagonist, Andreas Hartknopf, thin-blooded creature though he still is, has upon his shoes a little of the dust of the real highway, of the lanes of England and that hard road from Gotha to Erfurt. The innkeeper Knapp (reputedly based on Moritz's friendly host in Gotha) has actually chosen his vocation from 'a sense of pity for the poor despised wanderer, the errant son of the earth, for whom nobody cares ...' (*AH,* 86). Though his progress becomes increasingly allegorical, Moritz's tramping hero retains therefore to the end something of the texture of flesh.

ANDREAS HARTKNOPF AND THE PREDIGERJAHRE

Andreas Hartknopf: Eine Allegorie was probably written in the year 1784. Between it and *Andreas Hartknopfs Predigerjahre*, composed in 1789, one or two distinctions need to be made. Neither, we must note, postdates *Anton Reiser*. As different as they are from it, they and it were written exactly in parallel, and they do not constitute a sequel, but at most a complement, or conceivably an alternative, to it (like the two endings of *Blunt, oder der Gast*). Both the *Hartknopf* books are satires, and both stand under Masonic influence; but the *Allegorie* is the more improvised, an expressionistic miscellany of satirical and lyrical sketches, the *Predigerjahre* the more organised, and the more specifically a *roman à clef*. Klischnig explains that his friend began to write the *Allegorie* entirely without a plan, stringing together on a story-line, the end of which he did not know, a set of Masonic discourses and satirical cameos. 'Cetera sunt verba praeteraque nihil,' remarks Klischnig, adding that Moritz got the outrageous idea of pretending to utter profundities in this novel while actually saying nothing whatsoever.[33] With this information in mind, K.G. Lenz denounces *Hartknopf* as 'a confidence trick on the public,'[34] and it is no doubt not impossible that Moritz might have perpetrated such a thing. But Klischnig's statements are misleading. More perspicacious is Johann Christian Konrad Moritz's point that the *Allegorie* is planless only in the sense that Moritz would write whatever came into his head when the time came to send more manuscript to the printers; what he wrote, however, was in every case very much an intimate depiction of himself.[35] The ostentatiously eccentric style is a disguise for many things close to his heart, for which the proximity of much of it to what is expressed very differently in *Anton Reiser* is persuasive evidence. Moritz himself stated publicly that the Masonic symbolism was essentially a device for the covert expression of very personal ideas and experiences,[36] and *Andreas Hartknopf* is as much a projection of self as *Anton Reiser*, but refracted in the form of parable; in fact we can call it symbolic autobiography.

Both novels were published anonymously, and perhaps the first impression upon reading either is one of deliberate mystification and of egregious whimsy. There is a humouristic vein which occasionally suggests Sterne, but which swerves towards a more radical, sacrilegious, a black humour. Nervously suggesting that Goethe might condescend to read the *Allegorie*, Moritz told him it was 'a wild blasphemy against a great Unknown' (letter of June 7th, 1788). From this we may deduce that it was intended to be a work of revolt, also that the religious element in it is a significant one. The said blasphemy might be detected in the persistent banalisation of Christian symbols and motifs, but it really lies in the deeper act of defiance which both the *Allegorie* and subsequently the *Predigerjahre* embody. The rebel here portrayed has been defended as a secular saint, martyred for the sake of humanity,[37] but this perhaps overemphasises the nature of his tragedy as simply that of the Enlightenment prophet persecuted by ignorance and superstition. Andreas Hartknopf, it must be recognised, is also like Werther, a metaphysical insurgent, in rebellion against the universe as designed by God. Thus the *Hartknopf* novels transcend (as does *Anton Reiser*) the realm of the purely social and depict an existential dilemma with metaphysical implications: the lot of the anguished 'wanderer upon earth,' *homo peregrinator*, toiling on as best he can towards the East, exposed not only to the malevolence of men but also to the absurdities of Chance, the toy of the great unknown. Moritz is always trapped between the urge to drift and be wrecked upon the ocean of the great wide world, and a natural terror of such a destiny, and *Andreas Hartknopf* expresses something of this friction, the struggle between the need for order and the secret love of chaos.

Nothing could really be more subversive of the values of the Enlightenment than the words of Jeanne-Marie de Guyon in such a poem as *Abandon enfantain*[38] which speaks typically of the longing for formless oceanic liberation, submission to Providence, and the dissolution of all rational discipline in an 'insane' state. There was always much of this in Moritz. But Andreas Hartknopf is presented as an ideal figure, a practical saint, even though he becomes an outcast wanderer. He is also ironised, and like Anton Reiser he even has something in him of the pathetic fumbler, the *alazon*. The difference is that Andreas possesses spectacular perfections which entirely outweigh his blundering and put the blame for his failure squarely upon society, or upon the God of Chance. The *Hartknopf* novels are therefore bifocal as *Anton Reiser* is, social satire but also metaphysical lament, ironic and tragic at one and the same time. Unlike Anton, Andreas is not a compulsive actor, but the prophet of inner truth; only once does he compromise his integrity by staging a scene, and his punishment then is swift and severe. A man's life, *Anton Reiser* seems to say, may become a novel for two reasons: first of all because he wishes it to be, conditioning it by his unstable feelings and shaping it in the fertility of his self-delusion; but secondly because the adventitiousness of the novel is the very ground of existence. Andreas Hartknopf has the integrity to overcome this first danger, but even he cannot escape the second, which is inexorable. In this sense too, he is a martyr for humanity's sake.

The hero's story is simple and scanty enough. He is a smith, as was his father, a man eventually ruined by his lust for gold, and he sets off, as a journeyman, into the great wide world. In due course he turns to theology, and in the *Predigerjahre* we see him in office as the new pastor of Ribbeckenau. The *Allegorie* tells of his return, now well into his forties, to his birthplace of Gellenhausen, and its narrator recalls his contacts with Hartknopf in earlier years, especially in their student days together at Erfurt (here it was that they first met at the house of one Dr Sauer). On coming back to Gellenhausen, Andreas encounters some very old friends, the innkeeper Knapp of the Gasthof zum Paradies, and his sometime teacher, the Rector Emeritus. These two represent the force of good. Those of evil are incarnate, in the *Allegorie*, in Hagebuck, 'the world-reformer,' and his associate Küster, while in the *Predigerjahre* the verger Ehrenpreiss, the wicked spokesman of a malevolent society, is contrasted with Pächter Heil and his sister Sophie Erdmuth, whom Hartknopf eventually marries and with whom he enjoys a short period of happiness before being driven forth again into the vastness of the world, to find in the end – as the *Allegorie* tells us without giving any details – his martyr's death. The parable is therefore a fairly straightforward presentation of the struggle between good and evil, seen primarily in the devoted attempt of a prophet of the Enlightenment (and perhaps also of pansophistic wisdom) to help his fellow men, an endeavour which is frustrated by their obduracy, blindness, selfishness and brutality of mind. Hartknopf is a traveller and a wanderer not only because he is excluded from society, but also because he is committed to the service of man. The failure of the marriage idyll in the *Predigerjahre* is no doubt tragic, but it is also a necessary breaking loose. Expounding on the need for general education and the practical altruistic activity required to bring this about, the *Hartknopf* novels are a gospel of Enlightenment meliorism, their mystagogic elements a typical manifestation of the cult of Reason as a secularised religion with its own rituals (we might compare here Goethe's *Wilhelm Meister*, or even *The Magic Flute*). Andreas himself is the supreme pedagogue; though his words may often be 'without art or learning' (*AH*, 46), he possesses an uncanny power over the minds of others. He teaches no coherent system, but leads by means of hints and suggestions, and, very strikingly, sometimes through music. He combines a practical trade (though one having occult associations) with the priesthood, and for him religion is the acceptance and the exercise of resignation in service, submission in ceaseless activity.

He is however the prophet without honour, and will become the martyred saint. Society's rejection and exclusion of the unusual individual are carried in this fantasy further than they are in *Anton Reiser*, to the point of actual extermination. If the narrator is Hartknopf's rudimentary hagiographer or evangelist, the hero himself is unmistakably a transfiguration of Jesus. This basic allegorical element in the story went unremarked upon until quite recently,[39] and the author's inspiration for it may well have come from his noticing the analogies in *Werther* with the Passion according to John.[40] 'The secret of the earthly life of my Hartknopf,' the evangelist declares, 'is sacred to me. With veneration I gradually dare to draw back the veil that hides great deeds, worthy of eternity, for the eyes of the world, deeds which in time will shine forth with the highest brilliance, and eclipse those of kings' (*AH*, 17–18). Moritz uses a technique of sacrilegious comedy to develop his post-figuration. At the beginning of the *Allegorie* Andreas, on his way back to Gellenhausen, is overtaken by two drunken 'cosmopolitans,' one of whom shoves him into a ditch. This malefactor is compared to 'the wicked thief on the left hand,' and Andreas duly but sleepily observes to the one on his right: 'this day thou shalt be with me in Paradise' (by which, however, he means the Gasthof zum Paradies). In Gellenhausen, where this is to be found, there is also a quasi-Golgotha, the gallows on the hill which so puzzled him as a child for it seemed an 'open doorway in the open air' (*AH*, 52), and here one day Knapp and the Rector Emeritus meet their end (though it is not clear that Andreas does). There are also several references to what happened on the road to Emmaus, and the objectionable pastor of Gellenhausen actually writes a playlet about this, which is then crudely performed by Hagebuck and his associates, with the pastor himself as Christ; which sacred presentation is then followed, grotesquely, by 'a kind of picnic' (*AH*, 45). This vulgarisation is seen as a real blasphemy, and the narrator rejects it; more reverent is his own perusal of the Emmaus episode in Klopstock's *Messias*, as he lies in the grasses of Erfurt's Steigerwald in the setting sun. Andreas Hartknopf, as Christ, is sometimes beset by the threat of emptiness and of despair, but 'the cup ... still passed him by' (*AP*, 38); however, a Last Supper is duly celebrated before he leaves Erfurt to take up his pastorate in Ribbeckenau: 'The radish was brought on a plate – with a solemn expression Hartknopf peeled it, sliced round pieces from it, and passed me the first piece, sprinkled it slowly and reflectively with grains of salt, and looking at me seriously, said: as often as you do this, do it in remembrance of me' (*AP*, 5).

This passage caused some indignation. It is by no means an isolated scandal, for the radishes and the salt function throughout as occult leitmotifs. On the very first page of the *Allegorie* we hear that Hartknopf was 'a good soul – even though he thought that the Godhead was in four persons, and that the whole world was made out of alkaline salt' (*AH*, 1). As for the radishes, their seed is duly borne from Erfurt to Ribbeckenau, but it will not flourish there. The serious undertones are of course rather hard to miss: the salt is meant as the omnipresent Logos, while the radishes symbolise the Earth with which the Spirit blends. What we have, therefore, is a technique of whimsical blasphemous parody, which gives as it takes away. Fifty years later Heinrich Heine was to make capricious use of similar methods, but there are no very close parallels in Moritz's own day. The popular 'Pastorenromane' and 'Bundesromane' of the 1780s and 1790s, rich as they are in idealised wanderer figures with Masonic connections, seem to have no specific Christ transfigurations, nothing so indiscreet as this exploitation of the Gospel story. Nor can these ponderous works boast anything like the grotesque humour of *Andreas Hartknopf*. For Moritz treats here not merely of solemn spiritual challenge, but of the subversive absurdity of life. That groundwork of *Anton Reiser's* irony, the supreme spite of physical things, is found again in the *Hartknopf* novels. The hero's career is beset by mishaps, of which two ridiculous examples are described. His first all-important sermon at Ribbeckenau is fatally affected when his head bumps into a wooden dove over the pulpit and knocks it down. This thoroughly corporeal descent of the Holy Ghost results in a 'scornful, malevolent (*schadenfrohen*) smile' throughout the congregation when he has recovered himself determinedly and comes to speak of the Spirit. Recalling Moritz's own notorious clumsiness, we can perceive that what is involved here is the unspeakable misery of public ridicule. The incident has its exact complement when, in the middle of the festive celebrations for the centenary of the church at Ribbeckenau, a splendid golden angel comes crashing down from the top of the organ, while Hartknopf's carefully staged opening Hallelujah collides with the panting last syllables of the alto voice (who has lost the proper time). Andreas, who has organised this inauthentic scene, has to bear his share of the blame for it. Nevertheless, he is the victim of a universal spite, and though he is a far nobler creature than Anton Reiser, this is still by no means enough: 'the entire innate dignity of his nature could achieve nothing against the comic mask of mighty Chance' (*AP*, 11).

These ludicrous misfortunes put weapons into the hands of the world, which is ranged against him in the form of the smirking and malicious (*hämisch*) congregation of Ribbeckenau, led by the sinister verger Ehrenpreiss, a fanatically orthodox churchman. One might even go so far as to compare the primitive peasant society sketched in here, by means of a few Expressionist pencil strokes, with the animal-like villagers of a Franz Kafka or a Thomas Bernhard. In the nearby hamlet of Ribbeckenäuchen, approached over the sunless desolation of a peat-moor ('Das Torfmoor,' *AP*, 16–17), only Pächter Heil and Sophie Erdmuth gaze up at Andreas out of their pews with the serene features of a 'higher humanity'; the faces of the rest of the congregation 'were more or less deformed by brutality ... it was a chaotic mess ... It was as though a furrow had been drawn over these features making them all the same. ... A new creation had to take place here to give life to this dead mass sunk down to the earth ...' (*AP*, 24–25). These people are vicious, hostile, and bestial. If they surge up in Moritz's imagination from somewhere out of his neurotic personal memories, they come here to represent, in reflection of good Gnostic doctrine, the degeneration of Spirit and of Form into amorphous matter. The divine afflatus can return again only through some vehicle like Hartknopf, the inspired pedagogue of Enlightenment. In these two symbolic novels, therefore, the task of education becomes something far more dramatic and far-reaching than what was practised at the Graue Kloster in Berlin; it becomes a spiritual intervention, which communicates to an inert mass that divine spark from which alone Rationality can be born. Though the merciless spite of this debased world is terrifying, Andreas remains courageous and firm. Pushed into the ditch at the beginning of the story by the 'world-reformer,' he himself takes identical revenge at the end on the verger Ehrenpreiss. He is ready to fight against evil, with his own strong arm.

This evil, however, is not found alone in the primitive superstition of the peasantry, nor in the narrow tyranny of Protestant orthodoxy which considers him a heretic because he teaches a divine Quaternity (God, Son, Spirit *and* Word) and because, as his ever watchful enemies notice, he does not make the proper sign of the Cross but 'just a slanting line twice through the air' (*AP*, 34) – clearly the so-called Andreas Cross. In the *Allegorie* much space is devoted to a series of satirical sorties against another menace, the perversions of Enlightenment reformism, as specifically exemplified in the 'Philanthropist' movement in education. It is usually assumed that it is Basedow who is being pilloried as the 'thief of the left hand,' the drunken Hagebuck with his 'huge bushy black eyebrows and bristly hair, wearing a velvet suit from the sweat and blood of betrayed humanity' (*AH*, 10). The portrait is indeed transparent enough, though Hagebuck is in fact declared to be merely a pupil of Basedow's who is mentioned, as the Philanthropin, by name. Hagebuck pushes Andreas Hartknopf into a ditch. Later on he shows up upon Gellenhausen hill too late for the sunrise, but nonetheless holds forth to his assembled pupils about the beauties of the surrounding landscape, blotted out totally from their gaze by a suddenly descending fog. A former cobbler who has seen 'the light' (and his own importance too), Hagebuck stands for the errors of unrestricted theory, of an abstract ideology divorced from individual human beings, of which he regards himself as the authentic prophet and administrator. These 'men of pseudo-wisdom, the world-reformers, the Hagebucks get lost in idle fancies, in the enchanted lands of the better that is to come,' they do not recognise, as Andreas does, the need for patient work to change 'the bad that is' (*AH*, 149).

Hagebuck is fundamentally inhumane, he even kicks Knapp's lame one-eyed poodle to death. This seems on the whole an unreasonable attack upon

Basedow, and upon the Philanthropin 'which has made the heads of Germans spin' (*AH*, 20), though the ridicule of the fatuous ceremonies at sunrise, and of the vulgar morality play, is perhaps fair comment upon Basedow's ways. Certainly, the latter's fund-raising pursuit of the sons of the wealthy was easy to object to, while his overbearing nature and his flamboyance had evidently roused Moritz's antagonism from the start. But while the critique of abstract idealism is well founded, the personal blows at Basedow (and at Professor Wolke, who had after all helped Moritz in Dessau and is nonetheless satirised in the figure of Küster) are ill-judged, as were those at Jacobi on another occasion. After his initial positive response to the ideas of the philanthropists, Moritz had by 1785 come to perceive that an enlightened pedagogy, in order to achieve social change, must be gradual and empirical, must work above all 'from below' and address itself to the common people, but as individual beings. Pestalozzi is adduced as an example of how to proceed:

O you philanthropists (*Menschenfreunde*, not *Philanthropen!*), if you have the will and the strength to turn to work outside you, then begin at the bottom like Knapp and Hartknopf and the Emeritus, and the good Pestalozzi in Switzerland, if you wish to have some effect (*wirken*) – the sinking structure needs supports, and not statues ... (*AH*, 90).

This last iconoclastic observation might well not have been made after Goethe and Italy, but it is in this straightforward spirit of succour for the deprived that Knapp opens his inn, to receive 'the daily stream of people from the most abandoned and despised class' (*AH*, 87–88). Knapp is a true practical altruist, and the author describes his attempts to impart rationality to a deaf mute. Rousseau's *Emile* and Basedow's highly expensive *Elementarwerk* are not required reading for such good works as these.

In things political the *Allegorie* of 1784–5 is certainly one of the more uncompromising of Moritz's books. It speaks openly of 'the rights of man' (*AH*, 95) and furiously criticises the exploitation of people as mere objects or tools:

Woe unto you who robbed men of their individual genuine worth, to stop up holes with them ... who for the sake of a chimera, of an abstract, general notion, which you call the state, wish to have men exist no longer for themselves but simply for the sake of this chimera, this abstract notion (*AH*, 95).

Conceivably Hagebuck combines with those of Basedow some of the more dubious characteristics of Rousseau, whose revealing autobiography Moritz had probably just read when he composed the *Allegorie*. Of Hagebuck he says that 'the individual was as nothing to him ... but he could lovingly embrace the whole of mankind ...' (*AH*, 30). In this figure we find depicted the potential, even more perhaps than the actual, ideological excesses of the Enlightenment, as Moritz had come to perceive them, and he was not unperspicacious here. But the *Hartknopf* novels are far from being solely works of satire, they contain a number of ideal figures, incipient 'höhere Menschen,' beginning with Knapp and the Rector Emeritus, and including Pächter Heil and Sophie Erdmuth, the mystic Herr von G., and the Jew who chants a Hebrew psalm in the postchaise to Brunswick, giving such eloquent expression to a universal 'Humanitas.' Herr von G. is a particularly interesting figure. A nobleman of eighty, he has corresponded with Andreas for years, and he it is who bestows on him the living of Ribbeckenau. A friend of his father's, he is an unmistakeable combination of Tischer and Fleischbein. At first sight his views and those of Andreas may seem totally antithetical, which is expressed symbolically thus: 'Herr von G. loved the pyramidical form – Hartknopf the cube' (*AP*, 39). The former lives more in the vertical, the latter in the horizontal dimension. Herr von G.'s way of thought is said to have become 'pointed' (*zugespitzt*), it narrows as it rises towards heaven and thus shuts out the physical realities of this world. Herr von G., that is, preempts the results of all knowledge, as 'Über Mystik' complains such teachers always do. Even when he writes his script has this same momentum, so that 'the line underneath invaded the one above,' while the graphologist notes that Hartknopf's script is rather an agglutinative crowding together which makes a line look like a single word.[41] Yet in spite of the chasm between them, which Herr von G. does not see for in fact he stands in it, these two men are able to meet and in some degree blend. Herr von G. is portrayed with sympathy, even with a little humour. When he visits his château at Nesselrode, Andreas finds him soaping his beard. As he shaves his features, with their welcoming even youthful smile, gradually emerge from the soap. Herr von G. the mystic and Andreas Hartknopf the spiritualised Rationalist do still have certain things in common, and both, for example, believe in the necessity of mastering the passions. And this doctrine, and others of a similar quality, find expression in two songs Herr von G. has translated ('rather unpoetically') from the French.

The account of the visit of Andreas Hartknopf to Nesselrode may be regarded as Moritz's ultimate reckoning (though offered as fiction) with Pietistic mysticism in general. The results are the same as those summarised in 'Über Mystik.' Mysticism culminates in a condition which the novel calls 'swimming in bliss' [*In Entzücken schwimmen*] (*AP*, 113). But its attitude to scientific knowledge irritates Hartknopf. 'Taisez-vous ma sagesse,' Jeanne de Guyon had written, 'je veux devenir fou.' Andreas can tolerate mysticism only 'as far as the point at which it excludes human knowledge and calls it folly' (*AP*, 60). For he considers scientific knowledge an indispensable ladder on which one may 'ascend a little above the surface of the earth and gaze around one' (*AP*, 60). But apart from this major point of difference, Herr von G. is warmly defended against the criticism of carping rationalists of the orthodox kind. He was, declares the narrator, 'neither a hypocrite nor an idiot' (*AP*, 64), for it is possible to speak of hearing an inner voice without being either of these. Moreover there are many kinds of mystic, not just one. Moritz's position is therefore moderate and mediatory. And Hartknopf himself is a mediator, for he is a pedagogue with the aura of a religious teacher, like the Rector Emeritus, called 'Elias,' whose spiritual son and substitute Hartknopf becomes. The peculiar, indeed ambiguous nature of Hartknopf's pedagogy may be seen as well as anywhere in the importance for him of music.

The emergence of music, in the *Hartknopf* novels, out of the shadows of Moritz's life is a striking phenomenon, with its origins far back in his childhood.[42] Johann Gottlieb's performance of the songs of Mme de Guyon had provided the wretched little boy with a few rare moments of release. In *Andreas Hartknopf* music and religious feeling are still closely bound. In the *Allegorie* the hero teaches his friend, the narrator, a *Song to Wisdom* (*Lied an die Weisheit*), in which melody and word are perfectly blended, the notes in their gentle succession communicate 'the calm measured steps of life,' and the 'harmony of the whole' is so penetrating 'that a few lines of this song, when sung, have occasionally like a beneficent magic spell produced a sudden transformation in my feelings [*Gemüt*], and brought quiet to my roused passions once more' (*AH*, 157). As Andreas sits at Herr von G.'s piano he sings the so-called *Wiegenlied*, actually a version of *En una noche oscura*, the most famous poem of Juan de la Cruz.[43] He has discovered something of inestimable importance, the value of music as therapy for the modern mind, as a numinous teaching aid:

Hartknopf took his flute from his pocket, and accompanied the glorious recital of his teachings with appropriate harmonies, – he translated the language of the intellect [*Sprache des Verstandes*] into the language of the feelings [*Sprache der Empfindungen*] as he improvised. ... He breathed his thoughts, as he put them into the notes of the flute, from mind to heart (*AP*, 131).

A good deal of the passionate cult of music of the German Romantics is, as Minder makes clear, preempted in this passage. The 'language of the feelings' is one of wholeness, of a fullness unanalysed and undissected, for which 'the articulated notes are not as suitable as the unarticulated ones, which do not begin by dismembering [*zerstüchen*] the whole' (*AH*, 131). Harmony means coherence, it is the counterpoise to that empirical analysis which (unlike, for example, Novalis) Moritz was still prepared to advocate and employ. He puzzles over the relationship, in music, between sign and thing: how does musical notation come to express emotions? If this could be understood, he thinks one could invent 'an alphabet of the language of the feelings ... from which a thousand splendid works could be composed' (*AH*, 134). Music, he says, must learn to imitate Great Nature, and he observes that 'music and astronomy were closely linked for Hartknopf' (*AH*, 135). Moritz, in fact, had developed an interest in astronomy after his return to Berlin, and in his house in Spandau he had constructed a small observatory. This connection, between music and astronomy, is of course an expressive pointer to the 'cosmological aesthetic' to which he had in effect always adhered.[44] It might be said that the harmony of the universe, its perfection of design and its flawless coincidence with its own purpose, was the one main point on which Rationalist 'Aufklärer' and Pietist mystics invariably agreed. Throughout the seventeenth and eighteenth centuries, from Kepler's *Harmonicae Mundi* (1599), we can find signs of this analogy, sometimes directly expressed (for instance, in Johann Michael Schmidt's *Musico-Theologia*, of 1754). And therefore Moritz's favourite geometric metaphors are not unrelated to the apostrophe of music in *Andreas Hartknopf*, while that other common standpoint of rationalism and mysticism, the belief that the passions must be calmed, has to do with it too; the conviction is expressed that poetry too can bring peace to the soul, provided (and we may recall the *Deutsche Prosodie!*) it be *musical*, as for instance that of Horace is, 'because with his entrancing, balanced measures he communicates the proper rhythm of life' (*AH*, 138). In his curing of sick souls Andreas sometimes employs poetry, and it flows in perfect metre 'like balm from his lips' (*AH*, 135). And for those who seek it, music, and poetry as music, can open up a domain outside language: 'what an extensive region of ideas lies here beyond the limits of language: where is the new Columbus, who will make new discoveries to fill out this space, up till now empty and blank, on the great way of human knowledge?' (*AH*, 72).

In *Andreas Hartknopf*, more conspicuously perhaps than in any of the other writings of Moritz we become aware of the persistence of the occult tradition. Jakob Böhme receives a mention, while 'Elias' in the *Prediger-jahre* has turned into something like a real 'pansophist.' Hartknopf himself is the peripatetic blacksmith-philosopher, of the same family as the vinegar-brewer in *Anton Reiser*, as the mystical cobblers and vaticinal journeymen, in the portrayal of whom Moritz was simply reflecting an important feature in his society, a feature which was to have many reverberations in imagina-tive literature to come. The dominating imagery of morning (also to be found in the *Geisterseher*) may well have been reinforced by a superficial acquaint-ance with Böhme, but its chief sources lie in Masonic symbolism and also in the figurative vocabulary of Rationalism.[45] A similar eclecticism obtains in the case of the all but ubiquitous sun imagery, and in that of high noon. These devices constitute allegory only in Moritz's broad definition of the word, although a more narrow one would suffice to characterise the actual nomenclature of the characters in the novels. In the case of the hero, a complicated derivation has been suggested for the name 'Andreas' – first from the Greek ($\dot{\alpha}\nu\sigma\rho\check{o}\varsigma$), stressing the mature (and masculine) determina-tion of the *active* individual, and secondly from Christian hagiography, St Andreas the martyr.[46] Moritz certainly turns in this latter direction again later on, when composing *Die Neue Cecilia*. As for 'Hartknopf,' this sur-name, derived perhaps from the buttoned coat in which the hero sometimes appears, may equally be meant to suggest a certain dissonate awkwardness and toughness. The name 'Knapp,' as Moritz tells us, is appropriate for a man whose speech is unusually terse to the point of the inarticulate, an honest fellow whom fine words do not bemuse. 'Pächter Heil' speaks of pastoral care and salvation, 'Sophie Erdmuth' of a dark and mysterious Gnostic wisdom, and of the Earth which the Spirit must wed. 'The word,' Hartknopf pontificates, 'is the garment which shrouds the thought – but without the word the thought would be nothing – the word is almighty' (*AH*, 38). The word is therefore, in this work, conceived of as more than mere designation; it is the fourth element in the divine Quaternity. The 'words of life' are a music which, once heard and absorbed, dictate the harmonious rhythm of the soul (*AH*, 39). No mere signs for things, they partake in the nature of what they communicate.

Since this is so, it is justifiable to refer to *Andreas Hartknopf* as 'the first symbolical novel in German literature.'[47] Langen, who so describes it, notes the significance of the Masonic influence, as well as of the Egyptomania which emerged at this time and to which Moritz also made his small contribution.[48] The title pages of both the *Hartknopf* novels are duly adorned with a sphinx. But the most essential point is that the symbolism in these books is not something different for Moritz, which does not have its equivalent elsewhere in his work. On the contrary, it is for the most part merely a more extensive use of metanymic and synecdochal devices, like the city gates in *Anton Reiser*, together with a more persistent and intensive exploitation of stylised landscape, which is also to be found in the autobiography, and even *in nuce* in the *Reisen in England*, as the traveller descends into Castleton Hole. In *Andreas Hartknopf* the drive for analysis and dissection, so prominent in *Anton Reiser*, recedes in favour of its polar complement, the reaching after coherence. The parable of Andreas takes place against the background of a symbolic topography. Neither Ludwig Tieck nor even Philipp Otto Runge, claims Langen, invented the symbolic landscapes of the German Romantics, but Moritz.[49] The pointed spires of Ribbeckenau and Ribbeckenäuchen (two names of a truly sinister ugliness) push up like the twin towers of Gotha, but with a greater autonomy as symbol. The terrible peat-moor, dark and deserted, is in no need of allegorical elucidation. The gallows of Gellenhausen, that 'open gate' to eternity, look towards the East and are irradiated by the numinous sun. In the *Allegorie* the narrator speaks of the impression made upon his imagination by objects: a well, for example, always communicates a strange sense of rural simplicity and of the age of things, while a drawbridge signifies 'travel – cities afar off – beginning, end.' He goes on: 'In short there are certain physical objects the sight of which gives us a dark awareness of our whole life, and maybe of our whole being (*Dasein*)' (*AH*, 56). The line between allegory and symbolism is being crossed here at many points.

The closeness of the symbolic technique of *Andreas Hartknopf* to that frequently used in *Anton Reiser* has tended to be overlooked, since the works are so different in other ways. While the latter is a realistic novel-cum-autobiography, marked by incisive psychological analysis, the former is a parable set in a visionary domain. But the *Predigerjahre* reaches its climax in a passage almost indistinguishable in its main elements from the most overwhelming episode in *Anton Reiser*, the churchyard scene. Before this Andreas has turned away from his true destiny. Faced with the choice between a straight path and a winding one, he makes the mistake of selecting the second, for it meanders through pleasant fields and rouses sweet dreams of 'happy days ... the enjoyment of life and health in the harmonious change of the seasons' (*AP*, 72). It is the path which leads to the idyll with Sophie, which is really an illusion, and it is certainly possible that in this motif Moritz was finally disposing of his bond with the Bergrätin Standtke. What is required is to be resolute, like Kersting, also a smith, and a horse-doctor in Ribbeckenau, 'a straight and unbending wanderer through life' (*AP*, 80). Because of his failure to choose correctly, Hartknopf becomes enmeshed in fantasies, 'sweet deceptions' (*AP*, 72), which take no account of the hostility of society, nor of his inborn fate. In the chapter entitled 'Der schwüle Tag' menace begins to build: 'On the flat brown heath lay the night of the overcast sky' (*AP*, 115). The sandy soil is infertile, the few trees crooked. From the hill Andreas looks down upon the peat-moor, and sees the spires 'terrifyingly close ... In this sphere his life now lay, his circle of activity – here his career came to an end, and was plotted out for him as on a map' (*AP*, 116). It is ironic to find the autobiographer's normally wholesome vision, of his life marked out as space, employed on this occasion negatively, to convey a sense of conclusion and limitation, a claustrophobic end to the great traveller's career. The threatening atmosphere intensifies, the sky becomes 'a black evening over the earth,' a couple of woeful tree trunks stand bowed with old age, and as Andreas hastens down the hill in the fading light the horizon seems to close upon him. He has a vision of himself trapped for ever in this awful place, with the evil verger Ehrenpreiss always at his side, forced to live out his imprisonment for another forty years!

> Everything now ran out into a fearful tip, a mournful point.
>
> Ceaselessly the sand in the hourglass ran, and the end was there, there was nothing between except the monotonous repetition of what existed already. – Terrifyingly the chasm opened up right in front of the wanderer's feet.
>
> Now the narrow grave was there – the earth clumped upon the coffin – no outlook, no thought of the future belonged there.
>
> Everything was built up, closed off and hemmed in – between desolate walls which shut out the light of day (*AP*, 117).

Anton Reiser's dreadful moment outside the walls of Hanover is here relived and rewritten by his author some five years afterwards. To confirm this we need only notice the reference to the churchyard in the next paragraph, and to the graves crushed right together. The style is the same, to the point, practically, of self-quotation. Andreas Hartknopf then, like Anton Reiser, is pursued by dream-monsters of a closely similar species. He too has his moment when blackest melancholy impends, and when the grave seems to be at his very heels. His wanderings, like Anton's, can be seen as a flight away from 'pointedness,' from claustrophobia, from an unspeakable monotony. He cannot be regarded simply as an ideal figure who has supposedly transcended or resolved the misfortunes and miseries of his dissimilar twin.[50] The *Predigerjahre*, we should remember, is a book composed in Moritz's full maturity, after his return from Rome. But far from promoting a doctrine of tranquil self-containment, it ends in a gesture of separation and exile. Perhaps the idea of sacrifice, and of the transfiguration of suffering, was the true centre of the *Bildende Nachahmung* with which the *Predigerjahre* at first sight have so little to do. Parting, the author remarks, is 'the grave of love' (*AP*, 133), and the foundation of all wisdom. The wise man is one who has within him a stillness – not that of the grave, however, but that of high noon (*AP*, 137). But he must always be prepared to journey on, and to climb the rock face that rises up before him. If he succeeds, then 'the wanderer's step is unimpeded, and his view limitless' (*AP*, 138). When Pächter Heil and Sophie Erdmuth stand watching Hartknopf leave, they see the indefatigable traveller tramping away 'into his vast element again' (*AP*, 139).

The very last words of the *Predigerjahre* are unexpected. From behind a convenient bush Verger Ehrenpreiss rejoices to see the Pastor's departure, which he has engineered: 'I have morally destroyed Hartknopf,' he declares (*AP*, 140). The allusion is to Campe who is reported to have threatened to do this to Moritz, in so many words.[51] This ending therefore sheds a sharp light on the autobiographical relevance of the novel. It was written, after all, in 1789, at the very height of the quarrel with Campe, and just at the time when Moritz was working to establish his position in Berlin. Very likely it reflects something of the hostility, disapproval and envy he encountered on various sides. He may well, like Rousseau, have succumbed to paranoic visions of a conspiracy of 'Aufklärer,' led perhaps by Campe and Nicolai, and supported by professors, headmasters and orthodox rationalists en masse, against him and his appointment, and against the content of his teachings. There is, it is true, nothing in the *Predigerjahre* quite as explicitly autobiographical as the long Erfurt section in the *Allegorie*, which names names (Sauer, Froriep) and tells us a good deal about Moritz's encounter with the Carthusians, but Klischnig is prepared to assert that the sequel is the less 'planless' of the two novels, and that it is made up largely of 'hieroglyphics' of events in Moritz's life.[52] The term 'hieroglyphics,' which to Moritz and Klischnig meant an allegorical script, the code of a *roman à clef*, is also used by the latter as a general title for the four Moritz prose poems he publishes that are connected with the Standtke affair, and these four pieces have the same individual titles and are textually almost identical with four chapters at the end of the *Predigerjahre*.[53] It is clear that Berlin in 1789 opened old wounds, and the second part of *Andreas Hartknopf* is a significant document of its author's continued search for a stable philosophy, which might finally contain and make sense of the manifold conflicts in which he lived. Like its predecessor, it is a curious mixture of styles, varying from the elevated annunciatory and evangelical, to the whimsical and grotesque, from the Masonic and mystical to the urbane succession of Lawrence

Sterne. The dimension of psychological analysis has been largely abandoned, and prominent is a visionary, dream-like quality and a set of manneristic techniques which wholly transform the conventions of Enlightenment narrative. But the 'Aufklärung' remains in the didacticism of the book, and in its moral allegiances.

At the heart of the teachings of *Andreas Hartknopf* is the treatment of the problem of death. The innkeeper Knapp, a practical altruist and humanitarian untouched by mysticism, instructs his son not to forget the brevity of life, for only thus can a positive attitude be maintained. To recognise death's supremacy, and its omnipresence, is the real panacea for monotony and boredom, but Masonic resignation must be complemented by an insistence upon the irrefutability of the present moment, which alone is real: 'Just as there is no life without death, so also there is no true sense of life without a sense of death – the red of dawn breaks forth out of the midnight darkness – and the beauty of the day is formed out of the shadows of night' (*AH*, 101–102). Thus the *Allegorie* is the work in which Moritz says farewell to Young and his *Night Thoughts*. Young, we are told, was the narrator's favourite writer only in his days of gloom, Young 'cut night out of nature and set it up by itself' (*AH*, 125). The correct position is a constant awareness of the balance of night and day; and in this assertion we see once again an important difference between Moritz and his Romantic successors. Affirmation and denial are brought together by a technique of symbolism. Thus in the *Predigerjahre* the wedding of Andreas and Sophie is celebrated by Superintendent Tanatos, the descendant of a gentleman by the name of Tod who becomes a Master of Arts in Erfurt. Scarcely more than a skeleton in vestments, Tanatos stretches forth a bony hand to congratulate the happy pair, blithely unaware that this festival is to be his last. Perhaps, in the end, the underlying morbidity in *Andreas Hartknopf* is stronger than the beatific affirmation, for that was a wisdom Moritz could teach but could not live.

ULTIMATE DEPARTURE

The same proximity of life, love and death is expressed with somewhat more symbolic refinement in *Die Neue Cecilia*, Karl Philipp Moritz's final work. *Andreas Hartknopf*, fascinating though it still is, is ultimately a novel of phantoms, and almost wholly devoid of narrative power. Of this last virtue, *Die Neue Cecilia*, had it been completed, might have displayed more, for here is an entirely new undertaking for Moritz, the attempt to compose a short novel – possibly really a novella, as cannot be finally determined from the fragment – in a neo-Classical style. He was not dissuaded from this taxing endeavour by his own often professed belief that only genuinely creative minds, of which his was not one, should try to compose poetic works, and he wrote the story when he was extremely ill, dictating most of what there is of it from his death-bed. *Die Neue Cecilia* was published after his death in January 1794, with a preface by a friend of the deceased, F.L.W. Meyer.[54] It was, as we already noted, printed in the publisher Unger's new type-face, with a note by Unger on this experiment. Moritz took the theme from a story going the rounds when he was first in Rome, and recounted in the *Reisen in Italien* (*RI*, I, 133–36): it deals with a love affair between a member of the family of the reigning Pope and a middle class girl: the lover is incarcerated by his relatives, but is determined rather to waste away in prison than ever to renounce his love; to liberate him the girl makes a personal plea to the Pope, and then when that fails she poisons herself. The title Moritz chose is possibly copied from *La Nouvelle Héloise*, while the motif of saintly martyrdom is drawn from his knowledge of the legend of St Cecilia, of which there is evidence in his description of Domenichino's painting in the *Reisen in Italien* (*RI*, III, 182). Like the saint herself, Moritz's heroine is connected with painting and music.

Schrimpf calls this fragment the only genuine piece of pure creative writing (*Dichtung*) Moritz ever achieved.[55] It seems to me that this is too narrow a view. But *Die Neue Cecilia* is certainly very different from *Anton Reiser* and *Andreas Hartknopf*. An epistolary novel in imitation of *Werther*, but with several letter writers, it is carefully designed. Its formal restraint is sustained by an absence of auctorial intrusion, or indeed of moralising reflection except where the letter-writers ponder the problems raised by their lives. The style moreover is remarkably pictorial, a feature hardly found at all in Moritz's earlier work, except sometimes in the travelogues where the scenes are generally ended by reflective commentary. What is presented is in large measure a series of views: Cecilia, who lives with her elderly father, comforting him with her painting and music, pens letters to her intimate friend Augusta, from a balcony which looks out over Rome. The colourful details of the Tiber and its shipping are picked out, the dome of St Peter's is seen illuminated at night, this is a world of things (*Gegenstände*, a key word here). It is of course equally the world of Moritz's finest memories, and in these pages he brings forth once more his recollections of the glorious city, with a poignant, one might say a pathetic, vividness. It is a world devoted to aesthetic contemplation, to 'Anschauen': the steps of Trinita di Monte, the Corso lit up on Saints' Days with its excited crowds, the garden of the Villa Borghese where Cecilia responds to 'great and sublime Nature,' and where she is encouraged into 'renewed activity and the peaceful enjoyment of tranquil life' (*C*, 39). The entire work (as its editor, Meyer, suggests) is an attempt to create a painting (*Gemälde*), a term of particular resonance in eighteenth-century aesthetics,[56] which Moritz himself employs in his essay on *Werther*. In the contrapuntal structure of the story the philosophical discriminations of the *Bildende Nachahmung* may also be perceived for the two pairs of friends, the Marchese Mario and Carlo, Cecilia and Augusta, are contrasted in their relationship to art. The Marchese can only respond to beauty, not create it, and writes to his painter friend: 'You endeavour to reproduce the rose, which I delight in for its shape and scent' (*C*, 32). A similar passivity characterises Augusta, who admits that her desires and impulses lack the passion of Cecilia's. However, the Marchese Mario is a dilettante, as he also confesses: 'I sense that I shall not get anywhere in art, and yet I can't refrain from my botching' (*C*, 59), and this figure contributes importantly to Moritz's exposition of the dilettante problem so vitally significant in this period.[57] By contrast the creative genius, as represented by Cecilia, is also perceived to be the genius of sacrifice, and there can be no doubt that in *Die Neue Cecilia* Moritz was developing another version of his doctrine that only in the domain of forms, of beauty, can the miseries of the real world be harmoniously subsumed, and that martyrdom (spiritual and social) is finally perfected only in the art that portrays it.

That the tale was to end tragically follows not only from the summary of the plot found in the *Reisen in Italien* (and also provided by Meyer, *C*, 74–75), but equally from the actual symbolism of the work. Absolutely central are the symbols of death. When, for example, Cecilia describes Domenichino's painting of Diana, she is speaking of one who is a goddess of the arts *and* of death (as the *Götterlehre* makes clear, *G*, 109). Her first glimpse of the Marchese is in the gardens of the Villa Borghese, near the temple and pool of Asclepius; there he sits, sketching, 'before the urn which stands among the dark bushes, and on which the death of Phaeton is portrayed in bas-relief' (*C*, 53). He is dressed from top to toe in black. The technique seems more concrete, more objective than ever before in Moritz's writing, for the symbols communicate directly, and reflective commentary is entirely missing. The novelty amounts to this: objects do speak in *Andreas Hartknopf*, and most eloquently; so they do in *Anton Reiser*: the wall, the tower; but in both these works the narrator speaks as well, interprets and explains, sums up the meaning, even when 'sign and thing' are supposedly completely one. But in *Die Neue Cecilia* this interpretative voice has fallen silent, and the concrete symbols, like those of the later Goethe, have an opaque eloquence of their own. This is embryonic only, but it might have been a new beginning.

Immediately after Moritz's death, Unger sent the manuscript of *Die Neue Cecilia* to Goethe, with the request that someone might be found who could finish it.[58] Rather tactlessly perhaps, he suggested Wilhelm Heinse, whose lurid *Ardinghello*, with its Renaissance setting, does not bear that much resemblance to Moritz's dignified story set in eighteenth-century Rome. Goethe's reply to Unger has not survived, but we might have expected him to be pleased with *Die Neue Cecilia*, both for its style, and for the fact that so many of his own views were embodied in it. This is perhaps true even of the satire: the attack upon a commercialised, culturally profane society with no comprehension of the artist or his task. The Marchese's father writes to him in downright terms, telling him how to make his career in Rome, how to end up as a Monsignore at least: 'Prelates' bread is sweet; and the violet stocking is cool in summer and warmth-giving in winter' (*C*, 42). He warns Mario not to descend to being a mere artist or scholar, nor to waste his time in the company of such people. This, Moritz implies, is typical of the contempt in which wealth and aristocracy hold the arts; and indeed on the Roman upper classes, ensconced behind their protective net at the ball-games, no sympathy is lost. The tones are much the same as in the *Reisen in Italien*, finished not that long before. While the ideal society is perhaps that of bohemia, the plebs in general are respected for their honesty and vitality, in a city where oppression is exceptionally conspicuous and strong. Cecilia asks herself Rousseau's question whether education has not served to corrupt the innocence of man, and she also notes that the highest good fortune is something quite basic and primitive, 'a firm and continuing state of health' (*C*, 51). Such a thought must have seemed overwhelmingly pertinent to Moritz, as he lay so ill, and there is surely a very sad personal note in the very last sentence he ever dictated for print: 'From my dream,' writes the Marchese Mario to Carlo, 'I awoke with a feverish pulse' (*C*, 71).

'This much,' Meyer observes, 'Moritz spoke, and a day later he spoke no more. The story is unfinished, but not the presentation (*Darstellung*) ...' (*C*, 73). Had it been completed, it might have achieved an important place in the literary history of this period. As it was, it was not without immediate influence. Its likely impact upon Wackenroder has already been noted, and Tieck's *William Lovell* may well owe something to it, as it surely does to Moritz's other novels.[59] Jean Paul, his great admirer, must have known it well, and even Goethe, though he is silent on the subject, may have kept it in mind for some time (not too long afterwards he apparently toyed with the idea of writing a novel called *Cecilia*).[60] But at this moment Moritz was cut off, in the middle of *Die Neue Cecilia*, and in the middle of his *Grammatisches Wörterbuch* too. The end, when it came, was rather sudden, although it might have been anticipated for two or three years at least. Marcus Herz no doubt foresaw it, but other close friends such as Klischnig seem to have been rather obtuse in this regard. Though the sick man's lungs were by now in such a state that he often could hardly walk, Klischnig actually comments that 'he frequently took pleasure in pretending to be mortally ill and did this so admirably that people who did not know him well thought he couldn't live another day.'[61] So thoroughly had he managed to mix theatre and reality by now, that they could hardly be separated, least of all by himself. Goethe was one who may have seen more clearly, and of the visit Moritz paid him in Weimar in March 1791, he wrote to Reichardt, who had left Berlin:

Moritz gave me some very pleasant days. Ill though he was, his mind was cheerful and lively. In the very few years since I last saw him he has matured incredibly and is in all things he has undertaken, if not yet at the goal, at least on the right path. I have talked over with him almost everything I am doing in art and in natural philosophy and have received a good deal of help from his observations.[62]

Moritz must indeed have been in a bad way, for he was unable to see Frau von Stein during this visit,[63] which may have been the only one he paid to Goethe between 1789 and his death. During these four-and-a-half years his frenzied activity in Berlin can hardly have helped his condition, nor can the confusion into which his private life eventually disintegrated, in an episode which lends his last months some quality of macabre grotesquerie.

The story of Moritz's marriage, so far as it is known, reads like something from the pages of a fictionalised sequel to *Anton Reiser*. Thinking perhaps of Rousseau and Thérèse le Vasseur, but certainly rationalising his physical predilections as a form of pedagogical idealism, he hit upon the idea of selecting for himself some poor and simple girl of tender years, whom he could educate and mould.[64] He even dragged Klischnig along to an orphanage to inspect suitable candidates,[65] but finally his choice alighted upon Christiane Friederike Matzdorff, the daughter of a lottery collector and the sister of the bookseller and publisher Matzdorff. She was just fifteen years old. The wedding took place in August 1792, and Moritz, on presenting his wife to Henriette Herz, took his old friend into an adjoining chamber: 'Haven't I,' he asked, pointing to the room his bride was in, 'done something very stupid there?'[66] Such a question, as Henriette points out, is its own answer, and indeed the marriage was rapidly in deep water. What occurred that autumn is not entirely clear. The most sensational account of events is that by Varnhagen von Ense:[67] according to him Friederike, presumably finding her husband's pedagogical methods hard to bear, eloped with a lover called Siede (in some accounts Sydow or Zülow) who had (Eybisch tells us)[68] a previous hopeful foothold in the Matzdorff household, until Moritz unexpectedly intruded with his 'immature notion' as Siede put it, of marrying this young girl. The husband pursued the elopers to a spot a few miles from Berlin, where he caught up with them at an inn. Siede thereupon took refuge in a barrel in the wine-cellar, and his pursuer, poking in an unloaded pistol, demanded that he come out. This he did in terror, and Moritz then genially transported the couple back to the city in his carriage, after which, however, the adulterous gentleman was actually imprisoned for his act.

It has been simply suggested that Varnhagen's absurd tale is untrue,[69] but the evidence points to something of the kind having indeed occurred. Certainly, Varnhagen must have had it from Henriette Herz, who also tells it less circumstantially, and who is usually unreliable on points of detail. Varnhagen's own recollections were written down nearly twenty years after Moritz's death, and Henriette's dictated as late as the 1840s. However, this story was current in one form or another in Moritz's own time, and aroused a good deal of ridicule. Wackenroder for one (in Berlin just then) alludes to it: 'Siede (the revolting fellow) has made off with Moritz's wife, but they were overtaken and Siede is now in jail.'[70] One J.J. Horner, who visited Weimar in 1794, recalls how at supper at Herder's, in Goethe's presence, there was much mirth when a 'Professor Meyer (F.L.W. Meyer?) told the story of Hofrat Moritz's marriage and death in a scandalously witty manner, admittedly somewhat embroidered ...' Goethe, who had sat gloomily by, now livened up and began to relate equally funny stories about Moritz in Rome with a fine (and possibly a more tasteful?) species of wit.

It appears that Moritz was sincerely in love with his wife. He seems to have sought happiness in love with an almost childish trust. Klischnig prints love poems, in fact, which are essentially naive in tone. They seem to have been written after the separation which followed upon the elopement, and which Friederike appears to have exacted. Nine in number, they are all dated, and run from December 1792 to March 1793. Idealising his beloved, his 'Laura,' Moritz abases himself in regret and guilt. There is a tenth poem too, addressed to Klischnig, which is defensive in tone. He pleads for Klischnig's understanding in this step he was now (15 March) about to take. This was his remarriage to Friederike, and a letter to the King signed by the separated pair is extant (17 April) asking for permission to rewed. It refers to the desirability of speed, since Moritz now has to leave on a journey of several weeks. Duly remarried, he and Friederike set off for Dresden, where he was to inspect and study the contents of the galeries for the benefit of his courses at the Academy of the Arts. In Dresden Moritz was taken ill and the couple returned posthaste to Berlin, where he lingered for a number of weeks, able, apparently, until just before his death, to continue to dictate his last novel, *Die Neue Cecilia*. His wife seems to have cared for him devotedly, and Herz and Klischnig to have encouraged him, when they could not save him, to seek peace of mind in his own doctrine, that 'last freedom of the wise man,' resignation. He died on 26 June 1793, almost certainly from tuberculosis, a disease which was to claim his young widow a year or two afterwards. Friederike was plunged immediately into dire financial straits. Moritz had left no will and had in any case nothing to leave except debts and unfinished manuscripts (numerous publishers lost money). The very next day Matzdorf sent an appeal from his sister to von Heinitz, in which she says she does not even have the resources needed for the funeral. She was awarded the rather paltry sum of 75 Thaler, and Matzdorf himself with difficulty recovered from the Academy the 50 Thaler he had lent his brother-in-law to finance the trip to Dresden. This tight-fistedness, Proehle blandly remarks, was no doubt due 'to the bad reputation of the Hofrätin Moritz'![71]

Goethe, being away from home, probably did not hear of his friend's death immediately, and it is not mentioned in his letters until August. He and Schiller were to join in the controversy over his 'good journeyman's' reputation when it broke out openly on the publication of the Schlichtegroll obituary in 1795. Goethe wrote bitterly to Schiller of 'the necrological beak that hacks out our poor Moritz's eyes straight after his death.'[72] The famous *Xenie* reads thus:

> Armer Moritz! Wie viel hast du nicht im Leben erlitten.
> Äacus sei dir gerecht; Schlichtegroll war es dir nicht.

There can be no doubt that Goethe felt the loss as a deeply personal one. Friederike Brun, who on her visit to Goethe in 1795 at first found him stiff and lacking in courtesy, goes on to remark that when the conversation turned to Moritz 'he became so gentle and kind and praised Moritz and pitied him so like my own feelings that I forgave him all.'[73] No doubt in Berlin Moritz's departure was not regretted very much, though von Heinitz probably felt it a professional loss. There was an immediate move to get his job, by Gleim on behalf of a friend of his.[74] These last years must have been a time when, with the exception of Klischnig, Maimon and perhaps the Herzes, Moritz had rivals, listeners, even perhaps admirers, but no real friends. Asked before his marriage why he spent so much time alone, he answered laconically: 'In my lonely chamber I am always in the right.'[75] The ugly, eccentric raconteur and näve enthusiast who had so gripped the imagination of the Weimar court circle, this Moritz with his excellent elocution, his cheerful histrionics and capacity for mimicry and parody (he would deliver himself of lofty subjects, such as the story of David and Goliath, in Low German verses)[76] was increasingly worn down in Berlin by illness, and the pathetic episode of his marriage was a last grasping after refuge with a gesture that was gauche but perhaps moving as well.

Outside Berlin, one other person of note who took a deep interest in Karl Philipp Moritz's fate was Jean Paul Richter, who had sent him the manuscript of his first novel, *Die Unsichbare Loge*, with a request for his views.[77] In his capricious, nervous prose, Jean Paul introduces himself to this famous figure whom he very much admires and whose writings he knows so well. Encouraged by Moritz's enthusiastic response to the manuscript (its author, he apparently told his brother Konrad, 'is even better than Goethe, something quite new') Jean Paul expatiates in his second letter on his background and lonely existence, suggesting that perhaps his nature has some similarities with that of Moritz. Moritz arranged for *Die Unsichtbare Loge* to appear under Matzdorf's impression and enthused over *Schulmeisterlein Wuz*. Jean Paul, for his part, calls the author of *Anton Reiser* '(someone) whom the whole of Germany has learned to love,' and expresses his deep admiration for *Andreas Hartknopf*. Some time after Moritz's death, Konrad Moritz, who also works for the Matzdorf publishing firm, begins to correspond with Jean Paul about details of the publication of *Hesperus*. His letter of 1 August 1795 thanks Jean Paul for the Emmanuel figure in *Hesperus*, whom he believes to be based in part upon his brother: it makes him remember how the latter died, how death working in him gradually broke down his body, piece by piece. He recalls him feeling his irregular pulse in fascination, and at the same time planning more journeys, to Italy, Greece, even America. Such plans, such travels, however, could be of interest only if one returned, and otherwise not at all. The writer tells how the resurrection scene in *Die Unsichtbare Loge* was read out by Moritz to his two brothers as a special treat on Whitsunday 1793, in his little observatory. And in answer to a request by Jean Paul to write more about his brother, any details he can remember, he gives an account of his feverish and overhasty manner of working, the confusion and disorder of his days. He comments that Moritz, 'although he was of the firm opinion that the most important thing, the keystone of a beautifully rounded work must always be at its centre,' was equally keen on an interesting conclusion, and at the outset of a work often knew the words with which it would end. He makes the fascinating revelation that Moritz still, in the last years of his life, resorted for amusement to the games of yore, constructing cities of cardboard houses which he then destroyed by letting hot sealing wax drop upon them! 'He seemed to get a strangely melancholic feeling out of it, when the town was reduced to ashes.'

In his last letter to Konrad Moritz (30 October 1795), Jean Paul repeats how much he loves the *Hartknopf* novels, which Konrad has just discussed, and takes leave to criticise Klischnig's newly appeared 'biography.' It lacks coherence and individuality, as he very justly observes, and is merely 'an archipelago of floating, isolated islands.' He had in mind to write a biography of Karl Philipp Moritz himself, as had also Saloman Maimon, but neither of these works was ever composed. However, Jean Paul did address himself to the problem of Moritz in an important section of his *Vorschule der Ästhetik* (1804). Here he deals with Moritz as a 'Gränz-Genie,' suggesting Diderot, Rousseau, Bayle, even Lessing as examples of the type. Among poets he finds that Moritz had at least the beginnings of genius. He possessed a poetic sensitivity which might have taken him far, but he was unable to create. To this class of 'geniale Mannweiber,' Novalis too is said to have belonged. True or false, this definition is intriguing. At any rate it offers us an estimate of Moritz's character, a perception which is at least striking and revealing. It is a view not entirely possible to dismiss.

Conclusion

As the permanence of Moritz's literary reputation rests essentially on *Anton Reiser*, which is the only one of his works – with the solitary exception, perhaps, of the *Reisen eines Deutschen in England* – that is reprinted with any regularity today, so also that book probably contains the best analysis of his mind, the disturbances and excrescences of which are the real stuff of interest in his writings. Moritz stands revealed, certainly, as a second-rate intellect, but as an extremely intriguing and original one. The remorseless depiction of a paranoid illness which is found in his autobiography is hardly equalled in the literature of the period in fictional or in semi-fictional guise. The examination of the symptoms of claustrophobic aggression, of inferiority complex and of the significance of 'games' (played, as was noted earlier, right up to his death) is as revealing as it is new for its day, certainly in German literature and maybe in others too. Visions of wholeness and of circularity occur in his work, but states of *ennui*, boredom and restlessness are also abundant, a sense of rejection is frequent, a fight against coercion, a feeling of depression and of incipient manic qualities.

There is another side to the psychological traumas, the theatre-mania, the obsessional neurosis of walls, of tiny doors, of being shut out, worn down and inadequate, which are so obtrusive in him and particularly in *Anton Reiser*. This is the beginning of the empirical method, Moritz as the collector and displayer of evidence and even embryonically the conductor of experiments (e.g. on deaf mutes), appearing in *Anton Reiser* as the superior narrator who is at least sometimes the candid observer and the discoverer of empirical knowledge. There was indeed in this something which went beyond the concept of himself and of his role that was peculiar to him. This role remained in fact a curious mixture of antiquated views and new ones, still very much of the eighteenth century in its framework, yet with a realisation of the literarisation of his life which is prototypical in its way.

One of the most striking features about Moritz is the burgeoning in him of the Romantic genius. In the *Reisen in England* there emerges a Romantic view of the world, in the description of the cave at Castleton, in the discovery of a Kingdom of the Earth beneath. The silk-stockinged aesthete in the Berlin of 1792 is very much the Romantic in essence, in spite of the 'Classicism' of many of his appearances and doctrines. His influence upon the German Romantic movement, perhaps the richest and certainly the most intense and introverted of all versions of the phenomenon, was extensive; the Schlegels for instance were at one time much affected by his ideas. He played his part, there is no doubt, in the German Classical movement too, developing an interest in concrete works of art and their creation while in Rome. He conceived of the creative act (in *Über die bildende Nachahmung des Schönen*) as being of a unique quality, possible only for a very small number of poets and/or artists, whilst at the same time his notions about creativity have more than an analogy with the Sturm und Drang.

The gravamen of the charges often levelled against him – that he was no more than a charlatan, in essence a pretender whose mercurial and mercenary productivity was his only recourse – is surely untrue. He was doubtless a prolific dilettante, who worked against the clock for money, but he was also the author of one or two books which are really valuable, are read fairly widely and deserve to be read more. He was the inventor, or discoverer, of doctrines quite influential in their own day, although still not generally attributed to him. He was a born anti-Establishment man, struggling all his life, like many of his kind, to belong to the Establishment, in which he had a certain success. He was a Rationalist of a sort, with symptoms of a mystic, a Pietist *manqué* given to *a priori* reasoning, yet with inductive ways of thinking too. The empirical observation of facts is a significant feature of his work from 1780, and is particularly noticeable in his psychological writings. Goethe's influence upon him was profound, but he could reconcile this fairly easily with the persistent empiricism of his mind. He sought hard and, it must be admitted, vainly for a stable philosophy of life. One cannot but suppose that, had he been allotted a normal span, he would have turned towards empiricism again.

Notes

1 Peter Gay, *The Enlightenment*, 271
2 Goedeke, following contemporary sources such as Salzmann and Jordens (q.v.), gives the date as 1757, an error which has dogged subsequent historians. It is followed by Geiger in the *Allgemeine Deutsche Biographie*, by Proehle, and recently by Friedrichs. Eybisch has the correct date, which is to be found in the church register as published by Weisstein. See also Rudolf Steude, 'Wann wurde Karl Philipp Moritz geboren?'
3 Weisstein (5) records only one son by the first marriage.
4 Eybisch, 7
5 Eybisch, 4
6 See *La Vie de Madame J.M.B. de la Motte Guion, écrite par elle-même* (3 vols., Cologne, 1720).
7 See Minder, *Glaube, Skepsis, Rationalismus*, Chapter One, 'Quietismus.'
8 All references to: *Anton Reiser. Ein psychologischer Roman* (hrsg. Müller; München, Winkler, 1971)
9 This conclusion from 'Kindheitserinnerungen von K. St.,' *Magazin zur Erfahrungsseelenkunde*, VIII, 2, 107f – probably the reminiscences of Moritz's younger brother, Konrad
10 *Poesies et cantiques spirituels* (ed. Poiret, 4 vols, Cologne, 1722). They were translated by G. Teersteegen and others. Minder refers to an edition of the *Cantiques* in German which appeared in 1744 (Minder, 266).
11 *Italienische Reise*, 'Moritz als Etymolog,' *Weimarer Ausgabe*, Bd. 32, 182
12 In *Andreas Hartknopfs Predigerjahre* (1790) appears *Das Wiegenlied*, a poor version of the most famous poem of Juan de la Cruz, *En una noche oscura*, from *Subida del Monte Carmelo*.
13 Eybisch, 9
14 Minder, 138f

15 Boulby, 'The gates of Brunswick'

16 In Schlichtegroll's *Nekrolog* we learn that 'the written contributions of several people' were drawn upon, and the essay submitted for checking to a person who had known Moritz well. The references to Sextroh are invariably favourable and occasionally seem to imply the use of his own testimony. See e.g. Schichtegroll, 185.

17 'We were both,' writes Iffland, 'inspired with one passion, and about this, as well as all the events in his life which I know of until he left Hanover, he wrote with precision and the strictest truth.' *Werke*, Bd. I, 55.

18 Schlichtegroll, 259

19 Here were published excerpts of his work in progress; see *Mag*, 2, 76f.

20 Eybisch, 39. Eybisch's examination of the school records shows that Moritz, by March 1774, had fallen behind most of those who had entered the school when he did. See also Ulrich, 'Karl Philipp Moritz in Hannover.'

21 Compare Catholy, 24.

22 See Blumenthal, 'Moritz and *Werther*.'

23 Eybisch, 41

24 Henning, 12

25 See Catholy, 110–12, and Unger 164. The motif is widely found in eighteenth-century thinkers in various forms. See e.g. F. Pamp, *'Palingenesie' bei Charles Bonnet, Herder und Jean Paul*.

26 A protegé of Wieland's. See Eybisch, 65.

27 A weekly founded in 1776 and published by Hieronymus Gradelmuller. The magazine is lost.

28 Published in *Olla Potrida* (Berlin, 1780), IV, 7

29 See e.g. *Allgemeine deutsche Bibliothek*, Bd. 97, St. 2, 433.

30 For a full study of the matter see Garlick, *Novel or Autobiography. An Interpretation of Karl Philipp Moritz's Anton Reiser and the Problem of its Generic Identity*.

31 Compare, e.g., Pascal, 'Autobiography is ... an interplay, a collusion, between past and present,' *Design and Truth*, 11.

32 Booth, 71 & 74

33 See e.g. *Mag*, II, 2, 22–36, where there are certain discrepancies from the final text of the novel. In this earlier (and historically no doubt more authentic) version the journey lasts two days, and the travellers go part of the way with carters. The changes were presumably for reasons of narrative economy.

34 Compare Eybisch, 39.

35 In the *Allgemeine deutsche Bibliothek* the reviewer points out that the details of the book should be taken seriously, unlike the case of novels (Bd. 67, St. 2, 458–59). In the *Göttingische Gelehrte Anzeigen* (1785, St. 165), we are assured that the story is largely true, although the author's 'lively imagination' may have misled him for a time. In the Preface to Part Two Moritz is taking issue with the review in the *Gothaische gelehrte*

255 Notes to pages 37-51

Zeitung (1785, St. 68), which complained about the boring minutiae, believing the book to be fiction.

36 Schlichtegroll, 257

37 For a slightly more detailed exposition of the following argument, see Boulby, '*Anton Reiser* and the Concept of the Novel.'

38 'A psychological novel or rather biography the writer is currently working on,' *Berliner Monatsschrift* (hrsg. Fr. Gedike & J.E. Biester; Berlin, 1783), Bd. II, 357 ('Fragment aus Anton Reisers Lebensgeschichte').

39 Saine, *Ästhetik*, 120

40 Compare, e.g. Wieland, *Don Silvio von Rosalva* (1764), and Musäus, *Grandison der Zweite* (1760–1762).

41 F. Bruggemann, *Die Ironie als entwicklungsgeschichtliches Moment*, for this important point

42 Comparisons between Moritz and Lenz are frequently made. See e.g. recently John Osborne, *J.M.R. Lenz: The Renunciation of Heroism*.

43 For Heine on Moritz, see especially *Reisebilder*, Zweite Teil Dritte Abteilung, and *Zur Geschichte der Religion und der Philosophie in Deutschland*, Zweites Buch.

44 Cf. e.g. *Anton Reiser*, 209.

45 Compare here *Deutsche Prosodie* (26 & 30) where the identical expression is used.

46 Ruth Ghisler, *Gesellschaft und Gottesstaat*, especially 71 & 116. This author finds similar problems of alienation and inadequacy in the novels of Nicolai, Hermes and Wezel, as well as Goethe.

47 I translate the term 'bürgerliche Verhältnisse' in this way not in order to blur a point of social criticism but in order to clarify the meaning. Moritz is resentful of the whole social order, and is not class conscious in a modern way. Nevertheless, the phrase is striking, particularly in its association with a critique of property owners.

48 Saine notes that Leibniz uses the metaphor of a city to explicate the monad. *Ästhetik*, 58.

49 See especially Sørensen, *Symbol und Symbolismus*, Chapter 6, 'Die Autonomie des Symbols: Karl Philipp Moritz.'

50 It seems at least unlikely to have had much to do with Pastor Anton Reiser, who in 1681 wrote a pamphlet critical of the theatre! See Geiger, *Anton Reiser* xv.

51 For the symbolic landscapes in *Anton Reiser* see Stemme, *Moritz und die pietistische Autobiographie*, and Langen, 'Karl Philipp Moritz' Weg zur symbolischen Dichtung.'

52 Langen, 'Karl Philipp Moritz' Weg zur symbolischen Dichtung,' 174.

2 / ENLIGHTENED MAN EMERGENT

1 Karl Friedrich Klischnig: *Erinnerungen aus den zehn letzten Lebensjahren meines Freundes Anton Reiser. Als ein Beitrag zur Lebensgeschichte des Herrn Hofrat Moritz* (Berlin: Vieweg, 1794)

2 See *Denkwürdigkeiten, aufgezeichnet zur Beförderung des Edlen und Schönen*. Hrsg. von C.P. Moritz und C.F. Pockels (Berlin: Unger, 1786–8), I, 370–1.

3 The *Diarium* of the Brudergemeinde at Barby for 17 Feb. 1777, records as follows: 'Ein Studiosus theologiae von Erfurt, namens Moritz, der vor einigen Tagen in der Absicht hergekommen war, bei der Gemeinde zu bleiben, ging heute dahin zurück, nachdem ihm geraten war, seine Studia daselbst zu absolvieren und inzwischen die Gemeinde Neudietendorf bisweilen zu besuchen.' Quotes by Hans Henning: *Karl Philipp Moritz. Ein Beitrag zur Geschichte des Goethischen Zeitalters*, in: *Bericht des Livländischen Landesgymnasium zu Birkenruh*, 13.

4 Eybisch, 71. His sources are Moritz himself, *Denkwürdigkeiten*, I, 258ff, and Friedrich Nicolai: *Beschreibung einer Reise durch Deutschland* (Berlin & Stettin, 1781), I, 29.

5 Eybisch, 75. Klischnig, who claims that Moritz spent two years at Wittenberg, is incorrect.

6 Eybisch, 74

7 Eybisch, 89

8 See Christian Garve: *Neue Bibliothek der schönen Wissenschaften und der freyen Künste*, Bd. 12, 1 St., 282–324.

9 Johann Bernhard Basedow: *Das in Dessau errichtete Philanthropinum. Eine Schule der Menschenfreundschaft und guter Kenntnisse* (Leipzig: Crusius, 1774), XIII

10 'Zwischen Lavater und Basedow,' written in Bad Ems, July 1774. See *Dichtung und Wahrheit*, Book 14.

11 Basedow, *Philanthropinum*, 22

12 For these details see Klischnig, 21ff and Henning, 13–14.

13 First published in the *Berlinischer Musenalmanach für 1791*, hrsg. Karl Heinrich Jordens (Berlin: Matzdorff, 1791), 25–7

14 For these varied and conflicting explanations see Abbé Dénina: *La Prusse Littéraire sous Frederic II* (Tome III, Berlin 1791), 67 (generally a very unreliable source), Julius Friedrich Knüppeln: *Büsten berlinischer Gelehrten und Künstler mit Devisen* (Leipziger Ostermesse, 1787), 179, and Christoph Friedrich Rinck: *Studienreise 1783/84*. Nach dem Tagebuch des Verfassers herausgegeben von Moritz Geyer (Altenburg: Geibel, 1897), 170–1.

15 Weisstein, 6

16 *D. Anton Friedrich Büsching eigene Lebensgeschichte, in vier Stücken* (Halle: Curts, 1789), 552–3

17 For example: 'Würdiger Rath, lieber Getreuer! Eure Forderung vom 25sten ist schlecth überlegt. Um den Salpeter aus den Klassen des Gymnasii zum grauen Kloster wegzubringen, und solche über der Erde und im Lichten zu bauen, nachdem solche schon einige Jahrhunderte, der Gesundheit unbeschadet, besuchet worden, dazu kann, nach eurer Bitte, einige tausend Taler nicht verwilligen, euer sonst gnädiger König, Friderich.' Büsching, 570.

18 A copy of the second edition (1783) is in the Pestalozzianum, in Zürich. The title of this edition is *Unterhaltungen mit seinen* (*not* meinen) *Schülern*, unlike the first edition. I refer to this copy throughout.

19 Eybisch, 88, and 187–8 (letter to Herder of June 17, 1780)

20 Berlin, Wever, 1781

21 Klischnig, 43. Christian Boie commented to Gleim: 'Wie ist Friedrich für seine Vernachlässigung der deutschen Musen gestraft, dass er nun so mittelmäsigen Köpfen als Moritz öffentlich Beifall bezeugt.' See Friedrich der Grosse: *De la Littérature Allemande*, hrsg. Ludwig Geiger. XXVIII.

22 Weisstein, 7–9, for this material

23 Akselrad, 47

24 Schlichtegroll, 14

25 Rudolf Köpke: *Ludwig Tieck*, I, 89–90

26 Rinck, III

27 It is repeated by Dénina, 66.

28 Henning, 15

29 See Henriette Herz: *Ihr Leben und ihre Erinnerungen*. This is the main source. The reference to the play-reading group is found in *Jugenderinnerungen von Henriette Herz* (Mitteilungen aus dem Litteraturarchive in Berlin, 1896). See also K.A. Varnhagen von Ense: *Vermischte Schriften*, 20–26. Varnhagen drew chiefly on the anecdotes he had personally heard from Henriette.

30 Letter of 12 Sept. 1793 to Johann Gottwerth Müller (author of the popular novel *Siegfried von Lindenberg*). See Hans Schröder: *Johann Gottwerth Müller*, 115.

31 Sophie Becker, whose travel diary is a useful source of information on Berlin life in the eighties (and especially on Mendelssohn) describes a gathering at the latter's house on 24 November 1785: 'Um 5 Uhr holte uns Nicolai zu sich ab, wo wir mit dem Geheimen Rat Dohm und seiner Gemahlin, Gleim, Ramler, Moritz, Benzler, Klein und Engel den Abend sehr angenehm zubrachten.' *Vor hundert Jahren. Elise von der Reckes Reisen durch Deutschland 1784–86, nach dem Tagebuche ihrer Begleiterin Sophie Becker.*

32 Klischnig, 69–70

33 For Mendelssohn see especially Alexander Altmann's magnificently comprehensive study: *Moses Mendelssohn*.

34 Schlichtegroll, 240. We may contrast here Robert Minder's view that the two men got on well, and note the several signs of Mendelssohn's personal interest in Moritz and his work. See Minder 180.

35 Compare Ludwig Geiger: *Berlin 1688-1840. Geschichte des geistigen Lebens der preussischen Hauptstadt*, Bd. I, 393.

36 *Vossische Zeitung*, 24 January 1786. This was in the course of a review of Mendelssohn's opus postumus, *An die Freunde Lessings*, which appeared that same day. The review was

then re-published in the *Hamburger unpartheyischer Correspondent*. The acrimonious dispute thereby generated was continued by Moritz in the *Vossische Zeitung*, 11 Feb., and the *Correspondent*, 22 Feb. He stubbornly persisted in his allegations, that the pain caused Mendelssohn by Jacobi's behaviour contributed in a major way to the former's death. For the ins and outs of this disagreeable and complex quarrel see Altmann, *Moses Mendelssohn.*

37 Ferdinand Josef Schneider: *Die Freimaurerei und ihr Einfluss auf die geistige Kultur am Ende des achtzehnten Jahrhunderts*, 167

38 When he became Bruder Redner. See Eybisch, 306.

39 *Berlin 1688-1840*, I, 400

40 Berlin, Voss und Sohn, 1784

41 According to Eybisch, he left office sometime in the summer of 1785 (Eybisch, 120). We know that he and Klischnig departed from Berlin for the south in June.

42 21 July and 6 Sept. 1784. See Julius W. Braun: *Schiller und Goethe im Urtheile ihrer Zeitgenossen* (Erste Abtheilung, Schiller: Bd I, 1781-1793).

43 'Herr Moritz sei er doch kein Narr

Und mach er ein so gross Geplarr

Von meinen Akteurs und meinen Aktricen

In seinen Vossischen Avisen.

Lass er die Leute doch ruhig leben

Ich will ihn ja gern ein Freibillet geben.'

Knüppeln, 155-6. This is so execrable that one is forced to think the bad quality deliberate.

3 / POOR TRAVELLING CREATURE

1 Cf. e.g. *LP*, 368.

2 *Kleine Schriften, die deutsche Sprache betreffend* (Berlin: Wever, 1781)

3 *Magazin für die Deutsche Sprache*, 1782, II, 129

4 'eine gewisse eklektische oder ausgesuchte und auserlesene Art zu reden.' Quoted by Friedrich Müffelmann: *Karl-Philipp Moritz und die deutsche Sprache*, 39

5 Müffelmann, 105

6 *Über den märkischen Dialekt* (Berlin: Wever, 1781)

7 *Allgemeine deutsche Bibliothek*, Bd. 46, St. 2, 553-57

8 See Müffelmann, 144f. Moritz depends partly on Johann Friedrich Heynitz's *Die Lehre von der Interpunktion* (1773).

9 *KL*, 84-5

10 *Deutsche Monatsschrift*, 1793, Bd. 2, 221

11 'Vorbericht'

12 See Boulby, 'Karl-Philipp Moritz and the 'psychological' study of language.'

13 *DS*, 546

14 See *Mag*, I, 1, 92f; I, 2, 101f; I, 3, 123f; I, 1, 118f; III, 2, 110f; IV, 3, 95f. C.L. Bauer also contributes a piece with the same title (*Mag.*, IV, 1, 56f).

15 Specifically the term 'dunkle Begriffe'

16 See Karl Kindt: *Die Poetik von Karl-Philipp Moritz*, 108: 'Das Gewebe der rationalistischen Seele blosszulegen, ist die inhaltliche Aufgabe von Moritz' Grammatik ...'

17 See Robert Sommer: *Grundzüge der Geschichte der deutschen Psychologie und Ästhetik*, 311. The belief of the Sensualists that ideas derived from sensation led to an interest in the consequences, for conceptual thinking, of sense deprivation. Moritz however is concerned not so much with the negative results of such a defect, as with the nature of the mental power which transcends it.

18 *D*, I, 199

19 *D*, I, 202

20 *LP*, 265

21 Compare, for instance, Dietrich Mahnke: *Unendliche Sphäre und Allmittelpunkt. Beiträge zur Genealogie der mathematischen Mystik*. For Moritz's use of geometric metaphors see, e.g., August Langen: 'Karl-Philipp Moritz' Weg zur symbolischen Dichtung,' 169–218 and 402–44.

22 *Versuch einer kleinen praktischen Kinderlogik, welche auch zum Teil für Lehrer und Denker geschrieben ist* (Berlin: Mylius, 1786)

23 Here the German text reads as follows: 'Denn hier ist alles *in* – das Umfassende wird stets wieder umfasst – *Alles ist eins*. Das Eine trotzt der Zerstörung – Zerstörung ist *Entzweiung, Trennung* – Nichts ist in der Welt wirklich *eins*, als worin nichts auseinander, sondern alles ineinander ist – Die wahre Einheit ist also unsichtbar – Alles was wir sonst *eins* nennen, ist blosse Täuschung, weil wir dasjenige, was eigentlich auseinander ist, als ineinander denken – Nicht die Sache, sondern unsere Vorstellung von der Sache ist eins geworden – so ist das ganze Universum in unserer Vorstellung eins geworden.' *KL*, 112.

24 'Auch eine Hypothese über die Schöpfungsgeschichte Mosis'

25 'Die Pädagogen,' *LP*, 200–07

26 For a view strongly hostile to the spread of literacy among the common people, see esp. Freiherr von Knigge: *Über den Umgang mit Menschen* (1788).

27 See e.g. their principal organ, the periodical *Pädagogische Unterhandlungen*.

28 The first German translation of the *Confessions* is *J.-J. Rousseau's Bekenntnisse*, 2. Teile (Berlin, 1782).

29 Not all of the many examples of these autobiographies and journals now extant were at that time available to Moritz, even supposing he had tried to read them systematically, which is out of the question. Many remained in manuscript until the nineteenth century

or even later. However, Moritz may have been familiar with J.H. Reitz's compilatory *Historie der Wiedergeborenen* (Itzstein, 1717). Spener's *Eigenhändig aufgesetzter Lebenslauf* had been published in 1718. Haller's diary did not appear until 1787, but Lavater's *Geheimes Tagebuch von einem Beobachter seines Selbst* was published in 1771. For a full treatment of this rich tradition see Werner Mahrholz: *Deutsche Selbstbekenntnisse*. See also Minder, 37f.

30 *Aussichten zu einer Experimentalseelenlehre. An Herrn Direktor Gedike* (Berlin: Mylius, 1782), 26f

31 See above. Also published as 'Vorschlag zu einem Magazin der Erfahrungs=seelenkunde' (sic), *Deutsches Museum*, 1782, I, 499f.

32 *Psychologia empirica* (Frankfurt & Leipzig, 1732); *Psychologia rationalis* (Frankfurt & Leipzig, 1740)

33 Max Dessoir, *Geschichte der neueren deutschen Psychologie*, 118 & 210f

34 Compare, for instance, *Mahomets-Gesang* with *Les Torrents*, between which there is a connection. See Franz Saran: *Goethes Mahomet und Prometheus*, in: *Bausteine zur Geschichte der neueren deutschen Literatur*.

35 Thus Knüppeln, *Büsten*, 183 & Eybisch, 95

36 Moritz has a good word to say about Pestalozzi's *Lienhard und Gertrud*. See *AS*, 24.

37 Dessoir, *Geschichte*, 305. The short title of the work is *Adam Bernds eigne Lebensbeschreibung* (Leipzig, 1738).

38 The excerpts in the *Magazin* were published when Moritz was in Italy and Pockels was acting editor. Had Moritz known the work, it seems likely he would have used it or referred to it earlier.

39 Eybisch, 99

40 *Literatur und Theaterzeitung*, XXXIII, 12 August, 1780, 525

41 Ibid

42 Minder, *Religiöse Entwicklung*, 12

43 *Mag*, VII, 3, 42

44 Klischnig, 253

45 Ibid

46 Dénina, 69

47 See e.g. my '*Anton Reiser* and the Concept of the Novel'. The full implications of this problem must await further treatment.

48 The second edition has an engraving by Chodowiecki of a scene in an Oxford public house, with Moritz at the table. For a discussion of the journey, see W.D. Robson-Scott: *German Travellers in England 1400-1800*, 170-77

49 I cite two: J.A.G. Büschel, *Neue Reisen nach und in England im Jahr 1783, ein Pendant zu des Herrn Prof. Moritz Reisen* (Berlin, Maurer, 1784), and L.G--e, *Anmerkungen und Erinnerungen über Herrn Professor Moritzens Briefe aus England von einem Deutschen, der auch einmal in England gewesen ist* (Göttingen; Kübler, 1785).

50 *Travels, chiefly on foot, through several parts of England in 1782. Described in letters to a friend. By Charles P. Moritz, a literary gentleman of Berlin, translated by a Lady* (London; Robinson, 1795)

51 Hackemann, 626–7

52 *The Rise of the Novel*, 38

53 *The Gentleman's Magazine*, vol. 65, July–Dec., 1795, 758, and *The European Magazine*, vol. 28, July–Dec. 1795, 174–79. See also, for further evidence of the influence of this book in England, *The Quarterly Review*, April–July 1816, 542–44.

54 *Allgemeine deutsche Bibliothek*, Bd. 71, St. 1, 169–72. Eybisch's Wilhelminian comment (Eybisch, 112), that Moritz took little interest in the novelty of England and in political life there is quite untypically misleading.

55 Letter of 1 Dec. 1786, to Frau v. Stein

56 Henriette Herz, *Erinnerungen*, 130

57 Alexander v. Humboldt, *Briefe* (Stuttgart 1880)

58 Marcus Herz: 'Etwas Psychologisch-Medizinisches: Moritz' Krankengeschichte,' *Journal der praktischen Arzneykunde und Wundarzneykunst* (hrsg. W. Hufeland, Jena, 1798, Bd. 5, St. 2), 259–321. See also 'Eine vergessene Pathographie von Marcus Herz über Karl Philipp Moritz aus dem Jahre 1798,' Erich Ebstein, *Zeitschrift für die gesamte Neurologie und Psychiatrie*, Bd. 117, 513–15.

59 Marcus Herz, *Journal*, 279

60 Ebstein, 513

61 *Psychopathologische Dokumente*, 52, 68f, 80f

62 See Carl Friedrich Bahrdt: *Geschichte seines Lebens, seiner Meinungen und Schicksale* (Berlin: Vieweg, 1790–91, vier Teile), IV, 171f.

63 'D' (= T.G. Dittmar): 'Karakterzüge aus dem Leben des Prof. Hofraths Moritz in Berlin,' *Morgenblatt für gebildete Stände*, Nr. 170, 16 Julius, 1808, 678f

64 Letter of 10 Dec. 1788, to Caroline v. Beulitz

65 Geiger, in *Allgemeine deutsche Biographie*, Bd. 22, 314

66 Knüppeln, 185

67 Jördens relates the following anecdote, without giving a date: Moritz went to see his friend, General v. Knobelsdorf, at Stendal in the Altmark. He went dressed as a journeyman, and with his good clothes in a bag. At the gates he said he was indeed a travelling tradesman who had lost his papers. He was taken under guard to the general's quarters, who did not recognise him, gave him two weeks to produce the pass, and warned that if he did not do so he would be pressed into the army. In the cells Moritz changed clothes and then identified himself, to the delight and embarrassment of the general. This silly story is not flattering to Moritz, whether it actually occurred, or whether he invented it. See K.H. Jördens, *Denkwürdigkeiten, Characterzüge und Anekdoten aus dem Leben der vorzüglichsten deutschen Dichter und Prosaisten* (Leipzig: Kummer, 1812), 338–40.

68 *DM*, 497-8

4 / THE SMOKE AND THE LIGHT

1 Bd. 58, St. 1, 21f. See also 92f. These comments are quoted by K.H. Jördens, who knew Moritz well, with some approval. See *Lexikon deutscher Dichter und Prosaisten* (hrsg. K.H. Jördens, 6. Band. Supplemente. Leipzig, 1811), 880.

2 *Denkwürdigkeiten aus dem Leben ausgezeichneter Teutschen des achtzehnten Jahrhunderts* (Schnepfenthal: im Verlage der Erziehungsanstalt, 1802), 392

3 Rinck, 182–3

4 Letter to Johann Gottwerth Müller, 12 Sept. 1793. See Hans Schröder; *Johann Gottwerth Müller*, 115.

5 Wilhelm Heinrich Wackenroder: *Briefwechsel mit Ludwig Tieck*, 150–1.

6 Rudolf Köpke: *Ludwig Tieck*, I, 88f.

7 Letter to Caroline von Beulwitz, 3 January 1789

8 Henriette Herz, 129

9 Not only, it is alleged, did he fail to read Kant, but 'er würdigte auch die weniger Studium erfordernden und seiner Art zu räsonnieren nicht durchaus fremden Schriften eines Tetens, Eberhards, Platners, Feders, Garves u.a. kaum eines flüchtigen Anblicks, ob er sich gleich grosse Begriffe von den Fortschritten, die man diesen Männern zu verdanken habe, machte.' Schlichtegroll, *Nekrolog*, 246.

10 Schlichtegroll, *Nekrolog*, 255

11 Dessoir, *Geschichte*, VIII

12 *Dichtung und Wahrheit*, 14. Buch

13 Hartley's *Observations on Man* (1749, German translation 1772–3). For Bonnet see esp. his *Essai analytique sur les facultés de l'âme* (Copenhagen & Geneva, 1769), which refers in detail to Condillac's *Traité des Sensations*; also Michael Hissmann's *Geschichte der Lehre von der Association der Ideen* (Göttingen: Bossriegel, 1777); Hissmann alludes to English philosophers and to Malebranche, but claims that the theory of association may already be found in the Ancients.

14 See Johann Nicolas Tetens: *Philosophische Versuche über die menschliche Natur und ihre Entwicklung* (Leipzig, 1777). Dessoir states: 'Die rein wissenschaftliche Psychologie des 18. Jahrhunderts gipfelt tatsächlich in diesem Buch.' *Geschichte*, 356.

15 Though the word 'Unbewusstsein' is used by Ernst Plattner in his *Philosophische Aphorismen* (Leipzig, 1777). See Kurt Joachim Grau: *Die Entwicklung des Bewusstseinsbegriffes im 17. und 18. Jahrhundert*, 33.

16 See Michel Foucault: *Madness and Civilisation*, 127 & 129.

17 Dessoir, *Geschichte*, 320–1.

18 Johann August Unzer's periodical, which ran from 1759 to 1769, a somewhat confusedly edited magazine, raises such questions as the effect of emotional factors on the heart rate.

19 See Johann Gottlieb Krüger's *Versuch einer Experimental-Seelenlehre* (1756). An example of the newer terminology is Ludwig Heinrich von Jacob's *Grundriss der Erfahrungsseelenlehre* (1791).

20 These are: 'Aussichten zu einer Experimentalseelenlehre' (see Chapter 3, Note 30), written in congratulation of Gedike who had advanced rapidly to become Director of a Gymnasium, 'Vorschlag zu einem Magazin der Erfahrungsseelenkunde' (see Chapter Three, Note 31), and 'Ankündigung eines Magazins der Erfahrungsseelenkunde' (*Berlinisches Magazin der Wissenschaften und Künste*, 1782, I, St. 1, 183–7). This last is signed and dated 14 January 1782.

21 *J.J. Rousseau's Bekenntnisse*, Bd. I.

22 Full title: 'Psychologische Betrachtungen auf Veranlassung einer von dem Herrn Ober-konsistorialrath Spalding an sich selbst gemachten Erfahrung.'

23 See *Magazin*, V, 2,7.

24 Curiously enough, this episode is said to have occurred in the household of a family which subsequently became famous, the Brentanos (*Mag*, I, 1,9).

25 The story of Maimon first appeared under a pseudonym: 'Fragmente aus Ben Josua's Lebensgeschichte' (*Mag*, IX, 1, 24–69).

26 'Grundlinien zu einem ohngefähren Entwurf in Rücksicht auf die Seelenkrankheits-kunde,' (*Mag*, I, 1, 31–8).

27 Compare, for example, the views of Friedrich Hoffmann (1660–1742), a physician and a friend of Leibniz: 'Das Heil unserer Seele und die Glückseligkeit ist nichts anderes, als deren ruhiger und geregelter Verlauf, wie er von Gott bestimmt ist. Ist diese Harmonie vorhanden, so gibt es in den Handlungen der Menschen weder Fehler noch Gebrech-lichkeiten.' Quoted by Käthe Paulsen: *Die Auffassung von der 'Seelenkrankheit' im Magazin zur Erfahrungsseelenkunde*, 86.

28 Rinck, 171

29 All this in the polemic against Campe: *Über eine Schrift des Herrn Schulrath Campe, und über die Rechte des Schriftstellers und Buchhändlers* (Berlin: Maurer, 1789), 12–13

30 *Salomon Maimon's Lebensgeschichte von ihm selbst geschrieben und herausgegeben von K.P. Moritz* (Berlin: Vieweg, 1792 & 1793, 2 Teile)

31 Gerhardt, VI, 600

32 *Psychologia rationalis*, §20

33 See e.g. Sommer, 129–130 & passim.

34 See Foucault, 175–182.

35 Letter to Lotte v. Lengefeld & Caroline v. Beulwitz, 12 Dec. 1788

36 See Arno Schmidt: 'Die Schreckensmänner,' in: *Nachrichten von Büchern und Menschen*, Bd. 1. *Zur Literatur des 18. Jahrhunderts.*

37 As has been asserted, e.g. by Akselrad, 76

38 Geiger, in: *Allgemeine deutsche Biographie*, Bd. 22, 313

39 Schlichtegroll, *Nekrolog*, 205

40 *Moses Mendelssohn an die Freunde Lessings. Ein Anhang zu Herrn Jacobi Briefwechsel über die Lehre des Spinoza* (Berlin, 1786)

41 Altmann, *Moses Mendelssohn*, 739–41

42 Eybisch, 124. See also Eybisch, 125ff, for the further details summarised here.

43 K.G. Lenz refers to 'sein Liebling Klischnig.' Klischnig himself admits that his own jealousy was so obvious a friend felt obliged to utter a warning: 'Leut'chen, wenn ich euch nicht besser kannte, ihr könntet mich auf den Gedanken bringen, dass mehr als Freundschaft, dass griechische Liebe zwischen euch herrschte' (Klischnig, 161). Klischnig was ashamed at these suspicions. The friend in question was K.H. Jördens.

44 Schlichtegroll, *Nekrolog*, 209

45 Klischnig, 168f

46 For all these, see Eybisch 195–7.

47 Eybisch, 196

48 Klischnig, 172; Eybisch, 128

49 Eybisch, 199

50 Horace, *Odes*, II, 3, one of the most Epicurean in spirit. Moritz quotes:
'dum res et aetas et sororum
fila trium patiuntur atra.'
Perhaps the true quality of his Latin may be judged by the two errors (if they do in fact go back to him); he writes 'filia' for 'fila' (!) and 'patiantur' for 'patiuntur.'

51 *Allgemeine deutsche Biographie*, Bd. 3, 734

52 *Über eine Schrift*, 16–17

53 For all these references, see J.H. Campe: *Moritz. Ein abgenötigter trauriger Beitrag zur Erfahrungsseelenkunde* (Braunschweig: In der Schulbuchhandlung, 1789).

54 *Über eine Schrift*, 18

55 Klischnig's figure. Moritz mentions 100 Thaler. Campe gives no figure at all.

56 Berlin, Maurer, 1792

57 Berlin, Wever, 1786. *Nachdruck: mit einem Vorwort von Thomas P. Saine*. The only other edition appeared in 1815.

58 Saine comments: 'Hier, darf man wohl sagen, wird zum ersten Mal in der deutschen Poetik eine Trennungslinie zwischen der Sprache der Überzeugung (Rhetorik) und der der Selbstzweckhaftigkeit gezogen' (*Nachdruck*, XIII). As far as the dance metaphor is concerned, Moritz's use of it makes a curious contrast with that of Voltaire, who employs it to decry metaphysics, which always ends up on the spot from which it starts (See Peter Gay, *The Enlightenment. An Interpretation*, 135).

59 Andreas Heusler, *Deutsche Versgeschichte*, Bd. 3, 84f

60 Hans Joachim Schrimpf, 'Vers ist tanzhafte Rede,' in: *Festschrift für Jost Trier zum 70. Geburtstag*, 386–410

61 Schrimpf, 'Vers ist tanzhafte Rede,' 404 & 408

5 / AT THE FRINGE OF GENIUS

1 See e.g. Bengt Algot Sørensen, *Symbol und Symbolismus in den ästhetischen Theorien des 18. Jahrhunderts und der deutschen Romantik*, 80; also **Eduard Naef**, *Karl Philipp Moritz,*

seine Ästhetik und ihre menschlichen und weltanschaulichen Grundlagen, 103–104.
Abrams, in *The Mirror and the Lamp*, exemplifies the general unawareness of Moritz's
work and even of his existence.

2 Hans Pyritz, 'Goethes römische Ästhetik,' in *Goethe-Studien*, 17–33.

3 Introduction to *Über die bildende Nachahmung des Schönen,* in *Deutsche Litteraturdenk-
male* (1888), Bd. 31, XIX.

4 Compare here Alfred Baeumler, *Das Irrationalitätsproblem in der Ästhetik und Logik des
18. Jahrhunderts bis zur Kritik der Urteilskraft* (*Nachdruck von: Kants Kritik der Urteilskraft,* Bd. 1, 247); also Bruno Markwardt, *Geschichte der deutschen Poetik*, Bd. III, 48–52.

5 See Karl Heinrich Heydenreich, *System der Ästhetik* (Leipzig: Göschen, 1790), 137.

6 I am dependent for much of the following detail upon: Ferdinand Noack, *Deutsches Leben
in Rom. 1700 bis 1900*, Julius Vogel, *Aus Goethes Römischen Tagen*, and Johannes Nohl,
Goethe als Maler Möller in Rom.

7 *Italien und Deutschland. In Rücksicht auf Sitten, Gebräuche, Litteratur und Kunst* (Berlin,
1789–1791; four issues). The magazine never rose above triviality.

8 *Salomon Gessners Briefwechsel mit seinem Sohne* (Bern & Zürich: bei Heinrich Gessner,
1801), 187–90

9 Anon. (= Hagmann) *Fragmente über Italien, aus dem Tagebuch eines jungen Deutschen*
(1789, n.p.), Bd. 1, 105–106. According to Henriette Herz, an innkeeper in Tivoli still
remembered Goethe and Moritz some thirty years later (*Leben und Erinnerungen*, 133).

10 *Leben und Erinnerungen*, 132

11 *Italienische Reise*, WA, I, Bd. 30, 227 (All subsequent Goethe references in this chapter
are to the *Italienische Reise* unless otherwise indicated). 1 Dec. is also forty days from the
date of the unbandaging, 9 January, but see in this respect Nohl, *Goethe als Maler
Möller*, 25–26, who accepts a slightly earlier date.

12 *Wöchentliche Nachrichten*, 1786, 432; cited by Eybisch, 313. See also Moritz, *Über eine
Schrift*, 22–23.

13 Schlichtegroll, 213

14 Nohl, *Goethe als Maler Möller*, 26

15 According to Nohl (*Goethe als Maler Möller*, 41) there were indeed specific incidents of
this sort in Rome.

16 'Erste Bekanntschaft mit Schiller 1794' (1817)

17 They now have, in meticulous and all but excessive detail, by Egon Menz, without this
changing the overall picture much.

18 *Teutscher Merkur*, July 1789, 3, 105–111

19 In a letter to Caroline Herder, which she must have shown to Goethe, as was her wont.
See *Herders Reise nach Italien. Herders Briefwechsel mit seiner Gattin von August 1788 bis
Juli 1789*. Hrsg. von Heinrich Düntzer und Ferdinand Gottfried von Herder, 258.

20 Pyritz, 25

21 *Schriften*, Jubiläumsausgabe, Bd. I, 243

22 Compare here Chapter Three, 91.

23 See Menz, 67, for this point.

24 See especially the discussion of this matter by Saine, *Karl Philipp Moritz' Ästhetik*, 187–88, and *Ästhetische Theodizee*, 138f. Schrimpf takes the view (*Schriften zur Ästhetik und Poetik*, XIV) that the essay was most probably published somewhere else prior to its appearance in *Die grosse Loge* (1793). Menz points out (54) that it bears little enough resemblance to its author's post-Italian manner.

25 And reviewed enthusiastically by Lessing, *Berlinische Privilegierte Zeitung*, 30 May 1754. See also *Hamburgische Dramaturgie*, Bd. 1, St. 4, 12 May 1767.

26 Compare Baeumler, 244.

27 The title was probably borrowed from Kant's *Träume eines Geistersehers, erläutert durch Träume der Metaphysik* (1766).

28 *Magazin zur Erfahrungsseelenkunde*, VII, 2, 64–71

29 The *Ephemeriden* (1770) are evidence of his well-known youthful acquaintance with mystical and occult literature. His aunt, Frl von Klettenberg, may very well have introduced Goethe to Jeanne-Marie de Guyon's and to Fénelon's works. He certainly knew something of Gottfried Arnold and of Peter Poiret. Franz Saran (*Goethes Mahomet und Prometheus*) concludes that a borrowing from Guyon's *Les Torrents* is the most likely source for the central symbol of the poem *Mahometsgesang*. Proof of Goethe's early awareness of the existence of the sect in which Moritz had grown up came with the discovery of a letter of his to Herr von Fleischbein of 3 January 1774. See *Neue Züricher Zeitung*, 1921, No. 1592, and Martin Eckhardt, *Der Einfluss der Madame Guyon*, 18.

30 WA, IV, 9, 72

31 See, e.g., Abrams, *The Mirror and the Lamp*, 201.

32 See his *Inquiry into the Origins of our ideas of beauty and virtue* (1725).

33 See Abrams, 128.

34 'Vorbereitung des Edlern durch das Unedlere,' *Schriften*, 19–20.

35 For Leibniz, see, e.g., Ernst Cassirer, *Die Philosophie der Aufklärung*, 40. For Baumgarten, see Heinz Schwitzke, *Die Beziehungen zwischen Ästhetik und Metaphysik in der deutschen Philosophie vor Kant*, 36.

36 WA, II, 6, 321. Compare Menz, 189.

37 Gerhard, Bd. IV, 468ff

38 See Ernst Joachim Schaede, *Herders Schrift 'Gott' und ihre Aufnahme bei Goethe*, 27.

39 Suphan, Bd. 14, 250

40 Menz (165–66) has offered a detailed set of suggestions with regard to the composition of the *Bildende Nachahmung*, and the place of the several related essays in this process. While this is by no means free of unsubstantiated assumptions, I follow it in general outline.

41 In this connection see Carl Liederwald, *Der Begriff 'edel' bei Goethe*, and my article, 'Judgment by Epithet in Goethe's *Torquato Tasso*,' *PMLA* (March 1972), 167–81.

42 *Vorschule der Ästhetik*, §10

43 Saine's suggestion, *Ästhetik*, 225, and *Theodizee*, 162f

44 Compare Sørensen, 90: 'Der Gedanke des 'Symbols' lag wie gesagt in dieser Schrift gleichsam im Keim, wurde aber nicht von Moritz und erst ungefähr 10 Jahre später von Goethe klar erkannt und ausgesprochen.' See especially the Goethe-Meyer article: 'Über die Gegenstände der bildenden Kunst' (1798).

45 'Propyläen,' Bd. 2, St. 1, 16 (1799)

46 See Campe, *Moritz*, 10–11.

47 *Moritz*, 33

48 'Intelligenzblatt,' No. 65 (16 May 1789). Several further statements followed, ending with that in No. 101, 21 August 1789.

49 Schlichtegroll, 217–18

50 To Kanzler von Müller, 25 April 1819

51 Nohl, *Goethe als Maler Möller*, 111

52 *Ibid.*, 133–34

53 *Herders Reise nach Italien*, 107

54 *Ibid.*, 192–93

6 / SUBJUNCTIVES OF SUCCESS

1 Schlichtegroll, 214

2 Eybisch, 158

3 Nohl, 'Karl Philipp Moritz als Gast Goethes in Weimar,' upon which what follows is partly based.

4 *Herders Reise nach Italien*, 184–85. All references to Caroline Herder's letters are to this volume.

5 WA, IV, 9, 68

6 Düntzer, I, 307

7 See Weisstein, 10

8 Nohl, 'Moritz in Weimar,' 768

9 *Ibid.*, 769

10 Weisstein, 13–14

11 Schiller, *Briefe*, II, 198

12 See Schiller, *Briefe*, II, 177 & 180

13 Nohl, 'Moritz in Weimar,' 770

14 Schiller, *Werke*, Bd. 21, 77

15 Schiller, *Briefe*, II, 230; also Knebel, *Nachlass*, Bd. III, 300

16 No. 154, 417–21 (May 1789)

17 *Allgemeine deutsche Bibliothek*, 95 (1790), 453–56

18 One letter from Moritz to Kant survives (dated 4 October 1783). It requests the latter's help in publicising the *Magazin zur Erfahrungsseelenkunde*, and invites him to contribute to it (in fact he never did). Marcus Herz was probably Moritz's principal, and very competent, informant on the thought of Kant.

19 *Literaturgeschichte,* ²1923, Bd. III, 213

20 *August Wilhelm Schlegel's Vorlesungen über philosophische Kunstlehre,* 311ff

21 *Vorlesungen über Kunstlehre,* 311

22 *Vorlesungen über schöne Literatur und Kunst,* I, 103

23 Eichendorff, 'Der irre Spielmann'

24 'Wir befinden uns hier an einem Punkt, wo sich die Wege der klassischen und romantis-chen Ästhetik trennen.' Sørensen, 78.

25 Schrimpf, 'Die Sprache der Phantasie,' 171

26 *Ibid.,* 189

27 Körner to Schiller, 13 April 1791, *Briefwechsel Schiller und Körner,* II, 178–79

28 See Schrimpf, 'Die Sprache der Phantasie,' 171; also Karl Kerényi, 'Gedanken über die Zeitmässigkeit einer Darstellung der griechischen Mythologie,' 268–77.

29 *Vorlesungen über Kunstlehre,* 98

30 Cited after: 2te. Auflage, Berlin: Maurer, 1797

31 Zweiter Teil, ausgearbeitet von M. Friedrich Rambach (Berlin: Maurer, 1796), viii

32 Sigmund Auerbach, 'Karl Philipp Moritz,' in: Franz Kern (hrsg.), *Goethe: Torquato Tasso,* 384–85. Compare here also the highly significant notes for a never written section of Goethe's autobiography: 'Arrival of Moritz. Renewal of our Italian discussions. His essay On the Creative Imitation of the Beautiful, the real outcome of our contact, is being published in Brunswick. His part in my Tasso, which I just finished ...' Paralipomena to *Dichtung und Wahrheit,* WA, I, 53, 386.

33 *Herders Reise nach Italien,* 217. Compare Goethe's enthusiastic remarks to Jacobi on 2 February 1789. WA, IV, 9, 77.

34 See Boulby, 'Judgment by Epithet.'

35 It first appeared much later, in *Deutsche Monatsschrift* (1792), I, 243–50. But in a letter of 6 June 1789, he refers to a part of a MSS, obviously this short essay, which he hopes to send to Goethe.

36 See *Herders Reise nach Italien,* 203–205.

37 ' ... so ganz in dem Gefühl von ruhigem Dasein versunken, dass meine Kunst darunter leidet.'

38 See Erich That, *Goethe und Moritz,* and R. Lehmann, '*Anton Reiser* und die Entstehung des *Wilhelm Meister,*' 116–34.

39 WA, IV, 10, 105 (19 August 1793, after Moritz's death)

40 Klischnig tells us that Goethe remarked, with devastating effect: 'Good God, even you are weak enough to look for something in that.' Klischnig, 52.

41 Nohl, 'Moritz in Weimar,' 778

42 Campe, *Moritz,* 24

43 Pröhle, 156. Pröhle reprints most of the relevant documents in the Geheime Staatsar-chiv.

44 Weisstein, 13–14

45 *Monats-Schrift der Akademie der Künste und mechanischen Wissenschaften zu Berlin*

46 See Hans Müller, *Die Königliche Akademie der Künste zu Berlin, 1696 bis 1896*, esp. 166ff.

47 Klischnig, 199

48 Pröhle, 161

49 'My Sunday lectures, which Your Excellency honoured with the encouragement of your presence a year ago ...' *Anthusa*, v.

50 Schlichtegroll, 218

51 Akselrad, 138; see also *Die Gegenwart*, XXII (1802), 71.

52 Karamsin, *Briefe eines reisenden Russen*, 73

53 Karamsin, 79

54 'Entwurf zu einem vollständigen Vortrage einer Theorie der schönen Künste, für Zöglinge einer Akademie der Künste,' dated 8 February 1789, and written presumably on request immediately on arrival in Berlin. Preserved in the Geheime Staatsarchiv, and reprinted in *Schriften*, 123–24, Pröhle, 160–61 and Eybisch, 240–41.

55 'Bestimmung des Zwecks einer Theorie der schönen Künste. Vom verstorbenen Hofrat Moritz,' *Berlinisches Archiv der Zeit und ihres Geschmacks* (1795), I, 255ff. Reprinted in *Schriften*, 122–23; also Eybisch, 240–41. The fragment is analysed in detail by Dessoir, *Karl Philipp Moritz als Ästhetiker*, 44–54.

56 *Monats-Schrift der Akademie*, Jg. 2, Bd. 3 (1789), 74–77; also Klischnig, 192–96, and *Schriften*, 120–21

57 Menz, 255–60

58 The first section of this essay was published before Moritz's appointment.

59 Compare the important essay, 'Zufälligkeit und Bildung. Vom Isoliren, in Rücksicht auf die schönen Künste überhaupt,' *Monats-Schrift der Akademie*, Jg. 2, Bd. 3 (1789), 66–69 and *Schriften*, 116–17.

60 *Reisen in Italien*, II, 56–58 and *Schriften*, 226

61 Böttiger, *Literarische Zustände und Zeitgenossen*, I, 30

62 *Italienische Reise*, 6 September 1787

63 Compare the essay 'Einfachheit und Klarheit,' *Deutsche Monatschrift* (1792), II, 34–37, and *Schriften*, 148–51.

64 Compare the address 'Über den Einfluss des Studiums der schönen Künste auf Manufakturen und Gewerbe,' *Deutsche Monatschrift* (1791), I, 38–41, and *Schriften*, 158–60.

65 Klischnig, 207

66 Köpke, I, 89–90

67 *Morgenblatt für gebildete Stände*, No. 189 (8 August 1808), 756

68 Schlichtegroll, 231

69 Wackenroder, *Briefwechsel mit Tieck*, 150–51

70 Köpke, I, 89

71 Wackenroder, *Briefwechsel mit Tieck*, 163
72 *Ibid.*, 131–132
73 *Ibid.*, 163
74 Weisstein, 15

7 / DEPARTURE INTESTATE

1 Harnack, 1, 498
2 Quoted in Harnack, 1, 509
3 Proehle, 165–66
4 Henning's claim that Wöllner was directly responsible (Henning, 55) is based however on a mistaken dating of the letter in the Geheimes Staatsarchiv cited also by Harnack, 1, 509. This letter is dated 24 January 1791, at the time of von Heinitz' first recommendation.
5 Geiger, *Berlin*, 2, 32: 'Selbst in die Akademie nämlich drängten sich die Obscuranten ein' (although this sharp remark does not refer to Moritz).
6 Klischnig, 202
7 See Akselrad, 137, for this remark.
8 *Deutsche Monatsschrift* (1791), 1, 271
9 See the correspondence printed by Harnack, 2, 322–25.
10 See Rudolf Hildebrand: 'Vorwort' to *Grimms Wörterbuch*, Bd. v (1873), VIII.
11 'Über die Bildsamkeit der Deutschen Sprache,' and the report 'Über die bisherigen Beschäftigungen der akademischen Deputation zur Kultur der väterländischen Sprache.' *Deutsche Monatsschrift* (1792), 1, 168–72, and 3, 287–88.
12 *Deutsche Monatsschrift*, (1791), 1, 272
13 *Grammatisches Wörterbuch der deutschen Sprache* (Berlin, 1793)
14 *Vorlesungen über den Stil*, (2te Ausgabe), 122
15 For Campe's views on language see e.g. his prize winning *Über die Reinigung und Bereicherung der deutschen Sprache* (Braunschweig: in der Schulbuchhandlung, 1792).
16 'Über die Bildsamkeit der Deutschen Sprache,' *Deutsche Monatsschrift* 1, 172
17 'Der Dichter im Tempel der Natur,' *Deutsche Monatsschrift*, 1, 77–78
18 *Vorlesungen über den Stil, oder praktische Anweisung zu einer guten Schreibart mit Beispielen aus den vorzüglichsten Schriftstellern* (1793)
19 See e.g. Akselrad, 182.
20 Quoted by Enders, *Friedrich Schlegel*, 81.
21 See e.g. his 'Studienaufsatz' (*Jugendschriften*, 1, 109ff) for his early reactions.
22 The so called 'Unger-Fraktur,' in which the posthumously published *Die Neue Cecilia* (1794), *Wilhelm Meisters Lehrjahre* (1795) and *Herzensergiessungen eines kunstliebenden Klosterbruders* (1796) were all printed.

23 I cannot agree with Schrimpf that Moritz's attempts to contain and reduce the dangers of 'imaginative inwardness' can best be described as those of 'a sober social pedagogue' (Schrimpf, 'Wackenroder,' 407).

24 e.g. Langen, 'Wortschatz,' 143.

25 See especially the periodical *Archiv für Freimaurer und Rosenkreuzer* (Berlin, 1783/5). The *Fama* sold very well in this period (see Schneider, 110f).

26 See 'Die letzte Freiheit des Weisen,' *Launen und Phantasien*, 66–71.

27 'Das menschliche Elend'

28 Cf. e.g. *Mag*, VII, 3, 75–76.

29 Moritz mentions one entitled 'Der Mensch,' *Mag*, VIII, 2, 76–77.

30 Minder, 57

31 Cf. R.M.G. Nickisch, 'Karl Philipp Moritz als Stiltheoretiker,' 262–69.

32 Cf. especially Karl Grosse's *Der Genius* (1791–95), but also Hippel's *Kreuz- und Querzüge*, Jung-Stilling's *Heimweh*, Wieland's *Peregrinus Proteus* all contain wanderers. Meyer's *Dya-Na-Sore* has as its subtitle 'Der Wanderer.'

33 Klischnig, 257–58

34 Schlichtegroll, 255

35 Cf. e.g. Moritz, in Schrimpf: *Hartknopf*, 436.

36 Moritz, quoted in: Schrimpf, *Hartknopf*, 33–34, and *Hamburger Unparteischer Correspondent*, Nr. 114, 19 July 1786

37 Schrimpf, *Hartknopf*, 72

38 *Poèmes et cantiques* (1790), I, 247–48

39 See especially Schrimpf, *Hartknopf*, 30ff, and Langen, 'Karl Philipp Moritz' Weg,' 426ff. Schrimpf calls it a 'kontrafakturische, weltliche Christus-Allegorie.'

40 See here T.J. Ziolkowski, *Fictional Transfigurations of Jesus*.

41 Compare here Langen, 'Wortschatz,' who notes the presence of 'Vertikaldynamik' (57) as a conditioning factor in Pietistic vocabulary.

42 See e.g. Unger, 'Zur seelengeschichtlichen Genesis,' 176ff.

43 Cf. Juan de la Cruz, 'En una noche oscura.'

44 Minder, 231

45 Schwitzke, especially 11–30

46 Schrimpf, *Hartknopf*, 34f

47 Langen, 'Karl Philipp Moritz' Weg,' 174

48 We should note his edition of S.G. Bremer's book, *Die symbolische Weisheit der Ägypter* (Berlin, 1793).

49 Langen, 'Karl Philipp Moritz' Weg,' 421

50 Minder, 237

51 Campe apparently thought that Moritz's reputation would not survive this publication. See e.g. J.H. Campe, *Moritz. Ein abgenötigter trauriger Beitrag zur Erfahrungsseelenkunde*.

52 Klischnig, 262

53 I.e. 'Freundschaft und Zärtlichkeit,' 'Der geheimste Kummer,' 'Das höchste Opfer' and 'Die Trennung.' See Klischnig, 168–71.

54 The preface is unsigned. The name is given by Schrimpf, *Die Neue Cecilia*, 79, from which I quote. Schrimpf's excellent discussion of *Cecilia* is relied on for much of what follows.

55 Schrimpf, *Cecilia*, 85

56 See e.g. Langen, *Anschauungsformen*, 67–68.

57 Cf. e.g. H. Rudolf Vaget, 'Das Bild vom Dilettanten bei Moritz, Schelling und Goethe,' 1–30.

58 Schrimpf, *Cecilia*, 91

59 Schrimpf, 'Wackenroder,' 394

60 Cf. Schrimpf, *Cecilia*, 92

61 Klischnig, 209

62 To Reichart, 30 May 1791

63 Düntzer, 1, 350

64 Klischnig, 219–20

65 Klischnig, 220

66 Henriette Herz, *Leben und Erinnerungen*, 133

67 Varnhagen von Ense, *Vermischte Schriften*, 24–25

68 Eybisch, 256

69 Geiger, *Allgemeine deutsche Biographie*, Bd. 22, 319

70 *Briefwechsel mit Tieck*, 131

71 Proehle, 167

72 WA, IV, 11, 244 (26 Oct. 1796)

73 *Goethes Gespräche*, 126

74 Henning, 63

75 Jördens, 'Denkwürdigkeiten,' 343

76 Jördens, 343

77 Letters all in Eybisch. See also Schrimpf, *Hartknopf*, 425–38, where the complete correspondence between Jean Paul, Karl Philipp Moritz and Johann Christian Konrad Moritz, which covers the years 1792–1796, is published.

Select Bibliography

WORKS BY MORITZ

1779
C.P. Moritz *Tabelle von der Englischen Aussprache*. Berlin, gedruckt bey George Jacob
   Decker, Königl. Hofbuchdrucker, 1779.

1780
Unterhaltungen mit meinen Schülern. Erstes Bändchen. Berlin, 1780. Gedruckt und verlegt
   von Christ. Sigism. Spener, XII, 248pp.
Die Dankbarkeit gegen Gott erhöhet unsre Freuden auf Erden. Eine Predigt, in der St.
   Katharinen-Kirche zu Braunschweig am 27sten August 1780 gehalten. Berlin, bey
   Arnold Wever, 1780. 31pp.
Vom Unterschiede des Akkusativ's und Dativ's. In Briefen. Berlin, bei Arnold Wever. 1780.
   52pp.
Anhang zu den Briefen vom Unterschiede des Akkusativ's und Dativ's. Berlin, bei Arnold
   Wever 1781. 24pp.
Beiträge zur Philosophie des Lebens aus dem Tagebuche eines Freimäurers. Berlin, bey Arnold
   Wever, 1780. 120pp.
Beiträge zur Philosophie des Lebens. Herausgegeben von Carl Philipp Moritz. Zweite verbes-
   serte Auflage. Berlin, bey Arnold Wever, 1781. 167pp.
– *mit einem Anhang über Selbsttäuschung*. Dritte verbesserte Auflage, 1791, 168pp.
'Blunt oder der Gast.' *Litteratur- und Theaterzeitung*. Berlin 1780. II, pp. 385–99; III,
   449–56; 513–27 (Fragment).

1781
Sechs deutsche Gedichte, dem Könige von Preussen gewidmet. Berlin bey Arnold Wever 1781.
   16pp.

Rede am Geburtstage des Königs bei einer Gesellschaft patriotischer Freunde gehalten. Berlin, den 24sten Januar 1781. Bei G.J. Decker, Königl. Hofbuchdrucker. 15pp.

Blunt oder der Gast. Ein Schauspiel in einem Aufzuge. Berlin, bey Arnold Wever, 1781. 38pp.

Anweisung zur Englischen Accentuation nebst vermischten Aufsätzen die Englische Sprache betreffend von M. Carl Philipp Moritz Konrektor am grauen Kloster zu Berlin. Berlin, 1781. bei Arnold Wever, 80pp.

Über den märkischen Dialekt. In Briefen. Erstes Stück. Berlin bei Arnold Wever, 1781. 24pp.

Anweisung die gewöhnlichsten Fehler, im Reden, zu verbessern, nebst einigen Gesprächen. Berlin, bei Arnold Wever, 1781. 36pp.

Kleine Schriften die deutsche Sprache betreffend. Berlin, bei Arnold Wever 1781.

1782

Aussichten zu einer Experimentalseelenlehre an Herrn Direktor Gedike. Berlin, bei August Mylius, 1782. 32pp.

Vorschlag zu einem Magazin der Erfarungs-Seelenkunde. Deutsches Museum. 1782. 1, 485pp.

Allerneuste Mannigfaltigkeiten. Eine gemeinnützige Wochenschrift. Des ersten Jahrgangs Viertes Quartal. Berlin, 1781. pp. 775, 785.

Deutsche Sprachlehre für die Damen. In Briefen. Berlin, bei Arnold Wever, 1782.

1783

Anleitung zum Briefschreiben. Berlin, bei Arnold Wever, 1783.

Reisen eines Deutschen in England im Jahr 1782. In Briefen an Herrn Direktor Gedike. Berlin, 1783, bey Friedrich Maurer. 2 bl, 272pp.

ΓΝΩΘΙ ΣΑΥΤΟΝ *oder Magazin zur Erfahrungsseelenkunde Als ein Lesebuch für Gelehrte und Ungelehrte.* Herausgegeben von Carl Philipp Moritz. Erster Band. Berlin, bei August Mylius 1783. Zweiter Band 1784, Dritter Band 1785, Vierter Band 1786. Herausgegeben von C.P. Moritz und C.F. Pockels: Fünfter Band 1787, Sechster Band 1788. Herausgegeben von Karl Philipp Moritz: Siebenter Band 1789, Achter Band 1791. Herausgegeben von Karl Philipp Moritz und Salomon Maimon: Neunter Band 1792, Zehnter und letzter Band 1793.

J.D. Maucharts: *Anhang zu den sechs ersten Bänden des Magazins für Erfahrungsseelenkunde an die Herausgeber ... C.P. Moritz und C.F. Pockels. Stuttgart, 1789.*

1784

Englische Sprachlehere für die Deutschen. Berlin, bei Arnold Wever, 1784.

Von der deutschen Rechtschreibung. Berlin, 1784, bei Arnold Wever. 32pp.

Ideal einer vollkommnen Zeitung. Berlin, 1784, bey Christian Friedrich Voss und Sohn. 16pp. Umschlag des *Deutschen Museums*, 1784.

1785

Anton Reiser. Ein psychologischer Roman. Herausgegeben von Karl Philipp Moritz. Erster Theil. Berlin, 1785, bei Friedrich Maurer.

1786

Andreas Hartknopf. Eine Allegorie. Berlin, 1786, bei Johann Friedrich Unger.

Anton Reiser. Ein psychologischer Roman. Herausgegeben von Karl Philipp Moritz. Zweiter Theil. Berlin, 1786. bei Friedrich Maurer.

Versuch einer kleinen praktischen Kinderlogik. Berlin, bei August Mylius, 1786.

Denkwürdigkeiten, aufgezeichnet zur Beförderung des Edlen und Schönen. Herausgegeben von Carl Philipp Moritz. Berlin, 1786, bey Johann Friedrich Unger.

– Herausgegeben von C.P. Moritz und C.F. Pockels. Zweiten Bandes Erstes Stück. Berlin, 1787, bey Johann Friedrich Unger. Zweytes Stück. Berlin, 1788.

Anton Reiser. Ein psychologischer Roman. Herausgegeben von Karl Philipp Moritz. Dritter Theil. Berlin, 1786, bei Friedrich Maurer.

Versuch einer deutschen Prosodie. Dem Könige von Preussen gewidmet von Karl Philipp Moritz. Berlin, bei Arnold Wever, 1786.

1787

Fragmente aus dem Tagebuche eines Geistersehers. Berlin, 1787, bei Christian Friedrich Himburg.

1788

Ueber die bildende Nachahmung des Schönen. Braunschweig, 1788, in der Schul-Buchhandlung.

1789

Ueber eine Schrift des Herrn Schulrath Campe, und über die Rechte des Schriftstellers und Buchhändlers. Berlin, 1789, bei Friedrich Maurer.

Italien und Deutschland. Eine Zeitschrift. Herausgegeben von K.P. Moritz.

Monatsschrift der Akademie der Künste und mechanischen Wissenschaften zu Berlin. Herausgegeben von K.P. Moritz und J.A. Riem, 1789, 1790.

1790

Anton Reiser. Ein psychologischer Roman. Herausgegeben von Karl Philipp Moritz. Vierter Theil. Berlin, 1790, bei Friedrich Maurer.

Andreas Hartknopfs Predigerjahre. Berlin, 1790, bei Johann Friedrich Unger.

Neues A.B.C. Buch. Berlin, 1790, bei Christian Gottfried Schöne.

1791

Götterlehre oder mythologische Dichtungen der Alten. Berlin, bei Johann Friedrich Unger, 1791.

'Anthousa' oder Roms Alterthümer. Ein Buch für die Menschheit. Berlin, bei Friedrich Maurer, 1791.

Italiänische Sprachlehre für die Deutschen. Berlin, bei Arnold Wever, 1791.

Grundlinien zu meinen Vorlesungen über den Styl. Berlin, 1791, bei Friedrich Vieweg dem ältern. 8pp.

Annalen der Akademie der Künste und mechanischen Wissenschaften zu Berlin. Herausgegeben von Karl Philipp Moritz. Berlin, bei Johann Friedrich Unger, 1791.

1792

Mythologischer Almanach für Damen. Herausgegeben von Karl Philipp Moritz. Berlin, bei Johann Friedrich Unger, 1792.

Reisen eines Deutschen in Italien in den Jahren 1786 bis 1788. In Briefen. Erster Theil. Berlin, bei Friedrich Maurer, 1792. Zweiter Theil. Berlin, bei Friedrich Maurer, 1792. Dritter Theil. Berlin, bei Friedrich Maurer, 1792.

Vom richtigen deutschen Ausdruck. Berlin, 1792. Im Verlage der kgl. preuss. Kunst- und Buchhandlung.

Lesebuch für Kinder von K.P. Moritz. Berlin, 1792, bey Christian Gottfried Schöne.

Salomon Maimon's Lebensgeschichte. Von ihm selbst geschrieben und herausgegeben von K.P. Moritz. Berlin, 1792, bei Friedrich Vieweg dem ältern. Zweiter und letzter Theil. Berlin, 1793, bei Friedrich Vieweg dem ältern.

1793

Vorlesungen über den Styl oder praktische Anweisung zu einer guten Schreibart in Beispielen aus den vorzüglichsten Schriftstellern. Erster Theil. Berlin, 1793, bei Friedrich Vieweg, dem ältern. x, 260pp. Zweiter Theil. Berlin, 1794. x, 357pp. (only pp. 1–128 by Moritz).

Die grosse Loge oder der Freimaurer mit Wage und Senkblei. Von dem Verfasser der Beiträge zur Philosophie des Lebens. Berlin, bey Ernst Felisch, 1793.

Grammatisches Wörterbuch der deutschen Sprache. Erster Band. Berlin, bei Ernst Felisch, 1793.

Die symbolische Weisheit der Ägypter aus den verborgensten Denkmälern des Alterthums. Herausgegeben von Karl Philipp Moritz. Berlin, 1793, in Karl Matzdorffs Buchhandlung.

Vorbegriffe zu einer Theorie der Ornamente. Berlin, 1793, in Karl Matzdorff's Buchhandlung.

Allgemeiner deutscher Briefsteller. Berlin, 1793, bei Friedrich Maurer.

POSTHUMOUS WORKS

1794

Die neue Cecilia. Letzte Blätter, von Karl Philipp Moritz. Berlin, 1794. bey Johann Friedrich Unger.

1795

Bestimmung des Zwecks einer Theorie der schönen Künste. Vom verstorbenen Hofrath Moritz. Berlinisches Archiv der Zeit und ihres Geschmacks. 1795. I, p. 255.

1796

Launen und Phantasien von Carl Philipp Moritz. Herausgegeben von Carl Friedrich Klischnig. Berlin, bei Ernst Felisch, 1796.

POEMS

'Die empfindsame Schöne,' *Almanach der deutschen Musen auf das Jahr 1779.* Leipzig, Weygandsche Buchhandlung, p. 280.
Leipziger Musen Almanach auf das Jahr 1780. Leipzig, Schwickertscher Verlag: p. 36, 'Als am 23. Febr. 1779 in Berlin ein Friedensgerücht erscholl'; p. 38, 'Als am 17. May der Friede durch einen Herold verkündigt wurde'; p. 147, 'Morgenlied'; p. 196, 'Ode an die Stadt Berlin.'
Olla Potrida. Berlin, 1780: III, 3, 'Emma'; IV, 7, 'Das Kartheuserkloster. Erfurt 1776.'
'Probe einer Übersetzung von Popens Ode am St. Ceciliastage. Erste Stanze,' *Litteratur- und Theaterzeitung 1780,* IV, 658.
Leipziger Musen Almanach auf das Jahr 1781. Leipzig, Schwickertscher Verlag: p. 17, 'Das Manoevre'; p. 64, 'Gemälde von Sanssouci'; p. 71, 'Die Winternacht'; p. 194, 'Der Trost'; p. 208, 'Ode an den May'; p. 220, 'Die Klage.'
Almanach der deutschen Musen auf das Jahr 1781. Leipzig, Weygandsche Buchhandlung: p. 267, 'Gemälde von Sans-souci'; p. 275, 'Der Greis.'
Litteratur- und Theaterzeitung 1781: p. 3 'Am ersten Januar 1781'; p. 115, 'Der Wunsch'; p. 289, 'Leben und Trennung'; p. 353ff, 'Freundschaft. Mühe und Freude. Die Stütze'; p. 449, 'Lied beim Sonnenuntergang'; p. 529ff, 'Aus dem Tagebuche des unglücklichen, von der Welt verkannten P ... is'.
Olla Potrida. Berlin 1781: III, 8–10, 'Freundschaft,' 'Auf Lessings Tod. Berlin, den 24. Februar 1781,' 'An die Freude. Fragment'; IV, 17, 'Die Wiese.'
'Nach Swift,' *Musen Almanach für 1782,* Hamburg, p. 166.
Berlinischer Musenalmanach für 1791, hrsg. von C.H. Jördens: p. 25f, 'Die Stimme drinnen und der Fremdling draussen. Aus dem Altenglischen'; p. 148, 'Frühlingsgedanken.'

ARTICLES IN PERIODICALS

'Vorschlag zu einem Magazin einer Erfarungs-Seelenkunde,' *Deutsches Museum* 1782, p. 485ff.
'Ankündigung eines Magazines der Erfahrungsseelenkunde,' *Berlinisches Magazin der Künste und Wissenschaften* 1782, I, 1, p. 183ff.

'Versuch einer Entwickelung der Ideen, welche durch die einzeln Wörter in der Seele hervorgebracht werden,' *Berlinisches Magazin der Künste und Wissenschaften* 1782 I, I, p. 14ff. 'Ein Brief aus London,' *Berlinische Monatsschrift* 1783, I, p. 298ff.

'Fragment aus Anton Reisers Lebensgeschichte,' *Berlinische Monatsschrift* 1783, II, p. 357ff.

'An die Thätigkeit,' *Berlinische Monatsschrift* (1783), I, p. 298.

'Ein Brief aus London,' *Berlinische Monatsschrift* (1783), I, p. 298.

'Auch ein Hypothese zur Schöpfungsgeschichte Mosis,' *Berlinische Monatsschrift* 1784, III, p. 335ff.

'Versuch einer Vereinigung aller schönen Künste und Wissenschaften unter dem Begriff des in sich selbst Vollendeten.' 1785.

'In wie fern Kunstwerke beschrieben werden können.' *Monatsschrift der Akademie der Künste und mechanischen Wissenschaften*, 1788.

'Schreiben aus Rom,' *Deutsche Monatsschrift* 1790, I, p. 349ff.

'Die Villegiatura, und eine Seligsprechung auf dem Kapitol,' *Deutsche Monatsschrift* 1790, II, p. 267ff.

'Über die Bildsamkeit der Deutschen Sprache,' *Deutsche Monatsschrift* (1792), I, p. 168–72.

'Über ein Gemälde von Goethe,' *Deutsche Monatsschrift* (1792), I, p. 243–50.

'Einfachheit und Klarheit,' *Deutsche Monatsschrift* (1792), II, p. 34–37

'Über die bisherigen Beschäftigungen der akademischen Deputation zur Kultur der vaterländischen Sprache,' *Deutsche Monatsschrift* 1792. III, p. 282ff.

'Amint, oder kann die Vernunft beleidigt werden?' *Deutsche Monatsschrift* 1793, I, p. 187ff.

'Giebt es eine reine Uneigennützigkeit?,' *Deutsche Monatsschrift* 1793, I, p. 268f.

'Soll die Mode auch über die Sprache herrschen?,' *Deutsche Monatsschrift* 1793, II, p. 221ff.

'Über den Einfluss des Studiums der schönen Künste auf Manufakture und Gewerke,' *Deutsche Monatsschrift* (1793), I, p. 38–41.

'Der Dichter im Tempel der Natur,' *Deutsche Monatsschrift* (1793), I, p. 72–78.

MODERN EDITIONS

Anton Reiser (Stuttgart 1886).

Über die bildende Nachahmung des Schönen, hrsg. von Sigmund Auerbach (Stuttgart 1888).

Reisen eines Deutschen in England im Jahr 1782, hrsg. von Otto zur Linde, (Stuttgart 1903).

Anton Reiser (Leipzig 1959).

Anton Reiser (Augsburg 1961).

Die neue Cecilia, Faksimiledruck der Originalausgabe von 1794, (Stuttgart 1962).

Schriften zur Ästhetik und Poetik (Tübingen 1962).

Götterlehre oder mythologische Dichtungen der Alten (Leipzig 1966).

Andreas Hartknopf. Andreas Hartknopfs Predigerjahre. Fragmente aus dem Tagebuche eines Geistersehers, Faksimiledruck der Erstausgaben, hrsg. von Hans Joachim Schrimpf (Stuttgart 1968).

Anton Reiser (Kraus reprint 1968).

Anton Reiser (München 1971).

Versuch einer deutschen Prosodie, hrsg. Thomas P. Saine (Darmstadt 1973).

Moritz. *Werke in zwei Bänden* (Bibliothek deutscher Klassiker: Berlin und Weimar: Aufbau-Verlag, 1973, ausgewählt u. eingeleitet von Jürgen Jahn)

TRANSLATION

C.P. Moritz: *Journeys of a German in England in 1782*, ed. R. Nettel (1965).

SECONDARY WORKS

Abrams, Meier H. *The Mirror and the Lamp* (New York, 1953).

Akselrad, Rose-Marie. *Karl Philipp Moritz' Beziehungen zu seinen Zeitgenossen* (Dissertation, Texas, 1952).

Alexis, Willibald. 'Anton Reiser,' in *Litteraturhistorisches Taschenbuch*, hrsg. R.G. Prutz, 5 (Hannover, 1847), pp. 1–71.

Altenberger, Wilhelm. *Karl Philipp Moritz' pädagogische Ansichten* (Leipzig, 1907).

Altmann, Alexander. *Moses Mendelssohn* (University, Alabama: University of Alabama Press, 1973).

Auerbach, Sigmund. 'Schiller and Moritz,' *Vierteljahrschrift für Litteraturgeschichte*, 5 (1892) p. 143.

– (hrsg.) *Über die bildende Naturahmung des Schönen* (Heilbronn, 1888).

Baeumler, Alfred. *Das Irrationalitätsproblem in der Ästhetik und Logik des 18. Jahrhunderts bis zur Kritik der Urteilskraft* (rpr. Darmstadt, 1967).

Bahrdt, Carl Friedrich. *Geschichte seines Lebens, seiner Meinungen und Schicksale* (Berlin, 1790/91).

Basedow, Johann Bernhard. *Das in Dessau errichtete Philanthropinum* (Leipzig, 1774).

Becker, Eva D. *Der deutsche Roman um 1780* (Stuttgart, 1964).

Bernholdt-Thomson, Anke & Guzzoni, Alfred. *Magazin zur Erfahrungsseelenkunde* (Antique-Verlag, Lindau, 1978).

Beyer-Fröhlich, Marianne. *Die Entwicklung der deutschen Selbstzeugnisse* (Leipzig, 1930)./

Bisanz, Adam J. *Die Ursprünge der Seelenkrankheit bei Karl Philipp Moritz* (Heidelberg, 1970).

Blanckenburg, Christian F. von. *Versuch über den Roman*, hrsg. Lämmert, (rpr. Stuttgart, 1965).

Blei, Franz. *Fünf Sillouetten in einem Rahmen* (Berlin, n.d.).

Blumenthal, Hermann. 'Karl Philipp Moritz und Goethes *Werther*,' *Zeitschrift für Ästhetik und allgemeine Kunst* Bd. 30 (1936), pp. 28–64.

Bonnet, Charles. *Essai analytique sur les facultés de l'âme*, 2ième edition (Copenhagen et Génève, 1769).

Borcherdt, Hans Heinrich, *Der Roman der Goethezeit* (Urach-Stuttgart, 1949).

Böttiger, K.W. (hrsg.). *Literarische Zustände und Zeitgenossen*. In *Schilderungen aus Karl August Böttigers handschriftlichem Nachlass* (Leipzig, 1878).

Boxberger, R. 'Moritz in Erfurt,' *Jahrbucher der Koniglichen Akademie gemeinnutziger Wissenschaften zu Erfurt*, Neue Folge 6 (Erfurt, 1870), 142–69.

Brahm, Otto. *Goethe und Berlin* (Berlin, 1880).

Braun, Julius W. *Schiller und Goethe im Urteile ihrer Zeitgenossen*. Erster Abteilung: Schiller, Bd. 1, 1781–1793 (Leipzig, 1882).

Brück, Max von. 'Karl Philipp Moritz,' in: *Die Sphinx ist nicht tot. Figuren* (Köln-Berlin, 1956).

– 'Wiederbegegnung mit Anton Reiser,' *Die Gegenwart* 12 (1957) p. 829ff.

Bruford, W.H. *Germany in the Eighteenth Century. The Social Background of the Literary Revival* (repr.: Cambridge, 1965).

Brüggeman, Fritz. *Die Ironie als entwicklungsgeschichtliches Moment* (Jena, 1909).

Brümmer, Franz. *Deutsches Dichter-Lexikon* (Eichstadt und Stuttgart, 1877).

Bury, J.B., *The Idea of Progress* (New York, 1932).

Büsching, A.F. D. *Anton Friedrich Büsching eigene Lebensgeschichte, in vier Stücken* (Halle, 1789).

– *Geschichte und Grundsätze der schönen Künste und Wissenschaften im Grundriss*, 2 Bde (Berlin, 1772–1774).

Butler, E.M. *The Tyranny of Greece over Germany* (Cambridge, 1935).

Campe, Johann Heinrich. *Moritz. Ein abgenötigter trauriger Beitrag zur Erfahrungsseelenkunde* (Braunschweig, 1789).

– *Über die Reinigung und Bereicherung der Deutschen Sprache* (Braunschweig, 1790).

Cassirer, Ernst. *Die Philosophie der Aufklärung* (Tübingen, 1932).

– *Rousseau, Kant and Goethe* (Princeton, 1945).

Catholy, Eckehart. *Karl Philipp Moritz und die Ursprünge der deutschen Theaterleidenschaft* (Tübingen, 1962).

– 'Karl Philipp Moritz. Ein Beitrag zur "Theatromanie" der Goethezeit,' *Euphorion* 45 (1950) pp. 100–123.

– 'Schauspielertum als Lebensform,' *Hebbel Jahrbuch 1951*, pp. 97–112.

Croce, Benedetto. *Aesthetic* (New York, 1909).

Danton, George Henry. 'Anton Reiser and Asmus Semper,' *Modern Language Notes* XXIII (1908), pp. 77–78.

Dénina, Abbé. *La Prusse Littéraire sous Fréderic II*, Tome 3 (Berlin, 1791).

Dessoir, Max. *Geschichte der neueren deutschen Psychologie*, 2te Auflage, Bd. 1 (Berlin, 1902).

Dilthey, Wilhelm. *Leben Schleiermachers*, Bd. 1 (Berlin, 1870).

Dithmar, T.G. 'Karakterzüge aus dem Leben des Prof. Hofrath Moritz in Berlin,' *Morgenblatt für gebildete Stände*, 2. Jahrgang, pp. 678–80, 683–84, 743, 755–56 (July–August 1808).

Dunnington, Guy Waldo. *The Relationship of Jean Paul to Karl Philipp Moritz* (Dissertation, Illinois 1938).

Düntzer, Heinrich. *Charlotte von Stein* (Stuttgart, 1874).

- & Ferdinand Gottfried von Herder (Hrsg.), *Herders Reisen nach Italien. Herders Briefwechsel mit seiner Gattin von August 1788 bis July 1789* (Giessen, 1859).

Eberhard, Johann August. *Theorie der schönen Künste und Wissenschaften* 3te. Auflage (Halle, 1790).

- *Allgemeine Theorie des Denkens und Emp'ndens* (Berlin, 1776).

Ebstein, Erich, 'Eine vergessene Patholographie von Marcus Herz über Karl Philipp Moritz aus dem Jahre 1798,' *Zeitschrift für die gesamte Neurologie und Psychiatrie* (Berlin, 1928)p. 513–15.

Eckhart, Martin. *Der Einfluss der Madame Guyon auf die norddeutsche Laienwelt im 18. Jahrhundert* (Dissertation Köln, 1928).

Enders, Carl. *Friedrich Schlegel. Die Quellen seines Wesens und Werders* (Leipzig, 1913).

Engel, Eva J. *Carl Philipp Moritz. A Study of his Ethical and Aesthetic Concepts* (Dissertation, Cornell, 1954).

Ense, K.A. Varnhagen von. *Vermischte Schriften*, 2te. Auflage (Leipzig, 1843).

Ernst, Fritz. 'Karl Philipp Moritz,' *Corona*, 2. Jahrgang, 5 (1931–32), p. 562–71.

- 'Karl Philipp Moritz,' in: *Iphigenia und andere Essays* (München-Berlin- Zürich, 1933).

Eybisch, Hugo. *Anton Reiser. Untersuchungen zur Lebensgeschichte von K.Ph. Moritz und zur Kritik seiner Autobiographie* (Leipzig, 1909).

Fahrner, Rudolf. *K.Ph. Moritz' Götterlehre: Ein Dokument des Goetheschen Klassizismus* (Marburg, 1932).

Farmakis, Viola Marina. *Karl Philipp Moritz and His Conception of the Artist* (Dissertation, Chicago, 1948).

Feder, Johann Georg Heinrich & Meiners, Christoph. *Philosophische Bibliothek* (Göttingen, 1788–91).

Flemming, Willi. *Der Wandel des deutschen Naturgefühls vom 15. zum 18. Jahrhundert* (Halle, 1931).

Foucault, Michel. *Madness and Civilisation* (London, 1967).

Frels, Wilhelm. *Deutsche Dichterhandschriften von 1400 bis 1900* (Leipzig, 1934).

Friedrichs, Elisabeth. *Literarische Lokalgrössen 1700-1900* (Stuttgart, 1966).

Fritsch, Theodor (hrsg.). *J.B. Basedows Elementarbuch* (Leipzig, 1909).

Fürnkäs, Josef. *Der Ursprung des psychologischen Romans* (Stuttgart, 1977).

Garlick, David S. *Novel or Autobiography. An Interpretation of Karl Philipp Moritz's Anton Reiser and the Problem of its Generic Identity* (Stanford, 1973).

Gay, Peter. *The Enlightenment: An Interpretation* (New York, 1966).

Gedike, Friedrich. *Über 'Du' und 'Sie' in der deutschen Sprache* (Berlin, 1794).

Gehrig, Julia. *Karl Philipp Moritz als Pädagoge* (Dissertation, Zürich, 1950).

Geiger, Ludwig. *Berlin 1688-1840. Geschichte des geistigen Lebens der preussischen Hauptstadt* Bd. 1 (Berlin 1893) Bd. 2 (Berlin 1895).

- 'Karl Philipp Moritz,' *Allgemeine deutsche Biographie*, 22 p. 308–20.

Gerhard, Melitta. *Der deutsche Entwicklungsroman bis zu Goethes 'Wilhelm Meister'* (Halle, 1926).

Guion, J.M.B. de la Motte. *La Vie de Madame J.M.B. de la Motte Guion, écrite par elle-même* (3 vols. Cologne, 1720).

Gessner, Salomon. *Salomon Gessners Briefwechsel mit seinem Sohne* (Bern & Zürich, 1801).

Geyer, Moritz (hrsg.). *Vor hundert Jahren. Elise von der Reches Reisen durch Deutschland 1784–86, nach dem Tagebuch ihrer Begleiterin Sophie Becher* (Stuttgart, 1884).

Ghisler, Ruth. *Gesellschaft und Gottesstaat. Studien zum 'Anton Reiser'* (Winterthur, 1955).

Girschner, Wilhelm. 'Karl Philipp Moritz, der Freund Goethes und Mentor Jean Pauls,' *Monatsblätter für deutsche Literatur* VI (1902), pp. 59–68.

Glagau, Hans. *Die moderne Selbstbiographie als historische Quelle* (Marburg, 1903).

Goethe, Johann Wolfgang von. *Werke* (Weimar, 1887ff).

– *Goethes Gespräche* (hrsg. Floerard Freiherr von Biedermann, 1957).

Gottsched, Johann Christoph. *Versuch einer Critischen Dichtkunst*, (repr. Darmstadt, 1962).

Grau, Kurt Joachim. *Die Entstehung des Bewusstseinsbegriffes im XVII und XVIII Jahrhundert* (Dissertation, Berlin, 1914).

Grolimund, Joseph. *Das Menschenbild in den autobiographischen Schriften Karl Philipp Moritz'* (Zürich, 1967).

Hackemann, A. 'Goethe und sein Freund Karl Philipp Moritz,' *Zeitschrift für deutschen Unterricht*, XXI (1907), p. 624f.

Anon. (= Hagmann). *Fragmente über Italien, aus dem Tagebuch eines jungen Deutschen* (1798).

Haller, Albrecht von. *Gedichte*, (repr. Leipzig, 1923).

Harnack, Adolf. *Geschichte der königlichen Preussischen Akademie der Wissenschaften zu Berlin* (Berlin, 1900).

Heidemann, Julius. *Geschichte des Grauen Klosters zu Berlin* (Berlin, 1874).

Heil, Alfred. 'Karl Philipp Moritz als Romanschriftsteller,' *Die Grenzboten* 48 (1889), pp. 271–81.

Heine, Heinrich. *Historisch-kritische Gesamtausgabe der Werke*, hrsg. Wingführ, (Hamburg, 1973).

Henning, Hans. *Karl Philipp Moritz. Ein Beitrag zur Geschichte Goetheschen Zeitalters* (Riga 1908).

Herder, Johann Gottfried. *Sämmtliche Werke*, (Berlin, 1877–1913).

Herz, Henriette. *Jugenderinnerungen* (Berlin, 1896).

– *Ihr Leben und ihre Erinnerungen* (Berlin, 1850).

Herz, Marcus. *Betrachtungen aus der spekulativen Weltweisheit* (Königsberg, 1771).

– 'Etwas Psychologisch-Medizinisches: Moritz' Krankengeschichte,' *Journal der practischen Arzneykunde und Wundarzneykunde*, V, St. 2 (Jena, 1798).

– *Grundriss aller medizinischen Wissenschaften* (Berlin, 1782).

– *Versuch über den Schwindel* (Berlin, 1786).

– *Versuch über den Geschmack und die Ursachen seiner Verschiedenheit* (Berlin, 1790).

Heydenreich, Karl Heinrich. *System der Ästhetik* (Leipzig, 1790).

Hildebrand, Rudolf. 'Vorwort,' *Grimms Deutsches Wörterbuch*, Bd. 5 (1875).

Hillmer, G.F. *Bemerkungen und Vorschläge zur Berichtigung der Deutschen Sprache und des Deutschen Stils* (Berlin, 1793).

Hinrichsen, Otto. 'Zur Kasuistik und Psychologie der Pseudologia phantastica,' *Archiv für Kriminal-Anthropologie und Kriminalistik* 23 (1906), pp. 33–72.

Hinsche, Georg. *Karl Philipp Moritz als Psychologe* (Dissertation, Halle, 1912).

Hissmann, Michael. *Geschichte der Lehre von der Association der Ideen* (Göttingen, 1777).

Hoffman, Kurt. 'Karl Philipp Moritz' *Anton Reiser* und seine Bedeutung in der Geschichte des deutschen Bildungsromans,' *Schlesische Jahrbücher für Geistes- und Naturwissenschaften* II, 4 (1924), pp. 243–61.

Hogarth, William. *The Analysis of Beauty* (Oxford, 1955).

Humboldt, Alexander von. *Briefe Alexanders von Humboldt an seinen Bruder Wilhelm* (Stuttgart, 1880).

Iffland, A.W. *A.W. Ifflands dramatische Werke*, Bd. I (*Meine theatralische Laufbahn*) (Leipzig, 1798).

Jacobs, Noah Jonathan. *Salomon Maimon–Intellectual Vagabond 1754–1800* (Dissertation, Pittsburg, 1937)

Jördens, Karl Heinrich, (hrsg.). *Denkwürdigkeiten, Charakterzüge und Anekdoten aus dem Leben der vorzüglichsten deutschen Dichter und Prosaisten* (Leipzig, 1812).

– 'Karl Philipp Moritz,' *Lexikon deutscher Dichter und Prosaisten* VI. Supplement (Leipzig, 1811; rpt. Georg Olms Verlag, 1970).

Kant, Immanuel. *Werke in sechs Bänden* (Wiesbaden, 1956ff).

Karamsin, Nicolai M. *Briefe eines reisenden Russen* (Wien & Bern, 1922).

Kerényi, Karl. 'Gedanken über die Zeitmässigkeit einer Darstellung der griechischen Mythologie,' *Studium Generale* 8 (1955), pp. 268–72.

Kern, Franz (ed.), *Goethe: Torquato Tasso* (Berlin, 1893).

Kindt, Karl. *Die Poetik von Karl Philipp Moritz* (Dissertation, Rostock, 1924).

Klischnig, Karl Friedrich. *Erinnerungen aus den zehn letzten Lebensjahren meines Freundes Anton Reiser* (Berlin, 1794).

Koch, Franz. *Goethe und Plotin* (Leipzig, 1925).

– 'Lessing und der Irrationalismus,' *DVjs* 6 (1928), 114–43.

Köhler, Doris. *Karl Philipp Moritz und seine organische Kunstauffassung* (Dissertation, Berlin, 1941)

Köpke, Rudolf. *Ludwig Tieck* (Leipzig, 1855).

Küppeln, Julius Friedrich. *Büsten berlinischer Gelehrte und Künstler mit Devisen* (Leipzig, 1787).

Kuntze, Friedrich. *Die Philosophie Salomon Maimons* (Heidelberg, 1912).

Kurrelmeyer, William. 'A Fragment of an Earlier Version of *Anton Reiser*,' *Modern Language Notes* XXXIII, 1 (1918), pp. 1–7.

Langen, August. *Anschauungsformen in der deutschen Dichtung des 18. Jahrhunderts* (repr. Darmstadt, 1968).

- 'Der Wortschatz des 18. Jahrhunderts,' in: *Deutsche Wortgeschichte*, hrsg. Maurer & Stroh, 2te. Auflage (Berlin, 1959), II, pp. 23–222.

- 'Karl Philipp Moritz' Weg zur symbolischen Dichtung,' *Zeitschrift für deutsche Philologie*, 81 (1962), p. 166–218.

- *Der Wortschatz des deutschen Pietismus* (Tübingen, 1954).

Lehmann, Rudolf. 'Anton Reiser und die Entstehung des Wilhelm Meister,' *Jahrbuch der Goethe-Gesellschaft* 3 (1916), pp. 116–34.

Leibbrand, Werner. 'Karl Philipp Moritz und die Erfahrungsseelenkunde,' *Allgemeine Zeitschrift für Psychiatrie und ihre Grenzgebiete* 118 (1941), pp. 392–414.

Leibniz, Gottfried Wilhelm. *Die Philosophischen Schriften von G.W. Leibniz*, hrsg. C.I. Gerhardt (Berlin 1875–90).

Leyser, Jakob. *Joachim Heinrich Campe. Ein Lebensbild aus dem Zeitalter der Aufklärung*, 2 Bde. (Braunschweig, 1877).

Liederwald, Carl. *Der Begriff 'edel' bei Goethe* (Dissertation, Greifswald, 1913).

Mahnke, Dietrich. *Unendliche Sphäre und Allmittelpunkt* (Halle, 1937).

Maimon, Salomon. 'Über den Geschmack,' *Deutsche Monatsschrift* (1792), I, 204–26, 296–315.

Mahrholz, Werner. *Deutsche Selbstbekenntnisse* (Berlin, 1919).

Markwardt, Bruno. *Geschichte der deutschen Poetik* III. (Berlin, 1958), pp. 46–60.

Menck, Clara. '*Anton Reiser* – ein psychologischer Roman,' *Insel-Almanach auf das Jahr 1961*, pp. 52–59.

Mendelssohn, Moses. *Gesammelte Schriften* (Berlin 1929ff).

Menz, Egon. *Die Schrift Karl Philipp Moritzens 'Über die bildende Nachahmung des Schönen'* (Göppingen, 1968).

Menzer, Paul. 'Goethe – Moritz – Kant,' *Goethe. Viermonatsschrift der Goethe Gesellschaft* 7 (1942), pp. 169–98.

Meredith, Hugh Edwin. *Self-Education in the 18th Century: the Readings of Karl Philipp Moritz* (Dissertation, Texas 1963).

Meusel, Johann Georg. *Lexikon der vom Jahr 1750 bis 1800 verstorbenen teutschen Schriftsteller* (Leipzig, 1809).

Minder, Robert. *Die religiöse Entwicklung von Karl Philipp Moritz auf Grund seiner autobiographischen Schriften* (Berlin, 1936).

- *Glaube, Skepsis und Rationalismus* (Frankfurt, 1974).

Moritz, Eckart. *Karl Philipp Moritz und der Sturm und Drang* (Dissertation, Marburg, 1938).

Müffelmann, Friedrich. *Karl Philipp Moritz und die deutsche Sprache* (Dissertation, Greifswald, 1930).

Müller, Curt. *Die geschichtlichen Voraussetzungen des Symbolbegriffs in Goethes Kunstanschauung* (Leipzig, 1937), pp. 177–203.

Müller, Hans. *Die königliche Akademie der Künste zu Berlin. 1696 bis 1896. Erster Teil* (Berlin, 1896).

Muthmann, Joerge. *Der religiöse Wortschatz in der Dichtersprache des 18. Jahrhunderts* (Dissertation, Göttingen, 1949).

Naef, Eduard. *Karl Philipp Moritz. Seine Ästhetik und ihre menschlichen und weltanschaulichen Grundlagen* (Dissertation, Zürich, 1930).

Neumann, Johannes. 'Karl Philipp Moritz: *"Anton Reiser,* ein psychologischer Roman,"' *Psyche,* 1, 3 (1947–48), pp. 222–57 & 358–81.

Nickisch, Reinhard M.G. 'Karl Philipp Moritz als Stiltheoretiker,' *Germanisch-Romanische Monatsschrift,* Neue Folge, (1969), XIX, pp. 262–69.

Noack, Friedrich. *Deutsches Leben in Rom. 1700 bis 1900* (Stuttgart & Berlin, 1907).

Nohl, Johannes. 'Karl Philipp Moritz als Gast Goethes in Weimar,' *Sinn und Form,* 15 (1963), pp. 756–78).

– *Goethe als Maler Möller in Rom* (Weimar, 1955).

Oehrens, Wilhelm. *Über einige aesthetische Grundbegriffe bei Karl Philipp Moritz. Beitrag zur Geschichte der Aesthetik des 18. Jahrhunderts unter besonderer Berücksichtigung der Abhandlung 'Über die bildende Nachahmung des Schönen.'* (Dissertation, Hamburg, 1935).

Pamp, F. *'Palingenesie' bei Charles Bonnet. Herder und Jean Paul* (Dissertation, Münster, 1955).

Pascal, Roy. *The German Sturm und Drang* (New York, 1953).

– *Design and Truth in Autobiography* (Harvard, 1960).

Paulsen, Käthe. *Die Auffassung von der 'Seelenkrankheit' im Magazin zur Erfahrungsseelenkunde* (Dissertation, Hamburg, 1950).

Poiret, P. (ed.). *Poesies et cantiques spirituels* (4 vols., Cologne, 1722).

Pröhle, Heinrich. *Abhandlungen über Goethe, Schiller, Bürger und einige ihrer Freunde* (Potsdam, 1889).

Proskauer, Paul Frank. *The Phenomenon of Alienation in the Work of Karl Philipp Moritz, Wilhelm Heinrich Wackenroder, and in 'Nachtwachen' of Bonaventura* (Dissertation, Columbia, 1966).

Prüsener, Marlies. *Lesegesellschaften im 18. Jahrhundert* (Frankfurt, 1972).

Pyritz, Hans. 'Goethes römische Ästhetik' (1951), in: H.P. *Goethe-Studien* (Köln/Graz, 1962), p. 17–33.

Reichard, H.A.O. *Seine Selbstbiographie,* ed. Uhde (Stuttgart, 1877).

Richter, Jean Paul. *Werke* (München, 1963).

Rinck, Christoph Friedrich. *Studienreisen 1783–84,* hrsg. Geyer (Altenburg, 1897).

Robson-Scott, W.D. *German Travelers in England 1400–1800* (Oxford, 1959).

Rohm, Karl. *Traum ein Leben. Das Problem aufgezeigt bei Karl Philipp Moritz, als ein Beitrag zur Metaphysik der deutschen Romantik* (Dissertation, Wien, 1940).

Rousseau, Jean-Jacques. *Oeuvres Complètes* (Paris, 1964).

Saine, Thomas P. *Karl Philipp Moritz' Ästhetik als Lösung weltanschaulicher Probleme* (Dissertation, Yale, 1968).

- *Die ästhetische Theodizee* (München, 1971).

Salomon, Ludwig. *Geschichte des deutschen Zeitungswesens* (Oldenburg & Leipzig, 1900).

Salzmann, C.G. *Denkwürdigkeiten aus dem Leben ausgezeichneter Teutschen des achtzehnten Jahrhunderts* (Schnepfenthal, 1802).

Sandbach, Francis E. 'Karl Philipp Moritz' *Blunt* and Lillo's *Fatal Curiosity,' Modern Language Review* XVIII (1923), pp. 449–57.

Saran, Franz. *Goethe, Mahomet und Prometheus* (Halle, 1914).

Sawoff, Zwetan. *Der Haarausfall des Anton Reiser. Ueber den Zusammenhang des Ausfalles des Kopfhaares mit Erkrankungen des Körpers und die übrigen Alopecien* (Med. Dissertation, Berlin, 1926).

Schaede, Ernst Joachim. *Herders Schrift 'Gott' und ihre Aufnahme bei Goethe* (Berlin, 1934).

Schiller, Friedrich von. *Briefe* (Stuttgart, 1892–96).

- *Werke* (1943ff).

- *Briefwechsel Schiller und Körner* (Stuttgart, 1892).

Schlegel, August Wilhelm. *August Wilhelm Schlegels Vorlesungen über Philosophische Kunstlehre*, hrsg. A. Wünsche (Leipzig, 1911).

- *Vorlesungen über schöne Litteratur*, Erster Teil 1801–02 (Heilbronn, 1884).

- *Kritische Schriften und Briefe*, 6 Bde. (Stuttgart, 1962ff).

Schlegel, Friedrich. *Kritische Schriften* (München, 1964).

Schlichtegroll, Friedrich (ed.). 'Karl Philipp Moritz,' *Nekrolog auf das Jahr 1793* (Gotha, 1795), p. 169–276.

- *Supplement-Band des Nekrologs für die Jahre 1790, 91, 92 und 93* (Gotha, 1798), p. 182–218.

Schmidt, Arno. 'Die Schrechensmänner,' *Nachrichten von Büchern und Menschen*, Bd. 1 (Zur Literatur des 18. Jahrhunderts), (1971).

Schmidt, Erich. *Richardson, Rousseau und Goethe* (Jena, 1875).

Schneider, Ferdinand Josef. *Die Freimaurerei und ihr Einfluss auf die geistige Kultur in Deutschland am Ende des XVIII Jahrhunderts* (Prague, 1909).

Schnuchel, Hans-Ulrich. 'Die Behandlung bürgerlicher Problematik in den Romanen von Karl Philipp Moritz,' *Festschrift für Wolfgang Vulpius zu seinem 60. Geburtstag am 27. November 1957* (Weimar, 1957), pp. 85–99.

Schrimpf, Hans Joachim. 'Anton Reiser. Wege zum psychologischen Roman,' in: *Der Deutsche Roman*, hrsg. von Wiese, Bd. 1 (Düsseldorf, 1965), p. 95–131.

- 'Die Sprache der Phantasie. Karl Philipp Moritz' *Götterlehre,' Festschrift für Richard Alewyn*, hrsg. Singer & von Wiese, (Köln/Graz, 1967), pp. 165–92.

- 'Vers ist tanzhafte Rede. Ein Beitrag zur deutschen Prosodie aus dem achtzehnten Jahrhundert,' *Festschrift für Jost Trier zum 70. Geburtstag* (Köln/Graz, 1964), pp. 386–410.

- 'Karl Philipp Moritz,' in: *Deutsche Dichter des 18. Jahrhunderts*, hrsg. von Wiese (Berlin, 1977), p. 881–910.

- 'W.H. Wackenroder und K. Ph. Moritz. Ein Beitrag zur frühromantischen Selbstkritik,' *Zeitschrift für Deutsche Philologie* 83 (1964), pp. 385–409.

Schröder, Hans. *Johann Gottwerth Müller* (Itzehoe, 1843).

Schwinger, Reinhold. *Innere Form. Ein Beitrag zur Definition des Begriffes auf Grund seiner Geschichte von Shaftesbury bis Wilhelm von Humboldt* (Dissertation, Leipzig, 1934).

Schwitzke, Heinz. *Die Beziehungen zwischen Ästhetik und Metaphorik in der deutschen Philosophie vor Kant* (Dissertation Berlin, 1930).

Shaftesbury, Anthony, Earl of. *Characteristics of Men, Manners, Opinions, Times*, (rpr. New York, 1964).

Skorne, Hans J. *Der Wanderermotiv im Roman der Goethezeit* (Dissertation, Köln, 1961).

Sørensen, Bengt A. *Symbol und Symbolismus in der ästhetischen Theorien der 18. Jahrhunderts und der deutschen Romantik* (Copenhagen, 1963).

Stahl, Ernst Ludwig. *Die religiöse und die humanitätsphilosophische Bildungsidee* (Bern, 1934).

Stanzel, Frank K. *Typische Formen des Romans*, 2te Auflage, (Göttingen, 1965).

Staub, Hans. *Laterna Magica. Studien zum Problem der Innerlichkeit in der Literatur* (Giessen, o.J.).

Stemme, F. *Karl Philipp Moritz und die Entwicklung von der pietistischen Autobiographie zur Romanliteratur der Erfahrungsseelenkunde* (Dissertation, Marburg, 1950).

- 'Die Säkularisation des Pietismus zur Erfahrungsseelenkunde,' *Zeitschrift für Deutsche Philologie* 72 (1953), pp. 144–58.

Steude, Rudolf. 'Wann wurde Karl Philipp Moritz geboren?' *Germanisch-Romanische Monatsschrift*, Neue Folge, XVIII (1968), p. 313–14.

Thalmann, Marianne. *Der Trivialroman des 18. Jahrhunderts und der romantische Roman. Ein Beitrag zur Entwicklungsgeschichte der Geheimbundmystik* (Berlin, 1923).

That, Erich. *Goethe und Moritz* (Dissertation, Kiel, 1920; Auszug, 1921).

Tischbein, Johann Heinrich Wilhelm. *Aus meinem Leben*, hrsg. Schueler (Braunschweig, 1861).

Unger, Rudolf. 'Zur seelengeschichtlichen Genesis der Romantik. Karl Philipp Moritz als Vorläufer von Jean Paul und Novalis,' in: R.U., *Zur Dichtungs-und Geistesgeschichte der Goethezeit* (Berlin, 1944), pp. 144–80.

Vaget, Hans Rudolf. *Goethe und das Problem des Dilettantismus* (Dissertation, Columbia, 1969).

- *Dilettantismus und Meisterschaft. Zum Problem des Dilettantismus bei Goethe* (München, 1971).

- 'Das Bild vom Dilettanten bei Moritz, Schelling und Goethe.'

- *Jahrbuch des Freien deutschen Hochstifts* (1970), pp. 1–30.

Vogel, Julius. *Aus Goethes Römischen Tagen* (Leipzig, 1905).

Wackenroder, Wilhelm Heinrich. *Briefwechsel mit Ludwig Tieck* (Jena, 1910).

Wagner, Gertrud. *Die Entwicklung des psychologischen Romans in Deutschland von der Mitte des 18. Jahrhunderts bis zum Ausgang der Romantik* (Dissertation, Wien, 1965).

Walzel, Oskar. 'Goethe und K. Ph. Moritz,' *Jahrbuch der Goethe-Gesellschaft* I (1914), pp. 38–62.

Watt, Ian. *The Rise of the Novel* (University of California, 1967).

Weisstein, Gotthilf. *Carl Philipp Moritz. Beiträge zu seiner Lebensgeschichte* (Berlin, 1899).

Werner, Th. W. 'Der Roman Anton Reiser als musikgeschichtliche Quelle,' *Studien zur Musikgeschichte. Festschrift für Guido Adler* (Wien, 1930), pp. 207–15.

Werthmann, Maria. *Die Bedeutung des Romans 'Anton Reiser' von K. Ph. Moritz für die Erziehungsgeschichte und Theorie der Pädagogik* (Dissertation, Wien, 1932).

Wiese, Benno von. 'Karl Philip Moritz', *Anton Reiser,' Zeit und Leben. Eine Auslese aus der Kölnischen Volkszeitung* (Essen, 1940), pp. 55–59.

Wieser, Max. *Der sentimentale Mensch* (Gotha, 1924).

Windel, Rudolf. 'Karl Philipp Moritz als pädagogischer Schriftsteller,' *Neue Jahrbücher für das klassische Altertum* 18 (1906), pp. 44–59.

Zeydel, Edwin H. 'The Relation of Anton Reiser to German Romanticism,' *Germanic Review*, III (1926), pp. 295–347.

Ziegler, C. *Karl Philipp Moritz und sein psychologischer Roman 'Anton Reiser'* (Langensalza, 1913).

Ziolkowski, T.J. *Fictional Transfigurations of Jesus* (Princeton, 1972).

Chronology: Karl Philipp Moritz

1756	Born September 15
1763	In Hanover. End of the Seven Years' War
1768-70	In Brunswick, under Lobenstein
1771–June 1776	At the Gymnasium in Hanover
August 1776–	
January 1777	In Erfurt, where he matriculates at the university
1777	Early February, arrival in Leipzig. Final abandonment of actor's career. Visit to the Moravian seminary at Barby. Arrival in Wittenberg
1778	Leaves Wittenberg in May after two semesters. Visits Basedow in Dessau. Appointed at the Potsdam Orphanage in July, and at the Graue Kloster in Berlin in November
1779	A *Tabelle von der englischen Aussprache* is printed
1780	His first major book, *Unterhaltungen mit meinen Schülern*, published; also the *Beiträge zur Philosophie des Lebens*, and various works on language
1781	*Sechs deutsche Gedichte* and *Blunt oder der Gast* appear
1782	Visit to England (May-August). *Deutsche Sprachlehre für die Damen*. Appointed Conrector at the Kölnische Schule in December
1783	*Reisen eines Deutschen in England* appears; also the first volume of the *Magazin zur Erfahrungsseelenkunde*, which ran for ten years
1784	*Ideen einer vollkommenen Zeitung* (16 pages) published. Moritz appointed as editor of the *Berliner privilegierte Zeitung* on September 1. Also appointed Professor at the Graue Kloster
1785	First volume of *Anton Reiser*. Mid-summer sees a walking tour in Germany
1786	A productive year, in which *Andreas Hartknopf. Eine Allegorie*, *Anton Reiser*, volumes two and three, *Denkwürdigkeiten*, the *Kinderlogik* and the *Prosodie* all appear. The stay in Rome and the friendship with Goethe commence

1787   In Rome. *Fragmente aus dem Tagebuche eines Geistersehers* is the solitary production

1788   In Rome for the first ten months of the year. *Über die bildende Nachahmung des Schönen* appears, and Moritz returns, in December, to Weimar.

1789   *Über eine Schrift des Herrn Schulrath Campe* shows Moritz in a combative mood. He begins to edit the journal called *Monatsschrift der Akademie der Künste*, and is appointed to the Royal Academy of the Arts in Berlin

1790   *Anton Reiser*, volume four is published, also *Andreas Hartknopfs Predigerjahre*. Moritz settles down in his new role

1791   The *Götterlehre* and *Anthusa* are the principle works. Moritz becomes a Hofrat in April, and finally, in October, is elected to the Prussian Academy of Sciences

1792   The *Reisen eines Deutschen in Italien* is the outstanding production of this year. Moritz cuts a fine figure in Berlin

1793   The *Vorlesungen über den Stil* appears (only partly by Moritz), and *Die grosse Loge*. Moritz dies on June 26

1796   (posthumous) the *Launen und Phantasien*, edited by Klischnig, is published

Index